The Jews in the Renaissance

CECIL ROTH

The Jews
in the Renaissance

The Jewish Publication Society of America
PHILADELPHIA   1977/5738

Copyright ©, 1959, by The Jewish Publication Society of America
All Rights Reserved
Fifth Printing, 1977
ISBN 0-8276-0103-4
Library of Congress Catalog Card Number 59-8516

Contents

List of Illustrations

The following illustrations
will be found in a group following page 148

Preface

This work is an experimental study of the interaction of two societies and of two cultures at one of the seminal periods of the world's history. I had originally intended to interpret my terms of reference more rigidly and, taking the Jewish world as a whole into my survey, to restrict myself to the main tide of the Renaissance in the fifteenth century and the first half of the sixteenth. But I found that this would have conveyed a wholly false impression. For the essential contribution of the Jews, as Jews, to the Revival of Learning came not during the so-called Greek Renaissance which was stimulated by the fall of Constantinople in 1453, but at an earlier stage, in the original and in many ways more significant renewal based on the Latin (and ultimately Arabic) texts. On the other hand, in the history of music and the history of stagecraft—aspects in which the Renaissance was protracted into the age of the Catholic Reaction: the coincidence is not accidental—Italian Jewry's share was considerable, and in certain respects (according to some enthusiasts) fundamental.

In the early Middle Ages, the Jew, with a high standard of civilization which embraced the Arab version of ancient Hellenic science and philosophy, and with cosmopolitan elements such as no other section of the population enjoyed, was culturally in advance of Europe as a whole in many respects. Hence in the period of the Latin Renaissance he was in the Christian world a pioneer, venerated, and perhaps sometimes feared, as the custodian of a higher civilization. By the close of the fourteenth century, the world about him had absorbed most of these elements, partly in consequence of the activity of a remarkable band of Jewish intermediaries whose work will be described in the early chapters of this volume. In the fifteenth century, with the spread of a direct knowledge of the Greek language and literature, and the quickening of interest that resulted from this, Europe rose rapidly above its former cultural level, and the Jews were wholly outstripped. From now on, their participation was as individuals, and their preëminence (where it existed) was based on personal factors—

perhaps emphasized in some cases by their linguistic range, their cosmopolitan outlook, and their always advanced educational system, in all of which a positive Jewish element can be recognized.

On the other hand, in those areas of southern Europe with which the Renaissance was most closely associated, their participation was now retarded by a more acute discrimination than heretofore and by the close interaction of religious and social factors in the world about them. Henceforth, a new atmosphere prevailed. Previously Jewish culture had played a distinguished role in the reawakening of European intellectual life. Now Renaissance styles and conceptions begin to make their way timidly, and not very successfully, into the Hebraic outlook.

This does not imply that the change that had come to pass was universally or immediately appreciated. Some Jews were conscious of it relatively soon, and from the fourteenth century one finds them eagerly carrying out translations of essential scientific literature from Latin into Hebrew (this would formerly have seemed absurd), striving for admission to the newly-established universities instead of studying under Jewish or Arab teachers, and systematically laboring to avert the "reproach" that ignorance of European studies prevailed among their co-religionists. Highly characteristic is the story told by a Provençal physician of the period, Leon Joseph of Carcassonne, that, with the sole object of obtaining satisfactory medical texts for the use of Jewish students, he had learned Latin, attended lectures at the University of Montpellier, and for ten laborious years had striven in vain to obtain copies of the writings of certain eminent Christian scholars, the sale of which to unbelievers had been forbidden by the faculty of that great seat of learning: when ultimately he succeeded, he had to pay twice the normal price.

Nevertheless, the outside world did not realize how far the Jews' basic scientific knowledge had been outstripped, and still imagined quite wrongly that the Jews had access to stores of recondite information not available to other men. Some persons indeed were not loath to exploit the opportunities which were thereby opened to them. There was thus a debasement of the currency of Jewish participation in cultural life. In place of the unostentatious translators and learned scientists of a former age, the forefront of the stage was now occupied to some extent by picturesque charlatans (there will be more than one instance in these pages) who fit into the Renaissance pattern in a wholly different fashion.

In the same way as the origins of the Renaissance can be discerned as early as the twelfth century, so its echoes continued well into the seventeenth. Indeed, the extension of the New Birth into the realm of music came fully three centuries after the first exciting renewal of Italian art. In the Jewish sphere, the Renaissance environment may be said to have ended with the Catholic Reaction and the systematic repression that followed it. But this was a gradual process. Though in the Papal States it is to be dated precisely, with Pope Paul IV's melancholy bull, *Cum nimis absurdum*, of July 12, 1555, its introduction to other Italian cities and principalities extended over half a century or more. Moreover, the Italian Jews did not immediately change their outlook on life when the ill-fated institution of the ghetto was set up, any more than the German Jews automatically became different beings with the promulgation of the Nuremberg Laws in 1935. The former attitudes and interests continued among them as long as that generation survived—and there were friendly souls among the general population, clergy as well as laymen, of whom this was no less true. At the same time, it must be remembered that Venice, the city where the term "ghetto" had its origin (by reason of the segregation of the Jews in the area of the New Foundry or *geto nuovo* in 1516), was precisely where the institution as such—at all events, in its earlier days—had perhaps the slightest intensity and least validity in intellectual life. A man such as Leone Modena, the versatile though reprehensible rabbi of that community, stood between the two eras. It is impossible to depict a man who died in 1648 as a Renaissance figure (though some writers have fallen into that trap) and for that reason I do not propose to deal with his career consistently in this volume. But, born as he was in 1571, he cannot be wholly neglected and, as will be seen, I will constantly call his experience—especially his youthful experience—in evidence. On the one hand, he perpetuated the traditional Italian-Jewish cultural synthesis; on the other, he was a contemporary of Guercino, Cromwell, and Menasseh ben Israel—anything but Renaissance types—a precursor of the modern age, and an anticipator of the rabbis of our own time who are more actively interested in the interpretation of Judaism to Christians than in the spread of its knowledge among Jews. It happens, moreover, that Modena was exceptionally articulate, and in his letters and writings we have an unrivaled store of detail to illustrate the domestic and personal background of the sophisticated Italian Jew who grew up in the sixteenth century.

Of the two cultures with whose interaction this book deals, the Jewish element was inevitably, for the reasons that have been given, the active factor in the main before the fifteenth century and the passive one thereafter. There is a positive relevance for the present time. It is probably true to say that, with the one partial exception that will be mentioned below, there has never been any other period in history when the Jews achieved so successful a synthesis between their ancestral Hebraic culture and that of the environment. In Hellenistic Alexandria, as far as we can judge, the cultural outlook typified by Philo was confined to a very restricted circle. Moreover, it was incomplete—Philo was a loyal Jew, but his knowledge of essential Hebrew learning seems to have been scanty.

In nineteenth- and twentieth-century Germany and the European countries generally (and the same is true of America today), the extent of Jewish participation in general life was immeasurably greater than in Renaissance Italy. But, except in the case of a small group of professional scholars, the two interests were divorced. It is difficult to think of any outstanding modern instance in which the scientist was at the same time a talmudist, or the philosopher an exegete, even in those cases (perhaps a minority) in which fidelity to Judaism was wholly unimpaired.

In Renaissance Italy, we have the unique phenomenon of that successful synthesis which is the unfulfilled hope of many today. The Jews who translated Averroës achieved distinction as physicians, compiled astronomical treatises, wrote plays, directed the theater, composed music and so on, were in almost every case not merely loyal Jews, but intellectually active Jews, conversant with Hebrew, studying its literature and devoted to talmudic scholarship. The papal physicians who dabbled in Italian letters and were engaged in scientific investigation acted also as rabbis of their communities: the playwright-impresario was at the same time a Hebrew poet who founded a synagogue: the same individual plays a role of major importance in the history of Hebrew and of Italian printing: the financiers who mingled with the Medicean circle in Florence were students, patrons and sometimes workers in the field of Hebrew literature. It was perhaps the only period of history, with the exception of that of Arab predominance (at which time for obvious reasons different circumstances prevailed—among them a basic linguistic and cultural affinity), when absorption into the civilization of the environment had no corrosive effect on Jewish intellectual life. Unfortunately, the Catholic Reaction and the stranglehold of the ghetto system prevented this from achieving a lasting influence, and an obvious recession is discernible toward the end of the period here under consideration. By and large, the Italian Jew of the seventeenth century was a far less cultured person in both the Jewish and European sense than his ancestors of the fifteenth and sixteenth centuries.

In view of what I have said, it has been necessary for me to extend the purview of this book from the *duecento*, when the Jewish contribution was most intense, to the beginning of the *seicento*, when it was most characteristic—from the part played by Jewish culture in the early Renaissance of learning to the part played by individual Jews in the late Renaissance of music. And, because of this exceptionally wide extension in point of time, I have been compelled to restrict myself somewhat more severely than I might otherwise have done in point of geography. I have thus dealt in the main with Italy, the essential home of the Renaissance in its most characteristic manifestations: otherwise, this book would have become transformed into a general study of the inter-relations between the Jews and their neighbors in Europe in the later Middle Ages and after. Lands other than Italy have been taken into consideration only where it has seemed necessary for the development of my theme.

For "Renaissance" is in fact a subjective term, with connotations which it is easier to feel than to explain: it is used, as a recent inquirer has said, "to describe anything vague but splendid that happened in Italy between Dante and Michelangelo"—or indeed from certain points of view a good deal later than this. If I have preferred the picturesque to the drab, and devoted space to the curious as well as to the important, I do not feel that apology is needed.

Cecil Roth

Oxford, June 1959

ONE

The Background *of* Renaissance Jewish Life

The dazzling process that is known as the Italian Renaissance was enacted in an area not much larger than one of the lesser American states, or a group of English counties. Its essential stage was not in fact the whole of Italy, but part of the country only, from Rome northward: the south—the Kingdom of Naples and the island of Sicily—played only a sporadic part in certain aspects of the process. Even in the north, the share taken by the cities of Piedmont, or by those along the northeastern frontier beyond Venice, was of minor importance. But in the relatively small area between Rome and Milan and between Genoa and Venice, there was from the fourteenth to the sixteenth centuries an efflorescence of genius, of vitality, and of versatility, coupled with a universality of aesthetic appreciation, such as the world has never perhaps known at any other time—not even, it may be, in the great age of Greece. It happened that this area was at this period—as would not have been the case a century or so before—the seat of numerous Jewish communities, and it was impossible for them not to be affected by, and not to contribute in some measure toward, this intellectual turmoil. It is this reciprocal process that the present volume will endeavor to describe.

Italian Jewish history has certain characteristics which distinguish it from that of the Jews in any other country of the western world. Preëminent among them is its impressive antiquity and continuity. Jews are first mentioned in the peninsula in the Maccabaean age, two hundred years or more before the destruction of Jerusalem by the Romans; and from that time on their record has been unbroken. Hence in the Renaissance period the Italian Jews (of the older stratum, at least) were in no sense

3

aliens in the country. They were indigenous, as much as any of
their neighbors were, Italian cultural life having been part of their
normal environment for some fifteen hundred years.

The oldest center of Italian Jewry was of course Rome, where
there was an important colony already in Republican times. Subsequently other settlements were established, as might be expected,
along the trade-routes which connected the capital of the Empire
with Palestine and the eastern Mediterranean: that is, in the south
of the country, especially in the seaports. In antiquity, moreover,
this area—the subsequent Kingdom of Naples—was more fertile
and more prosperous by far than was the case in later history
and was thus able to support a far larger population. It is true
that we find casual references to Jewish individuals and even
groups in various places in the north as well at this time. But
such mentions are isolated and sporadic; and the center of organized and continuous Jewish life in Italy, down to relatively late
in the Middle Ages, was the area around Rome together with the
southern provinces of Calabria and Apulia. When the famous
Jewish globe-trotter Benjamin of Tudela (the first medieval
traveler, it has been said, who generally told the truth, his work
being for this reason of fundamental importance to historians)
traveled through Italy from north to south about 1169, he mentioned organized Jewish communities in only two places north of
Rome: Lucca and Pisa; whereas in the south of the country every
township that he visited had its Jewish group, whose numbers
and leading members he faithfully recorded. There is evidence
that even at this period there were little settlements in certain of
the northern cities. But the traces they have left are inconsiderable; and it is hardly possible that Benjamin would have failed
to mention them had they seemed in his eyes to be of any importance, numerical or otherwise.

This point is one of some significance for the historian, in particular for the economic historian. A good deal has been written
in the past, somewhat irresponsibly, about the participation of the
Jews in the development of the capitalist system, and it has been
asserted that they took an important part in the business activity
of the great Italian mercantile republics which had so profound
an influence on Europe in the Middle Ages. The hypothesis is
based on utterly erroneous data. Since there were no important

Jewish groups in northern Italy down to the close of the thirteenth century, it was impossible for Jews to participate in the economic life of the north Italian states. The reason for their absence is plain. Until the period of the Crusades the Jews had played an important (at some stages, certain scholars hold, a preponderant) part in international commerce, having by reason of their ubiquity and cosmopolitan sense special qualifications for such activities. Hence, at the close of the Dark Ages, when the Italian mercantile republics began to come to the fore, they regarded the Jews as their most dangerous rivals. We find the Venetians, not content with excluding them from their own city, trying to ban them from international commerce throughout Europe; we find the Genoese hermetically sealing themselves from infidel infection—and competition—throughout the centuries; we find the skeptical Florentines aghast at the idea of admitting any Jew to contaminate the purity of their faith. The independent Jewish traders naturally found themselves unable to compete against the new large-scale joint enterprises enjoying the political backing of the Italian republics. Thus, only slender remnants were left of their former trading hegemony, even before the Italian carrying-trade received the artificial impetus of the Crusades (fought, it may be said, between the Normans and the Saracens for the economic benefit of the Venetians and the Genoese). In the south of Italy, on the other hand, there was an old tradition of Jewish handicraft, and it seems that the communities whom Benjamin of Tudela found there depended for their livelihood largely on the two traditional callings of dyeing and silk-weaving. So much was this the case that when in 1231 the Emperor Frederick II set up a governmental monopoly in these branches of industry in Apulia, the processes and management were left in Jewish hands.

This then was the general condition and distribution of Italian Jewry until the thirteenth century. Then two almost simultaneous developments caused a radical change. One was an outbreak of persecution (a rare happening in Italian history) about the year 1290 in the Kingdom of Naples, which drove a large proportion of its Jewish communities ostensibly into baptism. Precise details are lacking—the whole story was recovered only recently—but what is clear is that, with this unhappy episode, the golden age of the Jews in the south of the country came to an end. Not all the communities were affected, and those that were affected became reëstablished in due course; but they never again attained their previous tranquil prosperity.

At this same period, a change in economic circumstances introduced a new chapter in Jewish history in the north. The Church had recently begun to intensify its campaign against the institution of "usury" (as all interest, however small, was designated) as being a crime against nature. For the major operations, for which they had become notorious throughout Europe, the Italians now found a way out, by subterfuge, legal fictions, or deliberate myopia. But by the same token, they began to view with horror the overt moneylending on a small scale whereby their own citizens and artisans tided over their urgent needs when sick or unemployed. There were no state social services to support the needy, the religious houses could not always help, and in effect there was now no alternative for the poor in times of stress except to have recourse to clandestine usurers, who in these circumstances charged fantastic rates of interest.

The situation would have been desperate in some cases, but for one thing. The practice of usury was considered to be a sin for any man, but seemed in Gentile eyes to be less so for Jews, who after all had so many sins on their infidel consciences that one more or less hardly mattered; moreover, the Popes, perhaps vaguely aware of the social problem involved, were prepared to grant them indulgences so as to permit them to carry on this activity. Hence, from the second half of the thirteenth century on, it became usual for the Italian communes, first in central Italy and then in the north, to invite Jews (in the earlier period originating from Rome, later from Germany or France also) to open "loan-banks"—in effect, pawnbroking establishments—preëminently for the benefit of the poor. Everyone was thus gratified—the city, which not only found its quandary obviated but also its coffers enriched by the fees exacted from the newcomers for their license to practice; the needy, whose requirements at time of emergency were thus satisfied (though they would have been more than human if they had felt as happy when the time arrived for repayment); the Papacy, whose indulgences were not issued *gratis;* and the Jews, who, now being squeezed out of their former activities as merchants and artisans, found compensation and in fact salvation in this new field of enterprise. Thus there emerged the paradoxical situation that the Italian cities, which had for so long excluded Jews who were engaged in blameless walks of life, threw their gates open eagerly to those who had to earn their living in this unlovable and unloved fashion. In many instances, in fact, Jews other than moneylenders continued for a long time to be excluded from the places in question as rigorously as before. But this paradoxical restriction could not be maintained indefinitely, and in due course the admission of the "loan-bankers" inevitably led in every (or almost every) case to the admission of Jews without restriction of occupation, and thus to the formation of a normal community. This then is the background in general terms of the establishment of the Jewish colonies in the historic centers of northern Italy in which the Renaissance was principally enacted.

In the course of the fifteenth century, the original native Italian element tended to be diluted more and more, especially in Lombardy, by fresh immigrants from Germany, and to a lesser degree from the south of France. After the expulsion of the Jews from Spain in 1492, there was a relatively considerable immigration from that country and later, throughout the sixteenth century, there was a small but steady influx of the so-called marranos (that is, persons who had been compelled to embrace Christianity but retained their Jewish loyalties), especially from Portugal. All of these elements enhanced the "international" outlook of the Jewish communities, introduced among them new values and new conceptions, and thus rendered Italian Jewry the more capable of participating in Renaissance intellectual life. The settlements in question were not large. None, even of the more important, probably exceeded a few hundred souls until the sixteenth century, or a couple of thousand at the period of their greatest development. But they were prominent and active out of proportion to their numbers.

It is desirable to pause at this point and survey very rapidly conditions in those parts of Italy in which the Jewish participation in Renaissance currents was most constant. It is hardly necessary to do more than mention briefly Sicily and Sardinia. (Corsica, for some reason, attracted no Jewish settlers at all and played no part in Jewish history at any time.) Over most of the period under consideration these islands were ruled by the House of Aragon and were under strong Spanish influence: a fact which was responsible for the tragedy of 1492, when the expulsion of the Jews from the Spanish dominions extended to these areas as well. Before this date the local Jewish communities, having been composed mainly of artisans and manual laborers, enjoyed scant leisure for intellectual activity; and though under the Norman rulers of the twelfth century the court of Palermo had been one of the most luxurious and cultured of all Europe, these areas played an inconsiderable part in the true Renaissance. Much the same may be said of the Kingdom of Naples, which extended over most of the south of the Peninsula, and was ruled successively by the Holy Roman Emperors of the House of Hohenstaufen, French rulers of the House of Anjou, and a cadet (later, illegitimate) branch of the House of Aragon. Naples itself, however, was always the seat of a brilliant court which, as we shall see, sometimes extended its patronage to Jewish savants as well. Moreover, after the expulsion from Spain at the end of the fifteenth century, some of the most cultured of the exiles settled here—especially the family of Don Isaac Abrabanel, the learned, devoted leader of Spanish Jewry, who had formerly been high in royal service both in Portugal and in Castile. Here they continued their former enlightened tradition, until they were driven out by the general edict of expulsion of 1541.

The nerve-center of Italian Jewry was Rome, under the eye and generally the protection of the Popes. From the middle of the fifteenth century on, the latter were among the leaders of Italian humanism—collectors of manuscripts, patrons of the arts, devotees of music, students of the humanities, enthusiasts for classical antiquity. Scholars and artists from all parts of Italy flocked to enjoy their enlightened patronage; and Jews too were able to take advantage of this benign atmosphere. The names of Nicholas V (1447-1455), Paul II (1467-1471), Sixtus IV (1471-1484), Innocent VIII (1484-1492), Leo X (1513-1521), and Clement VII (1523-1534)—the last two, members of the House of Medici—are especially memorable in this connection. In the middle of the sixteenth century, however, under the stress of the threat to the Church involved in the Reformation movement in Germany, the atmosphere changed; and as part of the Counter Reformation, a reaction set in against the Jews of the Papal States, later to spread to the whole of Italy. Yet even now there was among the Italian people a basic kindliness; and even now, the long acclimatization of the Jews in the country attuned them completely to the Italian outlook and Italian cultural life. Thus, in a certain sense, Renaissance conceptions prevailed even in the ghetto.

The Papal States extended over a considerable area of central Italy from sea to sea, and were greatly extended at the end of the sixteenth and beginning of the seventeenth century. It will be recalled how, during the pontificate of Alexander VI (1492-1503), his son, Cesare Borgia, attempted to subdue many of the lesser states in central Italy and to build up a principality on their ruins; in this volume, however, he will figure only as a patron of the arts. Of the secondary cities of the Papal States, two should be specially mentioned. The seaport of Ancona on the Adriatic coast, which later attracted a large number of Levantine merchants, was among the oldest Jewish communities in central Italy, going back probably beyond the thirteenth century. It was exceeded in importance by Bologna, ruled, one might say, alternately by the Popes and the enlightened "tyrants" of the House of Bentivoglio until the beginning of the sixteenth century, when it was joined definitely to the States of the Church. Until the brutal expulsion in 1569, as part of the general reaction which severed the connection of the Jews with so many minor centers under the papal rule, Bologna was from the cultural point of view one of the outstanding Italian communities.

East of this, the most important independent state was the Duchy of Urbino. The hill-town on which it centered had been intermittently, from the twelfth century, under the rule of the House of Montefeltro, which had gradually extended the area under its sway and in due course had been accorded the ducal title. Federigo da Montefeltro (1444-1482) had been the most enlightened patron of literature and art of his day, and under him and his son Guidubaldo (1482-1508) the court became one of the greatest centers of Renaissance enlightenment. Later, the duchy passed to the family of Della Rovere, and on its extinction in 1631 was joined with the Papal States, with unhappy consequences for the Jewish population. Toward the end, the administrative center of the duchy was removed to the seaport of Pesaro, which had formerly been (like Rimini, part of the Papal States from 1528 on) under the brawling, exuberant House of Malatesta, and at one time was the seat of a resplendent little court, like other independent city tyrannies in this region. Throughout this part of Italy, Jewish communities based on a nucleus of loan-bankers had been known from the close of the thirteenth or the beginning of the fourteenth century.

Bordering on this area was the Duchy (as it was after the middle of the fifteenth century) of Ferrara, under the enlightened rule of the Este family; in the period here under consideration, their territory extended also to Modena and Reggio. When the main line died out at the end of the sixteenth century, Ferrara itself passed to the States of the Church, but the family continued to rule, still with the ducal title, over the other places mentioned. The House of Este pursued a progressive economic policy, encouraging new immigrants from all parts to settle under their rule. Hence in all these cities there were relatively large Jewish colonies, including some originating from Germany. After 1492, refugees from Spain also were allowed to settle in Ferrara, this group being joined, after the expulsion of the Jews from the Kingdom of Naples, by the family of Abrabanel mentioned above. They were reinforced, later in the sixteenth century, by numerous marrano refugees from Portugal, some of them persons of very high intellectual attainments, so that the role of Ferrara in certain aspects of Jewish cultural life was, for a while, extremely significant.

As long as Florence was under a Republican regime, it piously excluded the Jews—as much probably from economic as from religious zeal. But with the establishment of the hegemony of the Medici family in 1437, loan-bankers were invited to set up their establishments for the benefit of the poor—part of the general policy of conciliating the populace. When toward the close of the century, the Republican regime was restored under Savonarola and the Medici were chased away, the Jews were expelled; when the ruling house returned in 1512, the Jews came back with them. When the Last Florentine Republic of 1527-30 renewed the tradition of Savonarola's day, they were again ejected; and they finally returned again to establish a settled community under the

auspices of the Medicean Grand Duchy of Tuscany in the middle
of the sixteenth century. Notwithstanding this tardy establishment
and these periodic interruptions, Jews were thus to be found in
that lovely city in its finest hour: and thanks to the researches of
the most distinguished of modern Italian Jewish scholars, Umberto
Cassuto, we are informed in detail of the manner in which they
both participated in and reflected its eager intellectual life.

The Republic of Siena lived in traditional rivalry with Florence
until it was subjugated by the Medicean grand dukes in the
middle of the sixteenth century. Here a highly-cultured Jewish
community had been in existence since the fourteenth century
at the latest. The community of Pisa, which had succumbed to
Florentine rule in 1406, was a good deal older, being one of the
few of those in the north of the county mentioned by Benjamin
of Tudela in his classic itinerary.

In the Duchy of Milan, Jews were barely known under the
tyrants of the House of Visconti; but under the Sforza dukes
(that is, from the middle of the fifteenth century) a number of
loan-banking communities were established—mainly of German
origin. Because of religious intolerance and jealousy, they were
still not allowed to install themselves permanently in the capital
city, Milan; but there was a community in Cremona—long an
important seat of Jewish learning—with others in secondary cities
such as Lodi and Alessandria.

Piedmont, under the House of Savoy, had numerous small
Jewish communities, notably in the capital city, Turin; but this
area of Italy played a relatively slight part both in Italian life,
and in its Jewish microcosm, during the Renaissance period. The
Republic of Genoa, outstanding in this respect for its intolerance
(as has been mentioned already), had, on the other hand, hardly
any first-hand knowledge of Jews.

The House of Gonzaga had established itself in Mantua as the
result of a series of bloody deeds at the beginning of the fifteenth
century, in 1428. It was about forty years after this that the first
agreement was entered into with a group of Jewish financiers to
set up their loan-banks in the city. In the course of time, other
Jewish groups—traders, goldsmiths and the like—established themselves at their side; but for a long while the entire control of
communal affairs was vested in the banking oligarchy who re-

tained a dominant voice even after they lost absolute control. By degrees, the Gonzaga consolidated their position. The rulers were raised to the rank of marquess in 1432, and in 1530 to that of duke. Their intellectual horizons also widened, and when in 1480 Giovanni Francesco II, who was to be the third marquess (1484-1519), married Isabella d'Este, the superbly cultured daughter of the Duke of Ferrara and one of the most distinguished women of Italian history, the city became one of the most notable seats of the Renaissance spirit in art and in letters. Their descendants lost something of the swashbuckler ardor of their forbears, and Mantua was *par excellence* the seat of sixteenth-century magnificence and luxury, its reputation reverberating even in the pages of Shakespeare. The Jewish community was of course affected by the prevailing atmosphere, and there was no city of Italy in which Renaissance currents so deeply influenced it. Mantuan Jewry unfortunately still lacks its historian, but it is remarkable how at every turn in our story—whether in the record of Jewish humanism, of participation in court magnificence, in the "modernistic" approach to Hebraic studies, or in the strength of the impact of secular life—this "joyous city" (*Kiriah ha'Alizah*, as Jewish writers of the age called it) seems to take a foremost place. Curiously enough, this hardly reflected the attitude of the Gonzaga themselves, who, though they befriended individuals and appreciated the intellectual collaboration of the Jewish community, sometimes followed in other respects a far from enlightened policy toward them.

Second it seems only to the community of Mantua, as regards participation in the Renaissance spirit and outlook, was the community of Venice. This community was not one of the more ancient in Italy, Jews having been known there only sporadically before the sixteenth century. At the time of the War of the League of Cambrai of 1509, however, many fugitives from the Venetian possessions on the *terra firma* sought refuge in the shelter of the lagoon, under the leadership of the wealthy Anselmo (Asher Meshullam) del Banco, formerly of Padua, and it was impossible to chase them away. This proved to be the origin of an established community which was subsequently to be perhaps the most important in Italy after that of Rome. The first settlers were either of native Italian or of German origin; later, they were reinforced by new "Sephardi" settlers—either traders from the Levant, or else marrano refugees from the fires of the Inquisition in Portugal. In other Italian cities, the Jews were allowed to settle more or less where they pleased, until the period of reaction which began in the middle of the sixteenth century. In Venice, however, one of the conditions on which the refugees were permitted to remain was that they should live together in a single area, that designated for them in 1516 being the former *geto nuovo* or "New Foundry" near the Church of S. Geremia; hence the term "ghetto," which subsequently spread throughout Italy—and beyond—to designate the Jewish quarter.

In some respects, however, the Venetian rule was relatively mild; and when reaction was in full swing elsewhere, it was here kept within bounds. Hence in the Venice of the sixteenth and seventeenth centuries, which became one of the luxury cities of Europe, Jews intermingled freely with non-Jews and were affected in an exceptional degree by the prevailing literary tendencies (as was the case also to some extent in other cities subject to Venetian rule, such as the throbbing university town of Padua, formerly under the House of Carrara, or Verona, long ruled by the family of Della Scala). The most famous and most typical of Venetian Jews was Rabbi Leone Modena, whom I have described elsewhere as "infant prodigy and hoary prodigal; Jack of twenty-six trades (which he enumerates with some satisfaction) though perhaps master of none: cynic enough to compose the memorial address to be delivered over his coffin, but yet so constitutionally unfortunate as to survive the person whom he had designated to give it; polemist against his own convictions, and practicer against his own precept . . . withal a scholar of unusual breadth, a prolific writer, and an eloquent preacher—the pride of the Venetian ghetto even though at times its shame." Though he survived to 1648, he was preëminently a product of late Renaissance influences as they manifested themselves in the Jewish community, and owing to his rare versatility his name will often recur, in various connotations, in the following pages.

It would be wrong indeed to think of the life of the Italian Jews in the Renaissance period as being invariably care-free and unchequered. It must always be borne in mind that there were two contrasting, almost contradictory, sides to the Renaissance:

so contrasting that, were it not for the versatility and volubility of the Italian character, they could hardly have coexisted. One may express the matter briefly by pointing out that Savonarola was as much a son of the Italian Renaissance as Lorenzo de' Medici, and that the reforming movement associated with his name is as characteristic of the period and of the country as, let us say, the career of Cesare Borgia. The general reader has the impression that the Savonarolan interlude in Florentine history was utterly exceptional. This is due partly to his extraordinary personality, partly to the fact that his activity took place in such a dramatic setting and had so poignant an end. But it is not far from the truth to say that other Savonarolas made their appearance from time to time in every Italian city, preaching repentance, creating a wave of religious feeling, and stimulating a momentary reaction which was often accompanied by a burning of the vanities similar to that in Florence which is so well remembered. And in almost every case this movement would be accompanied —as it was in Florence in his day—by some reaction against the Jews, more severe or less.

Such waves of religiosity took place in city after city throughout the country at intervals—especially at the time of the Lenten sermons, when some visiting preacher (generally of the "Observantine" branch of the Franciscan Order) would urge the people to repentance. The names of Bernardo da Siena, Giovanni da Capistrano, Bernardino da Feltre, Jacopo della Marca, Alberto da Sarteano, Roberto da Lecce, constantly recur in this connection; and the enthusiasm which they sometimes aroused among the masses was extraordinary.

Among the signs of repentance for which they generally pressed was the segregation of the Jews and the enforcement of the legislation against them; sometimes even (especially in the case of Bernardino da Feltre) their expulsion from the city and the establishment of a public loan-bank (*monte di pietà*) to provide alternative credit-facilities for the poor. This is not the place to go into an account of the details of this intermittent reaction. It is sufficient to say that there was perhaps no city in Italy in which there was no revulsion at all against the Jews at this time; that frequently there were temporary, and here and there final, expulsions; and that sometimes there were riots, even accompanied by loss of life—especially in the period after 1475, when Bernardino da Feltre managed to stir up a charge of ritual murder at Trent, which had repercussions throughout northern Italy.

The political variety and competitive spirit of the Italian city-states, which stimulated the Renaissance in its broader meaning, also in one sense made possible the Jews' participation, by saving them from disaster. In view of the country's fragmentary political condition, an outburst of bigotry, however severe, implied only an adverse local interlude. Suppression in one place frequently resulted in an artificial stimulus in another: the victims of persecution sought refuge elsewhere, across the border, until the storm blew over, when they returned and took up the threads of their former life again. In a unitary state, on the other hand, if disaster ever came, it was drastic and final. That was the reason why, for example, the record of the Jews in medieval Germany, though horribly stained with persecution, was unbroken, whereas in unified countries such as England or even Spain it was interrupted. Although there is hardly any part of Italy north of the Papal States, where the Jewish colony knew no disturbance at all between the thirteenth and the seventeenth centuries, there was no time during this period when there was a simultaneous attack. Normally, indeed, until the close of the period under consideration in this volume, when the Counter Reformation established its hold, the reactions were always of short duration, and strictly localized.

After the wave of feeling had ebbed, and the series of sermons was ended, and the friar had moved on to another city, the frenzy would die down as suddenly as it had risen. The Jew repaired his broken windows, and the needy artisan again began to bring along his valuables in the hope of raising money, and there would be laughter and singing and perhaps drinking in the streets, and somber ecclesiastics would again begin to mutter at the excessive cordiality, and it would again be true that in no part of the world did such a feeling of friendliness prevail as in Italy between the people and the Jews.[1]

Jews were thus solidly, or at the worst intermittently, estab-

---

[1] C. Roth, *The History of the Jews of Italy* (Philadelphia, 1946).

lished in the Renaissance period in those parts of Italy with which
the movement is especially associated. They were, as it might be
expressed, lapped in its atmosphere, and with their extraordinarily
high degree of receptiveness they could not fail to be affected
by it. This was so in two fashions. In externals, they, no less than
their Christian fellow-townsmen, absorbed and reflected the prevailing fashions, habits and mores: at the same time, in their
religious and cultural life, their outlook was affected and
modified by the new trends and tendencies that were affecting
the religious and cultural lives of their neighbors. In some ways,
indeed, the structure of the communities fostered this new interpretation. As we have seen, they were grouped around a family
or a few families of financiers who had been invited by the civil
authorities to open their loan-banks: the Italian Jewish community of this period thus started with an essentially "aristocratic"
structure, not too common in Jewish history. It is self-evident,
moreover, that the profession of moneylending is not what might
be called an exacting one, in terms of time. Like the merchant-
princes of the Italian city-states, the loan-bankers sat at home
and waited for the profits to accrue. Meanwhile, they had ample
leisure to busy themselves with cultural matters and, encouraged
all the more by the example of their Gentile neighbors, they
did so with all their might.

The households of these Jewish magnates thus reproduced on
a smaller scale those of their patrician neighbors. Their intellectual
purview extended beyond the "four ells" of traditional talmudic
lore to philosophy, poetry, belles-lettres and even art (so far as
this was possible). They scoured Italy for erudite tutors to instruct their children and to guide their own studies—obviously,
men of an enlightened outlook similar to their own, who could
write an Italian letter, turn an elegant sonnet, join in philosophical
speculation, read Cicero in the original and if necessary refer to
the works of the Church Fathers, as well as introduce their pupils
into the labyrinth of talmudical research. These scholars sometimes acted almost as domestic chaplains, or were called on to
serve as rabbis of the incipient communities; and it is curious to
see how in the scholastic disputes which racked Italian Jewry
from time to time they adopted the "liberal" and enlightened
point of view of their employers, as contrasted with the sterner

outlook of talmudists who acted as spiritual leaders of communities with a wider composition and less selective economic
basis.

The wealth of some of the loan-bankers in question, on whom
north Italian Jewry now centered, was very considerable: indeed,
it was necessary—and even obligatory—for them to command a
large capital (though not necessarily their own) before they
began their operations. In some instances, they were at the head
of a chain of establishments spread over a wide area. The Da
Pisa family, for example, with its headquarters in that city and
later in Florence and branches in at least half a dozen other places
in Tuscany (we will encounter their name frequently in the
following pages), is estimated to have commanded in the fifteenth
century a combined capital of 100,000 florins. This also is calculated to have been the amount of the fortune of their competitor,
Manuele da Volterra, in Florence. Anselmo del Banco who is
to be considered the founder of the Jewish community in Venice,
and maintained branch-establishments throughout the Venetian
territories in northeast Italy, must have been worth something
more, if contemporaries were justified in thinking him the
wealthiest Jew in Italy at the time. (The second was said to be
the blind, irascible Immanuel Norsa, of Ferrara, whose wife
belonged to the Da Pisa family.) Anselmo's charitable brother,
Hayim (Vita) Meshullam of Padua, left, however, only 30,000
ducats, which perhaps provides a sounder basis for the estimate.[2]
These figures must not be allowed in any case to convey a false
impression. Such fortunes did not compare even remotely with
that of the Roman banker Chigi, who bequeathed 800,000 ducats
to his heirs, or that of the Medici who, even after their decadence
had begun, commanded a capital of at least 500,000 florins, apart
from chattels and real estate. (The old legend, that the Florentine
Jewish moneylenders accumulated some 50,000,000 florins in
three-quarters of a century, has long since been disproved as a
piece of irresponsible chatter.) However that may be, the Jewish
loan-bankers could well afford to participate—on a smaller scale,

---

[2] In the middle of the sixteenth century, both Samuel Abrabanel of
Ferrara and Elhanan da Fano of Bologna were said to command fortunes of 200,000 ducats; but this seems to be a wild exaggeration.

indeed—in the luxuriance of living that characterized and conditioned their environment.

But the subject with which we must deal in these pages embraces far more than the Renaissance spirit within the Jewish community, or the influence of the Renaissance on Jewish intellectuals. Occasionally, they participated in some measure in the Renaissance, in its fullest sense. Sometimes, it is a question of Jews, still as always the great internationalists—if only because at this time the world was filled with Jewish refugees, forced to remove from one country to another—bringing with them new currents, ideas and conceptions; the great historic role of the Jewish people during the past two thousand years. In such cases, there is, one may say, an essential Jewish quality in the Jewish participation. But not infrequently we find also individual Jews —volatile, impressionable, perhaps ambitious, or forced to seek a livelihood by any means that offered itself—living in the purlieus of the Renaissance courts and acting there in the most unexpected capacities. The role they played in such cases was generally more colorful or curious than important: but sometimes it was important as well.

The political fragmentation which has been referred to above did much to facilitate and encourage this Jewish participation. Obviously, it involved what might be approximately termed a more democratic atmosphere. The Renaissance courts of which one speaks so readily were not remote centers of legendary splendor of the Byzantine type, inhabited by god-like beings who were raised high above their fellow-mortals. They were among the people, and of them. The rulers' *palazzi* in town were hardly more splendid than those of the rest of the bourgeois aristocracy on the other side of the square or in the same street; their villas in the country were much the same as the others which dotted the valleys of the Arno or of the Brenta. Their owners were normally (though of course there were exceptions) approachable and affable, as they had to be unless they were to live in utter isolation; everyone knew the families from which they were sprung, and many remembered perhaps when the grandfather of the present head of the state served in his counting-house, or had entered into the service of the city as a penniless mercenary—a public employee not wholly unlike the loan-banker. Obviously, this atmosphere reacted favorably on the position of the Jews. In northern Europe, they and the feudal nobility moved in different worlds. Here, they belonged from certain points of view to the same stratum of society as their lords. The Medici of Florence were after all in their origin cloth-merchants and bankers, of the same type as (though on a larger scale than) the leaders of the Florentine Jewish community; while the Visconti of Milan or the Malatesta of Rimini were *condottieri* risen out of the ranks of the soldiers of fortune who were among the regular clients of the Jewish financiers. Moreover, in the numerically restricted society of the Italian cities it was not easy to exclude anyone who could be an amusing or informative companion, merely because of the difference of faith.

In a certain sense, indeed, these Italian Jews of the Renaissance period led double lives. There was the life of the loan-bank and the city, and there was the life of the synagogue—the one recorded in administrative documents, the other in Hebrew records. In the latter case, we find the biblical names in use, in the former the Italian—and the correspondence is not always easy to recognize. It is obvious that the Italian *Abramo* represents the Hebrew Abraham, or that *Giacobbe* implies Jacob. But sometimes there was an intricate and remoter system of application, dependent on a vague assonance, or the meaning of the Hebrew term, or the similes in the Biblical Blessings of Jacob (Genesis 49) or Moses (Deuteronomy 32). Judah, for example, was almost always rendered Leo, or Leone, in view of the Patriarch's statement that his fourth son was a lion's whelp. That was common, and natural enough. But it was less obvious that Mordecai should become, by assonance, Marco, or else Angelo in view of the curious rabbinic legend that Esther's associate was identical with Malachi, which means "My [*sc.* God's] Angel": or that Isaac, implying laughter, was translated generally (at least in the earlier period) as Gaio: or that the unfamiliar Hebrew Menahem was rendered (perhaps via the German Mendel) by a vaguely homophonous, but more recognizable, Manuele—which seldom corresponds to Immanuel! Most curious of all is perhaps the invariable rendering of Benjamin (probably because in Jacob's Blessing he is compared with a wolf, which in Germanic dialects is vaguely like Wilhelm) by

Guglielmo [= William]; or Hezekiah, at least as far back as the seventeenth century, by the vaguely similar Cesare.[3]

It is only in the last generation that this name-correspondence has been fully recognized and established, with the result that there have emerged in the ranks of the Italian loan-bankers persons who were already familiar to us from Jewish records for their patronage or participation in Hebrew literary life. Thus, for example, Manuele di Bonaiuto, head of the Banco della Vacca in Florence, who nearly fell victim to the anti-Jewish riot there in 1488, has now been recognized as Immanuel ben Azriel de Camerino, a maecenas of Hebrew letters in his day. The most distinguished Jewish scientist in Italy at the close of the fifteenth century was Mordecai ben Abraham Finzi of Mantua, clearly to be identified with the local financier Angelo di Abramo, who received permission from the Gonzaga to open a loan-bank in 1435. We will have occasion to mention, too, Meshullam ben Menahem da Volterra, who wrote an absorbing account of his voyage to Palestine in 1481: in the records he figures, not always respectably, as Bonaventura di Manuele. Azariah min haAdumim, one of the most important figures in Jewish literary life at the period, signed his Italian letters as Bonaiuto de' Rossi. These unexpected equivalents must be borne in mind constantly by the student of the Renaissance scene.

Before the background that has been hastily sketched in the foregoing pages there took place, then, some of the most colorful chapters in the history of the Diaspora, which we may now proceed to describe.

---

[3] Mention should be made of the Jew "John the Baptist" (Giovanni Battista) in a name-list from Osimo!

TWO

The Jews *in* Renaissance Society

The term Renaissance is popularly associated not only with the revival in letters, learning, and art, but also with the luxurious living and hedonistic outlook which characterized this period, especially in Italy. Inevitably this attitude was shared by the Italian Jews, in whose narrower sphere was faithfully reflected every facet of outside life. The study of this scene is not merely picturesque: it demonstrates how in all ages, as in our own, the Jew has been essentially a child of his environment. Religious sanctions and religious solidarity were stronger then than now. But even so, not merely the harmless fashions, but also in some measure the crudest vices of the outside world penetrated into the Jewish circle. There is a Yiddish proverb *Vi es kristelt sich azoi yidlt sich* ("As the Gentile does, so does the Jew"). The pages that follow will amply exemplify that constant fact.

The personal relations between Jews and non-Jews—not excluding the aristocracy and even members of ruling families—were more intimate in the Renaissance period than was ever again to be the case in any land in Europe until the nineteenth century. The Medici, for example, were on very friendly terms, generation after generation, with members of the Volterra family, the affluent Florentine loan-bankers, who were able to call on their assistance or support at time of need. Bonaventura (Meshullam) da Volterra presented Lorenzo the Magnificent more than once with a gift of game from his own hunting; while his brother Lazzaro sent the other's son, Piero de' Medici, in 1492, six tarts of marzipan, with a letter expressing his regret that owing to his absence from the city they were unable to see one another regularly as in former times. Manuele da Camerino, this family's great business rival, was also familiar with members of the ruling house and able to call on Lorenzo's help when he was in trouble with the authorities.

The same was the case elsewhere in Italy. We see Vitale (Jehiel) da Pisa entertaining there a Portuguese nobleman who came to him with an introduction from Don Isaac Abrabanel; Ercole I, Duke of Ferrara, having a Jew as his favorite companion at the gaming-table; "Dattero ebreo" (probably Joab da Rieti) on intimate terms with Ottaviano de' Medici, and constantly seen about at Bologna in the company of the Florentine artists recommended by him; Ishmael (Laudadio) da Rieti, his brother, the wealthy Sienese banker, enjoying such influence with Duke Cosimo I of Florence that he was able to induce him to give his nephew an appointment on the faculty of the University of Pisa; the poet, Salamone Usque, in correspondence with Ottavio Farnese, Duke of Parma, and the savant, Azariah de' Rossi, with the Abbot of Monte Cassino; the Duke of Mantua and his train being magnificently entertained in the house of the balletomaniac Isacchino Massarano; Ippolito (Joseph) da Fano communicating to the same prince, as they strolled together after dinner, the news of the birth of a son to the ruler of Modena, and subsequently proving so useful in various ways that he was created a marquess. He was apparently the first Italian Jew, and almost the first in Europe, to be raised to the nobility, but he may have been anticipated by Noah Manuele Norsa, father of the irascible Immanuel (Manuele) mentioned above, who in a safe-conduct granted him by Borso d'Este in 1469 is referred to as a noble (*nobilem virum*) as well as a citizen of Ferrara. Later, the members of the Abrabanel family in Naples were on terms of intimacy with Gonzalo de Cordova, the Great Captain; and it was said that Doña Bienvenida Abrabanel was associated with the education of his daughter, later Grand Duchess of Tuscany. A beautiful synagogal Ark of the Law now in the Jewish Museum in New York, bearing the date 1451 (formerly in the collection of the Davanzati Palace in Florence), is said to have been the gift of the Duke of Urbino to the Jewish community of that city; and although there is nothing in the inscription to substantiate the report, it is not inherently impossible. Further details, and further instances, will be found scattered about elsewhere in this volume.

It was at the court of Clement VII that the friendly relations between Jews and Christians in Renaissance Italy reached their climax. The story is a fantastic one. A good deal of use will be made in these pages of the diary of that almost incredible figure David Reubeni, who suddenly appeared in the ghetto at Venice in 1524 with a pretended mission from his brother, Joseph, mythical king of the tribe of Reuben, to obtain military assistance from the Pope and the various potentates of Europe in his perpetual war against the Turk. Among those who believed implicitly in this strange story was the Jewish artist, Moses da Castellazzo, of whom more later on. Thanks partly to the latter's assistance, Reubeni was able to go to Rome, where he had a remarkable reception. He was received in audience by Cardinal Egidio da Viterbo, that cultured student of Jewish and cabalistic lore, of whom more will be said later. He, perhaps misguidedly, lavished attention on him, continued to display the greatest interest in him, introduced him to other princes of the Church and procured him an audience with the Pope, Clement VII, at the Vatican, whither he ostentatiously rode on a white horse. The Holy Father seems to have believed implicitly in his curious story and gave him letters of introduction to the various potentates of Europe. Thereafter, all the wealth and culture of the Roman Jewry was at his service. He was lavishly supplied with money. When he rode through the streets, he was accompanied by a mob of more than two hundred Christians, as well as his regular escort of ten Jews. In the picturesque annals of the Renaissance, there is hardly anything more picturesque.

Later he went on to Portugal, where he was received with high honor, and a scheme was outlined to transport munitions of war to the Orient for the arming of the mythical Jewish host. In due course, the negotiations broke down. But Reubeni's appearance had by now fired the imagination of a young marrano, Diogo Pires, who in consequence became converted to Judaism under the name of Solomon Molcho and embarked on a career more remarkable even than Reubeni's. He studied the Cabala in Salonica and Safed, aroused enthusiasm in the synagogues of Ancona by his eloquent preaching, sat at the gates of Rome among the beggars and the maimed in order to fulfil in his own person the rabbinical legend relating to the Messiah; and in due course fell in again with David Reubeni, attempted to convince the Emperor Charles V of his mission, and died a martyr. Meanwhile, however, he also gained the ear and favor of Pope Clement, who gave him hospitality for a long time at the Vatican and protected him when the Holy Office began proceedings against him. It is even recounted that, when he had been condemned to death as a renegade from the Holy Catholic Faith, the Supreme Pontiff gave over a condemned criminal to execution in his place. It was an amazing episode. But it was in the full line of tradition of the Renaissance spirit at its most tolerant.

The luxury among the upper classes at this time, Gentile as well as Jewish, was extreme. The latter, men and women, went about dressed in the height of contemporary fashion. We obtain a glimpse of the interior of the wardrobe of a Jewish home in the provisions of the synod of the communities held at Forlì, in 1418, which felt impelled to order that henceforth, in order to avoid arousing Gentile jealousy, no person of either sex should be permitted to wear a baldric with colored backing (*foderato cinto*), or robe with slashed sleeves and silk lining, or mantle of sable or of ermine, or cloak (*giubetta*) of silk or velvet, and so on—the clothing in fact that may be seen in the representations of domestic life in Italian paintings of the period, or for that matter in some illuminated Hebrew manuscripts. Above all, the women went about, as in other ages, bedecked in jewelry to an extent calculated not only to cause comment but also to arouse resentment, and the sumptuary laws passed by this same synod to control this abuse had many parallels, both before and after. The great historian of the Renaissance, Burckhardt, tells how in Italy at this time "the use of perfumes went beyond all reasonable limits." In this too the Jews were over-faithful imitators. The story was told of a blind man, who recognized a Jew on his way to synagogue one feast-day by the over-scented atmosphere, and spitefully belabored him with his staff.

Italy was famous for its pageants, and the Jews followed suit. If a bride came from one city to marry in another, an escort of friends of the family would come out to greet her, mounted or afoot, and it was regarded as a great restriction when, in order to prevent adverse criticism, the congress held at Forlì restricted the maximum number on such occasions to fourteen.[1] The election on Purim of a mock-king, with implicit rule over the Jewish quarter (a practice formerly associated with Provence), was introduced into Italy too, as Azariah de' Rossi informs us, and objections were raised when in the sixteenth century the picturesque custom was abolished at Alessandria. The Italian Purim Play became so elaborate that (as will be seen elsewhere in this volume) the performances were attended by many Gentiles and a Jewish drama and dramatic companies ultimately developed out of it. Jews of course thronged to see the public spectacles as well. In the seventeenth century, for example, we find a Venetian exerting himself to secure a good place for the regatta: not improperly, to be sure, for the Jewish community was expected to subscribe solidly to the expenses involved. For a Jew to be present at the carnival celebrations wearing a mask was forbidden in papal Rome, after the reaction; but elsewhere the sermons in the synagogue were actually suspended during the period of the masquerades, so as to permit the faithful to go about their pleasure without qualms of conscience—or to save the preacher from the indignity of addressing empty benches. On such occasions the Jews, too, joined the riotous throng, regardless of a possible forbidden admixture of material (*sha'atnez*) in their dominos. Some pious rabbis of the seventeenth century discussed whether the wearing of masks was permissible in accordance with Jewish law. On the other hand, the dukes of Mantua, surveying the problem from a different angle, prescribed that the badge, which Jews had to carry on their clothing in the age of reaction to distinguish them from Christians, was obligatory even when a mask was worn.

Some Italian Jews were obviously skilled in the use of arms. Those of the lower orders streamed out of Venice with the rest of the rabble to take part in the sack of Padua in 1509, and the studious youth of Siena joined their fellow-citizens in defending

---

[1] A similar mounted wedding cavalcade seems to have been usual among the Jews in France in the Middle Ages; see *Tosaphoth* on Succah, 45a. There is an attractive representation of such a scene in an illuminated Italian Hebrew prayer-book of the fifteenth century in the British Museum.

the ramparts during the siege of 1552. David Reubeni set down his opinion that the Italian Jews were intrepid and powerfully-built, better material as fighting-men for the Jewish army that he had in mind than those of any other country.

A common failing in Renaissance Italy was card-playing and gambling; and of this the Jews, their spirit of adventure partly diverted into such sordid channels, had more than their share. In every part of the country, from at least the fourteenth century on, the communal authorities exerted themselves to keep this tendency in check; but in vain. Time after time, restrictive laws were enacted by the communities, reinforced by the rabbis, and approved by the state, but they were obviously ineffective. One episode on record shows that sometimes obedience presented its own problems. During festivities at the court of Sardinia in Alghero, early in the fifteenth century, a well known Jewish gamester who was watching the gambling was ordered by the king to take a hand, notwithstanding the ban of excommunication which the local community had recently enacted against persons who indulged in the vice; and the rabbi, who happened to be present at the time (testimony, incidentally, to the degree of social emancipation enjoyed locally by the Jews), was sorely perplexed to know whether or not he was to be reckoned an offender. The synod of Forlì sternly forbade any gaming or card-playing, especially in any place where there was a convent of the vigilant Dominican Order, and local regulations reinforced this; but to no avail. At the Christmas festivities at Ferrara, in 1477, a Jew named Abraham (possibly Abraham Norsa) lost 3,000 ducats while playing with the duke, a circumstance which helps us to understand why in the same vicinity, a few years later, a luck-less gambler registered on the fly-leaf of a Hebrew manuscript Bible (British Museum MS. Add. 27210) an oath taken on the Ten Commandments, and repeated in the presence of a non-Jewish notary, that he would play no game of chance whatsoever for the next ten years. The sixteenth-century collector of curios-ities, Tommaso Garzoni, tells how "Leone Ebreo" of Mantua (perhaps the theatrical impresario, Leone de' Sommi, one of the most remarkable figures of Italian Jewry in the age of the Renaissance)[2] once gambled away his hose-cords, so that, having

---

[2] See below, pp. 258 f.

to go straight on to an entertainment, where that night he was to look after the entrance, he had to hold up his hose with one hand and the curtain with the other! Even scholars succumbed to the vice. The classical case is the scapegrace Venetian, Rabbi Leone Modena. Though he wrote a book in which he condemned gambling, and repeatedly vowed never to indulge in it again, he was never able to keep away from the cards for long, lost more than one small fortune at them, and brilliantly demonstrated, when the Venetian community tried to stem the vice, that the proceedings were contrary to talmudic law! One is forcibly reminded of the Christian polymath, Girolamo Cardano, of the previous generation—physician, mathematician and astrologer; for, though he also was an encyclopaedic scholar, whose collected works ran to ten intimidating folios, he, like Modena, was never able to refuse to take part in a game of cards, his all-absorbing passion. Unlike Modena, however, he usually won (this at least was his boast), and instead of penning a warning against the vice, he wrote an enthusiastic volume to commend his example and methods to those who shared it. Another expert at card-games, who put his aptitude, however, to less deadly use, was the protean Abraham Colorni of Ferrara—engineer, antiquarian, inventor, cabalist and military expert—who performed the most extraordinary feats of jugglery with them and has been described as the man who invented card-tricks.[3]

Jews not only played cards; they manufactured them as well—not only for domestic use: an occupation which, in the circumstances of the time, throws incidental light on their economic occupation and artistic aptitudes. In 1527, when a puritan reaction had forbidden card-playing in Florence, and when, to boot, Jews were not allowed within the gates, a couple of them were arrested there on a charge of manufacturing—that is, painting—playing-cards and smuggling them into the city. In the following year, another Jew was fined for importing the prohibited articles from Siena. But such interests were not confined to Italy. In Frankfort, in 1510, the *schulklopfer* who aroused the faithful for service each morning was also a painter of playing-cards, and on one occasion complained to the authorities that his livelihood was undermined by other Jews who imported them from elsewhere.

---

[3] For a fuller account of him, see below, pp. 240 ff.

So comprehensive is the Jewish code of law that even games sometimes gave rise to religious problems. In the sixteenth century, the game of tennis (of course, court tennis on a hard court and with a hard ball, and unlike the lawn-tennis of today in some other particulars as well) became very popular throughout Europe. The recreation is thought to have originated in the Egyptian rites for the Spring Festival, was introduced by the Arabs to Europe, was much played in France from the twelfth century on, and in Italy had now become a folk-sport, being a feature of popular festivities as well as a fashionable diversion. The young Jews followed the example of their neighbors and began to play the game with zest. But was it permissible according to Jewish religious law to play it on Sabbaths and holy days—the days when they had most leisure? That was the problem that was submitted in 1560 to the learned, enlightened Rabbi Moses Provenzal of Mantua, who gravely considered it from every angle. His reply gives a description of the game as played at this time, which is among the most important of the documents illustrating its history—more informative in some ways even than the pedantic philosophical treatise written just before, in 1555, by Antonio Scaino. We learn that two sorts of game were played—the one with the hand, the other with a scoop (like the modern pelota). Special courts were necessary, and it seems that the Jewish players hired or owned them outside the city. There was betting on the results, and the owner of the court would take a percentage of the winnings. The rabbi very probably objected to the size of the stakes, which by this time had increased so much that the tennis-court was almost converted sometimes into a gaming-house. Observant Jews would not handle money or deal in monetary terms on the Sabbath, so the bets were expressed in terms of food; this, however, made no real difference, as later on the stakes were converted into cash. Moreover, very often the game was played during the hour of the sermon in the synagogue—not then during the regular morning service, but a separate function—to which the rabbi naturally had a strong objection if only for professional reasons. With these reservations, however, he did not object to the game as a Sabbath occupation, provided only that the players used their hands and not rackets ("small bows laced with gut, and netted with string"), which might break and tempt the players to repair them: technically, a "forbidden work" on the day of rest.

The game continued in fashion among the Italian Jews for another two generations at least. By the time of Rabbi Moses Provenzal's grandson Eliezer, also a scholar of repute, the supply of rackets on the courts had become more plentiful, so that there was now no temptation to mend broken strings; and the tennis enthusiasts maintained, though unsuccessfully, that the former restriction should be removed. In Venice, however, at this time (notwithstanding the inevitable intervention of Leone Modena), the rabbinate forbade the playing with rackets on the Sabbath. It is obvious from the documents that the pastime had by now attained great popularity here, and Modena's responsum makes it appear that hard courts were then available in the ghetto.

A distinguishing feature of the Italian Renaissance was the rediscovery of nature, which found its expression in the universal urge of the urban patricians to spend at least part of their time at their villas in the country, a practice made easier by the normal prevalence of peaceful conditions, and almost imperative by the extremity of the summer heat. In the days before the ghetto system confined them rigorously to dank areas in the cities, the Italian Jews shared this passion to the full, and at least the wealthy among them—especially it seems in Tuscany—had rural retreats to which they repaired in the torrid season in much the same way as their Christian neighbors. When David Reubeni was in Italy in 1524, he was entertained by the learned Vitale (Jehiel Nissim) da Pisa (grandson of the Jehiel mentioned above) in his country seat ensconced among the olive orchards on a hillside not far from that city. Many of the local patricians came to visit them there, he tells us, and the cultured women-folk of the household used to entertain the company with music. The Florentine banker Manuele da Volterra had a villa facetiously called Polveroso ("Dusty"), where his lavish hospitality was affectionately remembered by a visiting magnate whom his son met in Egypt on his way to Palestine twenty years later. In an inventory of household property of this period, we find listed the hangings and utensils sent to the family villa at the beginning of the summer, and brought back at its end. There is extant an amusing Hebrew document written by a band of Florentine Jews relaxing during the summer in the country, apparently in a Jewish guest-house, in which they summon one of their friends, in the style of the Otto di Guardia (the police-commission of the Republic), to join them there forthwith, under direst penalties.

How did these fifteenth-century "vacationists" spend their leisure? Certainly (as we have seen) with music, doubtless in study, perhaps in admiring the countryside. But there can be no doubt that at least some of them followed the fashions of their neighbors down to the last detail, even in their pastimes. The German-Jewish statesman, Walter Rathenau, once asserted dogmatically that no Jew could possibly enjoy hunting, whatever he might pretend. The Italian Jews of the Renaissance period appear to belie this generalization. The signatories to the document just mentioned apologize for the absence of some of their number, who were out setting traps "for they spend all their time laying snares for kites and ravens"; one of them, however, arrived just in time to append his signature, accompanied by his attendant carrying his catch (one sparrow, they said!). Bonaventura da Volterra, having had a fortunate day's hunting in January 1471, sent his friend Lorenzo the Magnificent a buck and two fawns, and another present of the sort the following winter. But obviously everything was not given away in this fashion, and there is reason to suspect that these Florentine Jews on holiday were not always meticulous in their observance of the dietary laws. Nevertheless, long after the ghetto had established its stranglehold on Jewish life, the Rabbi of Ancona, Samson Morpurgo, had to discuss (*Responsa*, ii.18), in answer to a question, whether or not hunting was permitted to Jews who could not eat the meat of the animals they caught; incidentally he expressed in noble words his profound disapproval of the practice, on the ground that unnecessary suffering to the animals was caused thereby.

The love of, or rather yearning for, Palestine was at all times extremely marked among Italian Jews. But even this expressed itself in the time of the Renaissance in a characteristic fashion. It was easier for Italian Jews than for most others to go on pilgrimages to the Holy Land, both because they lived so much nearer to it and because communications between the two countries were relatively so well organized. Except during two interludes, from 1427 to 1430 and 1467 to 1487, when the Italian sea-captains were forbidden by the Popes to transport Jews to Palestine (though indeed even now ways were found to overcome the difficulty, by following a circuitous route), there was a constant stream of Italian Jewish pilgrims to the country, and they played a disproportionately large part in the renewal of its Jewish community in the fifteenth and sixteenth centuries. Impelled though they were by the immemorial mystical and religious urge, they looked about them with the acute Renaissance gaze. Several of them left behind graphic accounts of their experiences in which, in the pungent, nervous Hebrew prose characteristic of the Italian Jews of this period, they noted all of the relevant details. With them it was not merely a question of a list of the sites of pilgrimage in the Holy Land, such as had appealed to their medieval predecessors, but a lively day-to-day record of their journey to the country, their personal experiences on the way and after they arrived, whom they met and what they saw, local life and political circumstances, economic conditions and places—not only of Jewish interest—worthy of the tourist's inspection, sometimes accompanied by nostalgic comparisons with familiar sites in their native Italy. These are among the classics of Jewish geographical and travel literature. They include the descriptions by Elijah of Ferrara in 1435 and by Joseph of Montagnana in 1481; the letters sent back to his father in Città di Castello by Obadiah di Bertinoro, the commentator on the Mishnah and reorganizer of the Jewish community in Jerusalem, when he went to Palestine via Sicily and Egypt in 1487/8; the vivacious record of the Florentine Meshullam (Bonaventura) of Volterra, Lorenzo de' Medici's friend, who went on a pilgrimage in fulfilment of a vow in 1481; the story sent back by one of Bertinoro's pupils in 1495; the careful record of Rabbi Moses Basola of Ancona in 1521-23. None of these has indeed the importance of the accurate memoranda by the Spanish traveler, Benjamin of Tudela, of his journeys throughout the Mediterranean world and as far as Bagdad in 1168-72, but this greatest of medieval documents of this type, terse and factual, is in a category entirely by itself.

Some persons not only wrote down accounts of their travels, but even illustrated them with pictures of the Holy Sites in Palestine; others combined their pious pilgrimage with antiquarian research, and collected (for example) specimens of ancient Jewish coins which would be eagerly studied on their return. Highly characteristic of the Renaissance, moreover—and reminiscent indeed of the quest for Prester John by Gentile savants—was the systematic manner in which one Abraham of Perugia undertook to assemble the accounts of Jewish travelers, in the hope of being able to throw light on the secret of the Lost Ten Tribes. But, by the side of the mystical yearnings toward Palestine, one finds in the period an expression of what may be termed the classic anti-Zionist attitude—as exceptional in older sources as it was commonplace in assimilated circles four hundred years later. When David Reubeni was in Siena, he was brutally informed by his host, Ishmael da Rieti, the affluent loan-banker who had such influence with the Medici: "I have no desire for Jerusalem; I have no desire or affection except for my city of Siena."

The antiquarian interest which was a feature of Renaissance life was also shared by the Italian Jews, who indeed sometimes based their enthusiasms on similar faulty foundations. In 1465 there was found at Cividale in Friuli an ancient Hebrew tombstone, which was believed to bear the date 3156 according to the Hebrew reckoning—that is, 605 before the Christian era! In typical fashion, the Jewish community celebrated the find by a new inscription to commemorate their antiquity. This was set up by the side of the original tablet in the city gate, where it may still be seen—although the older one, which, if it existed, was certainly not pre-Roman, has long since disappeared. It was universally believed that four foremost Italian Jewish families—Min ha-Adumim (De' Rossi), Min haAnavim (Anau, Dei Piatelli) Min haZekenim (De' Vecchi) and Min haTapuhim (De' Pomi: but there is some uncertainty about this name—some versions list a different clan)—were descended from noble families of Judaea which had been brought back from his Palestinian campaign by Titus, after the destruction of Jerusalem. This obviously reflected the prevailing tendency of Italian families to trace back their descent, with the aid of fictitious pedigrees, to classical times, Latinizing their names so as to give verisimilitude to their claim. Indeed, according to recent ideas, the De' Rossi, those superbly cultured sons of their age, owed this appellation to nothing more romantic than the fact that their forebears had had been engaged in the dyeing industry.

Such patrician families, and others less exalted or of more recent vintage, flaunted quasi-heraldic badges—embryonic coats-of-arms, in fact—on their ritual appurtenances, manuscripts, tombstones and so on: not infrequently embodying the traditional lion of the tribe of Judah or the palm tree which symbolizes the upright, but generally more individual and more distinctive (for example, the three blackamoors' heads, blindfolded, in use by the Norsa family). Indeed, the chronicler Ibn Jacchia cheerfully asserted that coats-of-arms were first introduced to the world by the ancient Hebrews.

The Italian Jews of the Renaissance period were thus sunk to a great degree in the literary atmosphere and intellectual tradition of their environment. Their Hebraic training widened their intellectual horizons; it did not, as was the case in so many other lands later on, transfer them to a wholly different sphere. Any person with the slightest pretext to education was familiar with Dante and with Petrarch. Rabbis quoted them in their sermons, and exegetes mentioned them in their biblical commentaries. The *Divina Commedia* was even transliterated into Hebrew characters by some enthusiast to whom this method of writing was more familiar. Nor were the Jews ignorant of later poets, not yet of full classical status. Leone Modena's first serious experiment in Italian versification was a rendering into Hebrew of the first canto of Ariosto's *Orlando Furioso* from the original. It is characteristic that he translated similarly—and probably at the same tender age—the twenty-eighth canto, which was omitted in the standard editions after the end of the sixteenth century because of its moral laxity. Something of this spirit continued into the age of the ghetto. The eminent Italian Jewish poet of the late eighteenth century, Salamone Fiorentino, used to recount how his poetical appreciation was first aroused when he once heard a Jewish mother in Siena lulling her child to sleep to the strains of Petrarch.

Like so much else, the educational system among the Jews of Renaissance Italy was readjusted in accordance with the new conceptions that had come to prevail in the outside world. The old talmudic disciplines were by no means neglected. But these were supplemented by studies in accordance with the Renaissance attitudes—and this was the case even with the German immigrants, newly established in northern Italy, whose remoter background was hardly distinguished by the spirit of modernity. Hebrew grammar and composition were carefully imparted, so that the Italian Jews became distinguished for the purity and accuracy of their prose style. Even Latin was added to the curriculum: in the Yeshiva maintained at Siena by Rabbi Joseph Marli (that is, D'Arles) under the auspices of the lordly Ishmael da Rieti, there was, for example, a Christian teacher of "grammar" (presumably Latin and Italian) who held regular classes every afternoon, the Hebrew and talmudic studies being interrupted for this purpose. Of course, the vernacular was not neglected. In other countries, it was unusual to find a Jew reading the vernacular: in Italy, Leone Modena stood amazed at the obscurantists who deliberately confined their reading to Hebrew. On the other hand, Judah Asahel del Bene, writing in 1646, complained that Italian was being studied to the detriment of Hebrew, which was shamefully overlooked. Private teachers, at least, were supposed to add to all this instruction not only Hebrew versification, but also music and dancing. Toward the end of the fifteenth century, Jacob ben Judah Landau, an immigrant from Germany resident in Naples, composed his famous but not very original compendium of Jewish religious law entitled *Agur* ("The Bundle") for the benefit of a native-born pupil whose time was so taken up with the study of natural science and philosophy that he had no leisure for the Talmud.

Sometimes the knowledge of Latin, even in the upper classes, among Italian Jewry was elementary to a degree, and we find some Jewish writers apologizing for their poor equipment. But the better educated had in certain cases much the same introduction into classical training as their Christian fellow-citizens of the same social class. Manuele da S. Miniato, the scholarly loan-banker who taught Giannozzo Manetti Hebrew,[4] had a good knowledge of Latin, but was anxious to receive instruction in philosophy. Certain of the Italian Jewish writers show a fair knowledge of the classical literature, as we shall see in the cases of Judah Messer

---

[4] For all these names, see below, pp. 137-164.

Leon or Azariah de' Rossi or Leone Ebreo. Of course, the same was true for a handful of the upper class in Spain as well: Don Isaac Abrabanel, in a letter of condolence of 1470/1 to the Count of Faro (son of the Duke of Braganza) quoted not only Aristotle, but also Seneca, as he did long after in his Hebrew Commentary on the Prophets. It is more significant in a way that a comfort-loving businessman such as Bonaventura da Volterra, seeing a crocodile for the first time, in Egypt, was able to quote from memory Pliny's description of one. Recently there has come to light the library-catalogue of an Italian Jew of the sixteenth century. It is written in Hebrew characters and describes a small collection of works in various branches of knowledge, one-third of them in Italian or Latin. This would have been out of the question in any other country of Europe at that time.

Some Jewish scholars—especially those who had gone through the university—could speak Latin also, and to good effect. Leone Modena's uncle, Abtalion, when he was sent to Rome to plead on behalf of the Talmud, delivered an oration in Latin before Pope Gregory XIII and all his assembled cardinals, which lasted for two hours without interruption. Thomas Coryat, the English traveler, visiting the Venetian ghetto in 1608, had no difficulty in finding "a certaine learned Jewish Rabbin that spake good Latin," on whom he forced a religious controversy.

This was the golden age of the Italian sermon: and the Italian Jewish community too produced, in persons such as Judah Moscato and David del Bene and Azariah Picho,[5] eloquent preachers who commanded a degree of popularity hardly imaginable at present. Their pulpit addresses, normally delivered not at the "statutory" services but generally on Sabbath afternoons (when a couple of hours could be devoted to this and nothing else), attracted large and enthusiastic audiences and gained their authors a wide reputation. They did not concentrate preponderantly on points of rabbinic scholarship, as was the case in other countries, but were ethical, moral, and hortatory, not dissimilar in this to those of the friars who exhorted the multitudes to repentance during Lent. The structure too was greatly influenced by that

---

[5] Generally but inaccurately called "Figo"—a faulty retransliteration of the current Hebrew form פינ"ו.

of contemporary Italian homiletics: certainly artificial, being based on a rigorous pattern from the biblical citation at the beginning to the peroration at the end; but at the same time aesthetic in conception and harmonious in form. Not only were the classical Jewish sources quoted, but also, as we shall see, a wide range of classical and vernacular literature. Allusions to contemporary conditions, moreover, make these addresses a veritable mine of information for the social historian. Until the eighteenth century, they were invariably published, if they were deemed worthy of the honor, in Hebrew: but they were delivered in mellifluous Italian. Hence they sometimes attracted considerable numbers of non-Jews as well, including on occasion priests and friars or even visiting princes. Leone Modena in his autobiography tells, in his enthusiastic fashion, many tales to show how his sermons in the Venetian ghetto attracted the most distinguished audiences, and were sometimes referred to admiringly later on from the pulpits of neighboring churches. Giordano Bruno is recorded to have esteemed greatly a Jewish preacher of his day who (he observed) said nothing in his addresses that was not full of sense: he has been identified conjecturally with the Mantuan Rabbi Judah Moscato mentioned just above, author of the popular collection of sermons, *Nefuzoth Judah* or "The Dispersions of Judah" (first published in Venice in 1588, and often reprinted down to our own day) which first introduced the new standards and styles to the synagogue and thus inaugurated a new epoch in Jewish homiletic literature.

The Renaissance period coincided more or less with the first association of the Jews with the European university system. The reason is plain. In the early Middle Ages, when the level of the Jews in general and scientific culture (especially as regards medicine) was on the whole higher than that of their Christian neighbors, their own schools or those of Arab teachers were sufficient for their needs. When European culture began to advance, and the Arab culture to lag, the question of training began to be of great importance. The universities of the Christian lands at this time did their best to exclude Jews, or admitted them only reluctantly, the distinguished Jewish physicians of the Middle Ages in most instances having received their training privately. In the first half of the fourteenth century, the great jurist Bartolo de

Sassoferrato refused permission to two Jews, who had studied at the University of Bologna and successfully passed their examinations, to be admitted to their degree; for the doctorate was (he said) a dignity similar to that of knighthood, from which Jews were automatically excluded by canon law. Other legal experts agreed with this ruling.

In time, however, a more tolerant spirit began to prevail here and there. The earliest instance on record of the conferring of a degree on a Jew in an Italian university seems to be as late as 1409, when Leone Benaiah, of Imola, is said to have been admitted to the doctorate at Padua. There is some doubt as to the exact date, but from about this time, the Jewish physicians who were so prominent in Italy (even, as we shall see later, at the papal curia) generally seem to have held a doctor's degree from some university. Christian rigorists objected; and although the protective bull issued in 1429 by Pope Martin V (not without persuasion, solidly supported) included attendance at universities among the normal Jewish activities which should not be impeded, the Council of Basel in 1434 sternly prohibited Jews to be admitted to academic degrees. In Italy, however, its prescriptions were not obeyed very meticulously, or for long, and the Jewish graduates of the Italian universities at this period are relatively numerous. If any doubts arose as to the legality of the procedure, a papal dispensation or license could be obtained without much difficulty; or else there could be some slight change in the procedure, so as to deprive it of some of its pomp and make it less ecclesiastical in nature. Moreover, the Jews had various convivial burdens imposed on them by custom on such occasions. At Padua, for example, on the day of graduation they had to keep an open table with food and drink for all who cared to come: and one may readily imagine that some of the more impecunious Gentiles took care to arrange their diet on the previous days in such a way as to do justice to this enforced hospitality. In due course, however, this usage was compounded for by a fixed tribute. Every Jew on his graduation had to give the beadle of the university a quantity of sweet-meats for the academic attendants, and for each of the many "nations" into which the student body was divided. Thus, it was reckoned that it cost twice as much for a Jew as for a non-Jew to graduate. With local differences, this system probably applied elsewhere as well.

The Jews received on graduation the same elaborate diplomas as the Gentiles; a few are extant, lavishly illuminated and embodying the portrait of the graduate, though none is to hand earlier than the seventeenth century. We have records of eighty Jews who graduated (always in "philosophy and medicine") between 1517 and 1619 in Padua, as well as some in Naples (1490-1504), Perugia (1547-1551), Pisa (1554), Siena (1543-1695), Pavia (1563), Ferrara (c. 1540) and perhaps elsewhere. When Isaac Cohen da Viterbo graduated at Siena in 1543, the university authorities jubilantly escorted him with music to the house of his popular patron Ishmael da Rieti. In Bologna, indeed, a specific intervention of the papal governor was necessary when Angelo (Mordecai) Modena desired to graduate in 1528; for the university, never having admitted a Jew to a degree before, did not wish to create a precedent. They had to yield however; and the new doctor, like all others who took their degree while the Emperor Charles V was residing here for his nefarious conference with the Pope, was raised by him to the dignity of knight. There is extant the text of the eloquent oration made at the University of Ferrara about this time by a distinguished jurist, Caelio Calcagnini, when he conferred the degree upon a Jew named Reuben, in accordance with the usual formalities—handing him a closed book, placing a ring on his finger and a beretta on his head, and giving him the kiss in sign of affection. However, such broadmindedness was to disappear in most places after 1584, when Pope Gregory XIII stringently forbade the practice of medicine by Jews, except among their own co-religionists. From now on, it was only at Padua that the university retained a relatively tolerant attitude, becoming for the next two hundred years the main center of medical study for Jews from all over Europe.

Not only were there Jewish undergraduates, but in exceptional cases there were also Jewish teachers. Surprisingly enough, they had been known in the tolerant atmosphere of ancient Alexandria, where the Jews Adamantius and Domnus gave instruction in medicine in the Museum in the fifth century. In the Middle Ages, this was out of the question. It is true that there are a number of curious legends connecting Jewish scholars with the development of some of the most ancient European seats of learning—for example, that a Jew was associated in the eighth century, together with an Arab, a Greek and a Latin, in the founding of the famous medical school of Salerno, in south Italy, or that Jacob ibn Tibbon (Profiat Judaeus), the scientist whose astronomical works were used by Dante, was Regent of the Medical Faculty of Montpellier in the thirteenth. There is assuredly no basis for either of these tales which are manifestly quite improbable. In the Renaissance period, somewhat more plausible legends of this sort are current. Elijah del Medigo, for example, the tutor of Pico della Mirandola, may have taught informally in Padua, as we shall see; but there is no record of his name in the university archives as an official teacher. His kinsman, Samuel Menahem del Medigo, later rabbi in Candia (Crete), is also stated to have taught philosophy in Padua a few years later. Similarly, it is said that the learned and pious Rabbi Judah Minz, who died a centenarian in 1508 after officiating as rabbi in Padua for forty-seven years, had also lectured in philosophy at the university of that place, and that his statue was once to be seen on the main staircase. This tale, too, circumstantial though it is, has no documentary support.

On the other hand, there were various Jews who certainly did have teaching appointments in Italian universities in the period of the Renaissance. One may leave out of account one or two who taught Hebrew, such as Abraham Gallo, who lectured at Ferrara, or the nephew of Ishmael da Rieti (probably Simon Vitale, that is, Samuel ben Jehiel) who through his uncle's influence received an appointment at Pisa, with which seat of learning the name of one Hercules Judeus is also vaguely associated. Nor can one take into consideration in this connection marranos whose attachment to Judaism may or may not have been known, such as Amatus Lusitanus, who taught anatomy at Ferrara for a short while in the middle of the sixteenth century. There are in addition to these a small number of Jewish physicians, whose loyalties were notorious, who received official positions as university teachers. For example, that same Elias Sabot (Elijah ben Sabbetai), who at one time attended on Henry IV of England and was in service at many Italian courts, taught at the University of Pavia at the beginning of the fifteenth century; Don Judah Abrabanel (better remembered as Leone Ebreo, the author of the "Dialogues of Love") was reader in medicine and "astrology" (comprising, of course, astronomy) at Naples nearly a hundred years later; and—the best attested case of all—the Spanish-born Jacob Mantino, called Giacobbe Giudeo, an extremely versatile and in his day important figure, received official nomination in 1529 as Lecturer on Medicine at the University of Bologna, to be followed (probably in 1539-41) by appointment as Professor of Practical Medicine at the "Sapienza" organized not long before by Pope Leo X in Rome. On the former occasion, however, the post was a sinecure, for this was an ingenious device of his patron, Pope Clement VII, to secure him a regular source of income without cost to the papal treasury.[6]

Among the more conservative rabbis, university attendance raised certain specific problems. There was a great similarity between the academic robes and the normal Jewish costume worn at this time, to the distress of German anti-Semites, who alleged that sometimes a short-sighted student would reverently salute a Jew under the impression that he was a Master of Arts. The learned Italian Rabbi Joseph Colon on the other hand was asked whether the academic robes could be considered in the rabbinic sense "garb of the Gentiles," which a pious Jew should not wear. This he answered in the negative (*Responsa*, § 88). But another problem arose—the cloak was square-cut, with four corners: should the Jewish student not attach to it the ritual fringes, as prescribed in the Book of Numbers? This was perhaps a more ticklish matter. Colon was inclined to answer affirmatively (§ 149), though Judah Messer Leon of Mantua, a truer son of the Italian Renaissance, vigorously disagreed.

University education involved, however, more fundamental problems than this. In the first place, there was the question of obtaining admission, for the instances that have been quoted above were in fact exceptions proving the rule. Secondly, after

---

[6] According to the chronicler Gedaliah ibn Jacchia (who boasted that his uncle, Judah ibn Jacchia, was the third Jew to graduate at the University of Padua), the grammarian Abraham de' Balmes gave courses at that university, which were frequented by Christian students. The archives, however, provide no confirmation of this.

There are fuller details regarding all the persons mentioned above elsewhere in this volume, mainly in chapters VI and X.

the Jewish student was admitted, there was the problem of insuring that his secular training did not overwhelm or obscure his Jewish interests. In Sicily, there was a very strong medical tradition among the Jews, several court physicians and even some woman practitioners being recorded. As elsewhere in the Aragonese dominions, an examination before some competent authority, such as the Jewish *protomedico* Joseph Abenafia, was necessary before one could be licensed. As the tradition of Arab medicine waned here the problem of medical training became serious. The communities of the island determined, accordingly, on an amazing new venture—none other than to establish their own Jewish university, in order to satisfy the needs of young Jews who were thirsting for knowledge outside the "four ells" of rabbinical study. They presented their petition to this effect through their representative, Benjamin Romano of Syracuse, and on January 17, 1466, were formally authorized by King John to set up a university, or *studium generale*, in any city they might choose, to engage and discharge doctors, jurists, etc., "and in the said university to arrange instruction in all the approved sciences for those who seem proper thereto and to others." Moreover, the king took under his protection "all the doctors, jurists, masters, students and others who shall frequent the said *studium generale* . . . as well as the said *studium* itself." The precise object of the foundation is not stated. It is obvious, however, that it must have been intended in the main for the study of medicine and the conferring of academic degrees in that subject: not long before, in 1451, the practice of medicine among Christians had been thrown open to Jews, and there had perhaps been an influx into the profession. From the repeated mention of jurists, it is probable that civil law—in which Jewish experts were obviously needful for the domestic business of the communities—was to be another subject. That the humanities were envisaged, except incidentally, is most improbable, and Jewish studies would plainly have been superfluous. However that may be, the scheme was indubitably overambitious, and whether or not the Jewish university functioned for a short while, we hear nothing more about it. But the record is of exceptional interest. The University of Palermo was founded long after this date, at the close of the eighteenth century, and this is apparently the first episode in this aspect of the academic history of the island.

In north Italy precisely a hundred years after this Sicilian experiment, an analogous project was launched, though with a somewhat different slant. By this period, as we have seen, Jews had begun to frequent the Italian universities in some numbers. This involved two difficulties. One was that Jewish elementary education (using that term in a wider sense than would be applicable today), centered as it was on Jewish studies, provided an inadequate pre-university training. The other was that, once entered at the universities, the Jewish youths would be so much absorbed in the general courses that they would have no time to pursue futher their talmudic and Jewish studies, their progress in which was normally interrupted in these crucial years.

Accordingly, in the middle of the sixteenth century, Rabbi David Provenzal of Mantua and his physician-son Abraham, launched an ambitious scheme. Because of their eminent status as members of a rabbinical family outstanding in that city for many generations, which combined Jewish and secular culture to a remarkable degree (we have encountered them before), they proposed the establishment of a Jewish academy in a prospectus which was printed and circulated among the Italian Jewish communities in 1566. In this academy university instruction should be anticipated and in some measure supplemented; there were to be regular courses, not only in the Talmud and Hebrew studies generally (including philosophy on the one hand and calligraphy on the other), but also in secular subjects, in which Jewish students might be backward—Latin and Italian composition, logic, mathematics, rhetoric, astronomy, and of course (and preëminently) medicine. Those who could not as yet read Latin freely were to study in Hebrew translations "for in science the importance lies in the substance, not the language." Meanwhile, arrangements would be made for the students to have clinical training by attending on various physicians, Christians as well as Jews, in their practices. They would thus be enabled to leave the academy with a complete general culture, thoroughly imbued however with the Jewish spirit, and would be able to graduate at the university of their choice in the shortest possible period of time, without being submitted to an excessive assimilatory influence.[7]

Whether or not anything practical resulted from this is unknown: there is some evidence, though it is not quite conclusive, that this "university" was in fact established and did function for a little time. In any case, it was not until some three or four hundred years had elapsed that such conceptions as these were to be renewed in Jewish life.

---

[7] The spread of "modern" cultural conceptions among the Jews was, of course, not universal: nor was it unopposed. Just as some Christian religious revivalists of the period set themselves against the Renaissance tendencies, so some pietists and obscurantists among the Jews adopted a similar attitude. Thus a talmudist named Jacob ben David Provenzal, of Naples, wrote a letter in 1490 to David Messer Leon (published in *Dibre Hahamim*, Metz, 1849) in which he roundly condemned all secular learning, not excepting even the study of medicine. It is probable that he was the progenitor of the highly enlightened Mantuan family of a later generation! The episode illustrates the assimilative force of the Italian environment, even in a staunch rabbinic house.

THREE

Manners *and* Morals

In popular imagination the Renaissance figures prominently, if not preëminently, as a period of loose morality. The mere names of the Borgia and the Gonzaga, of Michelangelo and Benvenuto Cellini, of Machiavelli and Aretino, conjure up—not wholly un-justifiably—pictures of moral delinquency, not to say turpitude. The same attitude was reflected, though certainly not as universally as is sometimes thought, in every level of society. Not-withstanding the very different background and circumstances of life of the Italian Jews in this period, and the tenacity of the family tradition among them, this aspect was not entirely absent from their lives also. It is yet another example of what will be found so markedly throughout these pages: however strongly Jewish, they were at the same time profoundly Italian.

From early times, the Church had voiced the strongest possible objection to sexual relations between Jews and Christians, whether in or out of matrimony; such relations were considered almost as a species of perversion. Throughout Europe such intercourse—even though a prostitute were in question—was forbidden by the utmost rigors of the law; as late as the seventeenth century a Jewish girl was burned in Rome as the result of a love-affair with a young noble. Their own strict moral code should have prevented Jewish youths from succumbing to this hazardous temptation, even if considerations of this nature had not applied. Yet, out of a total of some eighty-eight condemnations of Jews recorded in Florence in the fifteenth century, no fewer than thirty-four were for sexual offences. There is reason to believe that the cultured Bonaventura da Volterra went on his pilgrimage to Palestine in 1481, of which he has left so vivid an account, in fulfilment of a vow that he had made some time before when he was in danger of sentence of death for such a misdemeanor.

No fewer than fifty Jewish prostitutes are said to have been burned in Rome in our period. At Padua, to the rabbis' horror, there were even disorderly houses in the Jewish quarter, the civic authorities considering the Jews' attempts to secure their suppression somewhat bizarre. In Florence, too, in 1460 the Jews were formally permitted to have their own prostitutes; and two "women of the town" are mentioned in the fifteenth-century records. (This, to be sure, is not so bad as were conditions in contemporary Spain where, if we are to believe the popular preacher Isaac Arama [§ 20], the leaders of the Jewish community actually encouraged prostitution in the Jewish quarter, so as to prevent worse abuses.) In 1416, a rabbinical synod held at Bologna took measures to stem what they regarded (it is to be hoped, with pardonable ecclesiastical exaggeration) as the general prevalence of immorality among the younger generation, especially with Gentile women. As a matter of fact, the whole question was complicated by the fact that Jews and prostitutes, fellow-pariahs, were sometimes segregated in the same area of the town, as a symbol of degradation—thus adding to the temptations of the Jewish youth and to the perplexity of their mentors. It may be observed that the criticisms of the rabbinical moralists are leveled mainly against the men; the traditional purity of Jewish womanhood seems to have been generally maintained, even in this licentious age and environment. But Rabbi Obadiah di Bertinoro, passing through Sicily on his way to Palestine in 1487, noted the low state of sexual morality, and dryly observed that most brides came under the marriage canopy when they were already pregnant. It is known that the learned, charitable, well-born Don Samuel Abrabanel, husband of one of the most esteemed Jewish women of the age, had a "natural" son—very much in the spirit of Gentile society in his beloved Ferrara.

From Urbino we have an almost unique document attesting the solemnization there in 1511 of a marriage in the most formal fashion by consummation—a method regarded by rabbinical law as legal but repugnant. What is most astonishing is that this took place in a room in the palace of the Duke of Urbino himself! There are even cases, in sixteenth-century Italy, hardly to be traced among the Jews at any other place or time, of condemnations for homosexual offences.

The moral outlook of the age is reflected in Italian Jewish literature. Immanuel of Rome, Dante's contemporary and imitator (of whom much will be said later in this volume) boasted immoderately in his poems, some of them highly erotic, of his amatory conquests. Even though these may have been fictitious, as such boasts frequently are, this would appear highly paradoxical according to modern lights in a scholar, exegete and synagogal employee—though it was not perhaps so regarded in a country where some of the classical erotic collections were compiled by persons who were in Holy Orders. He did not stand alone. Giuseppe Gallo (Joseph Sarfati), son of the sixteenth-century papal physician Samuel Sarfati, and a notable figure in his own right in Italian Jewish literary life, composed at least one Hebrew poem in honor of his mistress. There is extant, too, a delightful Hebrew ode written by Raphael da Faenza, the Florentine Jewish litterateur of the age of Lorenzo the Magnificent, to celebrate the frail beauty of one Galantina Morosina, whose name (unless it should be read *meRossena*, that is, Da Rossena, a fairly well known Italian Jewish family) reminds one of the lady-love who so long engaged the affections of Cardinal Bembo. This is in itself curious. But what is more curious is that it was copied on the flyleaves of a prayer-book, now in the great library of Parma, together with a hymn composed in honor of the same lady.

Nevertheless, there can be no doubt that in the vast majority of cases the traditional moral standards continued to prevail for ordinary men and women. This is vividly illustrated in an episode in the autobiography of Leone Modena, which contains one of the most moving love passages in the whole Jewish literature. At the age of seventeen, with his complete approval, his parents arranged for his betrothal to his cousin Esther, though he had a presentiment in a dream that she was not to be his bride. When in the following year he arrived in Venice for the marriage, he found her in bed, in a decline. Her state became worse and worse. On the day of her death she sent for Leone and threw her arms around him and kissed him and said: "Indeed I realize that this is shameless conduct on my part. But God knows that in the year we have been betrothed we have not touched one another even with the tips of our fingers. Now that I am to die, it is permitted me by death." Not long afterward, she passed away. A month later, Leone was reluctantly persuaded to marry her sister, with whom he lived almost from the first in perpetual friction.

Even the names borne by Italian Jewish women in this period emphasize their assimilation to the general population among whom they lived. The men all had biblical names, at least for synagogue and religious use, though they would be known familiarly by vernacular equivalents, as we have seen. But a very large proportion of the women had only Italian names, which were of a specifically non-biblical nature—Laura, Laudomia, Imperia, Diamante, Marchigiana, Virtudiosa, Armonia, and so on; sometimes even the names of pagan deities, such as Pomona. How widely this fashion prevailed may be indicated from one single instance. There is no need to apologize for adducing once again an example found in connection with Leone Modena, about whose background we have far more intimate details than is the case with any other person in this age. The woman whom he married after the episode recounted above bore the biblical name Rachel. But at a time of sickness and heightened religiosity, this was symbolically altered in accordance with the prescriptions of the cabalists. The new name chosen was Diana—which was, incidentally, the name borne also by a pious kinswoman of his who had a reputation as a talmudist, as well as by his daughter! Nothing can show more vividly than this curious anecdote, told by Modena in all innocence, the degree of cultural identification at this time between the Italian Jews and their neighbors, generation after generation, even in a rabbinical family outstanding for its piety and erudition.

The same spirit reflected itself in every other possible way: so much so that, according to one perhaps biased statement, Jewish women at Venice called on the Madonna in childbirth. Some exquisite household appurtenances made at this period are extant, wholly Italian in feeling but Jewish in symbolism, which show how profoundly Jewish women were affected by the aesthetic standards of their neighbors. The periodically-enacted Sumptuary Laws, such as the one passed in 1418 at the Synod of Forlì which has been spoken of above, prove how they also followed the prevailing fashion in dress and adornment—and how faithfully they shared the Italian tendency to excess in such matters; and from the fifteenth century on, many Jewish communities throughout the country, imitating the secular authority, periodically enacted codes, called *Pragmatiche*, to enforce moderation. The employment of adventitious aids to female beauty was a perpetual preoccupation of Renaissance preachers and moralists, and it is certain that Jewish women followed (or anticipated) the general fashion. During waves of repentance (such as that at Florence at the time of Savonarola) the Christian preachers succeeded in having such instruments of temptation publicly burned; there is no evidence that anything of this sort ever took place within the Jewish community, however much the rabbis may have fulminated. It is interesting to speculate whether the wearing of wigs by the pious Jewish matron, so as to prevent men other than her husband from being tempted by her crowning beauty, may not in fact have had precisely the reverse effect from what was intended; for in Italy generally no sort of ornament was more common than false hair, generally blond, to supplement that which nature had given, and the wealthy Jewess was able to keep abreast of fashion simply by remodeling her wig.

Jewish women were in fact thought to be experts in the theory and practice of cosmetics. In 1508, the aging Caterina Sforza, Countess of Imola, that virago of the Renaissance—widow of three husbands and mother of eight children living or dead—finding in her forty-sixth year that her once-famous physical attractions were waning, sent one of her esquires to an expert Jewish "beautician" in Rome, named Anna, asking for a fresh supply of face creams. The letter which Anna wrote to accompany the consignment is still extant. She sent "a black salve which removes roughness in the face, making it fresh and smooth. Apply this at night and allow it to remain until the morning; then wash yourself with pure river water; next, bathe your face in the lotion called Acqua da Canicare; then dab it with the white cream; afterwards take a pinch of this powder, dissolve it in the lotion labeled Acqua Dolce and apply it to your face, as thinly as possible." A price-list follows; the black salve cost four carlini an ounce, the Acqua da Canicare the same amount per bottle, the white cream twice as much, and the Acqua Dolce a gold ducat a bottle. The letter concludes: "If your illustrious highness will apply these preparations, I am sure that you will continue to order from me." The countess was certainly not a very good customer after this interchange, for she died in the following year. The letter in question has been preserved in a volume containing her cosmetic and medical recipes (copied at the close of her life by a Florentine soldier, the Count of Montefalco), which also contains advice on such important matters as how to make the hair blond or auburn: it is interesting to speculate how much more of this information may have been derived from Anna or her associates. For Caterina was by no means the only famous Italian beauty of the Renaissance period who had recourse to Jewish women for such objects. Bianca Capello, the upstart Grand Duchess of Tuscany who was to meet so tragic a fate, is said to have received unguents and supplies from them, and once, as a token of her gratitude, to have saved the Florentine community from expulsion by her infatuated husband. Naturally, such interests were not confined to Italy. A little after this, we find Esperanza Malchi, a Jewish woman at the court of Constantinople, writing to Queen Elizabeth of England on behalf of the Sultana and asking her for certain "distilled waters for the face and odoriferous oils for the hands," of English manufacture, as a partial return for a present of articles from the Levant for the royal wardrobe.

The Renaissance period in Italy was from certain points of view an age of feminine emancipation, in life if not in law. Indeed, Jacob Burckhardt, the great historian of the movement, emphasizes the fact that, in order to understand the higher forms of social intercourse at this period, we must remember that women then stood on a footing of perfect social equality with men. The generalization, though perhaps too sweeping, is true with certain reservations: and it was inevitable that this structure of society should be reflected in Jewish life as well. The Renaissance may thus be said to have witnessed in some measure in the Jewish community, too, an anticipation of the movement for the emancipation of women, at least in the social sense, which is associated with the nineteenth century.

Even the rabbinical correspondence of the period reflects this fact to some extent, as for example the inquiry addressed to one rabbi which shows how the Jewish women of Casalmaggior in Lombardy were accustomed to go unescorted about the fairs and markets in the surrounding countryside to dispose of their wares; or the problem addressed to another authority regarding a woman of Pavia who did not wish her husband to remain an innkeeper and ran away from him when he refused to change his calling.

There were women physicians too, such as we meet at this time also in Spain and in Provence; with the reservation that those in Italy did not apparently restrict their attentions to their own sex. One, Virdimura, wife of Pasquale di Medico of Catania, was authorized to practice in Sicily, after examination, in 1736, her intention being, it seems, to work especially among the poor; another, Perna, was licensed at Fano in 1460. Elsewhere in this work an account is given of the professional or semi-professional women singers who figured at Mantua and Venice and attained a considerable reputation—in one case, a member of a distinguished rabbinical house.

The education given to women in Italy at this period was modeled on that received by the men. Although some obscurantists objected, this was true, with certain reservations, in the Jewish community as well. Instruction in the Talmud was indeed considered a superfluity for the female (though as we shall see there were exceptions); but the humanistic element in education was enjoyed by both sexes. A separate institution, or *Talmud Torah*, for the elementary instruction of girls is said to have been established in Rome as early as 1475. The date is not quite certain, but it is obvious that female education was not overlooked: Jewish women of the upper class at least were initiated into elementary Hebrew studies—if no more than this—in the same way as their brothers. In the ghetto period the primary schools were normally kept by women, who taught reading and writing, and obviously must have studied before they instructed, and there is some evidence that the same applied from the beginning of the sixteenth century. Sometimes, the girls had private tutors: Hezekiah Rieti, dedicating his Judaeo-Italian[1] translation of the proverbs (Venice, 1617) to Isaiah Massarani of Mantua, told how his esteem for the family dated back to the time when he had been entrusted with the task of "educating in good letters" his patron's daughter-in-law, Sorellina Saraval. We know, too, of a teacher in Piedmont at this time, who seems to have specialized in the instruction of

---

[1] Italian printed in Hebrew letters, in the same fashion as Judaeo-German or Judaeo-Spanish.

girls. But the instructors might be women: David Reubeni mentions a woman teacher who taught Bible (of course in the original) to the daughter of a Roman Jew, whom he considered to have made remarkable progress in her studies. The fact that Hebrew poems were often written in honor of women obviously implied that they were able to read and understand them.

No doubt there were some who did not advance beyond the art of reading, and knew little of Hebrew except the words that had entered into everyday parlance. It was for their benefit that there were published at this time various translations of the prayer-book, and other such works, in Judaeo-Italian, a phenomenon which obviously reflects the limitations to their attainments. The fact that literature of this type disappears after the middle of the sixteenth century (the last edition was published at Mantua in 1561) suggests either that thereafter Hebrew became more widely known, or that instruction in literary Italian became more regular. (By this time, it would have been impossible to print such productions in Latin characters, accessible thus to non-Jews, because of the ecclesiastical censorship.)

Although, as has been mentioned, higher—that is, talmudic—education of the fairer sex was normally considered to be wasteful, if not actually harmful, in some cases women attained a grasp of the branches of Jewish learning usually considered to be a male preserve. Pomona da Modena, of Ferrara, was said to be as well versed in the Talmud as any man, and was honored by Rabbi David of Imola with a detailed responsum on Jewish law, which only a ripe scholar could have understood. Her son, Abraham ben Jehiel Modena, celebrated her piety in over a thousand liturgical poems, composed between 1536 and 1552. Another member of this family, Bathsheba or Fioretta, mother of the physician Mordecai (Marco) Modena and ancestress of a whole line of scholars (including not only the wayward Leone Modena, but also the cabalist Aaron Berechiah da Modena, one of the last of the inspired Italian hymnologists) was more remarkable still. She, we are told, constantly engaged in Hebrew and rabbinic learning, had a close acquaintance with the writings of Maimonides, mapped out for herself a regular sequence of advanced study week by week, and was considered to be largely responsible for the love of Jewish lore which distinguished her remarkable family. In her old age, she emigrated to Safed in Palestine, where she died.

Woman scribes too are not unknown. There are preserved a number of Hebrew manuscripts of rabbinic treatises and the like which were written at the outset of our period by Paola dei Piatelli (Anau), wife of Jehiel ben Solomon of Rome; and the mere fact of her copying such complicated texts, as well as her elaborate colophons, indicates a considerable degree of competence. Two centuries later, the physician Abraham Conat of Mantua, one of the earliest Hebrew printers, active at Mantua in 1476-80, was assisted in his work by his wife Estellina, who set up the type for at least one of the books which he produced. She was not the only woman intimately associated with early Hebrew printing. The widow of Meshullam Cuzi, founder, in 1475, of the primitive press at Piove di Sacco near Padua, was responsible for carrying on his work after his death. Much the same happened at Naples, where on the demise of Joseph Gunzenhauzen, in 1490, his daughter seems to have taken his place for a time as director of his press. The record of Estellina Conat however was never quite equaled.

Some women had so far mastered the codes that they were formally authorized to act as *shoḥet* or ritual slaughterer—hardly a feminine occupation, indeed, but one for which no ignoramus could qualify. It is probable that some of the illuminated Hebrew liturgical or biblical codices now extant—especially no doubt the Haggadah, or Passover liturgy—were written, like their counterparts in the secular sphere, for the use of women. When the daughter of the wealthy Hirtz Wertheim of Padua married Jacob, son of Anselmo del Banco, founder of the community of Venice, he wrote for her with his own hand a lovely illuminated prayer-book as a wedding present. But it was not a happy marriage—the bridegroom fell into evil ways and was in the end disinherited by his family.

Socially, the position of women was high, and they played a distinguished part in communal life. When David Reubeni visited Jehiel da Pisa in 1525, he was profoundly impressed not only by his learned, lavish host but also by the ladies of his household—especially his wife Diamante, daughter of the great Anselmo del

Banco (it had been a union of two great fortunes, not uncommon in those days in Italy: most of the prominent families were in fact interconnected by marriage). Noteworthy, too, were his mother Laura, and especially his grandmother, Sarah, the latter figuring in David's diary as an erudite, pious, somewhat overpowering matriarch, who attempted to control the lives of her numerous progeny down to the last detail. Leone de' Sommi, the playwright and impresario (whom we shall meet later) participated in the middle of the century in one of the artificial polemics in verse concerning women, *pro* and *contra*, so fashionable at the time. He was able to mention an entire roll of Jewish women of the lines of Rieti, Sforno, and so on—mainly in Mantua and Bologna—who were then considered to be of outstanding distinction, though we know little of them today. Women were not infrequently honored by receiving dedications of various works: Lazzaro da Viterbo, for example, inscribed some Italian translations from the Hebrew, which he published at Venice in 1585, to a daughter of Rabbi Samuel Corcos of that city.

Quite a number of contemporary Jewish writers devoted their learning and ingenuity to a consideration, not wholly Platonic, of the basic female charms—Judah Messer Leon in his *Nofet Zufim*, Abraham Jaghel in his *Moshe'a Hosim*, and the historian Joseph haCohen in an elaborate poem in which, in the spirit of his contemporary, Fiorenzuola, he enumerates chastely the thirty-three essential components of beauty in the fair sex.

Characteristic of the Renaissance was the remarkable political influence of women and the part they played in public life: and this was true in a certain sense of the Jewish woman as well. In Italian history at this period there stand out such characters as Lucrezia Borgia, Isabella d'Este, Caterina Sforza, Vittoria Colonna. It is not a coincidence that this, too, is the age when a succession of notable women emerge in Italian Jewry. There was indeed one outstanding difference. Those who attained eminence in European history at this time tended to be in a large proportion of instances not so much famous as notorious—a characteristic which, if only because of restricted opportunities, the Jewish women inevitably lacked.

Two persons in particular—both as it happens of Spanish

origin—strikingly illustrate this point: both associated incidentally with Ferrara, the city of Lucrezia Borgia's residence and Isabella d'Este's upbringing. Benvenida Abrabanel belonged both by birth and by marriage to what was perhaps the outstanding Jewish family in all Europe in that age. Her father was Jacob Abrabanel, brother of Don Isaac Abrabanel, the philosopher-statesman who had led the Jews of Spain into exile in 1492; her husband was Don Samuel, the latter's son, long the head of Neapolitan Jewry, of whom contemporaries said that he was like Hermes *Trismegistos* or thrice great—great in knowledge, great in nobility and great in wealth—and that he combined all the characteristics which according to Jewish tradition merit the gift of prophecy. His wife shared his qualities. Don Pedro de Toledo, viceroy of the kingdom of Naples, thought so highly of her that he associated her in the education of his second daughter, Leonora, who (it is told) called her "mother," and continued to turn to her for advice even after she became Grand Duchess of Tuscany. When disaster overwhelmed Neopolitan Jewry in 1541, the family removed to Ferrara. Here they lived in magnificent style, and their mansion, frequented by Christian and thronged by Jewish savants, was a center of cultural life.

When Don Samuel died in 1547 through an overdose of scammony, his widow continued his financial business on a grand scale, securing important commercial privileges in Tuscany, thanks to her relations with that court. Her Jewish sentiment was as profound and eager as might have been anticipated from a member of that great house. When David Reubeni arrived in Italy, she was his most devoted supporter, and he carried with him on his fabulous travels a magnificent silken banner, embroidered in gold with the Ten Commandments, which she had worked for him with her own hands. The report of her profound religious feelings and her acts of charity penetrated as far as Egypt and the Holy Land. She was a munificent patroness of learning. She is said to have ransomed over one thousand Jewish captives out of her private means. Immanuel Aboab, the chronicler, described her in his *Nomologia* in a passage that has become classical: "One of the most noble and high-spirited matrons who have existed in Israel since the time of our dispersion—such was the Señora Benvenida Abrabanel, pattern of

chastity, of piety, of prudence and of valor." And Leone de'
Sommi, in the poem mentioned above, devoted several stanzas to
this model of Jewish nobility and the qualities that she had
instilled in her children.

She was still alive and active when the most remarkable Jewish
woman of the Renaissance period, and perhaps of all ages, arrived
to settle for a while in Ferrara. This was the famous Gracia Nasi,
or Mendes, who had been born as a marrano in Portugal, had
lived for a time in Antwerp (where she cut a considerable figure
in fashionable life, and successfully defied the Spanish authorities
who wished to impose a husband of their own choice upon her
daughter), and then escaped to Italy. Hither she removed temporarily the seat of the banking and trading business of the
Mendes family, at one time among the greatest in Europe. From
1544 to 1550, she resided in Venice; in 1550, she transferred herself and her fortune to Ferrara, under a safe-conduct from the
duke, and declared herself openly as a Jewess. For two or three
years she remained here, living in great style, successfully managing the family business, and keeping an open house; we know
for example how on one occasion she entertained the French
Ambassador to the Venetian Republic when he came on a visit.
She supported scholars too. The famous Spanish translation of
the Bible printed by Abraham Usque and Yomtob Athias in
1553 (the "Ferrara Bible")[2] was dedicated to her in hyperbolic
terms "as being a person whose merits have always earned the
most sublime place among all of our people."

Later on, the former's kinsman, Samuel Usque, inscribed to her
his great Portuguese chronicle, "Consolation in the Tribulations of Israel," which he considered "proper to offer to your
Excellence, as the heart of this body" (that is, of the Jews of
Portuguese origin who had escaped the fires of the Inquisition)
"in whose bones your name, and your happy memory, will be
carved forever." For she had organized an amazing, incredible
"underground railway" (as it would have been termed later)
by which hundreds or even thousands of marranos had escaped
from the Peninsula, and were helped on by her agents from place
to place and station to station until they arrived in some haven of

---

[2] See pp. 183 ff.

refuge, in Italy or in Turkey—one of the most amazing episodes perhaps in the history of the time. In 1552 she settled in Constantinople. Here for nearly twenty years she tyrannized affectionately but redoubtably over the affairs of the Jewish community. When the persecution of the marranos took place in Ancona in 1555/6—the first fruits of the reaction against Italian Jewry—it was she who inspired and organized the movement among the Jews of the Levant to reduce the guilty city to ruin by means of a commercial boycott; and it was she who began the project for the establishment of a Jewish autonomous center in Tiberias in Palestine, afterwards associated with the name of her nephew, Joseph Nasi, Duke of Naxos.

Active literary work was not expected from the women of the Renaissance: it was rather in their lives that they found self-expression. It is not therefore to be expected that Jewish authoresses should come into prominence in this period. A Renaissance editor indeed published two sonnets by a certain Giustina Levi-Perotti (one directed to Petrarch, who answered it in the same medium, the other to a Pope at Avignon), and it was believed from her name that she must have been Jewish. But the evidence is insufficient ("Levi" is counterbalanced by the other two components, which are distinctly non-Jewish), and the lady's existence is now doubted, together with the authenticity of the poems ascribed to her. It is not in fact until late in the sixteenth century that the earliest Italian Jewish authoress makes her appearance in the person of Deborah Ascarelli, whose husband was the President of the Catalan Synagogue of Rome. She was one of the first persons in modern Europe who had the idea of translating Hebrew liturgical hymns into the vernacular (though, as we now know, the practice was already established in France in the twelfth or thirteenth century: a number of versions of synagogal poetry in Judaeo-French, in the meter of the originals, have recently come to light). Her greatest enterprise in this direction was a rendering of a section of Moses da Rieti's Dantesque imitation *Mikdash Meät*[3] that had entered into Italian devotional use, beginning "The Abode of the Suppliants." A certain David della Rocca, in gratitude for the favors he had received from the family,

---

[3] See p. 103.

published this at Venice in 1602 together with the Hebrew text, certain other translations from her pen, and some original verses of hers on the extremely proper subject of Susannah. This, unimportant in itself, is perhaps the earliest independently published work in Jewish literary history which was written by a woman.

While we know a good deal of the literary output of Deborah Ascarelli, but virtually nothing of her life, the reverse is true of her younger contemporary, Sarah Coppio Sullam, of Venice, who, although she belongs strictly to the post-Renaissance period, can hardly be overlooked in the present connection. Born in Venice in 1592, the daughter of Simon and Rebecca Coppio, she received a humanistic education of remarkable range, which shows how little the ghetto walls were able to keep at bay the spirit of Italian culture. By the time of her father's death, when she was in her fifteenth year, she could read Latin, Greek, and Spanish, as well as Hebrew and Italian. To these accomplishments, she added some poetical ability, an attractive personality, a sweet voice, and (if her admirers are to be believed) great beauty. In 1614, she married Jacob Sullam, member of an old and wealthy Italian Jewish family originating in Mantua, himself one of the leading spirits of the Venetian community. The position that she now occupied, coupled with her own abilities, rendered her a natural leader of society in the ghetto of this place, well known among non-Jews as well as Jews. Her home became something of a literary salon. Patricians and merchants, rabbis and priests, came to listen to her improvisations. Distinguished writers and visitors from other cities—not only from Rome but even from Paris—made a point of visiting this charming ghetto prodigy. Her verses, though unpublished, enjoyed no little vogue and established her reputation as a Venetian poetess. When Leone Modena produced his Italian *rifacimento* of Usque's Spanish drama on Esther (of which we shall speak later), it was natural for him to dedicate it to her.

Before this the Genoese poet-monk Ansaldo Seba, who had published a once-famous epic poem on that same subject, sent a copy to her as a matter of course, and had the satisfaction of learning that she slept with it under her pillow. This proved to be the beginning of a long correspondence between the two. Gifts, books, letters and verses proceeded from Venice to Genoa, and from Genoa to Venice, in an unending stream. Once, when the priest sent her a basket of fruit from his native Liguria, she reciprocated with a gift of her portrait; but the former's servant, who waited on her bearing his master's greetings, reported to him later that it did not do justice to her beauty.

Seba, however, was not satisfied with literary exchanges, and considered it to be his duty to secure her conversion. He had no difficulty (and this too is characteristic) in persuading her to read the New Testament, Plato, and even the writings of the Spanish mystic S. Luis de Granada. But, to his disappointment, her convictions were not affected by this pious literature; and when he died, five years after making her acquaintance, he could only commend her despairingly to the prayers of his friends. His letters to her were published posthumously in the following year.

Another Christian paladin with whom she had a brush was Baldassare Bonifaccio, later Bishop of Capo d'Istria, who accused her in a pamphlet of denying the immortality of the soul—a token at least of the importance which he attached to her opinions. She replied in a spirited manifesto, in which she implored her opponent not to rely on the precedent of Balaam's ass. This is the only one of her compositions to appear separately, though a number of her sonnets are scattered about in various publications. She was not quite fifty when she died, in 1641. Some generations were to pass before another Jewish authoress of her type was to reëmerge.

We have spoken above of the state of sexual morality among Italian Jewry in the age of the Renaissance, which certainly fell short of the traditional standard of perfection. Obviously then Italian Jews were not immune from other types of moral misdemeanor popularly associated with the period. Crimes of violence, elsewhere unusual (though not indeed so exceptional as apologists have maintained in the past), were common enough among them. The records make it apparent that some of them stabbed, killed and poisoned with their compatriots, though not perhaps quite so wholeheartedly. Acts of violence are reported, from time to time even in the synagogue. Both the rabbinate and the civil courts had their attention engaged at the close of the fifteenth century by an episode which took place at Verona, where a young man was beaten up during service, his ritual vestments torn from his back, and the pages of his prayer-book stained with his blood. In fifteenth-century Florence, the records reveal two cases of homicide and one of attempted poisoning in which Jews were implicated. The hand of the hot-headed young Italian Jew would fly to his dagger if he thought himself insulted, or he might go home and brood over more elaborate ways of revenge. Moreover, since quarrels take place obviously most among those who come into intimate contact, in many cases the Jews were the victims as well as the perpetrators. The diary of a Sienese Jew of the lower class that has recently been discovered shows us a ghetto society in which few persons seem to have objected to major acts of violence to avenge petty grudges. The converted papal musician, Giovanni Maria,[4] was condemned to death in Florence for a murder in 1492, though this did not prevent him from continuing long afterwards in the papal service. Another convert, who had been mortally offended by the notorious Gregorio Zampante, *capitano di giustizia* at Ferrara, was one of the little band who avenged themselves on him, amid popular jubilation, one afternoon in 1490, while he was taking his siesta. In 1477, a Jew offered his service to the *signoria* in Venice to rid them of their major enemy, the Grand Turk, with the aid of his personal physician Master Jacob of Gaeta, payment to be made, however, only after the completion of the task. The murder (or homicide) of Jews by Jews is recorded at this period in Florence, in Venice, and elsewhere. In Venice, it was found necessary to discuss the question whether it was proper to invoke divine vengeance in the prayers recited for the repose of the soul of one who had met his death at Jewish hands. There does not seem to be much reason to question *a priori* the story of Solomon Molcho, that personal enemies who thought his activities dangerous attempted to remove him from the scene by poison.

One of the paradoxes of intellectual life in this period was the manner in which skepticism and even rationalism of a kind were combined, sometimes in the same person, with the grossest super-

---

[4] See below, p. 281.

stition. To cite only one familiar episode, it will be recalled how even such a man as Benvenuto Cellini participated in a preposterous incantation performed by a Sicilian priest in the Coliseum at Rome, and believed that it was successful. The Italian Jews shared these tendencies. Even the most erudite and, as one would have imagined, level-headed scholars sometimes showed the utmost credulity and harbored the greatest superstitions, much as was the case with some of the leaders of Italian intellectual life at this time. Johanan Alemanno, friend and admirer of Pico della Mirandola, sought the elixir of life and was expert in magical writing: the geographer Abraham Farisol believed in satyrs, and the banker-economist Jehiel Nissim of Pisa in spirits; the grammarian Samuel Archevolti considered that there were lucky and unlucky numbers and guided his life by that belief. The autobiography of Leone Modena, the representative of Jewish enlightenment to the outside world, reveals to us an individual who was intensely superstitious, paid preposterous respect to omens, permitted his life to be governed by dreams and visions (an instance of this we have already seen) and displayed unswerving optimism in his belief in alchemy. The historian Gedaliah ibn Jacchia,[5] who also composed a book on chiromancy, has in his *magnum opus* a chapter on witchcraft, in which he tells among other things of a Jewish woman of Ferrara who was haunted by the *dibbuk* of a Gentile malefactor hanged for robbery. From all this, it may be imagined how steeped in superstition were men and women of a lower standard of erudition. This permeated even religious life. There were some Italian Jews who on the eve of Sabbaths and festivals would recite the Sanctification or *Kiddush* twice—once aloud and once in secret, so as to mislead the ever-present evil spirits!

The reputation which the Jews enjoyed in the outside world as exponents of the supernatural arts was considerable, and probably exaggerated. Ariosto describes one such person, by no means sympathetically, in his comedy of 1535, *Il Negromante:* one of the Spanish exiles familiar throughout Europe at this time, who however gives himself out to be a Greek or Egyptian or African,

[5] See below, chapter XIII for some account of this scholar; similarly for others mentioned in this paragraph.

and constantly changes both name and costume. He claims that he possesses the secret of invisibility, that his charms and incantations can darken the day or illumine the night, that he has the power of changing men into beasts, that he can move the earth itself. But it is all fraud, for his real ends are disreputable—to forward illicit love affairs, by persuading, for example, a jealous husband that a chest in which his wife's lover lies hidden cannot be touched because it is full of ghosts. Ortensio Landi, ("Philoletes Polytopiensis," as he designated himself in the absurd fashion of the time), too, gives an account of a Jewish magician in his so-called "Commentary," which he professed to have translated from the Aramaic: a worthless fellow who worked in conjunction with a Sicilian—another race which had as it seems a reputation in matters of this sort—with a panoply of magical mirrors, a talking skull, and birds stopped short in their flight. Again, in the *sacra rappresentazione* or morality play of "Teofilo" —"the Italian Faust," as it has been called—we are introduced to a Jewish sorcerer named Manovello, who takes the hero to a crossroad, raises the fiend Beelzebub, and, in the end, when Teofilo professes repentance, descends into Hell.

These imaginative accounts seem to have been based to some extent, if not on fact, at least on current belief. In Rome (where from classical times the Jews had a reputation for dabbling in charms, if the poet Juvenal is to be believed), the Jewish women are described in our period as telling fortunes in the homes of the nobility and brewing love-philters by night for languishing ladies. Even in the ghetto period, recourse was often made to the Jewish quarter for such purposes. Pietro Aretino (perhaps a reliable guide in disreputable matters of this sort) informs us that the courtesans, trying to supplement their natural attractions, resorted to Jewish women who were in the possession of loathsome charms, which he appreciatively describes. It is reported that Leone Modena's erudite and well-born pupil, Joseph Hamiz, used to write love-charms for the young sprigs of the Venetian aristocracy. Occasionally episodes of alleged witchcraft in the more restricted sense are reported, though it is difficult to say what degree of credence should be attached to them—whether, that is, the persons accused had really dabbled in the occult. In 1600, an aged Jewish woman of seventy-seven, named Judith Franchetti, was burned alive in the public square of Mantua on a charge of sorcery, the principal charge against her being that she had be-witched a nun recently converted from Judaism. An alleged pupil and accomplice, Jacob Fano, suffered with her, and two others who had fled were also implicated. At Reggio, an old woman was stoned to death in 1598 on the steps of the cathedral while she was carrying out the penance imposed on her for witch-craft. In Modena, about the same time, twenty-five Jews were punished for a similar offense by being made to go in procession, two by two, escorting a black-draped catafalque and an image of the Devil, their master. A woman in Venice, named Dianora, found it so difficult to escape a reputation for witchcraft—even among her co-religionists—that she obtained a certificate of exon-eration from the rabbinate. It was not long after this that the Austrian experimentalist, Johann Weihard Valvasor, learned from a Venetian Jew "how to make a Magical Glass which should represent any Person or thing according as he should desire." The clumsy baron, however, lost the secret through inattention. Many Hebrew manuscripts of this period contain magical or cabalistic recipes for achieving invisibility or for resisting temptation or for stimulating love and the like.

One of the pretexts for the expulsion of the Jews from the minor centers of the Papal States, by the bull *Hebraeorum gens* of 1569, was that they were alleged to seduce weak-minded Christians with their charms and tricks and witcheries, making them believe that the future could be foretold and stolen goods recovered and hidden treasure found. Gregory XIII's pronounce-ment, *Antiqua Judaeorum*, in 1581, attempted among other things to suppress the practice of magical arts by the Jews by giving jurisdiction in such cases to the Inquisition, even where their own co-religionists were involved. This was repeated at the height of the ghetto reaction in the eighteenth century, implying presum-ably that the suppression was not considered to be wholly effec-tive. That all these allegations were utterly baseless is hardly to be credited.

But to be sure, it was not merely a one-way traffic. We know from Leone Modena's correspondence how in his day some Venetian Jews resorted to a well known local witch. A late case is even on record at Urbino of a lovelorn young Jew having recourse to a Catholic priest to break an incantation which he believed to have been imposed on his intended bride, at a rival's request, by two Jews working in conjunction with a Gentile sorceress!

The wearing of amulets was at this time general, and among Jews was reinforced by the development of the Cabala, which involved credence in special mystical formulae of "undoubted" efficacy. It was regarded as part of the normal function of the rabbi to provide these, and even a scholar of the type of Leone Modena eked out his living by composing them. Even in this, the specific Italian aesthetic spirit was able to manifest itself. The fact that it was a Gentile habit to wear a decorative religious symbol naturally stimulated imitative Jews to have something of the same nature, as a container or as an independent adornment, usually bearing the divine name "Shaddai" and generally thus called by Italian Jews. These objects were frequently admirable specimens of the jeweler's art, in silver or in gold, sometimes even encrusted with precious stones, and bearing in addition to the Hebrew lettering representations of the classical symbols of Judaism—the candelabrum, priestly emblems and so on. Surprisingly enough, in view of the prevalence of this calling among Jews, they were often manufactured by non-Jewish silversmiths, this being stringently forbidden by the Popes at the height of the ghetto period of reaction.

We have dealt thus far with the background, and our attention has been perhaps distracted by some trivial details. It is time to turn to the positive achievement.

FOUR

The Latin Renaissance *and* the Jewish Translators

It was at one time usual to think of the Revival of Learning as a dramatic process which suddenly reached breathtaking maturity in the fifteenth century. We are today more moderate in our evaluation. Classical learning never died out in Europe quite so completely as was once believed, at least as regards Latin literature and scholarship; and the revival—if that is indeed the correct term to apply to it—was a gradual process, going back to the twelfth century, if not beyond. In the fifteenth century, a knowledge of the classical Greek literature in the original became widespread in Italy, and to some extent in western Europe, partly (though not wholly) through the medium of Byzantine scholars who fled from Constantinople at the time of the final onslaught by the Turks in 1453; at the same time, new standards of textual criticism and of aesthetic appreciation became general. Thus the literary Renaissance developed. But for practical purposes originals are not necessary, and literary form is superfluous. Translations, however poor, will serve, at least in part, to convey ideas, facts, theories, figures, problems, teachings. Hence the Revival of Learning really started, at least in philosophy and science, long before this time—when the lore rather than the literature of ancient Greece became available again in translation to western European scholars.

The cultural life of medieval Islam (apart from its literary aspect, in which Jewish participation was of some significance: but a consideration of this would take us far from the subject in hand) was based, as is well known, on the scientific and philosophical achievement of ancient Greece. This, forgotten or almost forgotten at this time in Europe, had been discovered by the

Arabs in the first flush of their expansion, and studied with tremendous enthusiasm in the schools of Damascus, Cairo, Kairouan and, at a later date, especially Cordova.

It was here, in Moorish Spain, that the medical wisdom of Hippocrates, the astronomical records of Ptolemy, and above all the science and philosophy of Aristotle, were revered, studied, commented on and further developed. The original texts indeed were inaccessible; the studies centered round Arabic renderings, in some cases made from Syriac versions that had been current in the Levant at the time of the Islamic invasion in the seventh century. The matter, however, was the same; and from the eleventh century on, when the breath of intellectual interest again began to stir in Christian Europe, it was to the academies of Andalusia that eager Christian students looked for some notion of the wisdom of the sages of ancient Hellas. Their Arabic exponents—Averroës, Avicenna and the rest—enjoyed a prestige barely less than theirs; and, if Christian Europe imagined that the Greeks had discovered the gate to wisdom, it was no less convinced that the Moors possessed the key. The history of European civilization in this period is to a great extent the record of the recovery of these treasures, by a curiously devious path.

But how to have access to them? There was at this time an almost insuperable barrier between the two spheres: the Moslem and the Christian—not merely religious, but cultural and linguistic as well; and the learned world that thought and wrote in Latin had no direct contact with the other learned world that thought and wrote in Arabic. The link between the two was the Jewish element, which was common to both, had an intellectual foothold in each, and now played its characteristic and all-important role in the history of civilization as the medium of understanding and communication between diverse and even opposing cultures.

Jews with their cosmopolitan sense and their wide economic interests have at all times tended to travel from land to land, and it was not unusual to find among them in northern Europe in the Middle Ages highly literate persons (an obvious example is the twelfth-century Spanish scientist and exegete Abraham ibn Ezra, who spent some time even in London) who had a knowledge of Arabic and were thus qualified to serve as cultural intermediaries. Moreover, the Jews, always sharing in the intellectual tastes of the environment, executed for their own use translations into Hebrew of many of the standard scientific and philosophical texts studied by the Arabs. These at once entered into literary currency among their co-religionists in non-Moslem lands. Thus the humblest Jewish scholar, in Italy or Provence, had access to intellectual resources of which the most erudite of his Christian neighbors was ignorant.

Hence it was to the Jews that Christian students would have recourse in very many instances for some inkling not only of the intellectual achievements of the Arabs, but also—the height of paradox—for the ideas of the sages of ancient Greece, whom their fathers of the age of the Talmud had so indignantly spurned. For this purpose, further renderings were now deliberately made from the Hebrew versions into Latin. The texts in question were barbarous, inelegant, often inaccurate. But the concepts of the originals were conveyed on the whole faithfully enough, and the result was sufficient to open up new horizons before the wondering eyes of students. There have survived hundreds, if not thousands, of such works, vividly illustrating the Jews' intense interest and fruitful participation in every branch of medieval intellectual activity. It was these Latin versions of the Greek classics and their Moslem exponents (whether made directly from the Arabic or through the medium of the Hebrew versions prepared by the Jews for their own use), which penetrated Christian Europe from the twelfth century on with such far-reaching results, constituting an important aspect of what is termed the Latin Renaissance.

The significance of this process must not of course be exaggerated, as has been done so often. Not all translations and versions came by the channel that has been described. Philosophical texts tended to be derived by the Latin world direct from the Arabic, whereas the scientific works were transmitted more frequently via the Hebrew. But in the former case, too, the Jewish participation was often close, and sometimes preponderant. As has been well expressed, when the civilization of the Arabs in Spain decayed, it was the Jews who took the torch of learning from their flagging hands and with magnificent success passed it on to the Christian world, avid for this new knowledge.

There were three main centers for this activity. One was of

course Spain, where the two cultures intermingled most signifi-
cantly—above all at Toledo, under the patronage of the arch-
bishops of the see and the kings of Castile; and at Barcelona,
where Abraham bar Hiyya "the Prince," one of the outstanding
medieval scientists, collaborated in the middle of the twelfth
century with the Italian Plato of Tivoli in the translation of the
treatises which introduced mathematics to the Latin world.
Another was Provence, the bridge between France and Spain,
where the local Jewish scholars (particularly of the family of
Ibn Tibbon, in successive generations) translated large numbers
of texts from the Arabic of their native Spain into Hebrew, for
the benefit of their co-religionists north of the Pyrenees. The
third—and it is this which interests us most here—was southern
Italy, whose successive rulers displayed in this respect a degree
of intellectual interest, expressed in an enlightened patronage,
unparalleled elsewhere in Europe at any time.

In the lands over which they held sway—where the Latin,
Italian, Byzantine and Moslem and Jewish influences intermingled
—there was then a remarkable intellectual ferment. No land, not
even Spain, was better fitted to transmit to renascent Europe both
the heritage of antiquity and the great contemporary Islamic
culture. From the time of Roger II, the Norman king of Sicily
(1101-1154) whose cosmopolitan court was the center for a
brilliant circle of savants, the process was stimulated by a succession of monarchs who, though of warring dynasties (Norman,
Hohenstaufen, Angevin), were all especially alive to the new
intellectual currents. Under the brilliant Frederick *stupor mundi*
("the world's wonder") King of Sicily and Apulia as well as
Holy Roman Emperor, the process attained its fullest development, largely as a result of his own intense personal interest. It
was not only that various Jewish translators were in his employ
and in receipt of regular payment for the work they did, but
that he was himself in correspondence or personal communication
with them on matters of common interest.

At his invitation, for example, the scholar-physician Jacob
Anatoli of Marseilles settled, perhaps as his medical attendant, in
Naples, where in 1224 the emperor had established a university.
Anatoli translated the most important philosophical writings of
the great Arab thinker Averroës into Hebrew, and it is probable

though not proven that the standard medieval Latin version depended on his work. In addition, he was responsible for the Hebrew renderings of numerous Arabic astronomical compositions. Of his personal relations with the emperor there is a curious relic in a volume of philosophical discourses of his in Hebrew, in which he cites a number of allegorical interpretations of the Bible which had been suggested to him, as he says, by "Our Lord, the great King, the Emperor Frederick (may he live long!)." He also cites with respect a Christian sage with whom he was on friendly terms, who is almost certainly to be identified with that almost legendary figure of medieval lore, Michael Scot. The importance of such personal intercourse in the history of the transmission of culture, even when it did not result in any specific literary expression, cannot be overestimated.

Another Jewish scholar who was in close touch with Emperor Frederick's court was Judah ben Solomon ibn Makta, of Toledo, author of a remarkable scientific encyclopaedia (largely dependent on Aristotle) which he issued both in Hebrew and in Arabic. Already at the age of eighteen, in 1233, he was in correspondence with the emperor's two court philosophers, John of Palermo and Theodore of Antioch. Later, Frederick himself corresponded with him on scientific and philosophical matters, and ultimately brought him to Italy for more convenient personal communication. In the same environment there was working another interesting figure: Moses ben Solomon of Salerno (known also for his polemical writings in defense of Judaism). Between 1240 and 1250 he was engaged in composing a Hebrew commentary on, or rather paraphrase of, Maimonides' philosophical classic, *The Guide for the Perplexed,* in which the technical terms were rendered into Italian. He is given special significance in the present connection by the fact that he meanwhile read that work in Latin with Fra Niccolò di Paglia of Giovenazzo, one of the most influential members of the Dominican Order (to which he had been admitted by St. Dominic himself). The version they studied had probably been commissioned by the emperor; for he, like many educated persons of that age, was (as we know from other sources) deeply interested in Maimonides' writings, which were having so profound an influence on contemporary scholastic thought.

Frederick II's wide intellectual interests were inherited by his successor in his Italian possessions, his ill-fated natural son, Manfred—himself, it seems, a student of Hebrew. He commissioned a number of renderings from Hebrew and Arabic into Latin—among them the famous dialogue ascribed in the Middle Ages to Aristotle, "The Book of the Apple," which was translated from the former tongue under his supervision, and perhaps with his immediate collaboration.

On his overthrow, the tradition was perpetuated by the rulers of the House of Anjou who established themselves as his successors, and who combined a remarkable intellectual alertness with their eager and sometimes fanatical devotion to the Church. Charles I of Anjou, King of Naples from 1265, worked on a more systematic basis than any of his predecessors, or indeed than any other medieval patron. He even engaged various professional Jewish translators to work for him full-time, as did also his son and successor Charles II.

The most active was Faraj (Faragut) of Girgenti, in Sicily, who settled in the famous intellectual center of Salerno, not far from Naples, and is referred to in the documents as a member of the royal household. His *magnum opus*, in the most literal sense, was a rendering of the great medical work of Rhazes, known as the *Liber continens*—one of the most bulky and most famous of medieval scientific compositions—a copy of which had been received by King Charles as a personal gift from the Arab ruler of Tunis. Illuminations in Faraj's final version, which is among the treasures of the Bibliothèque Nationale in Paris, show him engaged in the work on behalf of his royal patron and handing him the finished result of his labors: these are among the earliest portraits of a Jew now extant. The Angevin registers formerly in the Naples State Archives recorded many payments made to him for his translations; and when his native city in Sicily rebelled, he and his brothers were exonerated, since at the time they had been at court in the royal service. He also served as official expert in Jewish matters, being ordered, for example, to examine the religious qualifications of a functionary to whom (and this too is characteristic of the times) Charles wished to give a synagogal appointment at Palermo.

Another Jew in the service of the court in a similar capacity was Moses of Palermo, who was given instruction in Latin at the king's expense, so as to be able to translate for him various Arabic works assembled in the royal library at Naples. He was responsible for rendering into Latin, among many other works, a treatise ascribed to Hippocrates on the diseases of horses—one of the earliest compositions of the sort to become current in Europe. Even in the sixteenth century, an adaptation of this was frequently published and republished, under the title *Libro della natura di cavalli* (1517, 1519, 1537 and so on). Indeed, it has been stated that the terseness of expression and general absence of superstition and charms are a clear indication that Moses of Palermo was the source of most veterinary writings from his own day down to the close of the Renaissance period.

Meanwhile, in Capua, the Jew Samuel ben Jacob translated the most popular of all medieval books of remedies, which goes by the name of *Mesue*, from the Arabic into the Hebrew version from which it was subsequently rendered into Latin. His converted fellow-townsman, John of Capua, besides some similar work in the field of medicine, rendered into Latin from the Hebrew version, by one Joel, the Arab collection of stories called *Kallila and Dimna*, under the henceforth famous title *Directorium humanae vitae*. This, which he dedicated to Cardinal Matteo Orsini, was frequently published after the invention of printing (from 1483 on) and proved to be of singular importance, for it was the source of a great part of the European folk-tales of the Middle Ages and of the fairy tales of modern times which depend on them. Among the other works of this same translator was a version of Maimonides' treatise on diet, commissioned from him by a papal physician. Another converted Jew active in such work in the south of Italy was Paul the Convert ("Paulus neofidus") who assisted the Dominican friars Niccolò da Adria and Guido di Cipro in carrying out their versions of various texts from the Arabic.

Robert of Anjou, King of Naples from 1309 to 1343, not only continued the tradition of his house, but was actively interested in Hebrew scholarship for its own sake. It was on his behalf that Calonymus ben Calonymus of Arles, called in the records "the Jew Calo," translated various works of Averroës and others, having been brought by the king from Provence to Italy specifically to continue his labors. He had the run of the royal library, mentions various books that he found there, and refers to his master (though indeed he was by no means conspicuously pro-Jewish) as a second Solomon.

Another illustrious Jewish scholar who worked under Robert's auspices was Shemariah ben Elijah Ikriti, of Rome, whose name, however, suggests his Cretan—that is, Greek—origin. This introduces us to a new facet of the story. Normally, the Italian and west European Jews knew no Greek, and the renderings of the Greek masterpieces that they carried out were made from the Hebrew or the Arabic. The characteristic of the later Renaissance was, precisely, that recourse was now had directly to the Greek originals. For this, Jews seldom had any special linguistic qualification. But in this case, we have an instance of one Jew at least, who at the dawn of this new age played his part in the process. Unfortunately, we have no specific knowledge of his work in this sense. There is still extant, however, a Hebrew philosophical commentary on the Bible from his hand, of enormous bulk, carried out at the Neapolitan court and under the king's auspices, if not on his commission, and dedicated to him in extravagant language.

Meanwhile, similar activity had been taking place on a smaller scale and in a less systematic fashion in central and northern Italy as well: indeed, Calonymus ben Calonymus had done a good deal of his work in Rome, the foibles of whose Jewish community— its pomposities, its gluttony, its lack of proportion—he had brilliantly satirized in a parody of a talmudical tractate which he contributed to the hilariousness of the feast of Purim. Even before his day, we know how the Jewish physician, Master Bonacosa, translated the work known as "Colliget" (a rough phonetic transcription of the Arabic *kullijat* or "General Rules of Health") embodying Avicenna's famous attempt to found a system of medicine upon the neo-Platonic modification of Aristotle's philosophy. This he rendered directly from Arabic into Latin at Padua in 1255, *studio ibi vigente;* this phrase being incidentally most important testimony to the existence of that renowned university at this date. This version became classical, was long used as a medical textbook, and in the Renaissance period, after the invention of printing, was published time after time. Master Bonacosa may perhaps be the same person as the Master Jacob (sometimes identified, however, with the convert John of Padua) who assisted at Venice in 1280/1 in the translation of Avenzoar's Aid to Health (*Taysir*) from Hebrew into Latin, reading off from a manuscript in the one language a vernacular version which his Christian collaborator, a Paduan physician, set down in the other. This is of importance as one of the few specific accounts of what must have been a common practice among well-meaning scholars of the two faiths at this time.

Another very active worker, though in a somewhat different sphere, was Nathan haMeati ("of the Hundred," perhaps therefore of Cento, near Ferrara, though this is not certain: there is no evidence for the presence of Jews here at so early a date). With his son and grandson after him he systematically set about making Hebrew versions of the standard Arabic works in order to replace the medical writings which, he was convinced, had existed in the time of Solomon. Thus, as he naively informs us, he hoped to silence the mockery of the Gentiles, who said that the Jews possessed no such literature! Among those for whom he worked was the papal physician Isaac ben Mordecai, generally called Maestro Gaio—the first known in the long and distinguished series of papal physicians produced by Italian Jewry—who was in attendance at the end of the thirteenth century on either Pope Nicholas IV or else Boniface VIII. This family's versions were for the most part what has been called "terminal": that is to say, they were not retranslated subsequently from Hebrew into Latin, where by now such literature had become either familiar or superfluous.

By the middle of the fourteenth century, indeed, Christian Europe had acquired through the medium of translations, whether from the Hebrew or from the Arabic, most of the basic writings which it needed, both of the Greek classics and of their Moslem interpreters. Moreover, in Italy the Saracenic tradition had so far waned that not much more could be done in this sphere. Translations into Hebrew, especially of medical works, now began to be made from the Latin: for although the majority of cultured Italian Jews could (and did) read that language, this was not true of all, and in any case the tongue of the Bible appeared to them to be the proper medium of culture in just the same way as the tongue of Cicero was for their neighbors. Hence, from the period when European science began to be of some independent importance, the main stream of translations in Italy tended to be not as previously from Hebrew (sometimes *ex*-Arabic) into Latin, but vice versa.

Quite a number of the distinguished Italian Jewish physicians of this period were interested in such renderings. An outstanding example was the physician-philosopher Hillel of Verona, Dante's contemporary and a zealous champion of Moses Maimonides when his orthodoxy was impugned, who was in touch with the professors of the University of Bologna. He executed or commissioned much work of this sort. Yet the former tradition still persisted to some extent even now. This same scholar, for example, rendered (it seems) certain writings of Hippocrates, the father of Greek medicine, from Hebrew into a Latin version: this was printed in a trilingual edition at Rome in 1647 by the French scholar M. A. Gaiotius, and long passed for his own. At the beginning of the fourteenth century, Judah Romano (Leone de Ser Daniele), who taught King Robert of Naples Hebrew, justified the translation of certain Latin scholastics into the sacred tongue on the ground that "the Christians are not completely lacking in science."

The period of the High Renaissance introduced a wholly new atmosphere into such work. The treasures of ancient Greece had by now become accessible to the Italian scholars in the original language, and were being systematically explored. But, in the course of this process, it became apparent that there were some compositions which had been known to the medieval Arabs and Jews, the originals of which were no longer to be traced; some of them indeed had finally disappeared, being unknown even at the present time. Very great interest was aroused in humanistic circles when such instances were discovered, and retranslation into an accessible language was considered to be of primary importance for scholarship. Thus there again emerged in Italy at this period a little school of translators of philosophical texts of ultimate Greek origin from Hebrew into Latin, who occupy a special niche in the history of Renaissance literature. As before, the works in question mostly, if not exclusively, centered on the thought of Aristotle, for the simple reason that Plato, now popular, had been so neglected in the medieval world that few Platonic texts of this sort were available or needed. Hence some Jews became widely known at this time as exponents of the peripatetic philosophy, as we shall see when we deal with the relations of the Jews with the Florentine humanists at the time of Lorenzo de' Medici. This was especially the case in Padua, where—in contrast to Florence—a very strong scholastic and Aristotelian tradition persisted down to the close of the sixteenth century. Arab medicine was, moreover, unsuperseded as yet, and here, too, the role of Jewish intermediaries could be useful, for the importance of consulting the sources was becoming more and more appreciated. Andrea Alpago, of Belluno, one of the most eminent Italian physicians of the day (who had spent thirty years in the Levant) insisted in his lectures at the University of Padua on the importance of studying, in the original languages, the works of the Arab writers which still figured in that university's curriculum; he added that, if these were not available, recourse should be had to the Hebrew versions. Moreover, printing had by now become a commonplace, and a number of the renderings produced by this belated Aristotelian renaissance were immediately published and thus entered fothwith into literary currency.

The most noteworthy name in this connection is that of Elijah del Medigo of Crete, who was perhaps the most prolific of the school of translators in question as well as an original thinker of some reputation. In conjunction with his exposition of the Aristotelian philosophy for Pico della Mirandola and his circle, with which we must deal later on, he carried out an important series of translations not only of the texts of the Greek philosopher, but also of his great Arab exponent Averroës. He knew no Arabic, and all these works derived apparently from the Hebrew versions which were current among the Jews. His translation of Averroës' compendium of Aristotle's *Meteora* (after Samuel ibn Tibbon's Hebrew text), first published in the 1488 edition of Aristotle with Averroës' Commentaries, is among the first productions of a living Jewish writer to be printed. Without going into a catalogue of his work in this sphere, one may mention also his version of Averroës' commentaries on Book I of the *Prior Analytics* (published in a miscellaneous volume edited by the physician Lorenzo Maiolo, *Epiphyllides in dialecticis*, Venice, 1497) and on the first seven books of the *Metaphysics* (*ibid.*, 1560). Much more remains in manuscript, including his "medial" commentary on the same work based on the Hebrew of Calonymus ben Calonymus. Averroës' proem to his larger commentary on Book XII of the *Metaphysics* was translated twice by Del Medigo: once for Pico, and again later on for that great supporter of learning and Venetian patriot, Cardinal Domenico Grimani—the very names of these patrons have great significance in the story of cultural relations in the age of the Renaissance.

In the next generation, particularly important work along the same lines was done by the physician Calo Calonymus (in Hebrew, Calonymus ben David—not to be confused with the other translator, Calonymus ben Calonymus, of two centuries before). He belonged to a prominent family of south Italian medical practitioners, his father, David Calonymus of Bari having been a court physician and admitted with his sons to the citizenship of Naples, in recognition of his work for the city. Calo Calonymus, "doctor of the arts and of medicine," often receives mention in the Neapolitan records together with his father. When the condition of south Italian Jewry deteriorated, he moved to Venice, where he first figures in 1517. Here, too, he was much appreciated, if (as seems probable) he is identical with the Dr. Calonymus who in 1553 received from the senate a grant to keep his son at his studies, "so that he may be useful in the service of this most illustrious city." His astrological interests will be spoken of later. He is, however, best remembered today as translator of various Arabic scientific and philosophical texts into Latin, all from the Hebrew intermediaries. His published versions include one portion of Averroës' chief philosophical work, *Destructio destructionis* (Venice, 1526/7)—a vindication of reason and rationalism. He dedicated it to the future Cardinal Ercole Gonzaga, son of Isabella d'Este and Gianfrancesco Gonzaga. This prince of the Church will figure not infrequently in our story, for (perhaps as a result of the influence of his teacher, the Aristotelian philosopher Pompanazzo, who it is said had a strikingly Jewish appearance) he showed himself intensely sympathetic to everything Jewish. To this work, Calonymus appended an original philosophical treatise on the creation of the world (*Volumen de mundi creatione, physicis probata rationibus*). Four years later, his translation from Ibn Tibbon's Hebrew version of the famous *Theorica planetarum* by the twelfth-century Arab astronomer al-Bitruji ("Alpetragius"), which attempted to revive the theory of homocentric spheres, was included in an important collection of scientific texts published by Giunta (Venice, 1531). In addition, as we shall see, Calonymus collaborated solidly in the great Venice editions of Aristotle and Averroës produced in the middle years of the century.

His kinsman and fellow-countryman, Abraham de Balmes, author of one of the most popular grammatical works of the period, was engaged in a similar undertaking in moments of leisure from a busy practice: he was grandson perhaps of the Abraham de Balmes of Lecce who was appointed Court Physician at Naples in 1472, but was himself a resident of Padua, where he had graduated and is said to have lectured. Later he went to Venice, where he was body-physician to the Cardinal Grimani. It was under the latter's auspices that he carried out his work of translation into Latin of various works of medieval Arabic authors, of course from the Hebrew intermediate versions. Among these was the *Liber de mundo*, by the eleventh-century astronomer Ibn al-Heitham; and the *Epistola expeditionis* based on a version of a philosophical work by Ibn Badscha ("Avempace" as he was called by European scholars). Both of these are extant only in manuscript. He translated also Aristotle's "Posterior Analytics" with Averroës' "Major Commentary"—an extraordinarily rare work which was published at Venice about 1520, with his patron's arms on the title-page (*Liber posteriorum analiticorum Aristotelis: cum magnis commentariis Auverroys. Interprete Abramo de Balmes*). From the table of contents it would seem that this was intended to be the first part of a more ambitious project which was to have included, besides other versions, an original work of his own (*Liber de demonstratione Abrami de Balmes*). But both he and his patron died in 1523 within a few months of each other—he himself in straitened circumstances—so that the project was interrupted and nothing more of his was printed in his lifetime. Nevertheless, various Averroistic materials which he had rendered into Latin were also included, as we shall see, in the standard sixteenth-century edition of Aristotle.

A character of greater significance from this point of view, and a more typical son of the Renaissance, was Jacob Mantino, whose career presents many independent points of interest. He was of Spanish birth, studied medicine and philosophy at the universities of Padua and Bologna and subsequently established himself in the latter place, where he devoted his leisure to the translation of scientific works from Hebrew into Latin. These gained him something of a reputation, and he was befriended by some persons who stood high at the court of Pope Clement VII. In 1528 he received an official appointment at the Archiginnasio of Bologna as reader in Medicine and teacher of Hebrew.[1] Unsettled political conditions later drove him to settle in Verona, where he was befriended by the Bishop, Giovanni (Gian) Matteo Giberti, a great patron of learning; and when the latter was taken as hostage to Rome he settled in Venice. Here he attained an instantaneous success. He entered into relations with the doge, to whom he dedicated one of his books. He became medical attendant to many of the most aristocratic patrician houses and half the diplomatic corps, the "mystery" of his Jewish origin perhaps reinforcing his reputation. Giberti, now back in Verona, urged that he should be exempted from the Jewish badge and should be permitted to go about wearing a black *beretta* like any other practitioner, as being both an able physician and an excellent man. Notwithstanding the fact that this appeal was supported by the French and English envoys, it was granted only reluctantly and for a short period. The reason is plain: England and France were at this time in political opposition to Spain, and the color of the headgear of the Jewish physician was thus elevated for the moment into a minor diplomatic question. Ultimately, however, the concession was renewed, at the request of the famous soldier, Teodoro Trivulzio, Marshal of France and Governor of Genoa, another of his patients.

Among his other close associates was the noble Moorish traveler and exile, Al Hassan ibn Mohammed of Granada, who after traveling adventurously through Africa and beyond had been captured by pirates, enslaved, and given as a present to Pope Leo X. The latter had persuaded him to be baptized (not as it seems very effectively) under the name Giovanni Leo, so that he published his famous *Description of Africa* (Rome, 1526) and other works

---

[1] See, however, above, p. 40.

under the name Leo Africanus, by which he is best remembered. He took a great part in the diffusion of Oriental scholarship in Italy (Cardinal Egidio da Viterbo was among his pupils), and inevitably he came into close touch with Mantino, who perhaps studied with him also. It was for him, "the learned professor and celebrated physician," as he calls him, that Leo compiled his tri-lingual dictionary in Arabic, Hebrew and Latin, preserved at the Escurial, dedicating it to him in the most affectionate terms.

When the representatives of Italian Jewish scholarship were consulted regarding the legality according to biblical law of the first marriage of Henry VIII of England to Catherine of Aragon, widow of his deceased brother, Mantino was among those who gave an opinion, at the Pope's request, in opposition to the English thesis.[2] He also came into prominence by his determined, almost frenzied, opposition to the messianic dreamer, Solomon Molcho, whom he denounced as a danger to Jewry at large. Subsequently, he transferred himself to Rome, where he was body-physician to Pope Paul III. He received in 1539 an official appointment as Professor of Practical Medicine at the newly-organized university in the Sapienza, where his lectures were delivered in the afternoon. His prolonged association with academic teaching would of itself make him a memorable figure in our story, though indeed the teachers here at this time were said to be more numerous than the students. After a few years, however, we find him at work again in Venice. He died in the Levant in 1549 while acting as physician to the Venetian consul at Aleppo. It seems a lonely and lowly employment, after the glittering clientele on whom he had formerly attended. It may therefore be that his unquenchable intellectual curiosity had impelled him late in life to go eastward, to an Arabic-speaking environment—against the advice of his illustrious patient, Don Hurtado de Mendoza, the Spanish ambas-sador—in the hope of perfecting himself in that language and perhaps tracing more of the scientific classics of the Middle Ages, to the study and diffusion of which he was so devoted.

His translations of medical and philosophical works from the Hebrew into Latin were of considerable importance in the intel-lectual life of the age: from this point of view, he was unques-

---

[2] See below, p. 161.

tionably the most prolific Jewish writer of the Renaissance period. To mention only those that were published independently, they included Averroës' *De partibus et generatione animalium*, dedicated to Pope Leo X (Rome, 1521); his epitome of Aristotle's *Metaphysics* (after Moses ibn Tibbon's Hebrew version) which, published at Rome in 1521 with a dedication to Ercole Gonzaga, proved so popular that it appeared again two years later at Bologna; his paraphrase of Plato's *Republic*—a slight departure from the normal pattern—with an interesting prefatory epistle to Pope Paul III (Rome, 1539; Venice, 1552); and numerous other renderings which were incorporated subsequently in standard published editions, as we shall see. In addition, he published a version of Maimonides' ethical treatise popularly known as the "Eight Chapters" (Bologna, 1526) and assisted Bishop Agostino Giustiniani in his edition of the *Guide for the Perplexed* (Paris, 1520), which will be spoken of elsewhere.

These bibliographical details are heavy and meaningless, except to the expert who will perhaps find them trivial and inadequate. But they are necessary in order to demonstrate the main conclusions derivable from them—that the Jewish share in reconstituting the Aristotelian texts used in the Renaissance period was very marked. This may be strikingly demonstrated from a single memorable production. In 1550-52, the Giunta press produced in Venice, in eleven folio volumes, a splendid edition of the works of Aristotle in Latin, accompanied where possible by Averroës' commentaries: this is still the only source in which the whole body of the latter is readily available. In addition, the collection includes most of the other then-known works of Averroës, both philosophical and medical, and a number of minor texts and commentaries by various authors, some of them Jews. It is a work of the utmost rarity and importance: it is recounted that when in 1722 the King of France sent his copy through the Turkish ambassador as a gift to the sultan, only one other full set could be traced in the entire kingdom to replace it. The material of Jewish origin used in this great, though perhaps anachronistic, Renaissance achievement are of the utmost significance. Many texts, for example, are given in the version of Jacob Mantino, who has just been spoken of. The *Second Analytics* figures with Averroës' commentary which had been translated some time before by

Giovanni Francesco Burana from Calonymus ben Calonymus' medieval Hebrew version: in the margin the variants are given according to Mantino and De Balmes. The last-named was responsible also for the epitome of the *Organon*, while Averroës' medial commentary had been translated by Burana from the version of Jacob Anatoli. Other versions included were the work of a translator who is called Paul the Israelite ("Paulus Israelita")—believed to be identical with the German convert Paulus Riccius, formerly body-physician to the Emperor Maximilian, who had become professor of philosophy at Pavia. There also figures a commentary on Averroës' "Logic" and other materials by the medieval Jewish exegete, philosopher and scientist Levi ben Gershom of Bagnoles in Provence ("Ralbag"), rendered from the Hebrew by Mantino. Thus, each of the impressive volumes of which this classic edition consists (except the last, which comprises only Antonio Zimara's solution of apparent contradictions) contain compositions or versions by Jewish scholars—all of them famous (*celeberrimi omnes*) as the preface proudly states. In some volumes indeed (for example, the first and the tenth) their contributions constitute the greater part. Similarly, in the octavo edition of Aristotle and his Arab exponent produced in Venice in 1560, also in eleven volumes, Jewish versions figure in at least five. In this case, some of them (a commentary on Averroës' medial commentary, and a translation of his *De spermate*) are by Helias Cretensis—that is, Elijah del Medigo. (The theory has been advanced that one of the versions ascribed to Paul the Israelite is also based on earlier work of his.) In short, a great part—perhaps the majority—of the Latin Averroës, which still formed part of the curriculum of the University of Padua and other seats of learning well on into the seventeenth century, was the work of a group of Jews of the Renaissance period, most of them domiciled in Venice.

Not indeed that the leaning toward Aristotle and his philosophy was even now unquestioning and universal among the Jewish intelligentsia, any more than it had been during the Middle Ages. In the midst of this activity the rabbi-physician Obadiah Sforno of Bologna (who, as we shall see, at one time taught Hebrew to Johann von Reuchlin, on Cardinal Grimani's personal recommendation), distressed at the deference paid even by a man of the caliber and influence of Moses Maimonides to the Stagyrite and his writings, entered the lists on the other side. In a work which he entitled *Or Amim*, or "The Light of the Peoples" (Bologna, 1537), he endeavored to combat, with arguments drawn from Holy Writ, the latter's theories regarding the eternity of matter, the divine omniscience, and the universality of the soul, and such others of his opinions as seemed to him to be in opposition to Jewish doctrine. It would perhaps be out of place to mention the work here, were it not for the fact that, like so many of the writings of Jews on the other side, it was introduced to the Gentile world as well, the author himself translating it into Latin and getting it published in due course in that language, with a dedication to King Henry II of France, as a contribution to the defense of revealed religion in general, under the title *Lumen gentium* (Bologna, 1548).[3] It must have been received with some cordiality, as the author later inscribed to the same ruler the glosses on Canticles and Ecclesiastes which he appended to his lucid and rational *Commentary on the Pentateuch*–the work, even now constantly republished, for which he is still widely remembered among Jewish students of the old school.

Apart from these scholars, there were others who were continuing the old tradition of translating and commenting on philosophical and scientific classics in Hebrew. A Spanish Jew who settled in Padua after the Expulsion from his native country in 1492, Isaac ben Samuel Abu-l-Kheir, translated into Hebrew from the Latin the *Book of Nativities* by the Arab astronomer Albubather, as well as Rajil's *Completus;* in addition, he composed (or rather, plagiarized from Handali) a commentary on Al-Fergani's *Extract of the Almagest.* So, too, Rabbi Judah Messer Leon, one of the most humanistic of the Italian Jewish scholars of the age, composed Hebrew commentaries on Aristotle's *Ethics*, his *Ascoltatory Physics*, and his *Later Analytics* (the last said by one of his detractors–who replaced the opening lines of it by a statement to this effect–to be plagiarized from a composition of the medieval scholar Magister Paul). At the very end of the fifteenth century, the ill-fated Ludovico il Moro, Duke of Milan, gave orders for

---

[3] This work is stated by the bibliographers to have remained unpublished, but there is a copy in the library of the Jewish Theological Seminary of America, New York. The author's name is given as Servadeus Sphurnus.

the Jewish physician "Salamone Ebreo" to be given accommoda-
tion in the castle at Pavia, with a comfortable room and a couple
of scribes at his service and access to any Hebrew books he
pleased, the object being that he was to translate for his ducal
employer various works in that language useful for the study of
philosophy and theology, and thereby for the service of God.

Another somewhat evasive figure who participated in such work
appears in the eastern Mediterranean, in Cyprus—at that time
under Venetian rule, and in a certain sense a colony of Venetian
culture. In the Middle Ages, there had been current in Arabic a
treatise which attempted to "reconcile the Lyceum and the
Academy"—that is, to harmonize the doctrines of Plato and Aristotle. It is ascribed to Aristotle himself, but has nothing to do with
him: for it is probably a composition of the neo-Platonic school
of the late fifth century and has been described as the last native
work of the Hellenic genius. The original Greek is lost, but it was
early translated into Arabic, and in consequence of its hypothetical
authorship had a vast influence on the Arab thinkers of the Middle
Ages and through them on medieval Latin thought. The text of
the work, however, remained unknown to the European world
until the beginning of the sixteenth century. In 1516, a copy of
the Arabic was found in a library in Damascus. This was translated
into a rough-and-ready Italian by a certain Moses Rova or Roves,
an otherwise unknown Jewish physician-philosopher living in
Cyprus, who was probably of Italian birth. From the Italian it was
rendered literally into Latin by Pietro Niccolo de' Castellani of
Faenza, and published by Jacopo Mazochio in Rome in 1519,
under the title *Sapientissimi philosophi Aristotelis Stagiritae Theo-
logia sive Mistica Philosophia secundum Aegyptios* (there was another revised edition, Paris, 1572). It was a curious sixteenth-
century echo of the familiar medieval process, with the reservation that in this case the bridge between the Arabic text and the
Latin, executed by a Jewish scholar, was an Italian, not a Hebrew,
version.

The literary activity of Moses Alatino, in the second half of the
sixteenth century, illustrates in a remarkably vivid fashion both the
perpetuation of the tradition of the Latin Renaissance in the full
cinquecento setting and the position of the Jewish savant in Renaissance society. He belonged to a cultured Jewish family long

settled at Spoleto, in central Italy, where the church of S. Gregorio nella Sinagoga still perpetuates the memory of the former Jewish settlement. His half-brother Jehiel or, in Italian, Vitale (bisected into two separate individuals by savants and in works of reference of the last generation), was physician to Pope Julius III. Moses chose the same calling and entered the University of Perugia where, besides studying medicine, he attended the philosophical lectures of Francesco Piccolomini and made considerable progress. Owing to the religious restrictions, he was admitted to his degree in a private ceremony on July 7, 1556.

During the course of his studies, Moses Alatino came across an ancient Hebrew manuscript comprising the paraphrase of the four books of Aristotle's *De coelo* by the fourth-century statesman-rhetorician Themistius; this had been made from an Arabic translation of the lost Greek original, still untraced—a typical instance of the linguistic peregrinations of some of these classical texts. His teacher, the famous Bartolommeo Eustachi (who is reckoned one of the great reformers of anatomical study, with Vesalius and Fallopius, and was at the same time a competent Hebrew and Arabic scholar), was enthusiastic about the discovery. He had indeed good reason to show a benevolent interest in the finder, whose brother Vitale had been called from Rome to Perugia by the Cardinal of Urbino to attend on the professor in a very serious illness. Encouraged by his brother, and his teacher, Moses set about translating his find into Latin.

It turned out to be a very long task. At one time, owing to ill health, he felt inclined to give it up, but was urged to persevere by many scholars with whom he was in touch. Among these he mentions Benedetto Manzolo, of Modena, secretary of the Cardinal d'Este; he, nearly twenty years before, had incited a Jewish friend and fellow-townsman, Moses Finzi of the same place, to execute from the Hebrew version by Ibn Tibbon a translation of a similar work by Themistius (his paraphrase of Aristotle's *Metaphysics*) which had been dedicated to the Bishop of Gubbio. (*Themistii peripatetici lucidissimi paraphrasis in duodecimum librum Aristotelis de prima Philosophia. Moses Finzio Interprete*, Venice, 1558 and 1575. There is a copy of the former edition, the existence of which is questioned by some authorities, in the Bodleian Library in Oxford.) More practical help was forthcoming from a fellow philosopher-physician, Elijah de Nola, then functioning as rabbi in Rome. He proved useful especially in obscure passages where the Hebrew translator had used Arabic terms: for he had experience in dealing with such problems, having some time before translated from the Latin into Hebrew Robert Grosseteste's Aristotelian *Summa supra viii libros physicorum*, several manuscript copies of this version being preserved.

Moses Alatino finished his task after some years of intermittent labor. In 1572, he took his translation with him when he went to the baths near Padua for a cure, in the train of Camillo da Varano, a member of the former ducal House of Camerino. When the treatment was successfully completed, he betook himself to Padua to visit his former teacher, Francesco Piccolomini, now occupying the chair of philosophy at that university. Naturally, he was shown the manuscript, and, though it was still uncorrected, was very much interested in it and urged his pupil to make it generally accessible. Thus encouraged, Alatino at last had it published (Venice, 1574), the Cardinal d'Este accepting the dedication, probably through Manzolo's intervention. (*Themistii peripatetici lucidissimi paraphrasis in libros quatuor Aristotelis de coelo nunc primum in lucem edita. Moyse Hebraeo Spoletino medico, ac philosopho interprete*, Venice, 1574.) Alatino was also responsible for the translation from the Hebrew into Latin of Galen's commentary on Hippocrates' *De aere, aquis et locis*, which is included anonymously in the Paris edition of Galen's works published long after his death, in 1679. He also began a version, similarly from the Hebrew, of Avicenna's *Canon*.

Nothing could be more characteristic of the Renaissance than the scope of Alatino's literary activity and the cordial circumstances in which he was able to carry it out. But, while he was at work, he suffered personally from the deterioration of the conditions of Italian Jewry, and his life ended in a different and sadder world. In 1569, when Pope Pius V's *Hebraeorum gens* drove the Jews out of the minor places of the Papal States, he had to leave Spoleto, later settling in Ferrara: and he was living here when he addressed a letter in 1580 to the apostate censor, Andrea del Monte, begging him to be less severe in the exercise of his newly-established functions in respect to Hebrew literature. But full reaction was to extend before long to Ferrara too, when Duke

Alfonso d'Este II died in 1597 and the duchy was absorbed into the Papal States. It was now no place for a man of his temperament; as he wrote to the councillor of the Duke of Modena at the time, "it seemed to him that he was in another country and in another world, where there is a continuous flux and reflux of innovations." He accordingly took up his residence at Venice, where he died in 1605. His son and medical colleague, Bonaiuto (Asriel Petahia) remained, nevertheless, at Ferrara, being compelled to conduct a public disputation against a Jesuit in 1617 in the presence of the cardinal legate, and later being one of the Jewish commission sent to the Pope to attempt to avert the establishment of the ghetto. The record of father and son typifies the decline in the status of Italian Jewry at this time, paralleled in history only by the decline in the status of German Jewry in the period immediately following the rise of Nazism. Nevertheless, in this case too, before the relations between Jew and Christian were so brutally interrupted, they had affected the intellectual life of both for good.

FIVE

In the Steps *of* Dante

The Latin Renaissance culminated, and Italian literature burgeoned into sudden miraculous flower, in the superb genius of Dante Alighieri, whose *Divina commedia* is without question the greatest literary monument of the Middle Ages. It is not merely a vision of Heaven and Hell. It is a complete conspectus of the Universe—the world and the After-World—exactly delineated in accordance with a most elaborate plan through which the poet is guided, and guides us, step by step. In its unflagging stanzas there are conveyed, not only the aspirations and anguishes and petty resentments of a human being, but also the quintessence of the theology and eschatology, as well as a good part of the science and the learning, of the age.

As we have seen, in the texture of this there were many Jewish elements, or elements that had been transmitted through Jewish channels. Whether Dante ever met a Jew in the flesh is questionable; there were not many in north Italy in his day (though they were numerous in the south), and no community was established in Florence itself until more than a century after his death. A couple of passages of mysterious gibberish in his great poem ("Papé Satàn, papé Satàn aleppe," *Inferno*, vii.1: "Rafel mai amech zabi et almi," *ibid.*, xxxi.67) have received unsatisfactory interpretations through Hebrew; but there is no evidence that he knew a single word of that language, except for such as were universally familiar in theological writings and circles (*Hosanna, Sabaoth, El, Eli, Malacoth*); indeed he seems to deny explicitly in one passage that he had any knowledge of the sacred tongue. Nevertheless, the entire structure of his great poem is informed by philosophical, scientific and even theological conceptions which reached the Latin world largely through the intermediary of Jewish translators. The library that he used was a Latin one; yet Hebrew versions from the Arabic stood behind a good part of it.

He pays homage to Aristotle, whom he finds in the first circle of the Inferno at the head of the philosophers, as "Master of those who know" (*Inferno*, iv.131)—but, as we have seen, it was to a great extent through the intermediary of Hebrew that Aristotle's heritage came into the orbit of the European Middle Ages. Dante's theology and a great part of his philosophy are derived from the *Summa totius theologiae* of St. Thomas Aquinas: the latter, however, leaned heavily on Moses Maimonides, who thus influenced Dante too in an indirect fashion.

In the astrology and astronomy, which constitute such an important factor in the elaborate planning of the *Commedia*, the Judaic factor may be determined more precisely. For this purpose, Dante used the great series of astronomical tables or "Perpetual Almanac," drawn up by the Provençal Jewish scholar Jacob ben Makhir ibn Tibbon of Montpellier (c. 1236-1308), known in Gentile circles as Don Profiat ("one of the most honorable representatives of the progress of the human spirit in the thirteenth century," as Renan called him), which were translated into Latin during the author's lifetime. These tables start precisely with the period in which Dante placed his tremendous vision; and it seems that he had them by him constantly as a guide to the astronomical details which give his description so much of its specific coloring. The work has been published in full, as a companion to Dante studies, under the significant title *Almanach Dantis Alighierii, sive Profhacii judaei montispessulani almanach perpetuum ad annum 1300 inchoatum*.

This, in fact, solved one of the old, long-discussed difficulties regarding the precise year in which the action of the *Divina commedia* is staged. The historical data, and a good many of the internal references, seem to make it clear that it was supposed to be in 1300. Astronomical references, however (in particular the passage at the beginning of the ninth canto of the *Purgatorio*) give details that are reconcilable only with the year 1301. About this point there was long and involved argument, in which many eminent Dante scholars of the nineteenth century took part. One of the greatest of them concluded that "we feel almost inclined to take leave of the question in despair, with the cynical admission that 'there is nothing more deceptive than figures, except facts.' " However, after the publication of the volume referred to above it was found that an ambiguity in the arrangement of the Latin version of the *Almanach* (not inherited from the Hebrew original) could easily have led Dante to ascribe to 1300 the position actually occupied by Venus in the vernal equinox of 1301. This is now the accepted solution of the long-discussed problem.

Another, though more hypothetical, Judaic element in Dante's background was once suggested. Numerous parallels have been discovered in Moslem lore for various imaginative details in his elaborately-constructed After-World. Some years ago, the theory was put forward by a distinguished Spanish scholar, Migul Asin y Palacios, that these derive, not from Dante's fantasy or from eschatological elements which were familiar in Christian theology of the time, but from some Arabic source. In particular, attention was directed to the writings of the Spanish Moslem Ibn al-A'rabi, which incidentally seem to have embodied certain more remote rabbinical ideas. Obviously, some channel of transmission must have existed through which the Tuscan writer was made familiar with these concepts. It was natural, in the first instance, to suggest that this channel was Jewish, in view of the fact that Jews were the great intellectual intermediaries of the Middle Ages between the Moslem and the Christian worlds. In the original Spanish edition of his work, Father Asin suggested (in a passage omitted in the somewhat abbreviated English version) that the specific link in this case may have been the poet Immanuel of Rome, who was believed at one time to have been on terms of close intimacy with Dante. (It will be necessary to revert to him and his activity later on.) But it was recognized from the beginning that this was highly improbable both because this intimacy is more than hypothetical and because Immanuel, a child of the Italian environment, had hardly more access to Arabic lore than Dante himself. More recently, the suggestion was put forward that the intermediary may have been a Franciscan friar who returned to Florence early in the fourteenth century after long years of missionary activity in the Moslem lands. With this plausible alternative, the Hebraic thread running through this hypothetical bond wholly disappeared.

But at this point the story suddenly took a new twist, for the Arabic work which almost certainly served Dante as a model was actually rediscovered. This was a description of Mohammed's journey to Paradise, which enters into many details later incorporated by Dante into his vision. The work in question, entitled

The Ladder of Mohammed, had been translated into Spanish in Seville in 1264, on the instructions of King Alfonso the Wise of Castile, and had then been rendered into Latin and even into French. No element of mystery remains: Dante certainly had access to the work, and there is no reason to doubt that he used it. Now, as it happens, the original version from the Arabic into Spanish of this composition on which he relied and from which the later European versions were taken, was carried out by King Alfonso's Jewish astrologer, Don Abraham al-Faquim (that is, "the Physician") of Toledo, who was to be one of the hostages seized by the rebel barons in 1270. Thus the Jewish element in the transmission of the background of Dante's work reëmerges clearly, in the inevitable Jewish middleman who played such a vital part in medieval intellectual life.

The name of Immanuel of Rome is nevertheless one of importance—one might almost say, of primary importance—in connection with Dante studies. He was, indeed, from the literary point of view the most remarkable and the most important figure of the Renaissance period in the Jewish world. Like Dante, he stood at the forefront of it in time; like Dante, he was unsurpassed in his own field by any of his successors. But, whereas during the next three centuries there were Italian poets (Petrarch, Ariosto, Tasso) who can at least be mentioned in the same breath as Dante, Immanuel towers dizzily above the level of any of his Jewish competitors, in Italy at least, down to the dawn of modern times. Moreover, Dante, though the father of the new era in Italian literature which begins as well as culminates with him, was medieval through and through—the typical man, it may be said, of the Middle Ages. Immanuel, on the other hand, although in the full tide of the tradition of the Spanish Jewish school of poetry—in the direct line of succession to Judah Halevi and Solomon ibn Gabirol and Moses ibn Ezra—was basically a son of the New Age, and reflects the spirit of the Italian Renaissance more vividly than any other Hebrew writer whatsoever. At the same time, his poems in the vernacular were unsurpassed in importance by those of any other European Jew until the eighteenth century.

What we know about his background may be summed up very briefly. He was an almost exact contemporary of Dante, having been born four years before him, in 1261 (not, as was formerly believed, in 1270), perhaps at Ceprano in the Papal States, from which his Hebrew surname, Zifroni, may be derived. He seems to have been a rolling stone, wandering from place to place to earn his living, presumably as a house-tutor for the children of the wealthy Jewish loan-bankers who were establishing themselves throughout central Italy at this time. We find his traces in Perugia, Fabriano, Fermo, Camerino, Ancona and Verona, as well as outside Italy, in Vienne on the Rhône (though this is less certain). He dabbled in medicine, perhaps not seriously. He had some reputation as a Hebrew stylist, and was used from time to time by Jewish communities—those, for example, of Rome and of Ancona—to write official correspondence for them. It is probable that he acted from time to time as cantor in the synagogue. But generally speaking one receives the impression of the familiar type of the seedy, down-at-the-heels "literary genius," drifting aimlessly from town to town and from protector to protector, trying his hand at all things in turn, and never quite fulfilling his early promise.

His output was considerable, but in great part unimportant from the modern viewpoint. He wrote philosophical commentaries on almost every book of the Bible, though the only one published until recent times (that on Proverbs, which appeared at Naples in 1487) bore the name of another Immanuel—a characteristic piece of posthumous ill-fortune. A work of his on biblical hermeneutics, *Eben Boḥan*, is still unprinted; another, on the symbolism of the Hebrew alphabet, has been lost. But it is as a poet that Immanuel is best—it would be more accurate to say, solely—remembered today. Not as a Hebrew poet only; we shall have occasion elsewhere in this work to refer to his Italian writings: they comprise a curious *frottola*, or ballad, in which he described in an extraordinarily vivid fashion the feverish daily life at the court of Cangrande della Scala, Tyrant of Verona from 1311 to 1329, whose patronage he apparently enjoyed at one time; and a handful of sonnets, one of them slightly lewd, to which we will have to direct attention later. (It is enough to say for the present that at least one of them brings us, and the author, into touch with Dante's own literary circle.) There is reason to believe that this is the remnant of a considerable production in the Italian language that has disappeared.

The same might have happened to his mass of Hebrew poetical writing, but for the fact that toward the end of his life, in or about 1328, while he was living at Fermo in the Marches of Ancona, one of his patrons suggested to him that he should preserve his verses for posterity by collecting them in a single coherent corpus. This he did, using for the purpose a sort of rough narrative framework, basically autobiographical (in a highly idealized sense)—a system that had been used long before by the Arabic poet Ibn Ali al-Hariri of Basra for his *Maqamat* (literally "Assemblies," the unity in this literary genre being conferred by the participants).[1] Immanuel's similar compilation, entitled the *Miḥberoth Immanuel* or "Compositions of Immanuel," has some independent importance in literary history as being among the first works which introduced to a European environment, albeit in a Semitic tongue, that narrative framework embracing many independent episodes which was to be used not long after, with such magnificent effect, by Boccaccio in his *Decameron* and by Chaucer in the *Canterbury Tales*.

The "Compositions of Immanuel" are, however, a curious and in many ways bewildering compilation. The framework consists of somewhat inane conversations between the poet and his patron or "Prince"—presumably one of the loan-bankers who lorded it over the Jewish communities of central Italy at this time. This, however, was compiled merely to give some sort of organic unity to the contents, which are of the most varied description, and were brought together without much sense of congruity and still less of discrimination. The author crowded into it all of his poetical or semi-poetical writings that he could assemble or recall: epigrams, puns, satires, lampoons, elegies, epitaphs, religious poetry, narrative verses and anything else, even invitations to penitence and to asceticism. The work comprises various hymns, including what is apparently an experimental version of the famous synagogal poem based on Maimonides' Thirteen Articles of Faith, *Yigdal* ("The Living God O Magnify and Bless," in

---

[1] The *Maqamat* as a literary form was popularized first in Hebrew literature by the Spanish litterateur Judah al-Harizi in his Hebrew translation of that work under the title *Miḥberoth Ithiel* or "Compositions of Ithiel"; and subsequently renewed by the last-named in his own original, but obviously imitative, *Taḥkemoni* or "Apothecary."

Israel Zangwill's superb English version). The Italian influence is obvious on every page. The work contains the first sonnets in the Hebrew language, written in accordance with the formal rhyming scheme recently fixed by Guittone d'Arezzo (d. 1294). We find other Italian poetical conventions—the Alexandrine couplet, the *serventese*, and the traditional *envoi* so common in European poetry of the period. For example (§ viii).

> My song, if one doth see thee
>   And ask to whom dost wend,
> Say: "Manuel hath sent me,
>   To greet the Prince, his friend."

Everywhere, the spirit and influence of the poets of the circle of the *Dolce stil nuovo*, whose outstanding representative was Dante, may be discerned. Immanuel writes of his beloved as the angelic lady, who elevates her lover to a higher sphere. He first sees her in synagogue, just as Dante first sees his Beatrice in church; and he continues his adoration of her even after her demise:

> Corruption! Through thee now I love e'en death.
>   O happy, happy death, thus bound with her,
> Art sweeter now than aught that draweth breath,

he writes in his third "Composition": an obvious parallel to or imitation of Dante's famous lines in the *Vita nuova*, xxiii:—

> Io divenia nel dolor sì umile
>   veggendo in lei tanta umiltà formata,
>   ch'io dicea:—Morte, assai dolce ti tegno;
>   tu dei imai esser cosa gentile,
>   poi che tu se' ne la mia donna stata.[2]

---

[2] And I became so humble in my grief,
    Seeing in her such deep humility,
That I said: Death, I hold thee passing good
    Henceforth, and a most gentle sweet relief,
Since my dear love has chosen to dwell with thee.
                                    (Rossetti's version)

At one point, Immanuel indicates clearly enough that he had a secular model for his verses. His "Prince," or maecenas, tells him that he knew of a vernacular poem in which the author sang of all the arts and crafts and sciences and lands and peoples, and expressed the desire to read something of the same sort in Hebrew. He was obviously referring to the *Serventese del maestro di tutte l'arti* ("Serventese of the Master of all Arts") by an anonymous poet of the period:

> Heo so bene esser cavaleri
> Et doncello, et bo scuderi,
> Mercadante andari a feri,
> Cambiatore et usurieri
> Et so pensare.
>
> So piatari et avocare
> Clericu so et so cantare
> Fisica saczo et medicare,
> Et so di rampogni, et so zolare,
> Et bo sartore.

This was exactly imitated by Immanuel—in subject-matter, meter, and construction—in the highly amusing Hebrew version included in the *Miḥberoth* (Composition IX):—

> I'm a sailor and can row;
> I'm a weaver, I can sew;
> I can build and I can hoe;
> I can weigh and mix the dough;
> I'm a dentist-leach.
>
> I'm a burglar and a crook;
> I'm a tinker, I'm a cook;
> I can write and bind a book;
> I can give a dirty look,
> And can turn a speech.

It is not, however, only in its form, but still more in its spirit, that the *Miḥberoth Immanuel* betrays the Italian influence. It has

been said that the author decked out the decorous Hebrew muse
in the skirts of a ballet-dancer. He not only reflects Dante, but
also anticipates Boccaccio—and with the additional complication,
that by reason of the curious framework in which he included
poems of every sort, the two elements jostle one another in the
same work and sometimes on the same page. Alongside of hymns
there are lewd ditties. A dignified epistle written on behalf of the
Roman synagogue comes not long after a scabrous anecdote that
might have figured in the *Decameron*. Notwithstanding his ideal-
ization of his beloved *à la* Dante, the author a few pages later
boasts of his conquests *à la* Boccaccio and proudly styles himself
"the Prince of Love," or rather "Lust." He constantly boasts
(though to be sure without much conviction) of his amatory
adventures—of course, invariably successful. He displays an adolescent interest in the female anatomy, and indulges in characteristic undergraduate ribaldry whenever he has the opportunity:
for example, he wonders how the constellation Virgo has preserved her maiden state intact for so long—a theme reverted to by
Congreve in his *Love for Love* three centuries later. The following, after Composition XVI (in which he again uses a theme
common in the popular poetry of the time, as those who are
familiar with *Aucassin et Nicolette* will readily recall), may be
cited as one of the more decorous instances of his amatory verses:—

> My heart communes within me: Were it best
>   To give up Heaven and cast my lot in Hell?
>   There would I find most surely every belle,
> And all delights wherewith mankind is blest.
> For why should I choose Eden for my rest?
>   No love is there: only the features fell
>   Of antique hags, whose wrinkles dotage tell.
> In their abode, my soul would feel depressed.
>
> Aroint thee, Eden! thou dost specialize
>   But in the halt, the blemished and the maim.
> Naught are thy vaunted wonders in my eyes.
>   But Hell! what grace thy torments must enframe!
> In thee, all beauty yet, in loving guise,
>   Persists to charm, and still defies thy flame.

But it is not in his erotic writings only that Immanuel shows himself to be remote from the traditional pietistic spirit. The following sonnet, for example, the translation of which also preserves the rhyming-scheme of the original, is anticipatory of political activists of our own day: —

Haste on, Oh Prince Messiah! do not stay!
  We yearn upon thee. All our eyes well tears,
And bitter anguish rends us, night and day.
  Yet hope we ever, though the Gentile jeers.

Take thou the measuring-rod in hand, and span
  Zion, the crown of beauty. Calm her fears:
Let her sons know the peace of mortal man
  The while she stands full upright 'midst her peers.

Arouse thee, Oh Messiah! Gird thy blade,
  Harness thy prancing steed, prepare to mount:
For my heart is all broken and dismayed.

  But if thou wouldst come riding on an ass,
I prithee, Lord Messiah, to dismount.
  Put off thy coming to a brighter pass.

There is to be sure an air of unreality about all these erotic and skeptical verses of Immanuel—both those in which he endeavored to be sublime and those in which he succeeded in being lewd. One has the impression that he thought it fashionable to write love poems, and he wrote them; that he found that it was titillating both to himself and his hearers to describe amatory conquests, and he described them; but that in neither case did his compositions bear much relation to actuality. Romantic love, as distinct from marital devotion, was barely known in Jewish life at this time; and the social circles involved were too circumscribed for extra-marital adventure to be easy or even possible. The author, it seems to me, was simply following the conventions of the time, independent of his personal convictions; or he was setting out to be amusing, without much regard to verisimilitude or to veracity. He was a superb rhymester. But, if intensity of passion is a mark of great poetry, he is hardly to be reckoned a poet at all.

His reputation, however, suffered in consequence of his exhibitionism. It was no doubt characteristic of the Renaissance outlook that he was the first Jewish poet whose works were published more or less integrally, his *Mibberoth* appearing at Brescia in 1491. (Jehuda haLevi's collected poems were not printed until the nineteenth century!) They were, indeed, republished in 1535 in Constantinople; but two and a half centuries were to pass before they were to reappear. For meanwhile a strong opposition had developed to them on moral grounds. Already before this time Moses Rieti (who will be spoken of later in this chapter) excluded him from the hall of fame he erected to Jewish sages in his Dantesque imitation, *The Lesser Sanctuary*, "because of his language and gibes in his compositions of lust." Joseph Caro, in his authoritative sixteenth-century code, the *Shulḥan Arukh*, simply forbade the reading of his poems and considered that anyone who published them defiled public morals (*Oraḥ Ḥayim*, § cccvii.16), An Italian Jewish poet of the ghetto period, Immanuel Frances—close to him in spirit and otherwise—in his treatise on Hebrew prosody, *Metek Sefatayim*, censured his wanton songs and warned poets who took love as their theme against following his example. His reputation would have been more solid had his virtuosity been less apparent.

At the close of the *Mibberoth Immanuel* there is appended a final section (the twenty-eighth) which has no organic connection with the rest: Immanuel's famous vision of Heaven and Hell, written in obvious imitation of the *Divina commedia* of Dante and having a most important bearing on Dante studies. Much has been written—a good deal of it entirely fanciful—on this, called in Hebrew *Mibberoth haTophet vehaEden* or "The Composition of Tophet and Eden." Recent research however has thrown a new light upon its genesis and its background, and its dramatic and personal implications have thus at last fully emerged.

The *Divina commedia* was, as is well known, written while Dante was in exile, and it is impossible to understand its spirit without bearing this fact in mind. The same was the case apparently with Immanuel's "Vision of Heaven and Hell." In the spring of 1321, the Pope (then living in Avignon) was persuaded —probably by Sancha, wife of Robert d'Anjou, King of Naples and Count of Provence—to expel the Jews from Rome. When his

instructions reached the city, the Jews were seized with consterna-
tion. Not knowing where to turn, they sent a delegation, presumably well-furnished with funds, to induce the Pope to withdraw the edict: at its head was the versatile Calonymus ben
Calonymus, who had been in close contact with King Robert
because of the series of translations that he had carried out under
his auspices.[3] There is still preserved the Order of Service recited
on the occasion of the public fast observed by the Roman Jews,
to implore the divine protection, on the day that the delegation
left.

Their mission was successful in the end, though the cost was
very high. But the road from Rome to Avignon was long, and
before they could return—perhaps even before they arrived in
Avignon—the papal edict of expulsion was, it seems, temporarily
put into effect. The Roman Jews—men, women and children—set
out on the road of exile, Immanuel among them, the main body
going northward, toward Umbria. At this period the rural areas
around Rome were in a state of semi-anarchy, the local barons
terrorizing the entire region. The exiles found themselves harried
mercilessly on their path, and among those who lost their lives
was the poet's father-in-law, the learned Rabbi Samuel, on whom
he wrote a touching elegy (included in the *Miḥberoth*, xiii).

At this stage, succor came from an unexpected quarter. A handful of Jewish loan-bankers had recently been allowed to establish
themselves in Orvieto, and it seems that they sallied out, or even
organized an armed force, to succor their co-religionists, many
of whom they apparently brought back with them and entertained
hospitably in their homes. Among these was Immanuel, who never
forgot this service. But Orvieto did not allow him scope for his
normal activities, and he pushed up thence to Perugia, an older
and more important Jewish center. Here, too, he was hospitably
received by one of the local magnates. His objective, however,
was further north still, the lovely Umbrian hill-city of Gubbio,
famous today for its annual feast of flowers: for here was living
an old acquaintance of his, the wealthy loan-banker Daniel, known
as a patron of learning and of poetry, of whom he had good hopes.
A disappointment was in store for him: he had barely arrived,

---

[3] See above, pp. 70 f.

when his friend died, and Immanuel found himself abandoned, if not destitute.

He unexpectedly found an element of compensation and even of consolation. The most important person in Gubbio at this time was the poet Bosone (known today as Bosone da Gubbio) who, like so many others of that turbulent age, passed a good part of his life in exile, voluntary or otherwise, but had returned to his native city two years since. He was an intimate friend of Dante, who according to an ancient report had visited him there not long before. Moreover, a more important literary figure, the jurist and poet Cino da Pistoia—Dante's close friend, and one of the most prominent figures in the circle of the *dolce stil nuovo*—spent some time in Gubbio that summer, on his way from Camerino to take up an appointment at the University of Siena. Immanuel made their acquaintance, and at least with the former came to be on terms of real intimacy. A few of his sonnets written at this period, with the heading *Manuel Çudeo da Gobio*, have been preserved, probably in consequence of the accident of having been sent to one or the other of the above-named two. The sonnets are in part of the same character as some of his lighter Hebrew verses: one begins "Love never read the *Ave Maria*," in which he pleads for the overlooking of sectarian differences in matters amatory; while in another he professes his indifference to religious distinctions provided he could be a polygamous Moslem from the belt downwards. Obviously, he thought that this was the sort of thing that his Gentile friends might appreciate. Certainly, he made an impression on them, for when he died, there was an interchange of sonnets between the two, as we shall see.

Immanuel was in Gubbio at the end of September, 1321, when the news arrived that Dante Alighieri had died at Ravenna, and it was apparently just at this time that his own friend and protector, Daniel, passed away. Such was the esteem that he apparently enjoyed among the townsfolk, that Bosone actually addressed Immanuel a consolatory sonnet, in which he linked together the two deaths as similar losses to the world:—

> Two lamps of life have waxed dim and died,
>   Two souls for virtue loved and blessed grace.
>   Thou, friend, may'st smile no more with happy face:

I weep for *him*, sweet song's and learning's pride.
Weep thou for him now taken from thy side
    Whose cheerful mien bore virtue's own impress
    —Him thou hast sung so oft ere thy distress,
That is mine, too, and with me doth abide.

Not I alone bewail thy hapless lot,
    But others too: do thou bewail thine own
And then the grief that all of us have got
    In this, the direst year that e'er was known.
Yet Dante's soul, that erst to us was given,
Now taken from earth, shineth anew in heaven.

Immanuel replied in the same medium and the same spirit, something of Oriental poetic extravagance being perhaps discernible in
his hyperbole:—

    The floods of tears well from my inmost heart,
        Can they e'er quench my grief's eternal flame?
        I'll weep no more, though anguish is the same;
    For death alone can help to smooth the smart.
    Then Jew and Gentile weep, and sit with me,
        On mourning stool, for sin hath followed woe.
    I prayed to God to spare this misery,
        And now no more my trust in Him I show . . .

This interchange of sonnets was not all. Immanuel may well
have been introduced to, or if he already knew it may have discussed, Dante's *Divina commedia* with his Italian friends at Gubbio; and he determined to commemorate his own exile, and his
own sufferings, and his own loss, in a composition conceived along
the same lines. This was the origin of the "Composition of Tophet
and Eden," referred to above, which was appended to the *Miḥberoth Immanuel*. From the allusions to the tragic events in Italian
Jewish history in the summer of 1321, which have recently been
identified, there can be no doubt that it belongs to this period of
Immanuel's life—to the autumn, that is, of this year, within a short
period of Dante's own death. It is, indeed, of some significance in
Dante studies that his great poem was so generally known as to
be imitated at such an early date. There must, of course, be no

misunderstanding about this. To speak of Immanuel as "The Jewish Dante," as was done at one time, is misleading—it is more fitting
to call him "The Jewish Boccaccio." There is no comparison
between the two compositions in scale, in profundity, in majesty,
in finish, in literary value. Immanuel's is a by-product, dashed off
in a few days, and it wholly lacks the sublimity as well as the
elaborate construction of the original by which it was inspired.
The rhymed prose which he uses as his medium can hardly fail
to convey an impression of triviality even when it is solemn, in
contrast to the inexorable majesty of Dante's *terza rima*. Nevertheless, the dependence of the one composition on the other is
obvious throughout, beginning with the opening phrase which
indicates the poet's age ("When sixty years had clustered o'er my
head, / And I began to fear the ministers of dread," imitating
Dante's " 'Twas half-way through the span of human life"), down
to the last words with their reference to the constellations ("And
may my lot be set with those that are, / Adorned with light of
justice, like a star," following the other's "The Love that moves
the sun and moves the stars").

The action of Immanuel's *parergon* is ingenious, and links up
directly with the circumstances in which he found himself in the
year of Dante's death. He tells how at this time, when he had
just completed his sixtieth year, a most intimate friend of his,
named Daniel (obviously that is his patron, Daniel of Gubbio),
died in the flower of his days. This loss set the poet to thinking
of his latter end and of what would be his lot in the future world.
He accordingly called upon Daniel to inform him of this. In
answer to his ambiguous appeal, there appeared not his friend of
that name but the prophet Daniel, who guided him through the
After-World. (The suggestion, once made, that he is to be equated
with Dante, is wholly preposterous.) They go together down an
obscure and rugged pathway, pass over a torrent by a half-ruined
bridge, and arrive at a doorway inscribed with the words "Enter
who would herein, but not return" (cf. Dante's "Abandon hope,
all ye who enter here" over the gate of Hell). They see a crowd
of damned souls being conducted by demons to torment within
the bowels of the earth. Here large numbers of the sinful figures
of the Bible are being punished in fire. Then follow the ancient
philosophers—Aristotle for believing in the eternity of matter,

Galen for writing against Moses, Avicenna for believing that it is
possible to construct a synthetic man, and Hippocrates for being
niggardly with his wisdom (this last surely a characteristically
Jewish touch!). After this, they visit some twenty or more bands
of sinners: the lustful, hypocritical, suicides, defrauders, liars,
gamblers, misers, despisers of learning, and so on (divided into different categories), and make stereotyped inquiries of each. There
is none of the superb architecture of Dante's *Inferno*, nor of the
dramatic fitting of punishment to crime, let alone the tragic gran-
deur of those who command sympathy even in Hell—those elements that make Dante's poem so great. We read, however, a disproportionately long account of a miserly Jew of Ancona and the
luxury in which he had lived—an episode that must have been
familiar in Immanuel's circle. Without taking him any further (it
would have been a monotonous journey—how unlike Dante's!), his
mentor now describes the pains of twenty-five further classes of
the damned. Immanuel, on the other hand, is comforted by being
reminded of his "immortal" biblical commentaries, which would
insure his future felicity.

A ladder now leads to Paradise, where the sublimated souls of
those whose eternal bliss is certain sit tier by tier "enjoying the
radiance of the divine presence," in accordance with the rabbinic
picture of the Hereafter. (There is, of course, no intermediate
purgatory, which would be alien to Jewish concepts.) A long,
and it must be said highly uninteresting, roll of the biblical and
post-biblical characters of Jewish history now follows. Just as
Dante finds himself enlisted among the immortal poets, so Immanuel receives the thanks of the authors of the various biblical
works for his illuminating commentaries which, they tell him,
have alone fully penetrated their meaning! The story becomes a
little more interesting when Immanuel begins to enumerate his
contemporaries—the rabbis of Rome of his day, and his own
mother, and his kinsmen; this section culminates when he sees the
felicity that is to be enjoyed by his friend and patron, Daniel,
whose recent death was the cause of his voyage into the After-
World. There is another echo of recent events when he sees the
happy lot of a band who had lost their lives apparently during
the onslaughts that accompanied the exile from Rome, their sufferings at that time atoning for their misdeeds. This is followed

by an episode where Immanuel shows an imaginative force hardly inferior to Dante's own. He sees ten canopies, the seats under which are vacant, asks whose they are, and is informed that they are those of the "Ten Martyrs" of Jewish traditional lore—the group of rabbis who had been put to death by a Roman emperor and figure in Hebrew legend as the prototypes of Jewish martyrdom. "Where are they, then?" he inquires. And he is told that they have left their places and gone, together with his martyred father-in-law, Rabbi Samuel, to throw themselves before the Divine Throne and implore mercy and compassion for their exiled co-religionists who were then suffering on earth.

There is another characteristic episode in the Vision of Paradise which may be said to reflect the tolerant Jewish spirit and is in striking contrast to the attitude that had been forced on Dante by Christian theology. At one point Immanuel is shown a special section of glory in which the "Pious of the nations of the world," the righteous heathen and non-Jews, enjoy eternal felicity, in accordance with a famous talmudic dictum. It is legitimate to imagine that here we have an oblique allusion to the Christian friends who helped him in Gubbio. His recent Jewish benefactors are rewarded in a more direct fashion, when he describes the places reserved in Paradise for the valiant Jewish leader who had sallied out to help the exiles, and the hospitable householder of Perugia, and Calonymus ben Calonymus who had led the delegation to Rome, and above all the generous-hearted Jews of Orvieto, who had done so much to help the sufferers in their darkest hour.

With this, the vision ends, Immanuel being enjoined by his mentor, before the latter disappears, to write down all that he had seen, so that others might benefit. There is little doubt that the poet discussed the composition with his Italian friends, who not only knew of it, but even continued to associate him in their minds with the author of the *Divina commedia*. When Immanuel died (the date is not known, but it was some time between 1328 and 1336), Cino addressed a sonnet to Bosone in which he suggested that the Jewish poet was now in the Inferno together with Dante, both undergoing the penalties so graphically described by the latter, for their attitude toward women. Bosone, more tolerant if less orthodox, insists in his reply that nevertheless both will ultimately benefit by the Great Deliverance. The text is highly

obscure and the exact interpretation doubtful. What clearly
emerges, however, is that the Christian and the Jew who had
described the After-World have their names linked together for
that reason by the two poets who knew both of them and apparently were present at the birth of the "Vision of Tophet and
Eden."

Immanuel's composition is by far the most important and the
most interesting of the Hebrew works inspired by the *Divina
commedia*; it is, moreover, as we have seen, of some importance
in the history of Italian literature as one of the earliest evidences
of the diffusion of that work. There are, however, several other
Dantesque echoes in Hebrew. There is no need to linger over the
Vision of Paradise in the *Maḥberet heTene* (or "Book of the
Basket") in which the Sicilian poet-physician Aḥitub ben Isaac
of Palermo vaguely described in rhymed prose a visit to Paradise;
for there are no specific reminiscences here (indeed, the composition may have been written before the *Divina commedia*) and
from the viewpoint of Dante studies it is of interest chiefly as
demonstrating how prevalent at this time was the idea of a visit
to the After-World.

More important by far from this point of view is the Dantesque
imitation, *Mikdash Meät* ("The Lesser Sanctuary") of the fifteenth-century physician Moses di Rieti (c. 1388-1460). In him
we have a typical figure of Italian Jewry of the age—a physician
of note, who served the commune of Fabriano, in Umbria, in that
capacity even while attending on the humanist Pope Pius II who
must have appreciated his accomplishments. He was a prolific
writer in Hebrew on medicine, philosophy and apologetics; a
courageous polemist, who sustained the cause of Judaism against
the sermons of a friar who delivered a series of conversionist sermons in Rome (perhaps the humanist Giannozzo Manetti, according to the accepted view[4]), as well as in a public disputation with
certain converts at the court of Sigismondo Malatesta, Tyrant of
Rimini; and an active worker in the public life of Italian Jewry in
his day.

The *Divina commedia* exercised a powerful attraction on Moses

---

[4] See below, pp. 139 f. But Manetti was not a friar, and it seems
more probable that Rieti's opponent was John of Capistrano, who
staged a virulent anti-Jewish disputation in Rome in 1450.

di Rieti, as it did on all Italians of the time. He was no more than
twenty-one when he made up his mind to write an imitation of it
in the Hebrew language. Seven years later, he ended the task. His
Lesser Sanctuary is, however, conceived on an entirely different
plan. Before he embarks on his main theme, he provides an introduction to the entirety of theological and scientific knowledge
as he conceives it—from Aristotle and Porphyry and their commentators down to Maimonides and Levi ben Gershom: this,
which takes up five cantos of unequal length, he calls the *Ulam*
or "Hall." Then follows the main part of the work, the *Hechal* or
"Palace."

Here the Dantesque influence becomes apparent. The author,
omitting all consideration not only of the *Purgatorio* but also of
the *Inferno*, describes, in eight cantos, a visit to the abode of the
souls of the righteous, where the heroes of Israel and the sages of
olden time enjoy eternal bliss. In the first canto, he gives a general
description of the rabbinic "Academy on High:" the second,
beginning *Meon haShoalim* or "The Abode of the Suppliants,"
comprises a prayer, which though it did not enter into the synagogue liturgy (as is often stated) became very popular with
Italian Jewry. Thereafter, the poet enters the "City of God"
(that is, the Scriptures), on passing through which he reaches the
Ships of the Soul—that is, the talmudic literature described in
cantos iv and v. In the remaining sections of the work (vi-viii) he
enumerates the scholars and heroes who dwell for all time in the
City of God, together with an account of the miracles performed
by the pious and of the wonders of the Holy Land. In this section,
there are numerous sidelights on Jewish literary history, especially
as regards Italian Jewry of the later Middle Ages. Moreover, the
author had the forethought to provide some biographical notes,
from which we learn that he excluded from his Paradise some of
the Jewish philosophers (for example, Gersonides) because of
their erroneous conceptions of the Deity; and Immanuel of Rome,
his predecessor in this literary realm, because of his lascivious
writing. However, as has been wittily observed, it is doubtful
whether they (and especially the last named) suffered much by
their exclusion, as Rieti's Paradise was rather a dreary one.

The Dantesque reminiscence of the *Mikdash Meät* is accentuated by the use in it throughout of the same poetical instrument

that is characteristic of the *Divina commedia*—the *terza rima*, or inter-rhyming tercets, which Moses di Rieti first introduced to Hebrew poetry. It is in his hands a flawless but languid instrument, contrasting strikingly in this to the tremendous force that Dante's genius was able to infuse into it—though less to be sure in the *Paradiso*, which was Rieti's model, than in the other sections. It has been said of the *Lesser Sanctuary* that it is "as pure, as melodious, as forceful, and as profound—and therefore as difficult to understand—as Dante's own work"; but this is somewhat of an overstatement. It may be mentioned, however, that Rieti's prayer comprised in "The Abode of the Suppliants" has an importance of its own in literary annals, for it was repeatedly translated into Italian in the same medium—the version by the Roman poetess Deborah Ascarelli, of whom we have spoke above, being particularly noteworthy in this connection.[5]

A great deal more remarkable and more interesting than this, though far less known, is the audacious and highly original Dantesque imitation written by a young scholar named Abraham Jaghel, best remembered today (rather unfortunately) as the author of the earliest Hebrew catechism. He was a troubled soul, who loved learning but was thrust into business; who profoundly disapproved of the institution of the loan-banks, but nevertheless earned his livelihood by this means, and later was to become Master of the Mint to the Prince of Corregio; and late in life was once held to ransom by brigands. In 1587, when he was at the outset of his career, he composed in rhymed prose the fantastic work which he entitled *Ge Ḥizayyon* or "The Valley of Vision," in which he recounted with a wealth of graphic detail how the spirit of his father conducted him through the After-World. Here, in the intervals of being shown the sights and interviewing passing spirits, he recounted to his father the story of his somewhat adventurous life up to that point, those in Paradise having, curiously enough, no knowledge of what goes on in the earth below. What he hears from the spirits, on the other hand, comprises mainly exemplary tales, emphasizing the importance to a man's felicity of the virtues and vices. In some cases, interesting light

[5] There was another version (Venice, 1585), by Lazzaro da Viterbo (for whom see below, p. 332).

is thrown incidentally on contemporary social conditions and ideals; while in one case the story which he hears is of the highly-spiced Renaissance type, such as one might read in the pages of Fiorenzuola, if not of Boccaccio.

Two later Hebrew imitators of Dante deserve cursory mention before we leave this subject. Among the host of Italian writers of a later period who were inspired by him more or less directly was Moses Zacut, or Zacuto. Perhaps a descendant of the astronomer Abraham Zacuto who had flourished in the age of Columbus, and a fellow-student of Benedict Spinoza in Amsterdam, he had migrated to Italy, immersed himself in the mystical movement, and proliferated verses which for that decadent age may be considered as being on a fairly high level. He was the author of a religious drama, on the life of Abraham, which has some importance in the history of Jewish literature, and to which it will be necessary to refer elsewhere in this volume.[6] But in the field of belles-lettres his most important achievement was a long poem of 125 five-line stanzas entitled *Tofteh Arukh* or "Tophet Ordained" (cf. Isaiah 30.33: "For Tophet is ordained of old"). This is a sort of morality play describing the soul's fate in the After-World, the scene being laid first in the cemetery and then in Hell, and the dialogue being placed in the mouths of the dead man, and of the demon who leads him through the seven circles of Hell and shows him the type of suffering the sinners endure in each. It is said that Zacuto repented in his mystical old age of having wasted his time by learning Latin in his youth and fasted for forty days in the hope of forgetting that language; but it is obvious in this poem that he had read, and still remembered, his Dante. This work appeared posthumously at Venice in 1715; nearly thirty years later, it was republished by a pious Ferrara rabbi and poetaster, Jacob Daniel Olmo, together with a supplement of 277 stanzas in the same meter from his own pen, entitled *Eden Arukh*, or "Paradise Prepared" (Venice, 1743), in which he described in a similar vein the peregrinations in Heaven of a more fortunate departed soul. Incidentally, he mentions in Dantesque fashion some of the heroes of biblical literature and subsequent Jewish history—none, however, later than the classical

---

[6] Below, p. 333.

period—who were enjoying eternal bliss. But it is an unconvincing picture. None of Dante's Jewish imitators had anything approaching his poetic genius. None, moreover, was a good hater—and it was Dante's fierce passions that make his poem one of the greatest in all literature.

In the realm of Italian letters, in which so far as we can tell he was the pioneer among his co-religionists, Immanuel of Rome had many successors, but none whose reputation or ability equaled his. This is in itself noteworthy, for in Italy there was no intermission, as in other countries, in the tradition of writing in the language of the environment. Indeed, a considerable Jewish religious literature in Italian, both in prose and in verse, is extant—most of it translations, a little original—extending back as far as perhaps the twelfth century; and the mere list of such titles drawn up by Moritz Steinschneider, the greatest of Jewish bibliographers, fills a small volume. But, except for those verses of Immanuel that have engaged our attention, all or almost all of these compositions down to the middle of the sixteenth century were meant exclusively for Jews, and the great majority were written in Hebrew characters: for there was at one time a relatively considerable literature in Judaeo-Italian, comparable to the Judaeo-German (Yiddish) of northern Europe or the Judaeo-Spanish (Ladino) of the eastern and southern Mediterranean. This dialect (it is best to call it thus, though it approximated more closely to the accepted literary forms than its sisters) was the medium in which Moses di Rieti, after his Disputation in Rome, composed a religio-philosophical defense of Judaism—still unpublished—which is said to be the oldest extant work by a Jew in the Italian language.

Nevertheless, a few Jews ventured to appeal to a wider public. For example, there was living in Ferrara in the fifteenth century a Jewish poet named Solomon (Salamone), whose love-lyrics were highly esteemed and whom Giovanni Peregrini (secretary to Lionello d'Este, 1441-1450: this helps to fix the date) compared in an enthusiastic sonnet to the gifted poets of the *dolce stil nuovo*. Salamone's reply, also in sonnet form, is preserved. He boasts his knowledge of the writings of Sallust, Livy, Valerius Maximus (the moralist) and even of the Church Fathers Augustine, Ambrose, and Firmianus. But this vaunted erudition does not conceal the fact that he shows extraordinarily small poetical genius.

It is necessary to wait a half century longer before another Jewish name emerges in the purlieus of Italian literature. On the death in 1500, at the age of thirty-four, of the poet Serafino Aquilano, famous as a singer and improviser at the various Italian courts (including those of the Gonzaga and of Cesare Borgia), many Italian writers collaborated in a volume of poems in Latin, Greek and Italian which was published in his memory (*Collettanee Grece-Latine e vulgari per diversi authori nella morte de lardente Seraphino Aquilano*, Bologna, 1504, dedicated to the Duchess of Urbino). Among the contributors, who included persons of the eminence of (for example) Giuliano de'Medici, was one Jew, Judah ("Giuda Hebreo") of Mantua, from whose pen three sonnets in Italian are reproduced. No other record of this writer is preserved. If one may hazard a guess, it is likely that he too was a poet-improviser, who followed the same profession as Serafino himself; otherwise, it is difficult to imagine why he should have received this outstanding compliment. (His verses are not of so high a standard as to invite it otherwise.) This is in any case further evidence of the consideration with which Jews were treated in courtly as well as literary circles in Renaissance Italy.

The refugees who came to Italy from Spain after 1492, and the cultured marranos from Portugal who followed them, gave somewhat paradoxically a new stimulus to the vernacular literary interests of Italian Jews. Indeed, in the fourteenth century the Jews of Aragon and Castile had taken a direct part in the Spanish literary revival, their share in which cannot be overlooked; witness, for example, the Catalan aphorisms of Judah Bonsenior of Barcelona, based on Arabic and Hebrew sources, produced for Jaime II of Aragon shortly after 1300 and translated half a century later into Spanish by another Jew, Jacob Çadique (Zadik) of Veles; or the moral proverbs of Rabbi Santob of Carrion (identical as we now know with the synagogue poet Shem-tob ibn Ardutiel), originally dedicated to Pedro the Cruel of Castile (1337-1360). Or one can go back even further: the earliest known specimens of Castilian and Spanish poetry are the snatches and refrains preserved in Hebrew characters in the poems of the great Hebrew singer Jehudah Halevi, and dating back to the early years of the twelfth century. The family of Abrabanel brought something of this spirit with them when they settled in Italy; and the most memorable sixteenth-century contribution by a Jew to Italian literature, in whatever language it was originally composed, is Leone (Judah) Abrabanel's philosophical classic "The Dialogues of Love" of which we must speak elsewhere.

Judah Abrabanel did not stand alone. We will have occasion elsewhere in this work to deal with the famous marrano family of Usque, who established the earliest known Jewish press for printing books in the vernacular for the use of their co-religionists and produced the first published translations of Jewish liturgical and religious works. A member of this family was Solomon Usque, who, under the name of Salusque Lusitano (that is, *Salomon Usque* the Portuguese), published what is considered the finest Spanish translation of Petrarch's sonnets. (Part of the edition, however, appeared under his proper name—both Venice, 1567.) This—dedicated to the Duke of Parma—was one of the most notable productions of the revival of interest in Petrarch which marked the middle of the sixteenth century and did a good deal to spread his reputation abroad. "Salusque" had the rare gift of being able to write poetry in two languages. In Italian, his writings included a poem on the Creation of the World (*Canzone sull' opera de' sei giorni*) which he dedicated to the Cardinal Borromeo (later to be canonized, and never notorious for pro-Jewish sentiments). This was included in an anthology of writings of "divers fair spirits" published at Genoa by Cristoforo Zabato in 1572. Usque was also associated with one of the earliest Jewish experiments in the drama to be published and to be formally presented on the stage; but that is a point to which we will have to revert in another connection.

Another highly characteristic, and for that reason in this connection somewhat incongruous, Jewish contribution to Renaissance belles-lettres is left to the last. The vernacular Italian literary revival which reached so high a level in sixteenth-century Italy was accompanied by an artificial attempt to renew the vitality of the classical languages—not merely for theological or academic purposes, but as a vehicle of normal literary expression. There was a whole school of poets, some of them of considerable genius, whose productivity was confined to Latin, and who scorned to write Italian, such as Navagero or Sannazaro. Among them, and not the least in ability, was one of the marrano exiles from Portugal who were so common throughout Europe at this time. His Portuguese name was Diogo Pires, and he had been born at Evora: and he wrote therefore under the name of Pyrrhus Lusitanus (= the Portuguese) or sometimes Flavius Eborensis (= of Evora). He followed the course of so many others: adopted the career of medicine; settled in Antwerp in the hopes of escaping the unwelcome attentions of the Portuguese Inquisition; then migrated to Italy, practicing in succession in Venice and Ferrara, where he lived under the protection of the ducal House of Este and knew the great Tasso. Later he removed to Ancona; and finally, after the outbreak of persecution against the marranos here in 1555, he fled to the independent republic of Ragusa, a little Venice on the eastern shore of the Adriatic.

He found a congenial environment among the curious school of neo-Latin poets who flourished here at this time. Tired, how-ever, of a life of subterfuge, he now reverted to Judaism formally under the ancestral name of Isaiah Cohen. But there is very little indeed which would lead us to suspect any Jewish association or background to his work (though indeed he refers in one touching set of verses to his personal sufferings, and he composed the Latin hexameters, now lost, which were inscribed on the grave of the physician Amatus Lusitanus in the Jewish cemetery of Salonica). The Jew who attained distinction among the neo-Latin poets of the sixteenth century adds an unexpected new beam of light, from an unexpected direction, to the intellectual kaleidoscope of Jewish literary activity in this age.

SIX

With the Humanists *of* Florence

It is necessary to emphasize once again the fact that the settlement of the Jews in Florence was relatively late, even for a city of northern Italy. As we have seen, none was resident there so far as may be ascertained in the age of Dante: and, at the time when the citizens were acquiring notoriety throughout Europe for their rapacity as moneylenders, Jewish financiers and others were rigorously excluded from within its massive walls. The patricians, like those of more than one other Italian city-republic, seem in fact to have been nervous about Jewish competition, or perhaps found a salve for their breaches of the canonical laws as regards usury on a vast scale abroad by showing an ostentatious regard for them at home. It was thus only in 1437 (as we have pointed out) that the pressure of circumstances compelled the city to summon the inevitable group of Jewish financiers to open their loan-banks for the benefit of the poor. It is noteworthy that the personal rule of the Medici had just begun; for the change of policy was evidence not only of their personal enlightenment, but also of their policy of gaining the sympathy of the populace, the *popolo minuto*, however the moneyed classes might object.

Thereafter, the condition of the Florentine Jews was almost a barometer of the political regime of the city: whenever the Medici were under a temporary eclipse, the Jews were expelled; on the Medici's return, they were readmitted. Thus the heyday of the Florentine Jewish community was between the years 1347 and 1494—the most resplendent period in the history of Florence, or perhaps of any city in the world since recorded history began. That was the period when Cosimo de' Medici and Lorenzo the Magnificent dominated the political (and not only the political) scene; when Botticelli, Donatello, Ghirlandaio, Verrocchio and Leonardo da Vinci were beautifying the churches and palaces;

when Pulci was writing his verses and Macchiavelli beginning to write his prose; and when Marsilio Ficino was only one of the select band who discussed philosophy in the Platonic Academy which met in the palace of the Medici. In that scene Jews, too, were familiar figures. Elsewhere in this work there is a summary account of some of them. Here, attention will be devoted only to those who played their part in the ferment of intellectual activity which reached its climax at the close of this period.

Our story may conveniently start about the year 1480, at Padua. An amazing young prodigy, who had already begun to make his name known in academic circles in Italy, had come to study there at this time. Giovanni Pico, Count of Mirandola (near Parma), was the youngest son of the ruling prince of that minute state, which incidentally had long had a correspondingly minute Jewish community. Although he was even now no more than eighteen years of age, he had already spent two years at the University of Bologna, his appetite for learning being insatiable. It was natural for him to attend the lectures which were, it seems, being given at Padua by a hardly less remarkable Jewish scholar, Elijah del Medigo, now in his middle twenties.[1] Though of German descent, Elijah was a native of the island of Candia or Crete, which was under Venetian rule, and he had probably come to Italy to complete his studies in medicine, the hereditary profession of his family. He not only had an acute philosophical mind, but also had access to two non-Latin cultures, as was not too common in those days: to his ancestral Hebrew, and to the Greek of his native island. The traditional Averroistic bent of medieval Jewish philosophy accorded with the spirit that prevailed at this time in the University of Padua, which had not as yet succumbed to the rising tide of Platonism. In 1480, he composed in Venice a philosophical treatise, *Quaestio de efficentia mundi*, which, though published with other of his writings only some years later (Venice, 1488; several editions appeared subsequently), seems to have been widely read in manuscript and to have given him a considerable reputation. As a result of this, he is said to have been summoned to Padua to act as umpire in a philosophical dispute that had arisen

---

[1] See above, pp. 39, 74 f. and 80.

in the university. He fulfilled this function so satisfactorily that he was invited to remain in this ancient seat of learning to lecture. It is true that his name does not figure in any official university record in this connection, but there are numbers of contemporary references to him both in Hebrew and in Latin documents as a professor and academic teacher, and we must assume that he acted in this capacity, even though he may not have had a formal appointment.

It was thus that he came to make the acquaintance of the young Count of Mirandola, who, thirsty for knowledge, wanted from him more than could be obtained from public lectures. Del Medigo was one of the few persons in Padua at this time who had access to those Averroistic writings that were not as yet available in Latin. True, he knew no Arabic, but a considerable quantity of this literature was accessible as we have seen in medieval Hebrew versions. Pico accordingly commissioned him to carry out an entire series of translations or abstracts from the compositions of Averroës: his compendium of and commentary on Aristotle's *Meteorology,* and his commentary on parts of the *Metaphysics,* in addition to an original treatise (now extant only in a Hebrew translation or draft) on the Averroistic conception of the intellect. It is perhaps desirable to emphasize, in order to avoid any possibility of misunderstanding, that except for the last-mentioned work all these writings of Del Medigo were in Latin, some knowledge of which language was as necessary for the Jewish as for the Christian savant in Renaissance Italy. But, for the sake of truth, one must admit that in this case the Latinity left much to be desired.

On the outbreak of war between Venice and Ferrara, in the summer of 1482, Pico left Padua and spent a short while in travel. Del Medigo meanwhile returned to Venice. But the two remained in correspondence, and it may be that Del Medigo carried out some further translations from the Hebrew at this time. In the spring of 1485, Pico went to Florence, where he remained for over a year, now not merely intermingling with but leading the brilliant intellectual society of that place, and he sent for Del Medigo to join him. It was now that the relations between the two were at their closest. The Jewish scholar was commissioned to translate for him from the Hebrew a whole library of philosophical writings: Averroës' paraphrase of Plato's *Republic* (for under the influence of the newly-established academy at Florence, Pico was now beginning to immerse himself more and more in Platonic studies), his six treatises on Aristotle's *Logic*, and so on; moreover, at his patron's request, Del Medigo composed a series of annotations on the *Physics*, which constituted, as it were, a supercommentary on Averroës' glosses to that work.

But it was not a matter only of writing and translating in the seclusion of Pico's library, or even of private discussions between the eager young noble and the erudite visitor. The other Florentine savants too were anxious to enjoy the benefits of the latter's knowledge. He gave public lectures, probably in association with the "Studio" (as the then anaemic university was called), though once again without holding any official position. Moreover, he took part in the philosophical discussions which were held in Pico's house with the collaboration of scholars such as Marsilio Ficino the platonic philosopher, whose reputation at that time was superior even to that of Pico, and Domenico Benivieni, one of the foremost members of that cultured Florentine family. On several occasions, these two were present when Del Medigo and another Jewish physician named Abraham, also a peripatetic philosopher, engaged in a philosophico-religious discussion with the Sicilian convert Guglielmo Raimondo da Moncada, the distinguished Orientalist who had translated the Koran and other works for the Duke of Urbino and taught theology in the Sapienza at Rome.[2] Long after, Ficino recalled these memorable discussions in a letter to Benivieni. The intimacy between Pico and Del Medigo was so close that the latter is reported to have once contracted an infectious ailment from his noble patron.

Of Del Medigo's stay in Florence, there is possibly one interesting artistic record. In the chapel of the one-time Palazzo Riccardi in Florence, formerly the Medicean residence, there is a memorable fresco by Benozzo Gozzoli, which occupies the entire wall space, representing the Journey of the Three Kings to do homage to the infant Jesus. The main work was executed between 1459 and 1463, but there are some later modifications and additions. The setting is not that of Judaea, but the lovely hill-country

---

[2] See below, pp. 117 f. and 145 f.

around Florence; and the artist took pains to introduce all of the notable personalities who were to be found in that city at the time when he was working, including Lorenzo de' Medici, the Byzantine "Emperor" John Palaeologus, and the Patriarch of Constantinople. Pico della Mirandola, too, figures there, though when the fresco was originally executed he had not yet been born. It would be natural for his Hebrew tutor also to have been included, as one of the more remarkable of the foreign visitors to Florence in this period. Now, among the smaller figures riding in the procession, in the same train as Pico though well behind him, there is a bearded individual in the prime of life, wearing the broad-hooded headdress characteristic of Italian Jews of the day. There seems to be as good ground for identifying this figure with Elijah del Medigo as there is for many of the other identifications that have been made of characters in this great monument of Renaissance life.

When in the summer of 1485 Pico went on a visit to France, Del Medigo left Florence for Bassano, in northeast Italy, where he composed a treatise *De substantia orbis*, containing a summary of discussions on the subject between the two of them before they parted. He then went to Padua, where he apparently resumed his philosophical lectures. In the following year, Pico returned somewhat precipitately to Italy under unfortunate circumstances, and forthwith summoned the other to join him at Perugia—probably to assist in the preparation of those famous nine hundred theses which he intended to argue at Rome. Among the subjects that the two discussed here was that of Existence and Unity, which subject Elijah summed up afterwards in a brief treatise addressed to Pico, dealing with it again later on in fuller fashion. They then parted company, Pico going on to Rome (where the Pope intervened to prevent the intended disputation) and Elijah returning to Padua. They nevertheless remained in contact, the latter continuing to supply his eager pupil with information, with treatises, with letters, and with Hebrew books, for which he coyly but unconvincingly refused payment. "Your worship has asked me about the price," he wrote on one occasion, having managed to procure his patron a copy of Menahem Recanati's mystical commentary on the Pentateuch. "It has always seemed very strange to me that it should be possible to speak in such terms between us . . . However, so that you should not consider that I am a boor, if you send me a little present (not a great one as you usually do) I will be as happy with it as I would if the Grand Turk conferred a castle on me."

It seems that the two did not meet again after 1486. Before long, Elijah was back in Venice, where he came to be on terms of intimacy with Domenico Grimani (later Cardinal of S. Marco), one of the leaders of Italian humanism, and his inseparable friend the Venetian prothonotary Antonio Pizzamanni. For the former also he carried out a number of Aristotelian translations from the Hebrew—including a new version of Averroës' introduction to the twelfth book of the *Metaphysics*, as he had not retained a copy of that prepared for Pico. He also composed in Hebrew a treatise on the philosophy of Judaism, entitled *Beḥinat haDat* ("Examination of Religion"), in which he maintained that the philosopher must so interpret the evidence of revelation as to reconcile it with the teachings of philosophy—inevitably, in his view, that of Averroës. It is perhaps because of this work that he became embroiled with the rabbinic authorities of the age, led by Judah Minz or Minzi (that is, of Mainz), the aged head of the talmudical academy of Padua, who (it is said) went so far as to excommunicate him. This dissension may possibly have been the reason for his return to Crete, where he was again residing from 1490 on, apparently continuing his philosophical lectures to mixed audiences of Christians as well as Jews. He died still a relatively young man. None of his books was published independently in his lifetime; his "Examination of Religion," in fact, appeared only a century and a quarter after his death, through the devotion of his restless, erudite, quarrelsome descendant (hardly his grandson, as the current works of reference suggest, unless his father begat him in his hundredth year), Joseph Solomon del Medigo, memorable in literature as one of the first Jews to defend the discoveries of Copernicus and Galileo and to reconcile their philosophical consequences with Jewish thought.

Pico's intercourse with Del Medigo made him, as it were, aware of the potentialities of Hebrew literature and its possible bearing on his own researches. It may be that he learned from him the rudiments of Hebrew. But it was a long time after they had been first in contact that the implications of the study of Hebrew burst

on him. It is said that this happened as the result of his chance
purchase of a manuscript of the *Zohar*, the great Jewish mystical
classic. Another account, however, tells that having heard something of its nature he sought desperately for a copy and in the
end had to pay an extravagant price for it. However that may be,
the work immediately aroused his enthusiasm, and he became
convinced that in this, and in Jewish mystical lore or Cabala
(literally, "tradition") in general, he had discovered the key to
the essential verities of philosophy and of religion—even of the
Christian religion, which he considered to be specifically confirmed thereby. "In the Cabala," he wrote, "I find what I find in
Paul; in the Cabala I hear the voice of Plato—that strong bulwark
of the Christian faith. There is in short no subject of controversy
between Church and Synagogue but finds its support for our
Christian side in these books." And one of the theses which he
wished to defend in Rome—and which were pronounced heretical
by the Church—was that "there is no science that can more firmly
convince us of the divinity of Christ than magic and the Cabala."

The *Zohar* and the other cabalistic classics were not available,
however, except in the originals—in great part indeed not in
Hebrew, but in the closely-allied Aramaic, easily accessible to any
person with a knowledge of the Holy Tongue. Accordingly, the
whole of Pico's eager enthusiasm was devoted for a time to the
study of Hebrew and of the recondite literature to which it gave
access. In addition to Elijah del Medigo, he had a tutor for Hebrew
and the Cabala living with him in Perugia, and later in La Fratta
(where he retired after the outbreak of the plague in that city).
The scholar in question this time was not a professing Jew but a
convert, the son it was said of a rabbi. He went by the curious
name of Flavius Mithridates and translated various cabalistical
works from Hebrew into Latin (some of them for Pico himself);
he was in correspondence also with Marsilio Ficino: it is probable
that he is identical with the Sicilian Hebraist Guglielmo Raimondo
da Moncada mentioned elsewhere in these pages[3] for it was fashionable at this time to adopt classical pen-names of this type.
Mithridates certainly had a well-marked if not wholly agreeable
nature. When the poet Girolamo Benivieni (himself a Hebraist of

---

[3] See pp. 114 and 145 f.

some ability) went one day to visit Pico, he found Flavius Mithridates engaged in giving his lesson and wished to benefit from it. The pedagogue flew into a rage and chased him out, not desiring to allow the esoteric doctrine of the Cabala to become more widely known.

It may be that Mithridates was either too exigent, or not sufficiently erudite, for Pico's requirements, for he does not seem to have remained in the latter's service for long. He avenged himself for his dismissal, it seems, by appending to some of his Latin translations the most scurrilous observations regarding the private life and morals of his former employer, as well as of other contemporary patrons of letters. Pico's mentor in Jewish studies thereafter was a person of a different type and origin. The most affluent and probably most cultured of the Jewish loan-bankers in Florence at the close of the fifteenth century was Jehiel (or, as he was known in the secular sources, Vitale) da Pisa, the friend and correspondent of Don Isaac Abrabanel, whose family maintained a chain of branch banks throughout Tuscany. His combination of business acumen, Jewish loyalty, and cultural eagerness makes him represent perhaps the ideal of the Italian Jew of the Renaissance period. All these affluent Jewish businessmen maintained a scholarly pensioner in their households to instruct their children and to guide the fathers, too, maybe in more advanced studies, as well as to copy for them books which had taken their fancy. It was natural for Vitale da Pisa to employ for his purpose an outstanding scholarly personality. This was Johanan ben Isaac Alemanno, whose name indicates his remoter German origin, but whose more immediate forebears had come from Paris. In his youth, he had lived in Florence and had been brought up in Vitale's house. Later on, he began to live a wanderer's life, acting as tutor in patrician Jewish establishments in various places in northern Italy. At one time, for example, we know him to have been living in Mantua where he had an entrée to the palace of the ruling house, along with other eager students of every branch of human culture, not excepting Jewish lore. Here, as he records, he heard in 1470 a performance by the blind German musician who created something of a furor then at the court of the Marquess Luigi il Turco. In 1488, he returned to Florence, where he was hospitably received in the home of his old patron, Vitale da

Pisa. He remained here probably until the temporary expulsion of the Jews from the city in 1497; his later vicissitudes are obscure.

Almost contemporaneously with Alemanno, Pico della Mirandola also returned to Florence on the invitation of Lorenzo de' Medici, who placed his villa at Querceto at his disposal. The Jewish scholar, having no doubt heard of the other's interest in Hebrew studies, was, as he tells us, anxious to make his acquaintance—no difficult task in that small, however resplendent, society. Pico received him affably; he indeed urgently needed a Hebrew mentor to take the place of Elijah del Medigo, now returned to Venice. It seems as though for the next six years the two were in close and intimate contact. Not only did Alemanno act as Pico's tutor in Hebrew, but they had long and fruitful discussions on philosophical subjects—not presumably isolated, but with the collaboration of other members of that distinguished circle. This is apparent from Alemanno's writings, which reflect the same interests that were being discussed with such brilliant results in the Florentine palaces and villas.

Outstanding among these is Alemanno's commentary on the Song of Songs, which he called *Ḥeshek Shelomo* or "The Desire of Solomon." This is a philosophical treatise rather than a commentary, and is strongly influenced by the contemporary currents of Florentine thought. The author genially informs us about the genesis of the work. He had long contemplated writing something of the sort, but though he began he never made much progress with it. During one of the earliest conversations between them, Pico asked him whether there was any adequate Jewish treatment of the Song of Songs in this sense. Alemanno modestly replied that he knew of none except his own youthful attempt, which the other asked to be allowed to read (apparently, in the author's Hebrew manuscript). He found it so interesting that he begged him to finish it, which he did that same autumn in Vitale da Pisa's house (though he continued to revise it for another four years).

Nearly half of the work, unfortunately never as yet published in full, consists of an introduction in which, after speaking at length and with great erudition about King Solomon and the folklore that has gathered round him, Alemanno dealt with the nature of love: not only the carnal love of which the Song of Songs ostensibly speaks, but also the spiritual and divine love which can bring about the union of the human soul with God—the essential teaching of the biblical work according to his interpretation. In the commentary proper, the author gives first the literal sense of each verse and then its philosophical implications, with many digressions which demonstrate the wealth of his reading in all branches of contemporary literature. The language is Hebrew; but the treatment links up with that vast literature on the nature of love to which impetus had been given by Marsilio Ficino in 1474/5, was continued in the literary production of many other thinkers of that generation, and later on was to inspire (as we shall see) the most memorable Jewish contribution to Renaissance thought. Alemanno himself dealt with this same subject in a more systematic fashion in his *magnum opus*, on which he worked for a quarter of a century but is still unpublished, which he entitled "The Immortal One" or *Ḥai ha‘Olamim*. In this he delineates his ideal human type, perfect in knowledge and in virtue and thereby enabled to achieve the love of God and union with the Divine which is the supreme beatitude. Another of his works, of which only fragments are preserved (it was perhaps left unfinished), was a philosophical commentary on the Pentateuch, conceived according to much the same scheme as that on the Song of Songs, though less polished and less interesting in execution.

The *Ḥeshek Shelomo* acquires special interest through the naive but acute characterization of the Tuscan genius which the author includes somewhat inconsequentially in his preface. The Florentines, he writes, are distinguished by seven remarkable qualities. (i) All classes of society from their youth on received political training. Even those whose normal occupation was not with practical matters, such as musicians or artists, were thus qualified to serve the state if their names were drawn by lot to fill some public office. He himself, who had been brought up in Florence, had included such training in the course of study which he followed with his own pupils (that is, presumably, the Da Pisa family, unless he was employed also in some Christian household).[4] (ii) The Florentines loved liberty passionately, and would fight desperately to maintain their institutions and ideals inviolate. (iii)

---

[4] It may be mentioned that Alemanno gives his ideal curriculum of study in an Oxford MS. (Reggio 23: Catalogue, 2234) f. 64ᵇ.

They were conspicuously industrious, more than any other men. (iv) Unlike his fellow-Jews (!), they had a strong sense of unity and generally spoke with one voice. (v) Of all peoples, since history began, they had most fully developed the faculty of seizing the essential nature of any problem. (vi) At the same time, they were extremely quick-witted, able to grasp what was said from half sentences or indirect allusions. (vii) Finally, and above all, there was in all classes an eager love of knowledge, this having a profound influence both on their public and on their personal lives. It was his absorption of this same quality through his Florentine upbringing which (he informs us) had led him to seek out Pico della Mirandola when he returned to Florence, this being the genesis of the work to which he was now setting himself.

Already at the outset he had spoken with the warmest appreciation of Lorenzo de' Medici who, he said, "with his outstanding dexterity and exceptional intelligence, both of which are far above the common level, molds the course of events around him, to the very ends of the earth, so that all kings and rulers seek his alliance. But for him, there would be in the State of Florence no one to save and to guide—not with a strong hand and physical control, like other monarchs, princes and statesmen, but with intelligence, modesty, understanding, and piety. All his efforts are directed to doing good to those who come to his lovely city . . ." It will be obvious to those familiar with Renaissance literary fashions that the author hoped that this flattering characterization would come to the ears, if not to the eyes, of its object, and that the author was not therefore a complete stranger to the head of the Florentine state. Another incidental detail in the work is perhaps worthy of special note: among the virtues of King Solomon enumerated by the author is bodily cleanliness!

Another of the Jews who had access to the humanistic circle in Florence was the peripatetic philosopher named Abraham whom Marsilio Ficino encountered with Elijah del Medigo in Pico della Mirandola's home. He calls him a physician, but this may not be correct, as we can best identify him with Abraham Farisol who, so far as we know, had no training in the art of medicine. He, too, was a most interesting personality.[5] Like Del Medigo, he was an immigrant to Italy, having been born at Avignon in the Papal States in the south of France, in or about 1451. In Italy, he settled first it seems in Mantua, where he was at work copying manuscripts in 1470-1473, and then in Ferrara. Here and in the neighborhood he was active for several decades, not only as Reader (*ḥazan*) in one of the local synagogues, but also as a scribe. Large numbers of manuscripts from his hand, beautifully written and in some cases with fine Renaissance decoration, are extant; one or two are illuminated in a fuller sense, by artists of merit. Like other Jewish savants of the period, he had entrée to the ducal court; and in 1503-4 he had a religious disputation with two friars, one a Franciscan and one a Dominican, in the presence of Duke Ercole I. The substance of this he set down in writing in 1503-4, along with other polemical material, including a criticism of Islam, in a work to which he gave the title–*Magen Abraham* or the "Shield of Abraham," of which several manuscript copies are extant. He also composed a number of exegetical works, that on Job being included, in his lifetime, in the Rabbinic Bible of 1517.

But he is especially remembered today for his remarkable geographical work, *Orḥot 'Olam* or the "Paths of the World," completed in 1524 and published more than once after his death (Venice, 1586; Oxford, 1691; Prague, 1793, and so on)—the first work in Jewish literature (it is believed) in which the discovery of America is mentioned.[6]

There are in the work many contemporary allusions of great interest. He gives a long account, based upon first-hand contemporary reports, of that curious messianic pretender David Reubeni. He seems to have made it his business to inquire of foreign visitors to Ferrara, especially if they came from the Far East, concerning the position of the Jews in distant lands. Thus, he

---

[5] Formerly, it was usual to transliterate his Hebrew surname as "Peritzol," or something of the sort; but that the equivalent given here is correct is proved by the fact that he once gives the musical notes *fa, re, sol*, as a sort of rebus in one of his writings. (*Ferruziel*, or the like, was a common enough Jewish surname in medieval Spain.) His signature figures in French in Codex de' Rossi 145: "le scrivant abram farissol."

[6] See below, p. 311.

interrogated an Arab interpreter about conditions in Calicut, and heard a further account of his co-religionists there from the lips of travelers who reported to Duke Ercole on their experiences. In November 1487 he was in Florence; and he tells (Chapters xxi, xxix: the date is confused in the printed text) how he was present in Lorenzo the Magnificent's palace on the day when he received from the Sultan of Egypt that famous gift of a giraffe, spices and balsam, which attracted such attention at the time and was so long remembered. ("The *Camelopardis* or giraffe: the tallest, gentlest and most useless of mammals . . . has not been seen in Europe since the Revival of Learning," wrote Gibbon, three centuries later, with this episode in mind.[7]) Nor was he apparently at the back of the throng, for he heard the conversation, in which Lorenzo's son Piero also participated, in the course of which it was demonstrated that there must be a habitable land area south of the equator. This was ten years before Vasco da Gama rounded the Cape of Good Hope: later on, he was to meet at the ducal court at Ferrara a political exile from Piombino, who had actually explored this region. He did his best, however (not always indeed with success), to be skeptical about all such matters: "I am to be counted among the unbelievers in fables," he wrote, like a true son of his age.

We have no idea what brought Farisol to Florence, nor are any other details known regarding his visit. If he is to be identified with the Master Abraham, whom Ficino heard when he took part in the philosophico-religious disputation with Raimondo da Moncada, in Pico's house, he obviously must have been well known in the humanist circle. This identification is not, however, quite sure, and it may be that the *fisicus* in question was one of the local Jewish practitioners, such as Abraham ben Moses of Prato, whose name (though little else concerning him) is familiar to us from other sources.

-----

[7] Farisol does not record the melancholy sequel. The sentimental Florentines went mad about this "very fine and pleasing animal," which they estimated to be "seven yards high"; they stuffed it with food, followed it open-mouthed when it went on its daily walk through the streets, lighted a fire for it when colder weather set in, and made sure that it was taken round the local convents so that nuns, too, should not be deprived of so memorable an experience. As a result, the unfortunate creature died after a couple of months.

POLYGLOT PSALTER, GENOA, 1516

Dedicated to Agostino Giustiniani

וְהִקְפַּתֵּי עֵל־קְצוֹת &recurſo eiovſq ad ſumira Et occurſus eiovſq̃ ad ſummũ τὸ το ἀπάντημα αὐτῷ ἕως ἄκρα τε ὀρανε
וְאֵין נִסְתָּר מֵחַמָּתוֹ illu.&n̄ e q ſe abſcõdat (tē eius, nec eſt qui ſe abſcondat a ὁκ ἔϛιν ὃς ἀποκρυβήσεται τῆς ϲ̄, αὐτε
תּוֹרַת יְהוָֹה תְּמִימָה a calore eius. Lex Dei pfecta calore eius. Lex dn̄i immaculata Ὁ νόμος κυρίου ὅμωμος
מְשִׁיבַת נָפֶשׁ cõuertes aı̃as teſtimonium conuertens animas, teſtimoniũ ἐπιϛρέφων ψυχάς, ἡμαρτυρία
עֵדוּת יְהוָֹה נֶאֱמָנָה DEI fidele domini fidele κυρίου πιϛή
מַחְכִּימַת פֶּתִי ſapientiã preſtans inſipiēti. ſapientiamp̃reſtans paruulis. σοφίζουϲα νήπια,
פִּקּוּדֵי יְהוָֹה יְשָׁרִים Precepta DEI recta Iuſtitie domini recte Τὰ δικαιώματα κυρίου ὀρθὰ
מְשַׂמְּחֵי־לֵב מִצְוַת letificantia cor, mandatum letificantes corda preceptum εὐφραίνοντα καρδίαν, ἡ ἐντολὴ
יְהוָֹה בָּרָה מְאִירַת DEI lucidum illuminans domini lucidum illuminan̄ς κυρίε τηλαυγὴς φωτίζουϲα
עֵינָיִם יִרְאַת יְהוָֹה oculos, Timor DEI oculos. Timor domini ὀφθαλμούς. Ὁ φόβος κυρίου
טְהוֹרָה עֹמֶדֶת לָעַד mundus pſeueras in ſecula, ſanctus permanens in ſeculum ἀγνός, διαμένων εἰς αἰῶνα,
מִשְׁפְּטֵי־יְהוָֹה אֱמֶת iudicia DEI vera ſeculi, iudicia domini vera αἰῶνος. Τὰ κρίματα κυρίου ἀληθινὰ,
צָדְקוּ יַחְדָּו iuſtificata ſimul. iuſtificata in ſemetipſa. δεδικαιωμένα, ἐπὶ τὸ αὐτό.
הַנֶּחֱמָדִים מִזָּהָב Deſiderabilia ſuper aurum Deſiderabilia ſuper aurum Ἐπιθυμητὰ ὑπὲρ χρυσίον
וּמִפָּז רָב וּמְתוּקִים & obrizũ pcioſũ multũ,& & lapidē pcioſũ multũ,& dulc̃ κỹ λίθον τίμιον πολλυ̃. κỹ Γλυκύτερα
מִדְּבַשׁ וְנֹפֶת ſup mel & ſauũ (dulciora ſuper mel & fauum. (ciora ὑπὲρ μέλι κỹ κηρίον...
צוּפִים גַּם־עַבְדְּךָ redũdante. Vn̄ & fuus tuus Etenim feruus tuus Καὶ γὰρ ὁ δεῖλός σου
נִזְהָר בָּהֶם eſt ſollicitus in eis, cuſtodit ea, φυλάσσει αὐτά,
בְּשָׁמְרָם in cuſtodiendis illis in cuſtodiendis illis ἐν τῷ φυλάσσειν αὐτὰ
עֵקֶב רָב premium multum. retributio multa. ἀνταπόδοσις πολλή.
שְׁגִיאוֹת מִי־יָבִין Errores quis intelliget. Delicta quis intelligit Παραπτώματα τίς συνήσει,
מִנִּסְתָּרוֹת נַקֵּנִי ab occultis munda me, ab occultis meis munda me, ἐκ τῶν κρυφίων με καθάρισόν με
גַּם מִזֵּדִים חֲשֹׂךְ ab arrogãtiis quoq̃ libera. E & ab alienis parce κỹ ἀπὸ ἀλλοτρίων φεῖσαι
עֲבָדֶּךָ אַל־יִמְשְׁלוּ־בִי ſeruũ tuũ, nõ dominentur fuo tuo. Simei nõ fuerint dn̄ati τε δελου σου. Ἐὰν μή με κατακυριεύσωσι
אָז אֵיתָם in me, tunc perfectus ero tunc immaculatus ero, τότε ἄμωμος ἔσομαι, (λμ̄η,
וְנִקֵּיתִי מִפֶּשַׁע רָב & emũdabor a culpa multa. & emũdabor a delicto maximo. κỹ καθαρισθήσομαι ἀπὸ ἁμαρτίας μεγά
יִהְיוּ לְרָצוֹן אִמְרֵי־ Sint ad placẽ dũ ſermones Et erunt vt complaceãt eloqa Καὶ ἔσονται εἰς εὐδοκίαν τὰ λόγια
פִי וְהֶגְיוֹן לִבִּי oris mi, & meditatio cõdis mi oris mei, & meditatio cordis mi τὲ σόματός μου, κỹ ἡ μελέτη τῆς καρδίας μου
לְפָנֶיךָ יְהוָֹה צוּרִי i cõſpectu tuo, Deo fortituc̃ i cõſpectu tuo ſẽp. Dn̄e adiutor ἐνώπιόν σου διαπαντός. Κύριε βοηθός με
וְגֹאֲלִי & tredẽ ptor meus. (do mea, meus, & redemptor meus. κỹ λυτρωτά μου.

ceteriusquam luſitani feciſſent nouas terras, nouoſq̃ adire populos, regiones poſtremo ante hac incognitas penetrare. Fit celeriter de
re hac uerbum regi, qui tum regum luſitanorum emulatione, tum ſtudio huiuſmodi nouarum rerum & glorie, que ſibi ac poſteris poſſet
de ea re accedere pellectus diu re cum Columbo tractara, nauigia tandem exornari duo iubet quibus ſoluens Columbus ad inſulaıca
fortunatas nauigans curſum inſtituit paululum ab occidentali linea ſiniſter inter hibicum. ac zephirum remotior tamen longe a li-
bico & ferme zephiro iunctus. Vbi cõplurium dierum curſus exactus eſt & computata ratione cognitum quadragies ſe ſe iam cente
na paſſuum millia eſſe permenſum recto curſu ceteri quidem ſpe omni lapſi: referendum iam elle pedem & curſum in contrariam
partem flectendum contendebant, ipſe uerò in incepto perſiſtere & quantum coniectura aſſequi poſſet promittere haud longius diei
unius nauigatione abelle uel continentes aliquas terras, uel inſulas. Haud abſuit dictis fides. Quippe ſequẽti luce terras neſcio quas
conſpicati naute eum laudibus efferre, & maximam in hominis opinione fiduciam reponere. Inſule erant ut poſtea cognitum eſt ferme
innumere, non longe a continentibus quibuſdam terris ut preſe ferebat aſpectus. Ex huiuſmodi inſulis nonnullas ammaduer ſum fer
re homines incultos cognomento canibaclos, humanis ad eſum carnes minime abhorrentes, ac uicinos populos latrociniis infeſtantes,
cauaris quibuſdam magnarum arborum truncis quibus ad proximas trahicientes inſulas homines quais lupi in cibum uenentur. Nec
defuit fortuna ex his unam nauiculis cum ſuis huiuſmodi ductoribus comprehendendi. idcq̃ haud incruenta pugna qui poſtmodum
uſqꝫ in hiſpaniam ſoſpites uecti ſunt. Que prima eſt inuenta ex inſulis hiſpana uocata nuncupata. In eaꝗ inuenti mortales innumeri pu
pertate & nuditate cõſpicui, quos primo nutibus ad congreſſum comiter inuitatos donis eꝗ allectos, ubi propius acceſſerũt, facile ap
parebat & diſſimilem ſuo candorem. & habitum & inauditum antea ad eos acceſſum, ceteraꝗ omnia quali e celo aduenientium ob tu-
peſcere & mirari, quippe color illis lõge diſſimilis noſtro, minime tamen niger ſed auro perſimilis, lacerna illis collo pẽdebat herebatꝗ
pectori contegens pudenda quaſi uelamen, cui modicum annexi eſſet aurum, eaꝗ cõmunis manũ & feminarũ, no amplius uirginū.

Columbus' Discovery of America Is Mentioned in the Latin Commentary
Courtesy of the Jewish Theological Seminary of America

There were other Jews with whom Pico and his circle maintained a close contact. When he was at Ferrara on a visit in
1492/3, he heard that one of the Sicilian exiles who was passing
through the city had a number of books. He sought the man's
acquaintance, borrowed the collection, and shut himself up for
some weeks in order to read them before the owner left. A certain Dattilo (that is, Joab in Hebrew: the name-correspondence
is invariable), who subsequently taught Hebrew at Turin to the
German polymath-statesman Johann Albrecht Widmanstetter,[8]
had according to the latter formerly done the like for Pico. There
was, moreover, a young Jew who had carried out various translations for him in Florence, and later (according to a letter of 1489
from Lorenzo the Magnificent to one of his friends) yielded to
his persuasions and became converted to Christianity. Another of
his instructors in Hebrew (unless it is the same person) fell under
the influence of Savonarola and became a friar of S. Marco, under
the name of Clement (generally corrupted into Blemet). In his
correspondence, Pico tells—obviously with some exaggeration—of
the large number of Jews with whom he discussed points of common interest.

As a result of this concentrated attention, the young count
became far more than a dilettante in Hebrew studies. He had a
large library of Hebrew books, most of them of course in manuscript (for by the time of his death no more than a few dozen
Hebrew works had been printed); and he paid especially high
prices, as he informs us, for cabalistic treatises. The catalogue of
his Hebrew codices, some of them no longer traceable, was published in 1651 by the French scholar Jacques Gaffarel and is still
an important source for research. In addition to the *Zohar* and
the kindred mystical writings, he owned and studied the classics
of the rabbinic and medieval literature, citing in his writings
Maimonides, the Talmud, the Midrash, and much else, sometimes
in the original. And his Hebrew studies had a profound influence
on his own thought. His famous theses depended to a great degree
on his cabalistic convictions, this being one of the reasons for their
condemnation by the Pope; and his *Heptaplus*, dedicated to
Lorenzo the Magnificent, in which he dealt with the seven days

---

[8] See below.

of Creation, is based almost entirely on the *Zohar*, the first part of which concentrates to a great extent on this same vital subject.

Pico's example exercised a profound influence on the other members of the Florentine humanistic circle, though none of them had so remarkable a knowledge of Hebraic lore as he. Even before they met, Marsilio Ficino, later his close friend, had made much use of rabbinic literature in his writings—especially in his *De christiana religione*, of 1474, in which he cites Rashi, Maimonides, Gersonides, Sa'adia, though basing himself wholly on secondary sources or else on the inadequate translations which were then available. Later on, so he informs us, he preferred to leave to Pico the investigation of subjects that demanded some Hebrew knowledge. Nevertheless, he followed the latter's researches with deep interest and, as we have seen, was present at the discussions in his house in which his Jewish friends participated. He was, moreover, in correspondence with Pico's Hebrew mentor in Chaldaic studies, the convert Flavius Mithridates, and in a a well known letter records a Jew named Fortuna (=Mazzal-tob?) among those who attended his lectures.

The poet Angelo Poliziano, on the other hand, Lorenzo de' Medici's brilliant, unstable, somewhat contemptible favorite and amanuensis, obtained with Pico's help a fair knowledge of Hebrew at first hand and quoted the language and its literature in his writings. Another member of the circle was Girolamo Benivieni, the poet, Pico's closest friend, who was to be buried in his grave— the same who was so rudely repulsed by Flavius Mithridates when he wanted to participate in one of his lessons. He made such progress in his studies—also, it seems, with Johanan Alemanno—that he was able to compose a Hebrew-Latin and Latin-Hebrew dictionary, still preserved in manuscript. Fuller treatment of the progress of Hebrew studies in Italy in the Renaissance period is given below (Chapter VII). Nowhere, however, did these studies play so important a role as in Florence in those golden days.

The indirect importance of Pico's studies was perhaps even more important than the direct. In 1490, he received a visit from a German scholar and jurist named Johannes von Reuchlin—seven years his senior in age, but much his junior as yet in reputation— who had come to Italy on a diplomatic mission for the Duke of Württemberg (for in those days scholars were naturally used for such purposes). They discussed Orpheus, as Pico was to remember long after. What was far more important was that they obviously discussed the Cabala. In any case, Reuchlin returned to Germany all afire with enthusiasm for it, like Pico himself, and convinced like him that this esoteric doctrine of the Jews contained the key to the supreme verities of human existence. In order to master it, he threw himself into the study of Hebrew heart and soul—first in Germany with the imperial physician Jacob Loans, and later, when he returned to Italy in 1498 as ambassador of the Elector Palatine, with the learned Obadiah Sforno. (Reuchlin complained that Obadiah charged him the immoderate amount of one ducat for each lesson.) Later on, when the Hebrew literature was condemned in Germany as a result of the slanders of the apostate ex-butcher Johannes Pfefferkorn, Reuchlin in his passion for the Cabala valiantly took up arms in its defense; and the polemic against obscurantism that now began proved the prelude to, and gradually merged in, the Reformation movement. That meeting between Pico della Mirandola and Johannes von Reuchlin at Florence in 1490 had, it may be said, epoch-making results.

The most distinguished Jewish name associated with the Florentine circle of humanists is probably that of Don Judah Abrabanel, better known today as Leone Ebreo or "Leon the Jew." He was the eldest son of the Spanish scholar-statesman Don Isaac Abrabanel, whose posterity played so significant a part in Jewish life in Italy in the sixteenth century. Judah's own life was tinged with sadness. At the time of the expulsion of the Jews from Spain, a plot had been laid to kidnap his little son, in the expectation that this would weaken the family's determination and induce them to lead their co-religionists over to Christianity. To forestall this, the child was sent with his nurse to Portugal, where he was seized by order of the king and in the end was forcibly baptized. The recollection of this outrage remained poignant in the father's heart, and twelve years later he wrote a touching elegy—one of the classics of Hebrew literature of this genre—commemorating the tragedy that embittered his life.

As has been told, after they left Spain the family settled in Naples, where Don Isaac was once more summoned from literary retirement to enter royal service. Don Judah, too, was henceforth in the public eye—not as a man of affairs, like his father and brothers, but as a physician, who brought to Italy something of the legendary tradition of Andalusia. The French invasion of 1495 and the wars and disturbances that followed in its train caused the family to become wanderers once again. Don Judah lived successively at Genoa, Barletta, Venice, and (as we shall see) perhaps Florence. Ultimately, after order was restored, he was summoned back to Naples, where he became body-physician to the Spanish Viceroy, Don Gonsalvo de Cordova, the "Great Captain." (The readiness, not to say eagerness, of the Jews of the sixteenth century to overlook what they and their co-religionists had suffered at Spanish hands is depressingly obvious, though in this case it may be said in extenuation that Don Gonsalvo showed himself pro-Jewish on occasion.) In 1501 Don Judah was teaching medicine and "astrology" at the University of Naples; and on one occasion at this period of his life he offered his services to go on a diplomatic mission to the Grand Turk in Constantinople, where he had relations, on behalf of the Venetian Republic. The position that he now enjoyed is evidenced by a document of 1520 which informs us that, in recognition of his services, "Master Leon Abrabanel the physician" together with his family and household were exempted from the payment of tribute. This is almost the last reliable mention of Leone Ebreo that has so far been traced; and it is presumed that he died not long after.

In the course of his wanderings, Leone came in touch with some of the finest minds in the contemporary world. There can be little doubt that, before he left the Iberian Peninsula, he was acquainted with those leaders of Spanish intellectual life who clustered round the court of Ferdinand and Isabella. In Italy, he frequented (he informs us) the "Academies of the Gentiles." He certainly knew all the intellects of the Neapolitan court, at that time one of the centers of Italian humanism, and was on terms of friendship with the philosopher Mariano Lenzi who, in due course, was to publish his *magnum opus*. What we know of his Florentine relationships, indeed, is based on a single and much-discussed passage. The distinguished marrano physician, Amatus Lusitanus, has much to tell us in his famous collection of case-histories[9] about various

---

[9] See pp. 318-320 *infra* for this and its importance as an historical source.

members of the Abrabanel family whom he knew both in Italy
and later, after his formal return to Judaism, in the Levant. In
Salonica, toward the end of his life, Amatus treated for tertian
fever (unsuccessfully, in the final result), "Judah, the grandson
of that great Judah or Leo Abrabanel, the Platonic philosopher
who bequeathed us the divine 'Dialogues' "—that is, the *Dialoghi
di amore*, with which we will deal shortly (*Centuria* vii.98).
Amatus goes on to recount, in his chatty way, how his patient
possessed "a manuscript of some length, entitled *De coeli harmonia* ('About the harmony of the heavens'), written in a Lombard [that is, Italian?] hand, which was composed by the good
Leo aforementioned at the request of the illustrious Pico della
Mirandola, as appears from the preface. I had the book in my
hands and read it more than once. But for the grandson's untimely
death, which made it impossible, we had intended before long to
publish this work, which is not only learned but also very profound. In it, the good Leo, writing in the scholastic style, presented in a most satisfactory manner what is of permanent value
in philosophy." There is now no trace of the work in question,
which has completely disappeared. But what is most interesting
in the present connection about Amatus' statement is the evidence
that he gives of friendship between Leone Ebreo and Pico della
Mirandola, the leader of Florentine intellectual society when it
was at the height of its reputation.

Now, the Abrabanel family left Spain in the late summer of
1492; Pico della Mirandola died two years later in November 1494;
and nothing that we know of Leone Ebreo's movements (which
are fairly well documented) would indicate that he visited Florence during the relatively brief intervening period. It has therefore been suggested, and is now indeed fairly generally accepted,
that Amatus is here referring not to the famous Giovanni Pico
della Mirandola but to his less known, but still highly illustrious,
humanist nephew and namesake Giovanni Francesco who devoted
himself to similar studies and, surviving him by nearly forty years,
was murdered one night in 1533 by his own nephew—one of the
most notorious crimes of the Renaissance period. It seems, however, to the present writer that this conclusion is hardly justifiable.
It assumes that we are familiar with every detail of Leone's movements, both before he left Spain and especially in the first two

years he spent in Italy, which is certainly not the case. It postulates, moreover, that the highly cultivated Amatus Lusitanus, writing about half a century after the event, and knowing intimately many members of the family, used the most extravagant terms— "the Divine Pico della Mirandola" (*Divinus Mirandulensis Picus*) —to designate, not the person to whom such terms might almost legitimately have been applied in that age, but a relatively little-known homonym. The simplest interpretation—and there is no real objection to it—is that Amatus meant precisely what he said and that during his wanderings in Italy, in the first years after his arrival there as an exile, Judah Abrabanel spent some time in Florence and was among the Jewish scholars whom Pico so warmly welcomed.[10]

If Don Judah Abrabanel knew at first hand the humanistic circle in Florence, it becomes somewhat easier to understand the genesis of his famous work, the *Dialoghi di amore*. For the subject of love, in its philosophical aspect, was at this time extraordinarily popular in Italian, and especially in Florentine, literary and academic circles. Marsilio Ficino, Pico's intimate friend, had set the fashion when he published the final redaction of his famous commentary on Plato's *Symposium*, in 1474-75. In 1486, Girolamo Benivieni, another of the circle, had composed his *Canzone d'amore*, on which Pico della Mirandola had commented with much erudition shortly thereafter. About 1495, Mario Equicola of Ferrara had begun his *Libro della natura de' amore*—to be completed and published only in 1525—in which he depicted courtly love as the highest human ideal. While Don Judah was writing, Pietro Bembo (not yet a cardinal) was engaged in completing his remarkable discourse, *Gli Asolani*, of 1505—a classic of Italian literature—which he dedicated to Lucrezia Borgia and in

---

[10] It has been suggested that the meeting between Leone ebreo and Pico della Mirandola may have taken place, not in Florence, but during a visit to Ferrara; this would simplify the chronology to some extent.

A word of warning is perhaps necessary at this point. The "Leo hebraeus" referred to by Pico in his "Disputations on Astrology," whom some persons have identified with Judah Abrabanel, is obviously in this case the medieval philosopher-scientist Levi ben Gershom of Bagnoles ("Ralbag"), generally referred to at the time by this name. For him, see pp. 230, 273.

which Platonic affection is superbly delineated: a paradoxical production, to be sure, when one remembers the nature of his relations with the beautiful Morosina, the mother of his children, and other women, including Lucrezia herself. At much the same time Francesco Cattani de Diacceto was meditating on his less lively treatise on the same subject, *De amore*, to be published, however, long afterwards. Moreover, the Jewish writers like Johanan Alemanno, who basked in the intellectual radiance of the Medicean court, introduced the same conception in mystical dissertations on the Bible itself, as we have seen.

It was under this stimulus that Judah Abrabanel composed the greatest and most enduring of the works in this tradition, which is studied and reprinted even today. The *Dialoghi di amore* or "Dialogues of Love" were written, according to the author's own testimony, in the year 5262 of the Jewish reckoning, or 1501/2 of the current era; but it was not until 1535, after Judah's death, that his friend Mariano Lenzi "rescued the work from the shades in which it lay buried," and published it in Rome. In accordance with a well-established convention of the time, the external form is that of romantic fiction rather than philosophy, this approach giving it much of its charm. The work consists of three dialogues between Philo, the lover, and Sophia (that is, Wisdom), his beloved. It begins with a discussion between them, of the sort that repetition has never cloyed, on the distinction between love and physical desire. This leads naturally on to an attempt to define the various kinds of love and their nature. In the second Dialogue, it is shown how love is the principle that dominates existence, and how it operates in all human affairs. The third Dialogue—by far the longest and the most important—develops these points systematically. It describes the culmination of love in the love of God, which permeates the entire universe, radiating from the Deity down to the lowest creation. This involves incidentally a definition of beauty and a discussion of the nature and activity of the soul, which in turn provides opportunity for the exposition of the basic ideas of the Platonic philosophy. This, however, is secondary. The main theme throughout is that God is to be identified with love, which is the cosmic principle at the center of all life and activity and the source of the vigor which inspires every natural force. Knowledge of God is the knowledge of the workings of love, and it is through the intellectual love of God that the soul returns to Him. The idea of the supreme significance of the love and knowledge of God is, to be sure, fundamentally Jewish in the most strictly traditional sense, from the Bible, Talmud and Maimonides down. But Leone Ebreo's conception of the Deity and his views on God's connection with the universe brought him close to Pantheism. He shows throughout an intimate acquaintance, not only with Plato and Plotinus, but with the new speculative and scientific teachings of the fifteenth century. The great Spanish scholar, Menéndez y Pelayo, in his *History of Aesthetic Ideas in Spain,* pronounced the work the most notable monument of platonic philosophy in the sixteenth century, and the most beautiful in form from the days of Plotinus on. We are in the presence of a man who was abreast of the highest in his contemporary cultural life.

There is a controversy of long standing regarding the language in which the work was written. There is no reason why the erudite court physician, after ten years' residence in Italy, should not have been able to express himself in Italian. But the *Dialoghi* read a little stiffly, and there is reason to doubt that this is the primary text: indeed, in a letter of 1543, the editor's friend Claudio Tolomei wrote that the published version in Italian fell short of the original clarity. A strong case may be made out for imagining that they were written in Hebrew, of which language the author had a complete mastery, as his poems show; but in that case the original been lost, for the Hebrew version now extant is palpably a translation—possibly from the pen of Leone Modena. Modern Spanish authorities patriotically endeavor to win the original work (though not the published Spanish versions) for the language of the country from which its author had been ejected. But there is another possibility. The natural medium in which a Spanish Jew of the period would have expressed himself on a non-Hebraic subject was Ladino, or Castilian written in Hebrew characters. There is in fact in the British Museum a manuscript of the *Dialoghi* of this sort which, though not contemporary, may conceivably represent the author's original text.

The aura of mystery which surrounds the work is enhanced by the report, long accepted as true, that the author was converted to Christianity before his death. This is based solely on the state-

PHILOSOPHIE
D'AMOVR
DE M. LEON
HEBREV:

Contenant les grands & hauts poincts, desquels elle traite, tant pour les choses Morales & Naturelles, que pour les divines & supernaturelles.

Traduits d'Italien en François, par le Seigneur du Parc, Champenois.

D. C. L.

A LYON,
BENOIST RIGAVD.
M. D. XCV.

TITLE PAGE OF A FRENCH TRANSLATION OF LEONE EBREO'S *Dialogues of Love,* **WITH A PRESUMED PORTRAIT OF THE AUTHOR**

ment which is to be found in identical terms on the title-pages of the second and third editions, published at Venice by Aldus in 1541 and 1545 respectively: *Dialoghi di amore, composti per Leone Medico, di Natione Hebreo, et di poi fatto Christiano* ("The Dialogues of Love, composed by Leo the Physician, of the Jewish nation, but subsequently made a Christian"). This sentence is lacking, however, in the original edition, as well as in the fourth and fifth, and in the Latin version of 1564 with its long dedication to a church dignitary. It is pretty obvious that the Aldi considered that the sales of the book would be increased if it were believed that the author had accepted Christianity.

In the third Dialogue, there is indeed a casual mention of Saint John the Evangelist, which has been interpreted as a proof that the author was a professing Christian. But this suggestion takes no account of the prevailing sentiment in Italian Jewry at this time when, as we have seen, a remarkable degree of intellectual assimilation prevailed. The passage, moreover, is clearly counterbalanced by those passages in which the author speaks of the date of the composition of his work "according to the Hebrew truth," and alludes to "all of us who believe the Holy Law of Moses." In addition, he makes a couple of allusions in unmistakably proprietary terms to Jewish literature, speaking for example of "our Rabbi Moses" in reference to Maimonides, and of "our Albenzubron" (that is, Avicebron) in reference to Ibn Gabirol (whose authorship of the scholastic classic *Fons vitae*, which Salomon Munk demonstrated in the nineteenth century, was obviously no secret to him). His religious fidelity is further confirmed by the facts that the Jewish scholars of the age constantly reprinted his occasional verses to accompany the works of his venerated father, that he is lauded in extravagant terms by some contemporary Hebrew writers (in a manner unthinkable had he apostatized), and that a pious Jewish chronicler, Gedaliah ibn Yacchia, published at Venice in 1568 a Spanish version of the work which he ascribed to "the excellent philosopher and physician Master Leon Abrabanel."

For the *Dialoghi* were among the most popular philosophical works of the age. In the space of twenty years they went through at least five editions in the Italian form. They were twice translated into French—once by the poet, Pontus de Thiard—and no fewer than three times into Spanish. They were known to and used by Camoens and Montaigne. Burton cites them repeatedly in his *Anatomy of Melancholy*. It is believed that Baldassare Castiglione had read them in manuscript and used them in his *Cortegiano*, which taught Ariosto's Italy and Shakespeare's England the ideal of the gentleman. Traces of their influence may be discerned in the thought of Giordano Bruno (with whose ideas in particular they have many common elements), of Luís Vives, of Francesco Patrizzi, perhaps of Francis Bacon. They had a reputation, too, in Jewish circles. They were translated into Spanish by one Jewish savant and into Hebrew by another, as we have seen; and parts of the *Dialoghi* were actually incorporated early in the next century in a free translation by a Modenese rabbi, Isaac Alatrini, in his Hebrew philosophical commentary on the Song of Songs, *Kenaf Renanim* (preserved in manuscript in Oxford [MSS. 2220, 2222] and elsewhere). Benedict Spinoza had in his library a copy of the Spanish edition and, according to the opinion which has recently gained ground, derived from it his doctrine of the *Amor Dei intellectualis*. The influence on some other writers is less dubious: another work of the Renaissance period, *Tractado de la hermosura y del amor,* by M. Calvi (Milan, 1576) is little more than a barefaced plagiarism of it, copying even the dialogue form.

The third Spanish translation was executed not long after this by the Peruvian historian Garcilaso de la Vega, known as the Inca—in fact the nephew of the last Inca, Hulpa Tupac, who opened new perspectives in the intellectual life of his country. This (Madrid, 1590) was the first book ever published by a native American writer.

The influence of the work on the development of lyric poetry in Italy, France and Germany was very pronounced. In the present generation it has been republished more than once in Italian, as well as in English, German and yet again in Spanish.

Considered as pure literature, too, the *Dialoghi di amore* commands notice. It was one of the first original compositions in the vernacular by a Jew to be published in the western world, and thus has some importance in the history of European letters. Moreover, for all its strange garb and fine-drawn argument, it has a subtle charm which gives it a claim on our attention, apart from its importance as one of the significant philosophical productions of Renaissance Italy.

SEVEN

The Christian Hebraists

The Italian Renaissance was in one sense based upon a revival of interest in the languages and literatures of ancient Greece and Rome. But there was a third people of antiquity whose renown still lingered, and whose influence on European civilization was no less profound—the Jews. Inevitably therefore the renewed devotion to Latin and to Greek involved some sort of revival of interest of the same type in Hebrew. It was this literary and anti-quarian coloring that distinguishes the Christian Hebraists of Italy from those of northern Europe, and even of Spain.

Recent investigations have shown that there was far greater interest in this subject in Christian circles in the Middle Ages than was formerly imagined. In the twelfth and thirteenth centuries, a group of monkish scholars in France and England, centering upon the Abbey of St. Victoire in Paris, had attained with the help of Jewish instructors a high degree of proficiency in Hebrew, in order to be able to understand more satisfactorily the text of the Old Testament. To be sure, this revival did not last long, nor did the spirit prevail universally: it is instructive that in 1198, the Abbot of Clairvaux was ordered to take disciplinary action against a monk of the monastery of Poblet, in Catalonia, who was alleged to have taken lessons in Hebrew from a certain Jew. Nevertheless, in the fourteenth century, Hebrew was studied by the Dominicans in Spain, though purely for conversionist purposes; and owing to the influence of Raymond Lull the subject was included (though for the most part only nominally) in the curriculum of the principal European universities, in conformity with a decision made by the Council of Vienne in 1312 with the same object in view. Later on, the Reformation was to witness a great revival of Hebrew study in Germany and Northern Europe which had profound consequences; but this was to be based essentially on theological considerations. Only in Italy did Hebrew studies come into their own as a branch of humanism.

From what has been said, it follows that the revival here was relatively late. But there are indications of an interesting anticipation of it, to which little attention is generally paid, going back to the thirteenth century, to the heyday of the Latin Renaissance. We have already seen in a previous chapter the importance attached to Hebrew at this time at the court of Naples, as a key to the scientific and philosophical Graeco-Arabic classics to which it gave access. There is some evidence that Christian as well as Jewish scholars took part in the work of translation at this time. Moreover, the personal interest of certain of the rulers under whose auspices it was carried out seems to point to some knowledge of Hebrew, however slight, even in the highest stratum of society.

There is an old story that the Emperor Frederick II arranged for lectures to be given in Hebrew in the university which he founded at Naples in 1244, though it is not easy to determine whether there is any truth in this, or, if there is, for whom the lectures were intended. But it is certain in any case that this ruler was profoundly interested in Jewish studies. His son Manfred perhaps participated personally in the work of translation carried out under his auspices, as we have seen; and Moses di Rieti admiringly reports in his Dantesque imitation, *Mikdash Meät*, that King Robert of Naples of the rival House of Anjou read through the entire Hebrew Bible in the original with his Jewish teacher, Judah Romano, known as Leone de Ser Daniele (Immanuel of Rome's cousin). Nor was this interest restricted to the south of the country. It is told, for example, that the great Italian jurist Bartolo de Sassoferrato (1314-57) studied Hebrew with one Guido de Perusio—that is, presumably, Judah of Perugia: in any case, he mentions a religious discussion which he had with some Jews. A few other contemporary names can with some difficulty be assembled. Nevertheless, serious interest in Hebrew, on the part of a wider circle, began only with the fifteenth century, after Greek had come to be more or less firmly established.

In 1414, the learned Apostolic secretary Poggio Bracciolini was beguiling his leisure during the interminable sessions of the Coun-

cil of Constance by searching for manuscripts of the classical
Latin authors in all the ecclesiastical establishments within reach—
a most important chapter in the history of the revival of learning.
He had enough time on his hands to study Hebrew as well. He
found an instructor for the purpose in a baptized Jew, of whom
he had no high opinion—"stupid, peevish and ignorant, like most
Jewish converts," he described him in a letter to the Florentine
scholar-merchant Niccolò Niccoli. It is not therefore very surprising that, although he continued his studies with him for some
time, at Baden as well as at Constance, he did not make much
progress. What made matters worse, he had to defend his conduct
against his old friend Lionardo Bruni, the father of modern historiography, who considered that this branch of learning was not
merely useless, but potentially harmful; for to test the principles
on which Saint Jerome had carried out his translations presumably
demonstrated lack of faith. Others of the pioneers were, it seems,
no more fortunate in their researches. The scholar-diplomat Marco
Lippomani was reported to have studied Hebrew, to have been
in correspondence with a Jewish physician named Crescas Meir
about 1440, and to have discussed problems of semitic philology
with one Isaac Cohen. He, likewise, did not make much use of
his knowledge, while little more than the name is known of another reported Hebraist of the time, John of Lucca. Cardinal
Nicholas da Cusa (1401-64) who, though a German, had a considerable influence on Italian literary life, knew enough Hebrew
to cite the mystical *Book of Raziel* and to be aware of the varying
forms of the Divine name, besides being familiar (though probably
in translation) with the writings of Maimonides. So, too, Fra
Ambrogio Traversari, the general of the Camaldolensian Order,
though he included Hebrew in his library in Florence, had no
more than a superficial knowledge of the grammar and lexicon
of the Holy Tongue. With his pupil, the great Florentine scholar-
statesman Giannozzo Manetti, a new era began.

This remarkable son of the Renaissance, though he dedicated
himself to study only in his twenty-fifth year, soon obtained a
profound knowledge of the Latin and Greek literatures. He then
began to turn his attention to Hebrew as well—with theological
as well as humanistic objectives, to be sure, as he not only desired to

read the Holy Scriptures in the original, but also to use his knowledge for the purpose of propagating the Christian faith. With the
thoroughness which was characteristic of him, he engaged for
the purpose a Jew, who lived with him in his house for two years
while he was on a mission to Rome (he had two Greeks there
with him as well). With him, it is reported, he constantly spoke
Hebrew, in the same way presumably as other humanists spoke
Greek, in order to facilitate their mastery of that tongue: we can
hardly think of this as an anticipation of the Hebrew revival of
our own times, though indeed some Italian Jews attempted to use
the Holy Tongue for everyday purposes. This first instructor of
Manetti—apparently a person of no high culture—became converted in due course to Christianity, adopting his patron's name.

Fortunately, he was not Manetti's only teacher. One of the
wealthy Jewish loan-bankers in Florence, Manuello di Abraham
da San Miniato, who already had an adequate knowledge of Latin,
was anxious to perfect himself in philosophy. What could have
been more convenient than an interchange of lessons? Every
morning, therefore, Manetti sent his servant to fetch Manuello
before dawn, and again after nightfall, when they sat together for
three hours more. Day after day the two worked together, until
Manetti had gone through the Bible twice in the original and even
embarked on the study of the medieval commentators. To fulfil
the other side of the bargain, they read also the whole (or what
was considered the whole) of natural and moral philosophy.

We do not know how far Manuello benefited, but his Christian
friend attained sufficient competence at least to make a new translation of the Book of Psalms—an enterprise which was at the time
much criticized, and which he had to defend at great length—and
to compose a work of religious controversy, *Contra Judaeos et
Gentes*, which he dedicated to King Alfonso V of Naples. A
number of Hebrew manuscripts formerly owned by him—some
of them copied expressly for his collection—subsequently passed
into the Library of the Elector Palatine and are now in the Vatican. Moreover, his son, Agnolo, himself a distinguished humanist,
was also from his childhood taught Hebrew as well as Latin and
Greek, and in due course became a competent Hebraist. In 1448,
Giannozzo Manetti was on a mission to the diabolic Sigismondo
Malatesta, tyrant of Rimini, who though almost a pagan was never-

theless philosophically interested in religious discussion. He accordingly seized the opportunity to give a magnificent banquet to all the learned Jews of his territories and other distinguished persons, and afterwards persuaded them to engage in a polemical discussion with his guest on the merits of the two faiths—a characteristic Renaissance diversion, which lasted on this occasion for six hours.

Such episodes, it may be observed, were paradoxically common in Renaissance courts. Father Vicenzo Bandello held a controversy with the representatives of Judaism at Milan in the presence of Duke Ludovico il Moro; we have had occasion to mention how Abraham Farisol upheld the cause of his faith at Ferrara before Ercole d'Este; and such anecdotes constantly recur. It was the result of a conjunction of the inquiring Italian mind, constantly craving new intellectual experiences, with the strange phenomenon which combined in some of these potentates the greatest freedom of thought, the most debased personal behavior and the most complete fidelity to Christian doctrine and determination to serve its cause.

A great impetus to Manetti's collecting enthusiasm was given by Pope Nicholas V, himself an impassioned collector of manuscripts from his youth on. His imagination now stirred by the recent rediscovery of so many long-lost classical texts, he offered a reward of 5,000 ducats to any person who should produce the original text of the Gospel according to St. Matthew, which according to the Church Fathers derived from a Hebrew (or perhaps Aramaic) original. Obviously, this gave a great stimulus to the search for Hebrew manuscripts, and thus indirectly to Hebrew studies generally, even though the immediate quest was fruitless. (It was indeed only in the following century that what was optimistically believed to be the work in question was at last brought to light and published at Paris, in 1551: but there can be little doubt that this text was in fact a medieval translation from the Latin.)

By the close of the fifteenth century, interest in Hebrew studies had become general. Giovanni Annio (Nanni) of Viterbo, whom the Pope in 1499 made Master of the Sacred Palace in recognition of his fame as a scholar, had a reputation as a Hebraist and student of Oriental languages, though so far as is known his knowledge was not sufficiently profound for him to falsify Hebrew texts, as he was subsequently found to have done in the case of various classical authorities (including, in all probability, Philo of Alexandria). "Polifilo" (the name under which the Dominican Francesco Colonna wrote) quoted, as a matter of course, a short passage in Hebrew—perhaps picked up in the course of his travels in the Orient—in his extraordinary archaeological allegory *Hypnerotomachia* (written before 1479, though published only twenty years later—one of the most important of the Aldine productions). A priest named Pietro Montagnana, who died in Padua in 1478, is recorded even on his tombstone to have had in his library a collection of books in Hebrew, which he left to the library of the Monastery of S. Giovanni di Verdara in that city: they are now to be found in the Marciana in Venice. A little Hebrew grammar, *Introductio utilissima hebraice discere cupientibus*, produced about 1500 by the great Venetian printer Aldo Manuzio, was subsequently reissued for general use as an appendix to his Latin grammar of 1501, which was constantly reprinted. In addition to this, Aldo produced several issues of a separate brochure containing the Hebrew alphabet followed by a few phrases and a translation of the Lord's Prayer. This must have been almost thumbed out of existence, for not more than half a dozen copies are known to exist today.[1]

So popular did the subject become that some humanists (such as Benedetto Faleo, in his treatise on the origin of Hebrew, Greek and Latin letters, produced at Naples in 1520) actually preferred it to Greek. Its study was particularly widespread at Mantua, and Ortensio Landi pronounced it, in his *Forcianae quaestiones* of 1536, to be the characteristic feature of the city's intellectual life. In Venice so many students sat at the feet of Jewish scholars that in 1545 one of the latter, the fashionable physician Elijah Halfon,

---

[1] Aldo's grammar, plagiarized at Erfurt by Nicholas Marschalk (1501-02), was thus anterior to the more systematic treatment by Conrad Pelican (Strasbourg, 1504)—the first of any consequence written by a Christian scholar, if this "apostate in three languages" may legitimately be so defined. Nor could Italy, lacking theological enthusiasm, ever provide a public so eager as that which secured N. Clenard's grammar (first printed at Louvain in 1529) over twenty editions in the sixteenth century.

felt constrained to write a rabbinical responsum in order to demonstrate that it was permissible to teach Christians the Hebrew
language and Bible interpretation, though not in his opinion the
secret mystical lore.

A contemporary, Johanan Treves, who edited the prayer-book
according to the Roman rite, made an exception also as regards
the Talmud, which he thought should remain an exclusive possession of the Jewish community. Even so, there was a remarkable difference in attitude as compared with the pre-Renaissance
period, when Rabbi Isaiah di Trani II had restricted such instruction to parts of the Bible, exclusive of the Pentateuch.

All of this could no doubt be matched without much difficulty
by instances from other countries, particularly Germany, at this
period. In Italy, however, there was a humanistic approach which
created a unique atmosphere. A record from Ferrara indicates
in the most eloquent possible fashion the esteem in which Hebrew
studies were held. An enthusiastic Jew of that city, named Solomon Riva, desired to set up a Yeshiva, or rabbinical college, under
the direction of a scholar of some distinction named Jacob Reiner.
The founder applied for support of his project to Duke Ercole II,
who gave it readily, by a patent of August 4, 1556, in which he
authorized him to bring in one or more teachers, for the purpose
of instructing pupils in "all Jewish sciences," and exempted both
masters and pupils from customs dues on their property. "This
can only be for the honor and ornament of the city," he observed,
"because of the profit that many Jewish and Christian scholars,
both native and foreign, can derive therefrom." It would appear
from this that the duke expected Christian students to take advantage of these opportunities for purely rabbinic instruction.

When the Christian student penetrated to the Jewish quarter
for his lessons, he would sometimes find other things which he
considered to be worthy of attention. A curious instance comes
from this same place somewhat earlier than this. A Frenchman
named François Tissard, who was in Italy at the beginning of the
sixteenth century, was so influenced by the prevailing enthusiasm
that he too began to study Hebrew and attained a fair proficiency.
On his return home, he produced a Hebrew and Greek grammar
(*Grammatica hebraica et graeca*, Paris, 1508)—the first work of
the sort to appear in France, and the first (except an alphabet

probably produced by the same person in the previous year) to contain specimens of Hebrew type. In the prefatory matter, he gives some interesting sidelights on his travels and on Jewish life in Italy as he had observed it. Among other matters, he calls attention to what he considered the revolting habit of one of his Jewish teachers at Ferrara, who used to carry a piece of cloth about with him and would put it to his mouth to remove his spittle, instead of expectorating on the ground like a Christian. It was indeed once maintained that the earliest mention of the handkerchief (with the Italian equivalent, *fazzoletto*) is in the legal discussions of an Italian rabbi, Isaiah of Trani, of the beginning of the thirteenth century. Now it has been established that this probably is a marginal gloss of a later commentator. But a disciple of the Rhineland rabbi, Jacob Mölln or "Maharil" (d. 1427), tells us that his master kept a piece of cloth by him continually in a synagogue for the same purpose, so that the hygienic usage which so disgusted Tissard was apparently widespread among the Jews at this time. "I began to abhor this fellow for this to such an extent," he naively observed, "that I make an example of him." It may be observed for purposes of comparison that it was only at the end of the sixteenth century that the use of the handkerchief became general even among the ladies of the Venetian aristocracy.

Already in 1464 an attempt had been made to reëstablish the chair of Hebrew (with Chaldaic) at the University of Bologna, the oldest and at that time still the most distinguished in Europe. This turned out to be premature; but the chair came into existence effectively in 1488. The first incumbent was apparently a shadowy "Magister Vicentius," concerning whom we have no further information. His successor during the pontificate of Pope Leo X was the distinguished jurist and polymath Teseo Ambrogio—the earliest Ethiopic scholar in Europe—who filled the chair for some years: he showed his competence in Oriental studies by publishing an introduction to Chaldaic and twelve other languages. His instructor in Hebrew was Joseph Sarfatti of Fez (to be carefully distinguished from the poet-physician of the name, alias Giuseppe Gallo, who had died in 1527) who had acted in 1538 as the interpreter and intermediary between him and the first recorded

Syrian visitors to Rome in modern times. From 1520 to 1526, the Bologna chair was filled by Giovanni Flaminio, possibly the son of Antonio Flaminio of Rome, who will be mentioned below.

The ill-fated Ludovico il Moro, Duke of Milan (1481-99), founded a chair of Hebrew at the University of Pavia for one Benedetto Ispano, presumably a Spanish refugee, but it was abolished in 1491 as it did not seem to serve any useful purpose. In 1521, however, it was reëstablished, the first incumbent being that erudite apostate, Paolus Riccius.

In 1514, as part of the reorganization under Leo X's auspices of the Roman *studium* in the Sapienza (as the university building was called), the Holy Tongue began to be taught under the immediate auspices of the Vatican. The first teacher apparently was Agathon Guidacerio, a priest from Calabria, who records how he had begun his Hebrew studies in Rome under a Portuguese scholar named Jacob Gabbai, who had introduced him to the writings of Moses and David Kimhi. His *Grammatica hebraica* of 1514 (?) is quite a notable work of its type and one of the earliest to appear in Italy. In 1524, he produced an edition of Canticles, with Latin translation and commentary. With the sack of Rome in 1527, he was reduced to misery and transferred himself to Paris, where he also published a number of small works on Hebrew scholarship and another grammar which he called *Peculium Agathii* (1537-9)—a title obviously based on that of the Hebrew composition of Abraham de' Balmes, *Mikneh Abraham* (Venice, 1523), which in its Latin translation, published simultaneously for Gentile use, went by the similar name, *Peculium Abrahami*. In his first work Guidacerio gratefully records the interest shown in Hebrew studies not only by his patron, Pope Leo X, but also by Adriano de Castello, Cardinal of Bath—a famous humanist and prolific writer, whose fame has not been obscured by his implication in a plot to murder the Supreme Pontiff.

One other teacher at the Sapienza has already been mentioned— Guglielmo Raimondo da Moncada, alias Flavius Mithridates, a Sicilian by birth, who became converted to Christianity and lived ignobly for many years at the expense of his former co-religionists. He attained a considerable reputation for his knowledge of Arabic and other Semitic tongues, in addition to Hebrew and Aramaic. Among the slender roll of Italian Orientalists of the fifteenth century, he occupies an important place: he enjoyed the patronage of successive Popes and princes, was known in Germany as well as in Italy, taught theology in the Sapienza, and translated various works from the Arabic for the Duke of Urbino, one of them being the Koran—an achievement of importance in the history of oriental studies in Italy.[2]

In Florence, as we have already seen, Pico della Mirandola and his circle threw themselves heart and soul into this exciting new sphere of learning. Even persons who were far removed from theological interests, such as the scholar-poet Girolamo Benivieni and the scurrilous genius Angelo Poliziano, attained a fair competence—the former as we have seen sufficient to compose a Hebrew dictionary. The erudite bookdealer and biographer Vespasiano da Bisticci, whose stationer's shop was the hub of Florentine intellectual life, was reported to have a considerable knowledge of Hebrew literature, perhaps, however, only bibliographical. Savonarola prided himself on the fact that the sacred tongue was being taught together with Aramaic to the Dominicans of his convent of San Marco; and in 1497 he went to great pains to procure for their use, through his brother Albert, a number of copies of the "little" Hebrew Bible—presumably the second edition, in octavo, published three years before in Brescia by Gershom Soncino (the first, a folio, had appeared at Soncino in 1488). The teacher at San Marco was the ex-Jew named Clement ("Blemet") who had become converted as the result of the fiery friar's personal persuasion, and may formerly have been one of Pico della Mirandola's instructors. Savonarola records exegetical discussions with him which seem to display at least a smattering of Hebrew on his own part, as is the case also with some of the marginal notes on his copy of the Bible preserved in the National Library of Florence. One of Clement's pupils at this school was Sante Pagnini (Xanthus Pagninus) of Lucca (1470-1541), perhaps the most distinguished Italian Hebraist of the sixteenth century, who spent twenty-five years on a new translation of the Bible

---

[2] Another noteworthy linguist of Jewish birth in the Renaissance period was the Provençal Abraham de Lunel, who likewise became converted to Christianity, taught Hebrew at Avignon from 1537 onward, was reputed to have mastered no fewer than twenty-two languages, and reverted to Judaism at Venice, in extreme old age.

into Latin from the original; for he laid the foundation of his very considerable Hebrew knowledge when, in his youth, he was at the Dominican convent of Fiesole, just outside Florence. Apparently the direction of his studies can be attributed in the first instance to Savonarola himself. He was in close relations with the neo-Platonists of his day, including Giovanni Pico della Mirandola the younger, and in the preliminary matter to his Bible printed two letters from him, as well as expressions of approbation from two Popes. He published also a Hebrew grammar, the second edition of which (1546) was the first well-informed and correctly-printed work of the sort produced in Italy for the guidance of Christian students. Such was the prestige Pagnini enjoyed by virtue of his scholarship that, when his native Florence was besieged in 1530 by the combined forces of the emperor and the Pope, he could write from Lyons (where he had now settled) to Henry VIII of England beseeching his armed intervention.

Pagnini was the model for the ill-starred Florentine religious reformer, Antonio Brucioli (d. 1556), who relied on him to a great extent when he published in 1532 his own Bible translation into Italian—the first vernacular version by a single hand ever to appear, based so far as the Old Testament goes on the original Hebrew text. His fellow-Florentine Sante Marmochino also showed some Hebraic competence in his Bible version of 1538, produced a few years later, though it was in the main little other than a revised version of Brucioli's great achievement.

Every level of society shared the interest; and not merely in an abstract or academic fashion. Even in the early part of the fifteenth century Filippo Maria Visconti, Duke of Milan, was complimented by Gasparino Barzizza, one of the fathers of the revival of classical learning, on his attention to Hebrew studies. Federigo II of Urbino specifically commissioned the copying of Hebrew books, as we shall see. Giovanni Francesco II, Lord of Mirandola (Pico's nephew), studied Hebrew with the son of that same Johanan Alemanno who had taught his uncle. The general enthusiasm for the subject in Mantua was reflected in that court, from the close of the fifteenth century, when the Marquess Luigi Gonzaga III patronized Johanan Alemanno, down to a hundred years later, when Azariah de' Rossi taught the future Duke Ferdinand. One of the most remarkable illustrations of this interest here is provided by the strenuous efforts made by Isabella d'Este (who married the Marquess Giovanni Francesco II) to obtain a copy of the trivial work *Shimush Tehillim* (which, however, she may have needed for some cabalistical use!) for translation into Latin; after trying in vain to obtain the loan of it from a Jew at Governolo, she traced another copy at Scandiano, with which apparently she was more successful. Other daughters of princely houses had similar interests. Caterina Cybo, the daughter of the Count of Anguillara, who married Giovanni Maria da Varano, Duke of Camerino, and ruled the duchy for seven years (1527-34) after his death, was likewise reported to have attained a fair proficiency in the Hebrew tongue—as was the case with the ill-fated Lady Jane Grey, her slightly younger contemporary, the nine-day Queen of England in 1553.

The names of distinguished Italian Hebraists of this age, who occupied a high position in the world of politics or the world of letters, could be multiplied almost indefinitely. The warrior-humanist Count Guido Rangoni, a *condottiere* of noble family who served in succession or alternation the Pope of Rome, the Republic of Venice, the city of Florence and the King of France, was so interested in the subject as to take Hebrew lessons with the eminent Jewish physician, Jacob Mantino; and it was for him that the latter translated Maimonides' famous "Eight Chapters" on ethics into Latin. One of the most remarkable of the foreign humanists working in Italy at this time was the German, Johann Albrecht Widmanstadt or Widmanstetter, later Chancellor of Lower Austria and Rector of the University of Vienna, who went far beyond the rudiments of Jewish scholarship and enjoyed the advantage of instruction by a number of distinguished teachers. He was first introduced to the subject by Rabbi David ibn Jacchia about 1523, in Naples, in the house of Samuel Abrabanel; he studied the Cabala there with Baruch of Benevento, the translator of the *Zohar* into Latin; and in due course he worked in Rome with Rabbi Benjamin d'Arignano and in Turin with Pico's former teacher Dattilo (Joab). In consequence of all this, he became so expert that he was able to carry on correspondence in the tongue of the Bible, and so proud of the fact that he embodied Hebrew in his book-plate, together with Latin and Syriac. He once bor-

THE NORSA FAMILY

Detail from an altarpiece in the Basilica of S. Andrea, Mantua

GRACIA MENDES THE YOUNGER: BRONZE MEDAL, BY PASTORINO DE'
PASTORINI, C. 1553

*Courtesy of the Jewish Museum of the Jewish Theological Seminary,
New York*

ELIA DE LATTES AND HIS MOTHER RICA

Bronze Medal, 1552. Courtesy of Alfred Rubens, Esq.

A
SYNAGOGUE INTERIOR,
BY
ALESSANDRO MAGNASCO,
1667–1749

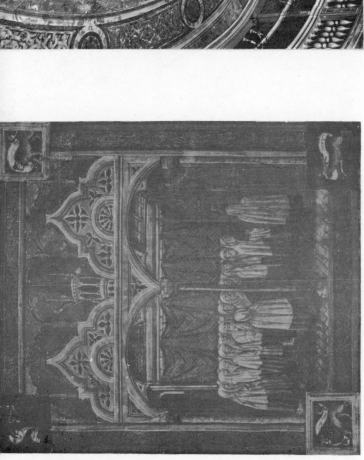

SEPHARDI SYNAGOGUE OF VENICE, CEILING

ITALIAN SYNAGOGUE, 15TH CENTURY

Vatican Library, Codex Rossi 555
Courtesy of J. Solis-Cohen, Jr.

JEWISH QUEEN AT THE SFORZA WEDDING PAGEANT, 1475

"MOUNTAIN OF THE JEWS" AT THE SFORZA WEDDING PAGEANT, 1475

ITALIAN WEDDING SCENE

Vatican Library, Codex Rossi 555
Courtesy of J. Solis-Cohen, Jr.

JEWISH BRIDAL COUPLE, RENAISSANCE ITALY

Courtesy of the Library of Jews College, London

Jncipit phemium libri elhauy ad
honorem dei cuius nomen sit bene
dictum inseculta seculorum amē.

velusis pr
sus omni
um uanis
et uarijs
phylosofo
rum erro
ribus om
niq3 huma
no intellec
tu ineoru

perscrupta; ttione que totam nature
faculratem excedunt penitus capti
uato Ventati pme firmiter inhere-
tes reatholice fidei lumine perlustrati

FARAJ OF GIRGENTI AND HIS EMPLOYER, KING CHARLES OF NAPLES

Miniature from manuscript, Latin 6192, Bibliothèque Nationale
Courtesy of the Bibliothèque Nationale, Paris

TRIAL SCENE IN RENAISSANCE ITALY

From an illuminated Italian 15th-century manuscript of Maimonides' Code

GUGLIELMO DA PESARO AND HIS PUPILS

Manuscript, Fonds Ital. 973, Bibliothèque Nationale
Courtesy of the Bibliothèque Nationale, Paris

TWO VIEWS OF AN IVORY
MEZUZAH CASE, C. 1500

Courtesy of the Jewish Museum, Londo

16TH-CENTURY SYNAGOGUE ARK, ITALIAN
Courtesy of the Jewish Museum, London

RENAISSANCE LAVER AND GRILL, PADUA SYNAGOGUE

HANUKKAH LAMP SHOWING THE LILY OF FLORENCE

Roth Collection

HANUKKAH LAMP SHOWING THE ARMS OF CARDINAL OTTAVIO RIDOLFI (1582-1624).

Formerly in the Lee M. Friedman Collection, Boston

STATUE OF MOSES BY ANTONIO FEDERIGHI, 15TH CENTURY

Formerly over the well-head in the ghetto at Siena
Courtesy of the Museum Civico, Siena

MEDAL COMMEMORATING BENJAMIN SON OF ELIJAH BE'ER THE
PHYSICIAN, 1497/1503

ELIJAH DEL MEDIGO, FROM THE FRESCO BY GOZZOLI IN THE PALAZZO
RICARDI, FLORENCE

ILLUMINATED PAGE OF A MANUSCRIPT OF THE HEBREW TRANSLATION
OF AVICENNA'S *Canon*, NORTHERN ITALY, C. 1480

Courtesy of the University Library, Bologna

DAGGER OF THE GONZAGAS,
BY SALAMONE DA SESSO

Courtesy of the Louvre, Paris

HOUSEWIFE'S CASKET, 15TH CENTURY,
BY JESHURUN TOVAR

Courtesy of the Bezalel Museum, Jerusalem

rowed from Jacob Mantino two manuscripts of the *Zohar*, so that
he could have a copy made for his famous private library, rich in
Hebrew manuscripts, which formed the nucleus of the splendid
collection now at Munich. (Among those who provided him with
books was the ingenious grammarian, Elias Levita.) Andreas Maes,
the Belgian scholar who, after a distinguished diplomatic career,
settled in Italy and devoted himself to the study of oriental languages, now calling himself Masius or Masio, became entirely
absorbed by Hebrew literature. His correspondents included Elias
Levita the grammarian, Daniel Bomberg the printer (who once
sent him an ancient Hebrew *shekel* as a present, as well as a translation of Maimonides' *Guide for the Perplexed*), and the latter's
technical adviser Cornelio Adelkind, with whom he was in close
epistolary contact. He, too, assembled an important Hebrew library, which included—a most unusual thing in those days—the
Talmud. The cultured secretary of the Signoria in Venice, Lorenzo
Massa, also prided himself on his knowledge of Hebrew, as did
the scholarly Federigo Campofregoso, brother of Ottaviano Campofregoso, Doge of Genoa from 1513 to 1515. Francesco Vis-
domini (1508-92) was so highly thought of, as Hebraist as well
as humanist, that he was the subject of a portrait-medal engraved
by Pastorino de' Pastorini.

About this time, Tommaso Aldobrandini, brother of the future
Pope Clement VIII, studied both language and literature under
the guidance of the Roman Jew, Menahem di Nola, whom, however, he persuaded to embrace Christianity, under the name of
Giovanni Paolo Eustachio. It may be that he adopted this name
in honor of Bartolommeo Eustachi, the distinguished anatomist of
the University of Perugia (mentioned already in another connection) who also enjoyed a reputation for his Hebrew scholarship.
The Mantuan theologian Francesco Stancaro (1501-74), who later
was to play so curious a role in the Reformation in Poland, also
had some little fame in his day as a Hebraist. At the close of
the century, Canon Marco Marini of Brescia—a pupil of the grammarian Samuel Archevolti—acquired sufficient knowledge, not
only to produce a Hebrew grammar (1580) and dictionary (1593),
but even to supervise the publication of the censored edition of
the Talmud of 1578-81. He was on fairly friendly terms with
Leone Modena, who at the age of fifteen had contributed a com-

mendatory poem to one of his books.

The latter was proud subsequently to count among his pupils in Hebrew various Christian scholars, including Vincenzo Noghera, "theologian" to the Cardinal of Bologna, and Giovanni Vislingio, Professor of Anatomy in Padua; and he was in touch on questions of Jewish scholarship with Giovanni Argoli, Reader of Fine Arts at Bologna and an authority on classical archaeology. Hebrew knowledge was still so fashionable at this time that Leone Modena furnished laudatory sonnets for a number of volumes by Christian scholars. These included at least one which specifically dealt with a recondite point of Roman Catholic theology, and— what was perhaps even more surprising—so wholly secular a work as the *Life of Federico Gonzaga,* by Count Alberto Pompeo, who must at least have had some appreciation of Hebrew studies. One episode throws remarkable light on both his status and that of Hebrew studies. When on one occasion the Doge of Venice visited the Seminary of San Antonio, he was greeted with a Hebrew speech and ode, which Modena had prepared at the request of the friars. He also had numerous non-Italian correspondents and pupils—some of them even Englishmen; but it would take us too far from the scope of the present volume to speak of them here.

Foreign nobles who visited Italy were naturally infected by the native example. Thus Rabbi Elijah di Nola, one of the outstanding scholars of Roman Jewry in the middle of the sixteenth century, is recorded to have copied a mystical work in Rome in 1555 (MS. Casanatense 65) for a person whom he designates as "the Duke"—apparently the Elector Palatine, Otto Heinrich— besides selling him a fine illuminated Hebrew Bible. When, in 1545, the Bolognese patrician Achille Bocchi built a palace in Via Goito for one of the literary societies in which the city abounded, the Accademia Ermatana, he pointedly had inscribed in bold letters at the entrance, by the side of verses from Horace, a familiar passage from the psalms in the original Hebrew: "What shall be given unto thee, and what shall be done more unto thee, thou deceitful tongue"—a warning against slanderous speech, obviously intended to be understood by the academicians. A recently-discovered chronicle, describing the sufferings of the Jews in the Papal States in the middle of the sixteenth century, tells us how a scholarly Jew, thrown into the dungeons of the Inquisition, found there two priests suspected of heresy, who not only had a considerable knowledge of Hebrew, but regularly read the Psalms and even prayed in the Holy Tongue.

Reverting to the earlier period, one should certainly mention the Franciscan friar, Cornelio da Montalcino, whose study of the Hebrew language and literature led him ultimately to embrace Judaism—an offense which he expiated on the pyre, in the Campo de' Fiori in Rome, in 1553, one of the harbingers of the impending reaction. No doubt it was nervousness that such an episode might recur which induced the Dominican chapter held in Rome in 1571 to decree that Hebrew might henceforth be studied by members of the Order only after obtaining written permission, in which the name of the teacher was specifically mentioned. Here we are in the full atmosphere of the Catholic Reaction: the Renaissance spirit has been left far behind.

Important collections of Hebrew manuscripts meanwhile began to be brought together by these Christian devotees, thus making possible further advances in the realm of scholarship. The greatest was that of the Holy See—probably the most ancient collection of its kind in any European library—which is said to have contained 116 Hebrew books when it was reorganized after the so-called "Babylonian Captivity," at the beginning of the fifteenth century. Pope Nicholas V's quest for the lost original of the Gospel according to St. Matthew resulted in new additions to this collection. There was a major development under Pope Sixtus IV, who erected the new building for what was now the Vatican Library and systematically added to its contents. Not only were old manuscripts extensively purchased, but new copies were made. For this purpose, according to one source, the Pope engaged for Hebrew as he did for Latin special scholarly *scrittori* (not the commonplace and moderately-paid *copisti*, who were mere clerks). This has been questioned, but it is certain that from the middle of the sixteenth century on the Vatican Library regularly employed a qualified Hebrew copyist, a second being appointed by Pope Paul V not long after his accession at the beginning of the seventeenth. The Dominican Zanobio Acciaiuoli, a close friend of Ficino and Poliziano (the only Florentine in Leo X's learned entourage), became Prefect of the Vatican

Library in 1518, toward the close of his life; he took some interest in Hebrew studies and did what he could to develop the collection in the few months that he still had to live. He was succeeded by Girolamo Aleandro, one of the greatest scholars of his time, under whose tutelage the Library greatly expanded. Religious zealot though he was (it was he who first kindled the fires of persecution against the Lutherans in Germany), he had a profound interest in Hebrew, which he had studied to such good effect that before he reached the age of thirty he taught the language in addition to the humanities at the University of Paris, where he became rector. It is with his period of activity there that French Renaissance scholarship may be said to begin. He enjoyed a reputation as a rabbinic expert, and as we shall see later, he was largely responsible for the authorization of Hebrew printing in Rome in 1536. Shortly after this date, he was succeeded by Agostino Steuco, Bishop of Gubbio ("Steuchus Eugubinus"), whose fame largely depended on his Old Testament studies: his *magnum opus* was a learned study of the biblical text "according to the Hebrew truth," published at Venice in 1529, in which he attempted to vindicate the accuracy of the Vulgate version against the criticism of the Jews and those (the Reformers) who followed them.

One group of the Hebrew and Oriental manuscripts in the Vatican Library, acquired apparently about this time, bears the signature (sometimes in Hebrew characters) of a former owner named Flaminius—probably the eccentric Sicilian humanist Antonio Flaminio, who taught in Rome early in the sixteenth century and was found dead among his books one day in 1512. The reputation of the collection was to culminate in the following century with the work of the learned Cistercian monk Giulio Bartolocci, whose *Magna bibliotheca rabbinica* (1675-93), based upon its accumulated treasures, was the first serious attempt to give the Christian world a really adequate account of Jewish literature, and has by no means lost its value or its importance even today.

At this period even Jews—most surprisingly—were admitted to the privileges of the Vatican Library. In 1539, a certain Beniamin Hebreo is recorded as borrowing a book entitled "Mibocar Apenidim" *(Mibḥar haPeninim* by Jedaiah of Béziers):

the reference is clearly to Widmanstadt's teacher, the bibliophile and scholar Benjamin d'Arignano, from whom the library is known to have purchased a couple of Hebrew volumes. Among the many Gentile scholars with whom he was in touch was Andrea Masio, for whom he found a copy of Maimonides' *Guide*, as well as Master Guglielmo, the latter's instructor in Arabic.

In other libraries, too, the papal example of paying attention to Hebrew literature together with that of the other classical languages was eagerly followed. The greatest of all princely collectors of the Renaissance period, Federigo da Montefeltro II, Duke of Urbino (*condottiere* though he was) was outstanding in this respect. He condemned, indeed, the newfangled invention of printing (he would have been ashamed, he said, to have a printed book in his possession), but maintained some thirty or forty *scrittori* in various places. One at least of these was a Jew— Aaron ben Gabriel—who copied for him in Florence in 1473 the Hebrew part of the trilingual codex of the Psalms, mentioned by Vespasiano da Bisticci, which is still extant. Ultimately, a memorable Hebrew section numbering over sixty codices figured in his library, which also was subsequently transferred to the Vatican. A good part of this came from the collection of Menahem ben Aaron di Volterra, of Bologna, which was apparently acquired *en bloc*. But the extent of the duke's interest is best illustrated by an anecdote told about him. When in 1472 he was in command of the Florentine forces which captured the city of Volterra, he did his best to prevent the sack of the city, but failed. He refused nevertheless to accept any of the loot, but evidently could not resist a fine Hebrew Bible for his personal library. It is conjectured that the manuscript in question may be the superb German codex of 1295, with the *Massorah* written in the margins in minuscular hand, in audacious decorative shapes, which is now in the Urbino collection in the Vatican Library—said to be one of the most ponderous volumes in existence, consisting as it does of nearly one thousand leaves measuring some two feet by one foot four inches, and so bulky that two men are required to carry it.

The Medici, too, paid some attention to Hebrew literature in assembling their superb collections. There were a number of Hebrew manuscripts in the original Medicean library, according to the catalogue of 1495; some had been acquired or commissioned through Giannozzo Manetti a generation before and drifted into the Vatican collection. Later on, the Grand Duke Cosimo I had a Mantuan Jew in his service as his Hebrew librarian. This was the origin of the important collection now in the Bibliotheca Laurenziana in Florence, which includes some codices of the greatest importance. The Cardinal Federigo Borromeo, Archbishop of Milan (nephew of St. Charles Borromeo), had a very considerable collection of Hebrew manuscripts, now in the Ambrosian library in that city, which he founded in 1609. Among these were copies of various codices copied or commissioned for him in Rome by the convert Giovanni Paolo Eustachio, formerly Menahem di Nola, who has been mentioned above. Another member of the family, Carlo Federico Borromeo, annotated several of the volumes and himself wrote independently on subjects connected with Hebrew learning. One of the earliest librarians of this collection was the noted Arabist Antonio Giggei, who had a reputation as a Hebrew scholar.

Similarly, Duke Carlo Emanuele I of Savoy, who introduced the full tide of Italian cultural life into his dominions late in our period, acquired in 1610 a considerable library of Hebrew books and manuscripts of Mantua from Solomon Rubiera, and had them put into order—in return for a license to act as broker!—by his own subject, Graziadio Treves.

This interest in Hebrew literature on the part of non-Jews had one somewhat bizarre result. In many cases, the manuscripts, copied by professing Jews, have nothing extraordinary about them except the mention of the name of the Christian maecenas in the colophon. Some, however, were written by converted Jews, or by erudite Christian students of Hebrew, and are characteristically Christian in feeling notwithstanding the language. A case in point is in two beautifully-written biblical codices, both by the same hand, in the Laurentian library in Florence, one of which begins with the phrase (in Hebrew) "For the honor and glory of our Lord Jesus of Nazareth, King of the Jews . . . in the name of the Father, the Son, and the Holy Ghost"; it has, in addition, illuminations (to be described later) which are thoroughly Christian in their inspiration.

Particular significance attaches to the interest in Hebrew

studies shown by princes of the Church, some instances of which
we have already seen. Already at the close of the fifteenth century,
the patrician humanist Domenico Grimani, patriarch of Aquileia
and later Cardinal of S. Marco, who had the Jewish grammarian
Abraham de Balmes in his employment as his personal physician
and accepted the dedication of his works, had patronized Elijah
del Medigo and commissioned him to carry out a number of
translations from the Hebrew. He was acquainted also with the
physician and exegete Obadiah Sforno (whose biblical commentaries are to this day published in standard editions of the
Hebrew Pentateuch). It was he who recommended the latter to
Johannes von Reuchlin when he was trying to find a competent
Hebrew teacher in Rome. Cardinal Grimani's direct competence
in Hebrew literature was not, so far as is known, particularly striking: otherwise, we might have hoped to find in his library some
Hebrew codex as richly illuminated as the famous Breviary which
he bequeathed to his beloved Venice. More striking from this
point of view was Agostino Giustiniani, Bishop of Nebbio in
Corsica, an eminent Orientalist, whose interests extended to
Hebrew as well. In his unrivaled library all the essential rabbinic
classics were to be found; and he naively prided himself upon
them, comparing them (if only for rarity) to pearls of the first
water. His most remarkable production was the polyglot Psalter
printed at Genoa in 1516 (the earliest work of its type), fifty
copies of which were specially produced on vellum for presentation to royalty. This volume is famous for one feature especially:
in the margin of Psalm 19 ("The heavens declare the glory of
God") he introduced somewhat redundantly a reference to
Christopher Columbus and his discoveries— the first in any document of Jewish literature! He also published (Paris, 1520) a Latin
translation of Maimonides' *Guide for the Perplexed*—unfortunately for his reputation, under his own name, although he
actually made unintelligent use of the old medieval version, faults
and all, which has been spoken of in a previous chapter.

The exiled English nobleman, Cardinal Reginald Pole, infected
by the general enthusiasm, was to derive a renewed enthusiasm for
biblical literature from the study of Hebrew originals. Among
those Jews with whom he was in touch was a young scholar in
Ferrara whom he persuaded to embrace Catholicism in 1540;

however, he later became a Protestant and, as Immanuel Tre-
mellius, was to teach Hebrew to the reformer Peter Martyr in
Lucca and then to be a notable figure in the Hebrew revival in
Germany and in England. Gian Matteo Giberti, Bishop of
Verona, gathered around him a number of savants in different
spheres, including Jacob Mantino, the learned Jewish physician,
and Johannes de Kampen (Campensis) the Belgian Hebraist, who
studied the language at Venice with Elias Levita, of whom we
will speak shortly.

Particularly great significance in the record of Jewish culture
at the Renaissance period attaches to the learned General of the
Augustinian Order, Fra Egidio da Viterbo, who was raised to the
Purple by Pope Leo X for his many qualities, and later showed
his genuinely religious spirit by consistently opposing the introduction of the Inquisition into Portugal. Even in splendid Rome,
before the calamity of 1527, his culture was outstanding and
Jewish studies constituted a great part of his interest. David
Reubeni, going to visit him in 1524, was surprised to find his
Hebrew teacher Joseph Ashkenazi among those in attendance on
him in the audience room. He patronized Hebrew learning as
eagerly as any Jewish enthusiast. Like Pico della Mirandola before
him, he conceived a great veneration for the Cabala and its principal classic, the Zohar. Not only did he have that work specially
copied for him by a Jewish scribe, but he even commissioned an
accomplished scholar, Baruch da Benevento, to translate it for
him into Latin. Moreover, unlike Pico, he extended his interests
to the more fundamental branches of Hebrew scholarship. For
some ten or thirteen years, he gave hospitality in his palace in
Rome to Elijah Bahur (= the Unmarried), known to Christian
scholars as Elias Levita (= the Levite)—that remarkable German
Jewish poet, grammarian and lexicographer, who more than any
other man linked together the medieval Jewish philologists with
the scientific Christian investigators of the age of the Reformation.
It was he, for example, who was responsible for the dissemination
of what was considered then the sensational if not heretical theory
that the Hebrew vowel-points were relatively modern. (In due
course, he was to be invited by King Francis I of France to
occupy the chair of Hebrew at Paris, though for one reason or
another he declined the offer.) Under Elijah's guidance, the

cardinal not only studied the Jewish mystical literature, but also became a competent Hebrew scholar, the other, meanwhile, being able to go on with his researches and his writing, and even to add Greek to his other accomplishments. This happy interlude in his life was ended by the Sack of Rome, when his patron was suddenly transformed by events into a man of action. When the cardinal's palace was sacked, a great part of the compositions on which Levita had spent so much time were destroyed.

Elijah Levita's wandering career in the north of Italy and Germany, in the twenty-two years which were to intervene before his death, has no place here; it belongs in the main to the history of the Germanic lands. But a nostalgic passage from the preface to his principal work, *Masoreth haMasoreth*, is worth quoting for the light which it throws on the intellectual atmosphere at this time in Italy:

> I swear by my Creator, that a certain Christian [that is, Cardinal Egidio da Viterbo] encouraged me and brought me thus far. For fully ten years without interruption he was my pupil. I meanwhile lived in his house and instructed him. On this account there was a great outcry against me [on the part of some Jews], for it was not considered proper. Some rabbis did not approve of what I had done, and pronounced woe on me, because I taught the Law to a Christian . . . However, when the Prince heard what I had to say, he came to me and kissed me with the kisses of his mouth, and said: "Blessed be the God of the Universe who hath brought thee hither to me. Now abide with me and be my teacher, and I shall be to thee as a father, and shall support thee and thy house, and give thee thy corn and thy wine and thy olives, and bear all thy needs." Thus we took sweet counsel together, iron sharpening iron. I imparted my spirit to him, and learned from him excellent and valuable things, which are in accordance with Truth. . . .

Latin and Greek scholarship in the age of the Renaissance concentrated on the literary study of originals of the classical texts. Inevitably, the same fashion colored the new-born enthusiasm for Hebrew. There was no need in those days, before the Reformation had cast its shadow, to insist unremittingly on the dogmatic importance of the Vulgate version—much less to suggest that it

would savor of heresy to supplement it. Indeed, when the converted Jew, Fra Felix of Prato, who had entered the Augustinian
Order, was contemplating his new Latin version of the Psalms
(Venice, 1515), he was cordially encouraged by Cardinal Bembo,
the illustrious humanist, and had an audience with the Pope,
Leo X, who wished him to continue with the other books of the
Bible. Similarly, Leo's kinsman, Pope Clement VII, at one time
had the idea of commissioning a new translation of the Old Testament from the original Hebrew into Latin, to be carried out by
six Jewish and six Christian scholars working together: a remarkable project, suggesting unexpected mastery of Latin by the one
side and of Hebrew by the other, in addition to cordial relations
between them all and a superbly tolerant attitude on the part of
the Supreme Pontiff. This new outlook resulted in renewed
enthusiasm for the literary qualities of the Hebrew Scriptures. No
higher tribute could be paid to them than to attempt to render
them into the style as well as the language of the classical poets. It
was now that Marcantonio Flaminio—a Hebraist as well as poet in
his own right—first translated the Psalter into Latin prose and then
into verse on the classical model (*Paraphrasis in triginta Psalmos*,
Venice, 1546), his renderings being later sung at the French court
by Marguerite de Valois and regarded almost in the light of a new
poetical revelation. Simultaneously, Gasparo Contarini of Venice
renewed (or, as it seemed to some contemporaries, surpassed) the
force of Isaiah in his lofty version. So, too, the poet and historian,
Bernardo Baldi of Urbino, was before long to execute a remarkable new literary translation of the Lamentations of Jeremiah.

The academic importance of Hebrew studies was already fully
recognized in Renaissance Italy when the personal vagaries of a
sensuous monarch and the exigencies of dynastic politics suddenly
gave them an unexpected practical significance. In 1509, Henry
VIII of England had been constrained for political reasons to
marry the Infanta Catherine of Aragon, daughter of Ferdinand
and Isabella of Spain and for a few months wife of his deceased
brother Arthur. Now, after a couple of decades of married life—
whether it was that he was seduced by the bright eyes of Anne
Boleyn or overwhelmingly eager to provide himself with a male
heir—he desired to have this marriage of such long standing

annulled. (The term "the Royal Divorce" generally applied to this case is quite misleading.) The Pope would no doubt have been prepared to grant the favor, but for his dependence on or fear of Catherine's nephew, the Emperor Charles V, who resented the slight on his house. Thus little by little the conflagration spread which in the end was to sever England from her traditional allegiance to the Roman Church.

On Henry's side in the dispute there was obvious biblical authority on which he mainly based his arguments: in the Book of Leviticus (18.16) in which marital relations between a man and his brother's wife are sternly and categorically forbidden. On the other hand, in Deuteronomy 25.5-6, such a union is expressly prescribed if the brother had died childless, in order that his name should be perpetuated. The problem of interpretation was indeed highly perplexing, and it was clearly necessary to go back to the primary sources. In consequence, the importance of the Hebrew tradition for the correct comprehension of Holy Writ was acutely realized. Since Jews were now excluded from both England and Spain, the two real protagonists in the dispute, it was to the Jewish quarters of Italy that both sides turned for guidance. Richard Croke, the eminent Cambridge humanist who had taught the king Greek, was sent to Italy to collect opinions from various canon lawyers on behalf of his royal pupil and master. Before he left, John Stokesley, later Bishop of London, advised him to put himself into contact also with the Jews, so as to ascertain what was their view regarding the interpretation and application of the Mosaic law in this delicate matter.

As soon as possible after his arrival, Croke applied for assistance to Fra Francesco Giorgi, the celebrated Venetian theologian, who was a Hebraist of some repute, besides being versed in the Cabala: this he had recently shown in his singular work *De harmonia mundi* (Venice, 1525), which in three "chants," each composed of eight "tones" and "melodies," propounded a philosophy concocted from biblical mysticism, Platonic speculation, cabalistic occultism, and musical theory. This versatile scholar had little difficulty in finding Jewish scholars who were willing to support the English thesis, for there was an increasing tendency in Jewish life to evade the Deuteronomical prescription of a levirate marriage by the legal formality of the so-called *Halizah* ceremony (laid down as an alternative in Deuteronomy 25.7-10). Hardly a day passed, reported Croke from Venice at the beginning of 1530, when he did not confer on the matter with some monk or some Jew. The names of half a dozen of the latter, conforming or converted, are mentioned in his dispatches. The most illustrious among them was Elijah Halfon, the fashionable physician, whose name we have already encountered. The latter even succeeded in collecting a few signatures to endorse his argument that the Deuteronomic regulation governing the levirate marriage need no longer be taken into account. Those who supported him in this included a German scholar named Benedict, living in Venice—perhaps to be identified with Rabbi (Baruch) Bendit Axelrad of that city,[3] and his own father-in-law, Maestro Calo (Calonymus ben David), the eminent physician and translator,[4] copies of whose published works were dispatched to Henry as an earnest of his scholastic reliability. There were some authorities in Padua too who were reported to have declared themselves in the same sense. The most useful of all, however, from the English point of view was a Venetian convert to Christianity named Marco Raphael, who some time previously had received a reward from the Senate for inventing a new invisible ink—obviously a useful adjunct in the famous secret diplomacy of the *Serenissima*. Meanwhile, the other English representatives were also active, including a priest named Francesco da Corte who acted on behalf of Girolamo Ghinucci, titular Bishop of Worcester and later cardinal. Among those whom he approached was one Jacob Raphael Peglione, rabbi at Modena, who drew up a closely argued rabbinical responsum in full form on the problem—but unfortunately arrived at a conclusion contrary to the English thesis.

It was characteristic of Henry VIII's keen interest in scholarship as well as in the case itself that he insisted on having these rabbinical opinions translated into Latin from the Hebrew originals by Giorgi and submitted to him for his perusal. Partly for this purpose the latter was dispatched to England, bringing with him

---

[3] Certainly not Baruch of Benevento, the translator of the *Zohar*, as has been suggested, who was neither a German nor of German extraction.

[4] See above, pp. 75 f. for him and his work.

Marco Raphael as Hebrew expert. Despite an attempt of the Spanish ambassador to waylay them, they arrived safely at the beginning of 1531; and there, after various audiences, conferences and consultations, the apostate drew up a further report, to the complete satisfaction of his patron: he remained thereafter attached to the English court.

But the question was not so simple. Indeed, as we have seen, some of those who had been approached on Henry's behalf had not responded in the manner that was hoped. Moreover, since the party favoring the annulment of the marriage had appealed to the Jewish tradition, its opponents were driven to do the same. In Venice, Halfon's professional rival and opponent in all things, Jacob Mantino, the outstanding scholar of the circle, had been courted in vain by the English representatives. But already at the outset of the controversy he had been approached on behalf of the Pope, to whom he was probably under personal obligation. This was not presumably the only reason why he declared himself wholeheartedly in favor of the papal thesis. Almost all the more important of the Italian rabbis consulted were ranged with him. The English thesis was in fact overwhelmed by weight of learning as well as number. Moreover, the Venetian government, now in alliance with Spain, actively discouraged the canvassing of opinions among the Jews in its territories by the English representatives. Worst of all, it came to light that a levirate marriage had taken place at this time at Bologna between a Jew and his brother's widow in accordance with the categorical precept in the Book of Deuteronomy. This obviously threw all the elaborate arguments on the other side into complete discredit. As far as England was concerned, the breach with Rome was drawn perceptibly nearer. Nevertheless, the episode was of real importance in Jewish intellectual history. For this, together with the "Battle of Books" which raged around the dispute of Reuchlin and Pfefferkorn in Germany, did much to rehabilitate Hebrew studies in Christian eyes in this critical age. Clearly, a fresh era had dawned when the King of England, the Holy Roman Emperor and the Pope of Rome, were paying such anxious deference to Jewish scholarship and scholars.

If Hebrew literature was a subject of study, obviously it had to be protected when the need arose. In the thirteenth century, the offensive against the Talmud, which had resulted in the burning of wagon-loads of precious manuscripts in Paris, had been approved if not instigated at the court of Rome, and there is evidence that it was imitated in Italy as well not long after. But now a wholly different spirit prevailed. When the great dispute about Hebrew literature to which reference has just been made raged in Germany from 1509 on, the obscurantist party received no encouragement from the Vatican, and Johannes von Reuchlin appealed to the Holy See (as we have seen, through the Jewish physician, Bonet de Lattes!) in justified confidence that here he would find support. Great writers, Pope Leo X said when he licensed the publication of the newly-found Tacitus, were a rule of life and a consolation in misfortune. Clearly, he considered that this was the case with Hebrew literature as well: for to the humanist nothing human was alien.

Leo's pontificate coincided with the most striking of all manifestations of Renaissance interest in Jewish scholarship. In 1516, the noble-hearted Christian enthusiast, Daniel Bomberg, founded at Venice that great printing-house which continued in amazing activity for the next thirty years, during which it produced the first or the standard editions of all manner of Jewish classics, from the great Rabbinic Bible of 1517-18 on. There is no single person whose name is more important in the annals of Hebrew printing: it might almost be said that there is no individual in the age of the Renaissance, Jew or Christian, to whom Hebrew scholarship owes so much. From what we know of his life and character, it is obvious that this was by no means a matter of merely finding an investment for capital. He was profoundly interested in the subject (and for that matter in Jews and in their welfare), and it is certain that he had himself a real understanding and appreciation of the literature which he produced so devotedly—and, it may be added, so elegantly. Joseph haCohen, the historian, recorded the beginning of his activity as a notable thing in contemporary Jewish life. "In this year," he wrote in his *Chronicles*, "Daniel Bomberg of Antwerp began to print; and he brought forth from darkness many works in the Holy Tongue. Learned men were always going and coming in his house, from as far as might be; and he turned not back his right hand from giving each one what he asked, according to the good hand of the Lord upon him. Now the said Daniel was a Christian born on his father's side and on his mother's and in all his ancestors; there was not in him one drop of Jewish blood."

Shortly after Bomberg began his printing activity in Venice, in the teeth of some opposition there, an appeal was made to Leo X to intervene, on the grounds that various heretical and blasphemous works had been produced. A Pope could not refuse to take some action, and in May 1518 Leo sent to Venice ordering that an inquiry should be made and those responsible punished if the accusations were justified. But it would appear that at the same time he gave a clear indication of his own feelings in the matter. Not only did no prosecution ensue, but Bomberg even obtained from the Pope at this time his formal authorization and license to publish the Talmud, the first collected edition of which began to appear from his press in 1519: the *editio princeps* of the complete work, and a landmark in Jewish intellectual life. Emboldened, moreover, by the clear manifestation of the Pope's sympathies, the Jews of Rome, too, now solicited and obtained authorization to set up a printing-press in the house of another interested Christian, Giovanni Giacomo Facciotto, in the Piazza Montanara. (Some Hebrew books had appeared here in the earliest days of Hebrew printing, but subsequently there was a prolonged interruption.) This, one may say, was the Pope's considered retort to the attempted suppression of Jewish literature in Germany.

This press was of very short duration, its production being in fact restricted to a couple of slight grammatical works by Elias Levita, the protégé of the Cardinal of Viterbo: for there was no one in Rome with Bomberg's drive and idealism. In 1536, how-ever, under Pope Paul III, the Roman Jews again applied for a papal privilege to print Hebrew books. It was highly characteristic of the age that they secured the support of the Pope's natural son, Pierluigi Farnese, the progenitor of the dukes of Parma—the same who figures luridly in the biography of Benvenuto Cellini and was to perish tragically so soon. In his eagerness—which was not necessarily venal, though it may have been—he went so far as to exert pressure on the Master of the Sacred Palace to secure his support, though without success. The application was referred to

Girolamo Aleandro, the learned Vatican librarian, recently created a cardinal, who as we have seen had a reputation as a Hebraist. With a show of ecclesiastical frigidity, the latter advised that the permission should be granted, but restricted to works which had already appeared in print, thus avoiding material against which theological difficulties could be raised. It was, however, notorious that this category must include the Talmud, of which more than one edition had by now appeared at Venice, so that this ostensibly cold approbation could hardly have been more comprehensive. Another Christian printer, Antonio Blado, official printer to the papal court for half a century, was associated with this venture, together with the Jewish enthusiast Benjamin d'Arignano, who has been mentioned above. But after a promising beginning in 1547, when five books were published, this press, too, closed down.

The amazing thing was that within a few years this attitude was to be wholly reversed, and the smoke from the copies of the Talmud and allied Jewish literature, destroyed by papal order, was to befoul the brilliant Roman sky, as will be decribed later. But even now the voice of enlightenment was not silenced. Andrea Masio (who was powerless to save even the Hebrew books in his private library) wrote that he considered it a godless sacrilege and an eternal disgrace in the eyes of posterity; for the cardinals' report condemning a literature of which they knew nothing was as valueless as a blind man's opinion of color. More remarkable was the fact that Isabella d'Este's splendid, enlightened son, Ercole Gonzaga, Cardinal of Mantua, actually sent to warn the Jews of his diocese of what was intended, so that they were able to take precautions in good time; while his brother Don Ferrante, Governor of the Duchy of Milan for the Spaniards, took advantage of the strained political situation and refused to put the edict into execution at all. For it was true then as at all times in Italian history that, although the spirit of reaction might triumph in the country, it could not prevail over the spirit of all its children.

EIGHT

The Printed Book

One of the most important agencies in the popularization of the New Learning, which brought the Renaissance within the reach of ordinary men and women, was the invention and diffusion of printing. The full story of the earliest Jewish participation in this is in part a mystery, the solution to which is still awaited.

It is well known that the first European printed book to which a date can be assigned (I am of course leaving out of account here the Chinese productions, which go back at least six centuries earlier) is the so-called Gutenberg Bible—in fact ascribable to Gutenberg only in part, and for that reason frequently called the Mazarin Bible, after the collection in which a copy was first recorded. This is undated, but was certainly in print before the end of 1455 and was presumably produced in the second half of that year. There is at least one earlier example of printing—an ecclesiastical Letter of Indulgence, on a single sheet, which was produced from type cast in a mold in this same place in 1454 (another is dated 1455).[1] The first mention of Hebrew printing goes back, however, ten years before this date, to the period of experiment of which only vague and tantalizing records survive.

A remarkable but little-known notarial document, found some years ago, illustrates the cordial relations that prevailed toward the end of the first half of the fifteenth century at Avignon, the papal city in southeastern France, between a goldsmith from

---

[1] The first printed volume which actually bears a date is the psalter published by Gutenberg's associates, Fust and Schoeffer, in 1457. The smaller of the two types used in this work appears also in an apparently more primitive form in an undated Missal according to the use of Constance (*Missale speciale Constantiense*) which is therefore considered by some scholars to have appeared some time between 1444 and 1448, thus anticipating the "Gutenberg" Bible.

INTRODV, ctio vtilissima, Hebrai= ce discere cupientibus: cum latiori emenda tione Iohãnis Bœ schenstain.

Oratio dominica Angelica salutatio Salue regina. Hebraice.

Matthæo Adriano Equi= te Aurato inter= prete.

TITLE PAGE OF BOESCHENSTAIN'S *Hebrew Grammar*, 1520

Prague appropriately named Procop, or Procopius Waldvogel (= Wild Fowl), and a member of the local Jewish community called Davin (= David) of Caderousse (a little place near Orange). Master Procopius had either anticipated the new ideas or else, while passing through Germany in the course of his travels, had heard of the invention, then in its experimental stage, and perhaps seen how it worked (if indeed its origins went back so far). He naturally spoke of this remarkable novelty to those whom he encountered on his travels. Among those who heard his description was the Jew Davin, a dyer by profession, who was accustomed, presumably by reason of his craft, to the operation of primitive mechanical appliances; the association of dyers and weavers with early Hebrew printing was in fact very significant. He immediately realized the implications of the new invention and began to study and practice it informally under the other's guidance. He was so satisfied with the experiment that he had the idea of applying the method to Hebrew. Accordingly, in 1446, the pair of them bound themselves by a formal contract before a notary. Davin now promised to teach Procopius the art of dyeing, that ancient and traditional Jewish activity so widely followed in the south of Europe. In return, the other undertook to provide him with the twenty-seven letters of the Hebrew alphabet (the number is correct, for the five final letters are to be added to the alphabet of twenty-two letters), in accordance with the "science and practice of writing" which he had been teaching him during the past two years. *This brings the date for the beginning of this activity back to 1444—fully ten years before Gutenberg.* The letters were to be "well cut in iron," and Davin was to be provided with the necessary "instruments of timber, lead and iron" for performing the work. Similar contracts, not so detailed and without any stipulation of reciprocity or mention of previous experiment, were made contemporaneously with two non-Jews. In another contract, of April 26, 1446, Davin acknowledged that he had received the specified material in connection with the "art of artificial writing."

The precise significance of this phrase, and the implications therefore of the agreement, are not quite beyond dispute. The suggestion has been made that a sort of primitive typewriting-machine is in question, which did in fact "write artificially," or even a crude anticipation of the linotype for setting up lines of type together—of course, without its mechanical element. But all this seems a needless complication. It is evident that the idea of printing in the present-day sense was in the air in 1444. The obvious deduction is that Waldvogel had either anticipated, participated in, or become acquainted with the invention and tried to apply it—one must imagine with some success, for otherwise he would not have continued for so long, nor would he have been able to derive benefit from it. Davin de Caderousse, with the Jewish aptitude for scenting out a new idea, obviously hoped to use it for the production of Hebrew books. The papal registers make it clear that in the previous century the Jews of Avignon had been closely connected with the book trade—providing parchment, binding codices, buying and selling even strictly ecclesiastical works such as missals and pandects. Thus Davin is seen to be working within the framework of a well established local tradition. If what he attempted was not an experiment in Hebrew printing, ten years before the Gutenberg Bible, it is difficult to know how it should be described.

Unfortunately, the arrangement did not work out as anticipated. The Gentile was dissatisfied with the instruction in the art of dyeing that he had received; the Jew was possibly disappointed in the other's degree of mastery of the new art of writing and its results. A lawsuit ensued, and Davin was ordered to return the forty-eight (!) characters that he had received, and to bind himself not to impart the knowledge that he had learned to any person within a radius of thirty miles around Avignon. Whether in fact anything had actually been printed during the intervening period is unknown; certainly, nothing has survived. Nevertheless, it is natural to imagine that at least some experimental attempts were made in the course of the two years involved. In any case the documents in question are of the utmost significance to the history of printing, suggesting as they do at least the possibility that its record in Europe goes back fully ten years farther than was formerly suspected, and even that the primacy in the art belongs to France, and not to Germany. And it is of far more than merely casual interest that this remarkable anticipation is in part associated with a Jew, and with Hebrew printing.

Apart from this tantalizing glimpse (for it is nothing more), we have to wait another thirty years—twenty years, that is, after the publication of the "Gutenberg" Bible—for the earliest authenticated Hebrew printing. In 1464, the new art had been introduced by wandering German craftsmen to Italy, and soon became firmly established there: it is said that, in consequence, the price of mass-books was so much reduced that many Jewish loan-bankers incurred great losses! It was with this country that the assured beginnings of Hebrew typography are associated. In 1475, two presses were at work at opposite ends of the peninsula, certainly in complete ignorance of each other's existence. At tiny Piove di Sacco in the north, not far from Padua, in the area of German influence, the physician Meshullam Cuzi was superintending the production of the code *Arba'a Turim* of Jacob ben Asher of Toledo. In the extreme south, at the city of Reggio di Calabria, on the straits of Messina, Abraham ben Garton was at work on an edition of the classical commentary of Rashi on the Pentateuch. It was a less ambitious production and, although he may have begun later, he was the first to finish, on Adar 10th 5235 (= February 17, 1474/5: this is the correct date given in the colophon, which is quoted inaccurately by some authorities); the first of the four volumes of the other work appeared only in July. Only one copy of the Rashi survives—that in the famous De' Rossi collection of Parma; and even this is not quite complete, the first leaves having been supplied from another early edition. At one time, however, De' Rossi, that great eighteenth-century Christian Hebraist, owned another copy; but it was lost in the River Po while in transit to his library.[2]

Abraham ben Garton, then, has the distinction of having produced the earliest dated Hebrew book. Whether it is in fact the earliest in time is questionable. It may be that some other volumes

---

[2] The present writer must, however, place on record the fact that one day during the war of 1939-45 he had, to his amazement, a copy offered to him, with an entire collection of similar rarities. While he was excitedly exploring some means of acquiring the collection, it transpired that an ignorant clerk had copied the marked items out of a printed list of incunabula; these, however, denoting not the works for disposal, but the desiderata—including every unicum and impossible rarity in early Hebrew typography!

which do not bear a date preceded it, and it is believed by some experts that perhaps the oldest Hebrew printing of which specimens survive was executed in Rome—the cradle of Italian printing—where certain works, obviously (even to the least expert eye) very early indeed, are believed to have been produced not later than 1470.

No more than two years after the first recorded Hebrew printing, we find our first mention of a Jewish printer of non-Jewish books. His name is not known, but the work with which he was associated was one of supreme importance—none other than Dante's *Divina commedia*, printed in Naples in 1477—preceded only by the three editions (Foligno, Mantua and Venice) of 1472, and generally considered to be superior to them. The work was anonymously produced, but the fact that the date is given *adi xii del mese di Aprile, M.CCCC.LXXVII*, without the habitual (though not indeed invariable) *anno domini* or *anno salutis*, and that the volume ends with the religiously neutral valediction, *Laus Deo* (without any Christological flavor) seems to indicate Jewish association. This, however, is not the reason for, though it is confirmation of, the ascription of the work to a Jewish printer. In the following year or soon thereafter (the date is not given, but the indications are clear enough), the famous Neapolitan printer Francesco del Tuppo, who was later to be associated with some of the loveliest achievements of Italian printing, also published in this same city an edition of Dante's ever-popular work. The methodical reader must have been mystified when he found at the end of the *Purgatorio*, after the normal pious valedictory, the words: "Let the unhappy Jew blush for shame" (*Erubescat Judeus infelix*). He would have found the explanation when he reached the end of the volume where, by way of colophon, there is appended a letter of thanks from the printer to the representatives (*electi*) of the city of Naples, in which the printer gave an obviously one-sided account of the circumstances in which the work had been produced. After a virulent attack on the Jews, from the time of the capture of Jerusalem by Titus down to the Ritual Murder accusation at Trent "not long since" (1475), he delivered a virulent tirade on a Jewish business rival. This "arrogant Jew" (*fiero Iudio*), it seems, had had the temerity to engage in similar activity as his own and had apparently re-

Quale ilgeometra che tutto saffige
permisurar locerchio & non ritroua
pensando quel principio ondelli indige
T alera io aquella uista noua
ueder uolea come siconuenne
limago alcerchio & come uisindona
M a non eran daccio lepropie penne
se non chelamia mente fu percossa
da unfulgore inche sua uolglia uenne
A lalta fantasia qui manco possa
magia uolgea ilmio disio iluelle
sicome rota cheigualmente e mossa
L amor chemuouel sole & laltre stelle

Finisse la tertia & ultima Comedia di
Paradiso. delo excellentissimo poeta
laureato Dante: alleghien di firenze.
Impresso nela magnifica cipta di Na
poli: cū ogni diligentia & fede. Sotto
lo inuictissimo Re Ferdinande inclito
Re de Sicilia. &cť. Adi XII. dil mese
di Aprile. M. CCCC. LXXVII.

LAVSDEO

COLOPHON OF THE EDITION OF THE *Divina Commedia*, PRINTED IN
1477 IN NAPLES BY A JEWISH PRINTER

ceived a copyright for an edition of the *Commedia*. When Del Tuppo's was announced, he procured some sort of judicial or administrative injunction for the printing to be stopped, "finding plausible reason for his action." It was only as a result of the support of the *electi* of the city that the order was rescinded, and Del Tuppo was able to resume his work. The only edition of Dante that can possibly be referred to in this curious document is that which appeared anonymously in Naples in 1477, referred to above. Can Abraham ben Garton, the Hebrew printer of Reggio di Calabria (who disappears from view after 1475), have been responsible for it? It is possible, though hardly more than this. But it is interesting to note that in Naples too there is some evidence of Jewish participation in the general book trade in this early period.

The conventional ascription of the beginning of Hebrew typography to Reggio di Calabria in 1475 gives rise to certain problems. This backward and remote area is in fact an unlikely one for an innovation of this sort. Moreover, the printer does not seem to suggest in his colophon that there was anything strikingly novel in his enterprise. He was, as he implies, an immigrant—very likely a Spaniard, for Spanish influence was strong throughout this area— and uses a Spanish rather than Italian type of character. It is thus conceivable, at least, that Hebrew printing was being carried on in Spain before this date, being transported thence into Italy, where it flourished so remarkably in the first generations of its existence. The association of Jews with the art of printing in Spain and in the Iberian Peninsula was certainly of the utmost importance. At one time, about ninety out of the hundred known Hebrew incunabula (that is, books printed before 1500) were from Italian presses. During the last generation, their number has been supplemented by a large number of works or (especially) fragments of works mostly printed in Spain. With the recent discoveries the total number has now risen to approximately 150, of which 103 (or some two-thirds) are of Italian origin; and it is thus conceivable that the Spanish productivity before the expulsion of 1492, which wrought such havoc and destroyed so much, may have equaled the Italian. The reader must be reminded that the new evidence that has accumulated (as indeed some of the old) is based to a considerable degree on single copies or fragments—or even single leaves. A trivial accident would have destroyed many of these as well, so that the argument from silence is in this case by no means final.

On the basis of our state of knowledge a few years since, such early productivity in Spain would have seemed improbable, for it was formerly believed that the history of general printing in this country went back only to 1475—the same year as the recorded beginning of Hebrew printing in Italy—when Lambert Palmert set up his press in Valencia. We now know, however, that he was anticipated at least two, and perhaps five, years earlier by a press in Segovia. The first dated production of the Hebrew press in the country belongs apparently to 1476, but there is a little doubt about the precise details. In any case, is this the earliest product of a Spanish-Jewish printing-press? Here, we are plunged immediately into fresh mystification, the final solution to which has yet to be found.

In August 1481, in the course of proceedings before the Inquisition at Seville, a certain Diego Fernandez testified that, at Montalban (near Toledo) some four or five years before, he had been acquainted with a converted Jew named Juan de Lucena, now living as a refugee in Rome. At the time in question, the Jew was engaged in producing "many printed books in Hebrew" (*muchos libros de ebrayco de molde*), some of which he took with him to sell in Granada. In a later process, two of his assistants (one of them a locksmith) gave evidence, being described as "writers and typographers of printed books." They too testified how, some time previously, they had worked for a period of two years with Juan de Lucena in his Hebrew printing-press in Toledo and Montalban. His daughters Teresa and Catalina, moreover, at their subsequent trials by the Inquisition (in the latter case, as late as 1531), confessed that they had helped their father in his work of printing books in Hebrew characters.

Precisely when this took place is not stated. But, as has been indicated, Diego Fernandez makes it clear that Lucena had been engaged in it four or five years before his deposition—that is, in 1476-77; nor is it suggested here that this was necessarily the period of the beginning of his activity, which, as we know from the other testimonies, continued for at least two years. In any case, we now have evidence of the existence of an active Hebrew typography in Spain at a period very shortly after the origins of

Spanish printing in Latin characters. Moreover, Abraham ben Garton's activity at Reggio in 1475 seems to suggest, as we have seen, an anterior press in Spain, whose productions have been lost. The exciting and by no means preposterous possibility opens up that the Jews may in fact have been the pioneers of printing in that country.

All this however is conjectural; and the first product of the Hebrew printing-press in Spain that has survived is the commentary of Rashi on the Bible (the same much-loved work as was chosen by Abraham ben Garton) completed by Solomon Alkabez at Guadalajara on September 1, 1476. Unfortunately, the year of publication of this work is not indicated quite clearly, but the printer's colophon makes it certain that it was his first production. The characters were cut for him, as he gratefully records, by a Christian craftsman, Pedro de Guadalajara, presumably that same Maestro Pedro who was responsible for the Gothic type used by Antonio Martinez at Seville in 1486 for Cavalca's *Espejo de la Cruz*. The collaboration of Jewish technicians and Christian craftsmen, which recurs throughout the early history of Hebrew printing, is noteworthy. This Hebrew volume is, it seems, the first known work printed in Spain of a purely Spanish character, with native and not imported type, as was the case with the earliest non-Jewish books produced here.

The most memorable link between Hebrew and non-Hebrew printing in Spain in this adventurous period is a certain scholarly silversmith named Solomon Zalmati, a native of Jativa in Aragon. This place is itself of very great interest in book history, because the earliest known paper-mill in Christian Europe was one run by the Jews in this place in 1273.[3] It is unnecessary to emphasize

---

[3] The original document referring to the tax levied by King Jaime I to protect the native paper industry refers to the *aljame Saracenorum Xative*, but the heading refers to the Jewish community, and André Blum (*Origin of Paper*, New York, 1934, pp. 26-27, which should be referred to also for other details) is confident that the allusion is to them. It is of interest in this connection that in the fifteenth century the Jews of the Duchy of Urbino dealt on a large scale in paper acquired in bulk from the ducal mills (G. Luzzatti, *I Banchieri ebrei in Urbino*, pp. 26-27). The oldest dated Hebrew MS. on paper is apparently one in the British Museum of 977 (MS. Or. 5538); but it is claimed that some specimens extant are of the eighth century.

the importance which the replacement of vellum by paper had for the diffusion of culture; for paper, unlike the other substance, was available in unlimited quantities. But in the twelfth century Peter the Venerable, Abbot of Cluny, had regarded the use in books of a writing material made of rags as an objectionable Jewish innovation, fit only for their preposterous Talmud!

In 1483, Zalmati was living in Murcia, where he entered into relations with Alfonso Fernandez de Córdoba—one of the important figures in early Spanish typography, who cut some exceptionally lovely types and was associated with many memorable productions, including Lambert Palmert's Valencian Bible of 1477/8. On July 31, 1483, Zalmati, De Córdoba and another Christian, Gabriel Luis Arinyo, entered into a partnership for printing certain theological works. This consortium apparently produced the commentary on the Psalms by Jaime Perez, Bishop of Cristopoli (Valencia, 1484), and probably his minor writings (*Opuscula*) in the following year—these including an anti-Jewish polemic by him, *Tractatus contra judaeos!*—as well as a life of Saint Anna. In the course of these transactions, De Córdoba spoke of Zalmati in such terms as to make it clear that he, great master though he was, considered him an expert in the art of printing.

Shortly thereafter, another work of very great importance appeared, also of exclusive theological significance, in which De Córdoba and Zalmati (though not Arinyo) were apparently associated. This was the Church Ritual according to the usage of Saragossa (*Manuale Caesaraugustanum*), believed to have been printed at Hijar in 1486 by De Córdoba, the characters and decorations being very similar to those which he designed and used. The association of this beautiful work with Zalmati seems to be made certain by one curious fact. Around the first page there is a superb decorative border, which has been described as being of a Jewish type, and was presumably designed and engraved by De Córdoba himself. As it happens, this same border appears again, around the Song of Moses in Exodus, in a Hebrew Pentateuch produced about the same time at Hijar by Zalmati's partner in Hebrew printing, Eliezer Alantansi. This seems to make it certain that Zalmati was associated with De Córdoba in the production of the *Manuale* (as he had been in earlier works). It suggests, moreover, the likelihood that De Córdoba, conversely, may have cut the types and the decorations (some of them very lovely) used in Alantansi's press.

But we have not yet finished with the story of the decorative border that has been mentioned. We find it used again in Lisbon by Eleazar Toledano in two Hebrew works produced in 1489. When the Jews were expelled from Portugal in 1497, it was apparently taken, with other printing materials, to the East, and here it was used in Constantinople in various works produced between 1505 and 1509. It is an extraordinary odyssey, unparalleled in typographical history.

The sharing of decorative borders by Hebrew and non-Hebrew books at this period was not confined to Spain. A border which appears in Francesco del Tuppo's *Aesop* (Naples, 1485)—one of the loveliest of fifteenth-century publications—occurs also in the first complete edition of the Hebrew Bible (Soncino, 1488) and in various other Hebrew works produced here at this time. The *Aquila volante* ascribed to Leonardo Aretino, published at Naples by Ayolfus de Cantono in 1492, has a very pleasing border depicting a fanciful hunting scene which was used almost simultaneously in the same place by the Jew Asriel Gunzenhausen in printing his edition of Bahya's commentary on the Pentateuch. We are informed in the colophon to this work that the craftsman who collaborated in it, "an able engraver, skilled in the art of wood-engraving, for everything connected with printing," was the publisher's brother-in-law, Moses ben Isaac. It is obviously implied that he was responsible for the border mentioned above, in which case he was the artist to whom the Italian publisher, too, had turned in the first instance. This border, also, was later used in certain Hebrew books printed in Constantinople. The whole story illustrates the close association and collaboration in certain circumstances between Jewish and non-Jewish enthusiasts who were engaged in this exciting new profession, which was probably not confined to these few cases that can be definitely proved.

After the Expulsion of the Jews from Spain in 1492, an important center still flourished on the peninsula for some few years in Portugal, where a large proportion of the exiles found temporary refuge. Here indeed the share of the Jews in cultural

THE SECOND PRINTED HEBREW BIBLE, NAPLES, 1491: BEGINNING OF
THE BOOK OF JOSHUA
(Engraved border ascribed to Moses ben Isaac)

life at this time was in some respects of such importance that
Dom Manuel, the last monarch of the country, in his monumental
work written in exile, *Early Portuguese Books* (London, 1932),
was able to say that "the Renaissance found Portugal ready to
receive its impetus because the ground had already been prepared
partly by the learned Portuguese Jews." This was the case particularly in connection with the art of printing: it is indeed the
only country of the Christian world (in the non-Christian world
matters were different, as we shall see) in which the part played
by Jews in the art of typography in these early days was of de-
cisive importance. Hebrew printing began in Portugal in 1487,
non-Hebrew printing only in 1494; and, of the twenty-four
known Portuguese incunabula, the first eleven in chronological
sequence are those printed in Hebrew. Ninety-five copies of
Hebrew incunables printed in Portugal were known to exist according to a census made in 1932; but only twenty-two of Portuguese. Imported printed books were indeed known in Portugal
from 1481, while there is a vague and probably inaccurate reference to a non-Hebrew work produced there in 1490, but even
this would be three years later than the Hebrew Pentateuch published at Faro by Samuel Gacon in 1487. For purposes of comparison, it must be added that no Latin work printed in the
country before 1494, or Portuguese book printed before 1495,
is known to exist. It is thus apparent that, whereas in other European countries (with the reservations indicated above) the Jewish
printers followed in the path blazed out by their non-Jewish
fellow-workers, in Portugal they were indubitably the pioneers.

Not only did they pioneer in Hebrew printing, but they made
their contribution to non-Hebrew printing as well. For, within
two years of the production of the first Latin work in the country,
and within one year of the appearance of the first in Portuguese,
one of the Hebrew printers produced what is from some points
of view the most important production of the early Portuguese
printing-press. Samuel d'Ortas (perhaps of Orthez in Navarre,
for he indicates that he was a stranger from a distant place) was
engaged in Hebrew printing at Leiria north of Lisbon from 1492
to 1497. In 1496, there appeared in this place, from the press of
the *vir solers Magister Orta*, one of the fundamental works of
Renaissance science, which has been referred to already in another

connection—the astronomical tables and perpetual almanac (*Tabulae tabularum coelestium motuum: sive almanach perpetuum*) by Abraham Zacuto, which, intended no doubt for astrological use, became invaluable for navigators in the great period of maritime discovery that had now dawned. This work was edited, translated and prepared for the press by the author's pupil, Joseph Vecinho (later to be dragooned into Christianity, under the name of Diego Mendes), and several extant copies, perhaps given to him for distribution, bear his badge. It actually appeared in two distinct editions, for some copies have the twenty folios which contain the *canones*, or general material, not in Latin but in Spanish. These are of special interest in typographical history, for they constitute the only known incunable printed in the country whose text is neither in Latin, nor in Hebrew, nor in Portuguese. It may be observed that a copy of this work is in the Bibliotheca Colombina in Seville which embodies the collection of Christopher Columbus, and may have been owned by him (it bears manuscript annotations in the hand of his son). Indeed, it is believed that it was with the aid of this work that he "prophesied" an imminent eclipse of the moon, when he was threatened by the natives in Jamaica in 1504, thus extricating himself from a very dangerous predicament. Apart from this, it is likely enough that Columbus carried with him on his first journeys the manuscript copy of Zacuto's *Tables* now in this same library—an invaluable aid for navigation.

When in 1497 the Jews were driven out of Portugal, they conveyed some of their types and perhaps their presses with them to Fez. The well known commentary on the ritual by David Abudrahim was produced here with this material in 1516. This is the first work printed in Africa, anticipating by well over a century the volume believed (and even this is not certain) to have been printed in Funchal, on the island of Madeira, in 1637, or the other hypothetical instance perhaps produced on the mainland, at Loanda on the west coast of Africa, in 1641. Similarly, printing was introduced to the Near East by the Hebrew press set up in Constantinople in 1493, and the earliest work printed by the European method anywhere in Asia is a Hebrew commentary on the Book of Esther which appeared in Safed in Palestine, the great center of cabalistic studies, in 1577. In Egypt, where a European press was started only in 1798, during Napoleon's expedition, and

Arabic printing began later still, Hebrew printers had been active at least as early as 1557.

Essentially the home of Hebrew publishing in the early days was, as has been indicated, Italy, which had become the great center of the printing craft in general. Indeed, a vast majority not merely of Hebrew incunabula before 1500, but of all Hebrew works published up to the end of the sixteenth century, was produced in that country, to a great extent by non-Jews, such as the Flemish merchant Daniel Bomberg, with whom the story of Hebrew printing in Venice is inextricably associated, and who has been spoken of in the previous chapter as one of the outstanding Christian Hebraists of that age. But the most famous name in the annals of Hebrew printing in Italy is that of Soncino—a small place in Lombardy, whence the family which began its activity there derived its surname. Its most prolific member at the outset was Joshua Solomon Soncino, who (at the beginning in association with his father, Israel Nathan) was active at Soncino, Casalmaggiore, and then Naples between 1484 and 1492, printing in all about forty volumes. He was, however, far outdone ultimately, both in productivity and in ubiquity, by his nephew, Gershom ben Moses Soncino, who produced some seventeen incunabula before 1500, and between that date and 1534 a further eighty or more Hebrew works in Italy, in addition to others later on in the Levant. A single family thus produced more than one-third of all Hebrew incunabula—more than one-half of those known until a few years ago.

Gershom Soncino's itinerary can be marked by the places associated with his imprint: Soncino, Brescia, Barco, Fano, Pesaro, Ortona, Rimini, and then Salonica and Constantinople, where his son Eliezer continued his activity for some years after his death. He was succeeded in turn by a grandson, a second Gershom. (I mention only the most important members of this family, whose name commands respect even after this long interval of time.)

Gershom Soncino the elder was born in Italy and brought up in the versatile humanistic tradition of Italian Jewry. His interests extended beyond the bounds of the traditional Jewish literature that had engaged the attention of his uncle and the other members of his family. In 1502, accordingly, while his press was situated in Fano, he produced the first of a series of Latin and Italian works through which his name is memorable in the history of general printing in Italy, and (it may be said) in the cultural history of the Renaissance in its wider sense. In the course of the next quarter of a century, he published something like one hundred such volumes (approximately the same as the total of his Hebrew productions, which were, however, spread over a longer period) bearing the imprints Fano, Pesaro, Ancona, Ortona, Rimini and Cesena. It will be noticed that in two of these places (Ancona and Cesena) he did no Hebrew printing. In these works, his name figures in a Latin form, as Hieronymus (= Geronimo [Jerome]) or Girolamo; it is perhaps worth while to observe that he never actually mentions the Italian form generally used in references to him. Any lingering doubts as to the identification of the printer of the Hebrew and non-Hebrew works are settled by the fact that in one case both forms of the name, Latin and Hebrew, figure together, while in one Hebrew publication he specifically mentions his activity in Latin and the vernacular.

Much has been written about Gershom Soncino and his work, and it is needless to do more here than to mention briefly a few points of special interest, which illustrate his role in Italian cultural life. For example, Francesco Griffo da Bologna cut for him an "improved" version of the italic type he had made just before for the great Aldo in Venice, thus understandably arousing the latter's ire and initiating a virulent polemic. In this type he produced at Fano a new edition of Petrarch in competition with Aldo's, embodying material never previously used which has now entered into the canon of the poet's writings. This he dedicated to no less a person than Cesare Borgia, then at the height of his power, to whom he owed his right of residence.[4] He inscribed other

---

[4] In the Dedication to Borgia, Soncino stated the facts as he saw them: "It was Francesco of Bologna who conceived the new form of letters, known as Cursive or Chancery, of which neither Aldus, nor those who wish to trick themselves out in borrowed plumes, are the authors, but assuredly the said Francesco, who invented and designed them. Indeed, he designed all the types of which Aldo has at any time made use, as also that in which this book is printed, from which the reader may judge their excellence."

works to such personages as the Bishop of Fossombrone, or the Duke and Duchess of Urbino. He employed as literary editor the well known humanist Lorenzo Bevilaqua (= Drink-water: better known by his semi-jocular name of Abstemio) the former librarian of the Duke of Urbino, who after the rise of the Borgia had left that city and settled in Fano as a teacher of grammar. This conscientious scholar exhorted all those who owned manuscripts of good Latinity to insure immortality by sending them to his employer for publication. In 1508, Gershom was summoned back to Fano after a brief absence specifically to print the City Statutes, for which purpose a house and proofreaders were placed at his disposal by the Priors. He carried this task out so satisfactorily that later he was entrusted with the publication of the statutes of the cities of Jesi (1516) and of Rimini (1525). He produced, in addition to literary works, certain volumes of specifically Christian and narrowly theological significance—for example, his beautiful edition of Cardinal Vigerio's *Decachordum christianum*, illustrated with engravings ascribed to Florio Vavassore (Pesaro, 1507), or the "Rules of the Franciscan Order" (Pesaro, 1507), or the "Privileges of the Eremite Friars" (Pesaro, 1515). He even published an anti-Jewish polemic, Galatinus' *Arcana catholicae veritatis* (Ortona, 1518), enriched with Hebrew verses in praise of the author. He had obviously been unable to refuse this kind of work, even if it had not been redeemed to some extent by the favorable attitude which the author adopted toward Johannes von Reuchlin, the great German defender of Hebrew literature.[5] He produced in addition some contemporary works of belles-lettres by persons such as Lorenzo de' Medici or Ariosto.

He made use also of an elegant Greek type, and even of Ethiopic characters, thus being a pioneer in remoter branches of study. A member of his family, Alberto Soncino (perhaps to be identified with his son, in Hebrew, Eliezer) contributed a laudatory Latin dystich to his publication of Pindar's *De bello troiano* (Fano, 1515), notwithstanding the fact that this work is disfigured by a

---

[5] It was this book which was discussed at the encounter between Amatus Lusitanus and Azariah de' Rossi: see below, p. 228.

vulgar anti-Jewish poem by Battista Guarini, and an Italian sonnet to Andrea Senofonte's delightful formulary of love letters, *Flos amoris* (Cesena, 1527). This last work—unusual phenomenon—was actually dedicated by the author to his publisher in an affectionate letter. An Italian scholar has written of Gershom Soncino that he was second only to Aldo in the sumptuous novelty and perfection of his productions.

In the long run, however, the difficulties against which Soncino had to contend, faced as he was with the competition of Aldo in the general sphere and of Bomberg in the Hebrew, proved excessive for him. In a rabbinic volume published at Rimini in 1525/6, he announced his intention of giving up his non-Hebrew printing, as he did very shortly thereafter, the *Flos amoris* being one of his last productions. In 1529, we find him at work in Salonica, and in the next year in Constantinople, complaining how unfair competition had driven him from his native land. In the quarter of a century in which he had been engaged in his general printing work in Italy he had, however, made an imperishable name in typographical history and exemplified, as perhaps no other single individual had done, how closely Jewish and Italian cultural life could be integrated in this age.

Just a quarter of a century after Geronimo Soncino left Italy, the tradition of vernacular printing was resumed, though under quite different circumstances, in Ferrara. He had published works in Latin and in Italian, specifically for the non-Jewish public. The Ferrara publications, on the other hand, were intended predominantly for a category of Jews who were ignorant of Hebrew but were desperately in need of Jewish literature—that is to say, for the marranos of Spain, and especially of Portugal, who were at this time beginning to establish themselves in Italy in such great numbers. For their use, a scholarly enthusiast belonging to this same category, Yom-tob Athias (known, before he escaped from Portugal, as Jeronimo de Vargas) began to publish at Ferrara in 1552 a series of liturgical translations in Spanish: later on, he was first joined and then (perhaps on his death) superseded by the more enterprising and more prolific Abraham Usque, alias Duarte Pinhel. The works issued from this press are memorable by reason of the fact that they initiated the tradition of the printed vernacular literature of the Jews which in our own days has produced some noteworthy fruits. The most important of the publications in question was the great Ferrara Bible, in Spanish, of 1553, which is one of the classics in this field of literature. These volumes, of a religious nature and intended expressly for Jewish use (though the Bible appeared also in a form adapted to some extent for Christian readers), need not detain us in our present survey. Three works of the series, however, are noteworthy in the field of general letters. One is the great historical threnody by the publisher's kinsman, Samuel Usque, *Consolaçam as tribulaçoens de Israel* ("Consolation for the Tribulations of Israel," 1553) which, though written for a Jewish public, is now considered a classic of Portuguese literature.[6] Another is *Vysion delectable de la philosophia* (1554) by Alfonso de la Torre, a noteworthy humanistic production of the Spanish Renaissance, whose author (who made considerable use of Maimonides' *Guide for the Perplexed*) was probably himself a marrano. The third, and from this point of view the most important, was the first known edition (1554) of the famous pastoral and chivalrous romance, *Menina e Moça*, by Bernardim Ribeiro, the father of bucolic prose and verse in Portugal. This seductive work is unquestionably among the most important imaginative productions of the sixteenth century. The fact that the Jew Abraham Usque should have interested himself in it, and that he should have been, so far as is known, the first to publish it, is remarkable, and various hypotheses have been put forward to explain the fact. Ribeiro is known to have been banished from the Portuguese court in consequence of a romantic episode of youth; and it has been conjectured that in the course of his wanderings he found himself in Italy, where his marrano compatriots befriended him, undertaking also the publication of his work. Another hypothesis is that the Usques brought the volume with them in manuscript when they fled from Lisbon, that its style and composition may be traced in the pastoral dialogue which is the setting of Samuel Usque's *Consolaçam*, and that Abraham Usque published it when he heard of the author's unhappy death in 1552. But an even more remarkable theory has

---

[6] See below.

been put forward: that the latter was in fact identical with the Jewish pastoral writer, Samuel Usque, under which name he returned to Judaism in maturity. It is indubitable in any case that the family stood in close relationship to the writer who "introduced the suave pastoral style and a deep love of nature into Portuguese letters."[7]

Abraham Usque's activity as a printer in the vernacular ended at the beginning of the great counter-offensive of the Popes against the marranos in Italy in 1555. The sequence was broken. It is true that Dr. Jacob Marcaria, who had published a number of Hebrew books in Riva di Trento between 1539 and 1562 under the protection of Cardinal Cristoforo Madrucci (whose coat-of-arms surmounted by a tasseled hat often decorated the title-pages), had his services utilized in 1562-63 by some of the assembled prelates for printing various Latin opuscula concerning the newly-reassembled Council of Trent. The chief value of these publications is as curiosities, though under the circumstances the curiosity is considerable. To find a Jewish publisher of vernacular works in the full tradition of Geronimo Soncino it is necessary to wait until the nineteenth century; one who combined his warm Jewish interests and scholarship with significant vernacular activity has never yet reëmerged.

By this time, a new atmosphere prevailed in Italy so far as Hebrew publications were concerned. In 1548, the Bomberg press in Venice had closed its doors, after some thirty years of fruitful activity. In its last days it had encountered a good deal of competition, especially from Marcantonio Giustiniani, a member of a famous patrician family, who in 1545 had established a Hebrew press near the Rialto and now enjoyed a monopoly for a few years. Hebrew types were cut for him by craftsmen of the ability and reputation of Michel Dubois and Guillaume le Bé, great names

---

[7] It may be mentioned at this point that marrano descent is generally ascribed to another of the great Portuguese writers of the period—Jorge de Montemayor (c. 1520-61) whose *Diana* of 1559 (written in Spanish) was perhaps the most important pastoral novel of the sixteenth century. The first work of the sort published in Spain, it was the starting point of a universal literary fashion and the indirect source of an episode in Shakespeare's *Two Gentlemen of Verona.*

in the history of typography.[8] The last-named mentions in a letter how he was conducted to Giustiniani's press near the Rialto by a certain Master Leon, a Jew, whom he describes as a queer person, possessed of a great knowledge of the finer points of Hebrew calligraphy and literature, although by calling he was a dealer in second-hand clothing.

For a year or so, Giustiniani's press was one of three in the entire world engaged in Hebrew printing; it somewhat abused the special position which it enjoyed. At this time Rabbi Meir of Padua, one of the most distinguished of the contemporary Italian scholars of the old school, had ready for publication a new edition of Maimonides' legal code. Finding the conditions imposed by Giustiniani too onerous, he came to an agreement with another Venetian aristocrat, named Alvise Bragadini, under whose name a new press was founded which published the work in 1550. Giustiniani promptly had another edition prepared, which he threw on the market, no doubt at a low price, in the hope of ruining the rival enterprise. Rabbi Meir obtained therefore a copyright for his edition from some of his rabbinical colleagues, who banned the other one. Giustiniani retorted by denouncing the rival work to Rome, as containing material offensive to the Holy Catholic faith. It was not difficult for him to find apostates who would support this point of view and indicate passages which, by

---

[8] Guillaume le Bé, a native of Troyes (the place of residence of the great medieval French Jewish scholar, Rashi) worked in Venice from 1545 to 1550, when he went to Rome at the time of the solemnization of the Jubilee. Afterwards he returned to France, and continued to work at his craft until his death there in 1598. In his scrapbooks, in which he pasted specimens of his work, there are notes such as the following: "In the year 1573 I made this likeness and drawing of the Hebrew alphabet, preserving its best characteristics as it has been handed down from antiquity, in the judgment of the persons most experienced in Hebrew lettering among those of their religion and nation in the city of Venice, where I dwelled five years or more, on the basis of the sketches and rough scribblings I made whilst I was there." He retained his interest until his last years: in another note he informs us that "in the year 1591, after the siege of Paris, during the great troubles, I amused myself by making these likenesses of big (Hebrew) letters: one for text and the other for glosses. This second is a running letter, which the Hebrews use for their accounts and business. . . ."

dint of some dialectical effort and the suppression of the context, could be interpreted in an objectionable fashion. Bragadini was not long in following suit, denouncing on similar grounds and through similar means the works published by his competitor. Soon there were two rival sets of renegades at Rome working on behalf of the one printer or the other and systematically maligning, partly from interest and partly from spite, some of the noblest products of the Jewish intellect—especially the Talmud, republished by Giustiniani a few years before.

At Rome, under the threat of the Reformation, the spirit of the Catholic Reaction was now beginning to triumph, and the censorship of heretical publications had recently begun under the supervision of the Inquisition. The atmosphere was thus highly propitious for action. On August 12, 1553, after a commission of cardinals had formally reported in an adverse sense, the Pope issued a decree stigmatizing the Talmud and the kindred works as blasphemous, and condemning it to be burned. A month later, on the Jewish New Year's Day, an auto-da-fè was held on the Campo de' Fiori in Rome, at which Hebrew books in enormous number, seized almost haphazardly from the Jewish houses, were committed to the flames. Immediately afterwards, an edict was issued by the Inquisition summoning all rulers, bishops and inquisitors throughout Italy to take similar steps. The Renaissance spirit was belied by the implicit obedience with which this order was obeyed in almost every state of the country. Especially drastic was the action in Venice, where the accumulated stocks in the printers' warehouses afforded special opportunities for destruction, and where orders were issued that not merely the Talmud but all "compendia, summaries, and other works dependent thereon" were to be surrendered. The phraseology was so comprehensive as to embrace almost all Jewish books, so that sometimes even copies of the Bible itself were added to the pyre.

The Jewish communities could not look on idly while this was happening. The rabbis of Rome made counter-representations to the Pope and found support from at least one enlightened member of the Sacred College, Cardinal Sacristo; nevertheless, they could obtain only minor concessions. In June 1554, representatives of the Italian rabbinate met together in Ferrara to consider the new situation, which implied disaster to the entire community if anything henceforth appeared which could be interpreted in an anti-Christian sense. They coped with the problem by instituting a preliminary censorship of their own, ordering that no book should be printed without the license of three duly ordained rabbis and the lay leaders of the nearest large community. The system, clearly modeled on that which had by now become familiar in the outside world, obviously lent itself to abuses; instituted to prevent the publication of what might be considered objectionable by the Church, it came to be used in the end as a means of suppressing what one scholar or another happened to consider contrary to the doctrine of the Synagogue.

This was the first of the series of blows which ended the bright Renaissance noonday of Italian Jewry. In May 1555, Cardinal Caraffa, embodiment and inspirer of the Catholic Reaction, was elected Pope, taking the name of Paul IV; his bull *Cum nimis absurdum*, of July 12 of that same year, initiated the ghetto system and all its horrors for the Jews of his states. Thereafter, except for one or two brief interludes of relative mildness—preëminently under Sixtus V (1585-90), under whom the former spirit temporarily revived—Italian Jewry lay under an ever-thickening cloud. The spirit of the Renaissance had merged into the Baroque.

But it was not dead among the Jews of Italy. Now that the Talmud was banned, sneered a moralist of the next generation, his co-religionists could use Boccaccio's *Decameron* as a handbook to morality and religion.

NINE

Art *and* Artists

In a former generation, it was generally assumed that representational art had been unknown among the Jews before the Age of Emancipation, because of their over-literal interpretation of the prohibition in the Ten Commandments: "Thou shalt not make unto thee any graven image, or any likeness of anything that is in heaven above or that is in the earth beneath or that is in the waters under the earth." There were, of course, certain periods in Jewish history when this injunction was minutely obeyed, and Jews would not tolerate even in their homes any representation, however crude, of any living thing. But recent archaeological discoveries in Palestine and elsewhere have made it clear that this attitude did not prevail universally, or at all times. There were more liberal interludes, when the interpretation of the biblical passage was conditioned by the ensuing verse: "Thou shalt not bow down to them, nor serve them," implying that the prohibition extended only to the creation of graven images *for worship*. At such times, representational art was used with relative freedom for decorative or illustrative objects—occasionally even for purposes closely associated with divine worship, or in the synagogue itself. The actual practice was naturally affected to a great extent by the environment. This, however, could act in two diametrically reverse directions—by revulsion or by attraction. If the Jew's neighbors venerated images, as in the Graeco-Roman or later in the Catholic world, he might regard them as a heinous religious offense (as was the case in first-century Judaea or nineteenth-century Poland); or, on the other hand, he might adopt the prevailing fashion and make use of pictorial art without restriction (as we find, for example, in the now-famous third-century synagogue frescoes of Dura Europos). Where, on the other hand, the Jew's neighbors did not countenance the use of images for religious purposes, he generally followed suit—as in Moslem Spain,

where representational art was taboo also in Jewish circles. Sometimes, however, as later on in a Protestant environment, he could
in such circumstances regard the question, as it were, from the
purely aesthetic angle, divorced from religious significance, this
being in general terms the background of the remarkable twentieth-century revival.

Notwithstanding these considerations, it is obvious that in the
period with which we are here dealing the Jew who had an
artistic bent suffered from grave disadvantages. This was especially the case as regards painters. For in the Renaissance environment art was still basically, if not as in a former era exclusively,
ecclesiastical and used for Church purposes—and not merely for
Church purposes, but for Church services. There was no basic
reason why a Jew should not have been employed to decorate a
Christian place of worship. But an artist was expected to create
images of the Madonna, of the Savior, of the saints, for the veneration (not to say the adoration) of the faithful. I suspect that in
this period there were among the Italian Jews a few who would
have had no objection to this, for like so many of their Christian
compatriots they could divide their minds into two separate and
almost water-tight compartments. Indeed, their action would have
been no more paradoxical than that of the painter who scribbled an
assignation with his mistress on the back of a painting of the
Madonna on which he was engaged. Moreover a traditional calling
of Roman Jews, going back to the Dark Ages and persisting in
our own day, was the sale of holy images on the steps of the
churches. On the other hand, it was clearly preposterous for a
Christian to commission a sacred painting from one who *ex
hypothesi* could not have executed it with the proper feelings of
reverence. Nor, under the circumstances, would it have been
likely for an Italian painter of note to receive a Jewish assistant
into his *bottega* for training, even had social prejudice been wholly
absent. Thus, it was almost impossible for the young Italian Jew
to graduate (as one might put it) as an artist, or to participate
in the most usual and most lucrative aspect of artistic activity,
which provided him moreover with the publicity and the practice
that might enable him to go on to other art types.

For these reasons (and assuredly for these reasons only, since the
record of recent generations has abundantly demonstrated the
degree of pent-up artistic enthusiasm and ability among them)

the participation of Jews in Renaissance art was slight. But it was not wholly absent; nor was it confined to Italy. In Spain quite a few Jewish painters are mentioned in contemporary documents, such as Abraham ben Yomtob de Salinas (1406), his son Bonastruch (1406), and Moses Aben-Forma of Saragossa (1438). Unfortunately, none of their productions has survived and they remain mere names. But the fact that Jewish artists were at work at this period makes it at least possible that the two brothers, Guillen and Juan de Levi, whose productions are beginning to attract the notice of students of the newly-revealed fifteenth-century Aragonese school of painting, were Jews, as the name seems to imply. It is a matter about which it is necessary to keep an open mind. "De Levi" is not the same as "Levi," the prefix possibly implying a place of origin; the first names are pronouncedly non-Jewish: and it is almost certain that, whatever their origin, the two professed Christianity. Nevertheless, Spanish writers have no hesitation in considering them to be of Jewish descent, at all events. From the fifteenth century onward, all callings were represented among the marranos; and it is therefore inevitable that there were artists and painters too among them. One, named Just, appeared in an auto-da-fè at this period, but there were probably others. Indeed, it has been said that one of the greatest of Spanish primitives, Bartolomé Bermejo of Cordova, was a marrano, though the evidence is feeble, being in part based on his use of Hebrew lettering in his religious paintings, a practice which was common enough elsewhere. In 1480, Queen Isabella of Castile appointed a court painter, one of whose duties it was to ensure that "no Jew or Moor paint the figure of our Lord and Redeemer, Jesus Christ, or of Holy Mary the Glorious." This certainly implies that the "infidels" had hitherto shown an unreasonable tendency to indulge in such activity. A Jewish painter of Church images, however paradoxical he might seem to us, would not therefore have occasioned excessive surprise among the Mediterranean peoples of the age of the Renaissance.[1]

However that may be, the number of Jewish painters who may be traced in Italy at this period is extremely small, and even so there is not a single name of the slightest distinction. Indeed, in

---

[1] For Jewish sculptors, etc. who were employed for ecclesiastical work, see below.

the heyday of the Renaissance only one name emerges with any clarity. At the beginning of the sixteenth century there lived in north Italy—at Venice, Mestre, and Ferrara—a certain Moses da Castelazzo, son of a German immigrant named Rabbi Abraham Sachs, who had a certain reputation as a portrait-painter and engraver. It has recently emerged that he was in close and friendly contact with Pietro Bembo, later to be a cardinal and one of the most famous men in Italy, but then young and irresponsible. A number of communications which passed between the two—partly through the intermediacy of Bembo's lady-love of the hour, Maria Savorgnan—have been preserved. On one occasion, when Moses, writing to complain of the vexations suffered by his wife, apologized for his bad Italian composition (in fact, fantastically inelegant and inaccurate), Maria snatched the pen from his hand, expressed her complete agreement, and added a few vivacious lines of her own before permitting him to resume. From this correspondence, it appears that at this time Messer Moses was at work on a medallion of Ercole I, Duke of Ferrara—unfortunately, now untraceable. For Bembo himself, he once executed a magnifying-glass.

Late in life, he apparently turned his attention to Hebraic themes, and executed (or began to execute) a series of illustrations to the Pentateuch, which he intended to have engraved on wood by his sons, artists like himself, and then to publish. In 1521, he received copyrights for this work from the Council of Ten in Venice and from the Marquess of Mantua. In the biographical details included in his petition to the Signoria, Moses stated that he had applied himself "for many years past in this happy city in making portraits of gentlemen and other famous men, so that their memory should remain for all time, and similarly in other parts of Italy."[2]

---

[2] In the original petition, he piously intimated that it was his desire to launch this achievement on the world "in laude de Messer Domenedio" or "for the praise of the Lord God." The very eminent scholar who published this document, David Kaufmann, misunderstood this common Italian idiom and observed that "A maecenas had offered himself to accept the translation of this illustrated Pentateuch: it was a certain Messer Domenedio"—one of the most amusing blunders ever made by a great savant.

Unfortunately, not a single specimen of the production of this Jewish artist is now identifiable. The same is the case with the two Jews named Angelo d'Elia (= Mordecai ben Elijah) and Giacobbe di Vitale (= Jacob ben Hayyim), who were admitted at about this same period to membership in the Painters' Guild in Perugia. To pass over into the following century, Jonah Ostiglia, of Florence, is recorded by a contemporary chronicler as a painter in the style of Salvatore Rosa; though he turned to art only when he was thirty-six years old, he was able to achieve results which could be taken for those of the master himself. There may be some works by these Jewish artists still awaiting identification, but thus far none has come to light. For the sixteenth century we are hence restricted thus far to a single not very memorable achievement—the engraved map and plans which add to the beauty of Antonio Campi's handsome volume, *Cremona fidelissima città* (Cremona, 1583). This is considered one of the most elaborately illustrated Italian works of the sixteenth century, containing as it does thirty-four portraits of rulers of the city of Cremona engraved by Annibale Carracci. The other engravings to which we have referred were the work of the Jew David da Lodi, being clearly signed "David de Laude Crem. hebreus incidi," or the like. But engraving was a different branch of art, at which it was possible to arrive by a separate route.[3]

---

[3] According to a statement made, perhaps carelessly, a generation ago, there is one outstanding exception to the generalization that no Jewish painters were at work in Italy in the Renaissance period. Umberto Cassuto, the most distinguished Italian Jewish scholar of our day, in one of his earliest articles (writing upwards of forty years ago) mentioned that a certain art historian from Ferrara had informed him that the painter Cosmè Tura (1430-98), the founder of the Ferrarese school of painting (who worked also for the counts of Mirandola) was possibly a Jew (by which he presumably meant of Jewish origin). No evidence in substantiation of this statement has been published, and it is believed the hypothesis was based only on the fact that Tura embodies Hebrew words in the architectural and decorative background of some of his paintings. One is content to accept this conclusion. Tura was the son of a cobbler, and most of his paintings were religious in character. But there is a small point, hitherto overlooked, which is worth while taking into account in connection with this discussion. Tura's masterpiece is a painting "The

194 THE JEWS IN THE RENAISSANCE

It is obvious that both the social and the religious impediment disappeared if a Jew became converted to Christianity, and there were presumably quite a number of baptized Jewish artists. There was one minor Veronese painter of the sixteenth century, Giovanni Battista Levi (c. 1552–*post* 1605), some of whose competent altar-pictures may be seen in Legnano. It is very probable that he was of Jewish extraction, though his Christian name proved clearly that he was not a professing Jew. In the next generation, two other painters of Jewish origin rose above mediocrity, at least in the eyes of contemporaries. One of the busiest church painters in Venice at this time was Francesco Ruschi, son of a once-Jewish physician (probably of Roman ghetto origin). A pupil of the popular Roman artist Giuseppe Cesari ("Il Cavaliere d'Arpino": 1568-1640), he was influenced by Caravaggio in his dramatic sense of illumination and by Pietro da Cortona in his decorative treatment of space, and was a forerunner of the specific style of the minor Venetian Renaissance of the eighteenth century; it has been said of him that he breathed new life into all the younger generation. It is interesting to note that he showed a predilection for Old Testament themes. His contemporary Pietro Liberi (1614-87), baptized son of a Paduan Jew, who settled in Venice in 1659, was more interested in altar pictures and church decoration. His eminence was such that, while working in Vienna before this,

Virgin and Christ Enthroned" in the National Gallery in London. In this work, the Ten Commandments are shown with Hebrew wording —no evidence, to be sure, that the artist was a Jew. But a close inspection demonstrates a curious fact. The first commandment begins not with the words "I am the Lord thy God who . . ." but (omitting "the Lord thy God") with "I am . . . who" (אנכי ה' אלהיך אשר not אנכי אשר). In, and for, a Christian, this alteration of wording would be incomprehensible. But a Jew, who religiously eschewed the indiscriminate use of the Hebrew Name of God and changed it wherever possible, and who would presumably have considered it sacrilegious (or nearly so) to introduce it into a church, might well have made this change. Who was responsible? Was it the painter? Or did some Jewish scholar, to whose assistance he had recourse for tracing the Hebrew letters, perform the pious fraud? The latter, in all probability; but in either case the detail does something to illustrate the relations between the Italian artists of the Renaissance period and their Jewish neighbors.

he had received from the emperor the title of count. We are now almost verging on the eighteenth century, when Anton Raphael Mengs (1728-79), similarly the son of a converted Jew, was in his day a very great figure. But this brings us too far away from the age of the Renaissance; and indeed any artist more alien to the essential Renaissance spirit it is not easy to conceive.

We have seen that in order to become a painter, it was necessary for the Jew of the Renaissance to graduate, as it were, by way of Christian religious art. There was, however, another branch of artistic activity to which this did not apply. Metalworking derived from the goldsmith's craft; and in this, from a remote antiquity, Jews had been very actively engaged. Indeed, we find Jewish goldsmiths all over the world from the Dark Ages onward. King John of England even had one in his employment at the beginning of the thirteenth century. The same was the case elsewhere: in 1345, for example, a silversmith named Moses Jacob, of Perpignan, was summoned to Barcelona by the King of Aragon to execute the ornamental metal-work for his clocks. It must be recalled that gem-dealing is one of the traditional Jewish occupations, and this inevitably led to the manufacture of the setting for gems—that is, jewelry-work in the wider sense. Large numbers of Jewish goldsmiths and jewelers may be identified in Renaissance Italy, and in Mantua there was even a "Street of the Jewish Goldsmiths," which continued in existence as late as the eighteenth century. The Formiggini family, who owned a private synagogue at Modena, were court jewelers to the dukes of the House of Este, generation after generation, for centuries, though it is unascertainable how far this tradition goes back.

These Jewish goldsmiths' main work was clearly the manufacture of articles of personal adornment. But personal adornment was more lavish then than in our day. The settings of the precious stones could sometimes be most elaborate; and in the long run there was a point where sculpture and metal-working almost overlapped. Unfortunately, such productions were in a majority of cases unsigned; but it is probable that a relatively large number of the anonymous specimens of the goldsmith's craft of the Renaissance period are of Jewish workmanship. This was the case presumably above all with objects intended for Jewish use—such as the splendid chased or enameled betrothal rings, often decorated with a representation of the Temple in Jerusalem, which were produced in great numbers in Venice in the sixteenth century. A few names, indeed, emerge of persons who worked for the Italian courts and for other secular patrons: for example, Master Isaac of Bologna, who was employed by the court of Naples in 1484. And from Bologna, too, came another person, who links up with one of the greatest names in this field. In his *Autobiography*, Benvenuto Cellini, speaking of his training and early days, records his experiences at the age of sixteen:

> When I reached Bologna, I put myself under a certain Ercole del Piffero, and began to earn something by my trade. In the meantime, I used to go every day to take my music lesson, and in a few weeks made considerable progress in that accursed art. However, I made still greater in my trade of goldsmith; for the Cardinal having given me no assistance, I went to live with a Bolognese illuminator called Scipione Cavaletti; and whilst there I devoted myself to drawing and working for one Graziadio, a Jew, with whom I earned considerably.

Graziadio (= "Thank God": that is, Elhanan, or else Judah) was, it seems, one of the local goldsmiths, who employed the gifted Florentine apprentice who had already shown his ability to design for him settings which he presumably executed himself. There can be little doubt that he guided his young employee in his work. The most famous goldsmith of the Italian Renaissance thus numbered a Jew among those who helped train him in his formative years.

Among the other eminent workers in this field of the heyday of the Renaissance there was one gifted Jew whose work emerges from the rut of anonymity. This was Salamone da Sesso, named after his native place, Sesso (near Reggio in northern Italy) where he was born in or about 1465. He was brought up as a Jew, and it was as a Jew that he learned his craft, in which he became so proficient that in 1487 he entered the service of Ercole d'Este, Duke of Ferrara. At this stage, he was persuaded to accept baptism, the duke serving as god-father; so that he was afterwards known by the latter's name, as Ercole "dei Fedeli" ("The Faith-

ful"). He remained in the service of the court of Ferrara until
his death, upwards of thirty years later. He worked occasionally
in addition for the duke's brother-in-law, the Marquess of Mantua
and at one time also for Pope Julius II. He is referred to now
as Ercole "da Pesaro," having perhaps been active at that resplendent little court as well. He was especially noted for the magnificent swords and daggers which he produced—not, as it has been
put, mere instruments for killing, but superb articles of personal
adornment, encrusted with pagan (never biblical!) scenes, classical
symbols and nude figures in the spirit of the age. He specialized
in the short swords known as *cinquedee*, of which some thirty
can now be traced, and specimens of his work are to be found
in most of the great collections of Renaissance goldsmiths' art.
The most famous is the exquisite but sinister weapon manufactured for no less eminent a person than Cesare Borgia, which has
been designated "the Queen of Swords" (long in the Gaetani collection in Rome). As has been mentioned, the artist was baptized
on entering the ducal service. His two sons, Alfonso and Ferrante
(named like himself after members of the ducal house), were also
metal-workers who enjoyed some reputation.

There were also of course others, whose work was in a humbler
sphere. A Jewish master-craftsman from Ferrara, named Jeshurun
"Tovar" (?), executed about 1460-80 for a Jewish housewife an
exquisite little box (now in the Bezalel Museum, Jerusalem), to
hold the keys of her linen cupboards; it is chased with representations of Jewish domestic scenes in niello-work. When, later on,
the Duke of Modena on one occasion sent a brace of dogs as a
present to the Duke of Savoy, a Jewish goldsmith named Samson
was entrusted with the task of making the armorial shields which
were to be affixed to their collars.

For Jewish craftsmen to execute specifically ecclesiastical work
for church use is obviously paradoxical: it suggests a degree of
tolerance, or of indifference, which before the nineteenth century would hardly be imaginable. But the paradoxical sometimes
happens. In 1415, the anti-Pope Benedict XIII, then resident in
Spain, foiled in his hope of bringing about a mass conversion of
the Jews, had issued a bull which (among many other restrictions)
forbade them to be employed in the making of ceremonial objects
for Christian use, such as chalices or crucifixes. It would be

natural to imagine that this was simply an expression of an excess of zeal. But, as it happens, we have a fully authenticated instance of the manufacture of a reliquary for the Augustinian priory in Barcelona, a few years before this, by a Jewish goldsmith, and a reliquary is specifically associated with Catholic ritual. So, too, we are informed of a certain "Rabbi" Samuel, silversmith, of Murcia, who in 1378 was given a safe conduct for three months by the Infant Juan of Aragon to travel with Jaime Sanchez, *sculptor imaginum*, whom he presumably assisted in his work; two Jewish goldsmiths, who undertook to provide a crucifix before the ensuing Christmas, are referred to in a contract made at Huesca in Spain in 1402. We thus have ample documentary evidence that Jews were in fact employed for Christian ritual art, at least in metal-working, for which they had specific qualifications.[4] Hence an unexpected verisimilitude is acquired by such curious reports as that a painting of the Madonna was executed for Edward I of England by a Jew named Marlibrun (according to her own prescriptions!), or that a Jew made a statue of St. Francis—the first of which there is any record—when he visited Guete in Spain in 1214. And it becomes more probable, or at the least less improbable, that the two distinguished Veronese bronze-workers of the seventeenth century, Joseph di Levi and Angelo de' Rossi were Jews, notwithstanding the essentially non-Jewish, and sometimes ecclesiastical, nature of their work. The one Jewish name may indeed be fortuitous. But that two persons with specifically Jewish names should work in collaboration (for Angelo de' Rossi would have been the inevitable and invariable equivalent of the Hebrew Mordecai *min haAdumim*) seems somewhat more than coincidence. It is perhaps significant that the former invariably signed his name "Joseph," not "Giuseppe," in the biblical rather than Italian form.

One of the glories of Italian handicraft in the Renaissance and

---

[4] It may be pointed out that such services were reciprocal: one of the earliest references we have to the silver ornaments for the Scroll of the Law is a contract made at Arles in 1439 between the Jewish community and a local silversmith (who bound himself not to work on the Sabbath) for the manufacture of a "Crown" for the *Sepher Torah*.

post-Renaissance periods was the manufacture of ceramics. With this the Jews had some contact; but this work too was largely anonymous, and their share in it may have been somewhat more extensive, and of more general appeal, than the positive evidence demonstrates. It is known that in 1626 a Jew named Lazzaro (= Eleazar) Levi was licensed to manufacture majolica at Mantua. No specimen of his work is recorded, though he may have been responsible for some dishes for Jewish ritual use recently found in that city. But, for a century before and after this date, we have a record of Jewish majolica makers who were active in Italy, working in the style and with the methods of the age, and in the places in which the industry reached its highest pitch of achievement. The Azulai family was active in Padua, Faenza, and Pesaro for fully two centuries (1532-1730); and there was a Cohen family in Pesaro and Ancona between 1614 and 1673, in addition to a Moses Fano who was at work in Urbino in 1556. Of their production, we know only of a series of magnificent Passover plates for use in the seder ceremony, increasingly stylized as the generations passed, and designed in the eighteenth century precisely as they had been in the seventeenth. But the manufacture of these was clearly insufficient to provide a livelihood, and presumably these craftsmen produced much more than this for general use. At the same time, the possibility suggests itself that some of the numerous specimens of Italian majolica dishes and jars bearing Old Testament and Apocryphal scenes (for example, Judith with the head of Holophernes, associated with the Hanukkah feast, and very popular in the lore of Italian Jews) may at least in some cases have been manufactured by Jewish artisans, and for a Jewish clientele. It was long since conjectured[5] that the ornamental marriage-chests, or *cassoni*, bearing representations of Mordecai and Esther, or similar Old Testament scenes, were made for Jewish usage, as may well be the case.

There was one branch of handicraft for which there was certainly no need for Jews to have recourse to Gentile assistance. This was embroidery. In every branch of the textile industry, from time immemorial, the Jews had been profoundly interested (this, rather than finance, was their characteristic employment!),

---

[5] *Burlington Magazine*, 1903.

and even in the Dark Ages the "Jewish Weave," or tapestry, was famous. The beautiful Renaissance textiles from Italy which were used as the basis of the synagogal embroideries in the rich collection formerly owned by the Prague Jewish community may well have been manufactured by Jewish craftsmen as well as purchased from Jewish dealers. Above all, the Jewish women were famous for their embroidery. We know of a Jewish master-craftsman who executed a number of superb Torah-curtains for various Ashkenazi communities of central and western Europe at the beginning of the eighteenth century. But there can be no doubt that normally work of this sort was carried out by the pious mothers and grandmothers of the community in the long winter evenings, as they exchanged the gossip and legends of the ghetto, while their husbands immersed themselves in their books. Some such objects—wrappers for the Scroll of the Law, covers for the synagogue reading-desk—are signed by the pious makers, one example in Ancona being, for instance, by an ancestress of the Montefiore family, another (now in the Jewish Museum, New York) by a proud child who gives her age as six years. Exceptionally lovely is the textile collection of the Jewish community of Rome, with which the Great Synagogue there is now hung on festive occasions, many of the weaves—perhaps from Jewish looms —dating back to the Renaissance period.[6]

Unfortunately, textiles are more subject to normal wear, to decay and to destruction than metal objects, and the more precious the materials, the less likely they are to be preserved. Thus no such object is recorded which in its present form antedates the seventeenth century. We know, for example, only by report of the curtain for the Ark and mantle for the Scroll of the Law which the affluent loan-banker Hirtz Wertheim had made for his private synagogue at Padua at the beginning of the sixteenth century; it was said to be worth five hundred ducats. These sacred appurtenances were embroidered with Wertheim's crest (for every well-to-do Jewish family at this time had its *stemma*, or armorial badge, much in the same way as their neighbors). In

---

[6] This collection escaped destruction or sack during the war of 1939-45 through the presence of mind of a devoted non-Jewish custodian, who informed a predatory German patrol that the door leading to the strong-room was only an emergency exit.

this case, it embodied a stag's head, symbolizing Hirtz's name, though this scandalized some of the highly orthodox, who alleged or suspected a breach of the Ten Commandments. To be sure, this immigrant zeal was regarded by most Italian Jews as excessive.

Lace-making is said to have been a specialty of the Jews in Spain—at Barcelona, Toledo and Majorca. Sometimes the work was interwoven with gold and silver thread, though this was periodically forbidden by the sumptuary laws which restricted extravagance and display. Certainly, this occupation was known also among Italian Jews, who down to the end of the ghetto period were famous for such needle-craft. In Avignon at the beginning of the fifteenth century, the work of a Jewish woman named Blanquette was so highly valued that she was employed to make the surplices and albs for the use of the Supreme Pontiff— that same anti-Pope, Benedict XIII, who was later to inveigh against the entrusting of even semi-sacred work to Jewish hands!

That there were Jewish bookbinders at this period, when book-binding was an art rather than a craft, was inevitable. At the papal court in Avignon in the fourteenth century, the official book-binder was frequently a Jew; indeed, of five persons thus employed there between 1336 and 1362, two were Jewish. Cases are even recorded when they were commissioned to see to the binding of a missal, or a codex of Canon Law, which the Pontiff wished to present to a friend or relative. In Spain, too, bookbinding seems to have been a common Jewish occupation. We know of one Jew, Meir (Mahir) Salomo, who was employed to bind the registers of the Aragonese royal treasury from 1367 to 1389, and obviously gave satisfaction. The bull of the anti-Pope Benedict XIII of 1415 spoken of above, which among other restrictions forbade Jews to bind books containing the names of Jesus or the Virgin Mary (a category which at this time included most litera-ture), demonstrates how closely associated the Jews of the Peninsula were with this craft. In Germany, the work known as *cuir ciselé*, with the use of damped leather as a basis for carved designs, is regarded by some authorities as having been a Jewish specialty. We know here of at least one bookbinder of high ability and reputation. This was Meir Jaffe, competent also as a scribe and illuminator of Hebrew manuscripts, who in 1468 bound a

Bible for the City Council of Nuremberg, where patronage of a Jew was unlikely unless he had exceptional qualifications. One authority, who ascribes to him a number of other works bearing a somewhat similar signature, calls him a "supreme artist." A number of other Jewish artists in leather-work of this period are known, none of them, however, as it happens, closely associated with Italy.

That the Italian Jews of the Renaissance period patronized the arts, to some degree at least, was inevitable; for it could not have been otherwise with persons so strongly imbued as they were with the spirit of the environment. Their households were in externals very similar to those of their Gentile neighbors of the same social class, and were adorned in much the same manner. The masterpieces which came into their hands in the way of business were sometimes retained, at least temporarily, to add to their domestic resplendence. It is recorded how, on the capture of Padua in 1509, the Jewish community hopefully presented the imperial commander with an enormous silver basin of splendid workmanship, and when he grumbled that it was useless without the jug, tactfully informed him that the companion-piece was still at the silversmith's but would be ready in a few days. There can be little doubt that many specimens of Renaissance handicrafts for domestic use still extant were commissioned or purchased by some of those affluent and discriminating loan-bankers who dominated Italian Jewry at the time. In the nature of things, there would be little evidence of this, any more than there would of their having been in the hands of members of the Christian merchant-class of the same standing; though from time to time one comes across fine specimens of Renaissance craftsmanship which bear Hebrew inscriptions, testifying to the fact that at some period in their history they passed through Jewish hands. It is true that the famous Florentine metal-worker of the fifteenth century, Niccolò Grosso, known as "Il Caparrà," or "ready-money," refused to work for Jews, saying that their money was dirty and stank. But this was regarded as a sign of his notorious eccentricity, and Vasari tells the story in a manner which makes it obvious that others similarly engaged had no such inhibitions. Patronage and appreciation would obviously lead on occasion to personal intimacy: and of this too we have adequate evidence. When in 1539 the Florentine artists Cristofano Gherardi (called "Doceno") and Battista Cungi arrived in Bologna on a visit, they brought with them letters of recommendation from Ottaviano de' Medici, a member of the ruling house, to his "friend" (so he is described), the Jewish banker Dattero—probably identical with the ex-Florentine Joab da Rieti, who figures prominently in Jewish records—who treated them with the utmost consideration and kindliness. Vasari informs us how the three were constantly seen about together in the streets, so that the two painters (one of whom had a cast in his eye, while the other's eyes were exceptionally large) were taken by the Bolognese to be Jews themselves, these being considered Jewish characteristics!

When Michelangelo was at work on his famous statue of Moses for the grave of Pope Julius II in the Church of S. Pietro in Vincoli in Rome, the Jews would stream out of their quarter on the Sabbath afternoon (once again, Vasari, the great contemporary chronicler of Renaissance art, is our authority) to admire his progress and gaze on the features of their venerated lawgiver as they emerged from the marble under his chisel. Obviously, they did not share the "orthodox" inhibitions in this matter: nor did many of their compatriots. In the synagogue of Ascoli, two gilded lions guarded the approach to the Ark containing the sacred scrolls, without arousing any protest even from the most meticulous—as was the case afterwards also at Pesaro, whither in due course they were transferred.

In the Jewish quarter at Siena there was a water fountain over which, appositely enough, a statue of Moses stood for centuries, executed by (and, in view of the subject, presumably commissioned by the community from) the distinguished local sculptor Antonio Federighi dei Tolomei (c. 1420-90); so high was its merit that it has now been transferred to the Civic Museum. It is noteworthy that no objections were raised, so far as is known, even among the most pious, to the presence of this "graven image" in the Piazza del Ghetto until some Polish pietists happened to visit the city, almost on the eve of the French Revolution.

The walls of the Jewish homes would sometimes be decorated with paintings, perhaps by a master-hand. Thus in the more elegant houses of the Florentine ghetto, established in 1570, there were frescoes of some merit representing Old Testament scenes, which unfortunately perished without proper record when the area was so ruthlessly reconstructed at the close of the last century. It was conventional, it seems, for the interiors of the synagogues, too, to be similarly decorated at this time—perhaps a heritage of the practice of the classical period exemplified in the now-famous ruins of Dura Europos and repeated contemporaneously in the eastern European tradition. The Scuola del Tempio at Rome (1555?) embodied in its wall decorations representations of the sacred vessels of the Temple; the sixteenth-century oratory of Casale displayed the city of Jerusalem. But it seems that sometimes the scope was more ambitious. When early in the seventeenth century the synagogue at Carpi was enlarged, the Duke of Modena was asked for permission to have it decorated with frescoes, since "in all synagogues fine paintings are made without stint for adornment," and in this new one it would be proper to have some "more charming and more precious" than in the old. In the little township of Luzzara in the same region the sixteenth-century synagogue was established in two adjoining rooms, decorated with very old paintings, perhaps antedating the place of worship but not considered to be inconsistent with it. The rabbi-grammarian Samuel Archevolti, to be sure, was opposed to the practice—in part because in his opinion it made the house of worship look like a comedy theater!

It is probable enough that these decorations were not made by Jewish hands, for even for purposes most intimately associated with religious observance, the services of Christian masters of their craft were frequently employed. For example, it is known that the superb "Ponentine" synagogue in Venice, which dates back to 1584 but was reconstructed in 1655, was the work of Baldassare Longhena, the most eminent Venetian architect of the day, whose magnificent church of Santa Maria della Salute is one of the most prominent features of the lagoon. Other Italian synagogues dating back to this period (some of them, such as that of Pesaro, veritable jewels of the baroque style) were no doubt constructed similarly by Christian architects. There is only one ancient Italian synagogue which we have reason to believe was designed by a Jew—that of Trani, of 1247, still standing though converted many centuries ago into a church. On the other hand, one of the seventeenth-century Prague synagogues is known to have been the work of a Jewish architect, as were probably several of those in eastern Europe.

In the same way, there is no doubt that Christian workmen were employed for many of the interior appurtenances of the synagogue, for which only the finest and the best would serve. Much has been dispersed or destroyed in recent years; but still there may be found in the various public collections and in the ancient Italian synagogues lovely specimens of silver and metal work of the Baroque and even the Renaissance periods. The Rome community, for example, owns a dish and ewer of chased silver, in the style of Cellini and popularly ascribed to that master, which has been in its possession for centuries past. The work which "Il Caparrà" refused to do for the Jews of Florence may well have been intended for the adornment of their synagogue rather than their private houses.

More because of the influence of the environment than the inclination of the non-Jewish craftsmen (who would have carried out whatever instructions they received), the motifs and decoration to be found on the objets d'art executed even for religious and synagogal use tended sometimes to be not merely non-Jewish, but even un-Jewish in inspiration. This may be studied for example in the eight-burnered lamps kindled in the home on the Maccabean feast of Hanukkah—of which very large numbers from the Renaissance period, both in precious and in base metals, are to be found in private and public collections. One may leave out of account the fact that some of them bore human figures—such as Judith bearing the head of Holophernes, an episode associated with this celebration in Jewish folklore; for the inhibition against portraiture was not strong in Italy (as we have seen) and this was at least a Jewish motif. Similarly, there is no need to pay specific attention to those bearing as their central decoration such motifs as the Lily of Florence, for the local patriotism of the Italian Jews was noteworthy. But it is certainly somewhat incongruous to find them lavishly decorated—as so many of them were—with naked *putti*, mermaids, or sea-monsters, in the normal Italian tradition of this age; or to find as the central decoration a pagan scene, such as Orpheus playing his lyre to an attentive group of wild animals—a subject which it is impossible to correlate with the

festival even by the most agile argumentation, but which figures
on more than one such lamp and therefore can hardly have been
inserted accidentally.[7] Most remarkable of all is an entire series of
Hanukkah lamps, which bear as their central design the coats-of-
arms of various cardinals of the Holy Catholic Church, surmounted by their characteristic hat with the tassels falling grace-
fully on either side: those, for example, of the Spaniard Inigo
Avalo de Aragona, who was admitted to the Sacred College in
1561; of Cesare Baronio, the great ecclesiastical historian; or—the
most remarkable—of Cardinal Ippolito Aldobrandini, who was
to become Pope in 1592 as Clement VIII. (I mention only three
out of perhaps a dozen which are traceable.) The reason for this
extraordinary choice of subject is mysterious. For them to have
been presented to the prelates whose device they bear is hardly
to be imagined: as gifts they were trivial, and either side in that
age would have considered such a presentation of a religious object
as verging on sacrilege or insult. The most likely explanation is
the least dramatic. Often, Princes of the Church extended their
patronage to individual Jews, who became their agents and enjoyed their protection: and probably some of them, proud of the
association, had their patrons' arms embodied in these decorative
religious objects so as to blazon the connection abroad. However
that may be, the fact has perhaps a symbolical value, besides illustrating, once again, the cordial relations and the close integration
between the Italian Jew of the age of the Renaissance and the
world around him.

It was in connection with their profoundest love—their libraries
—that the Jews were brought into closest contact with the artists
of their day. For they transferred to their Hebrew books too the
aesthetic standards and fashions of the environment. That they
were elegantly written and beautifully bound need not be emphasized. But they were also in many cases illuminated, sometimes
exquisitely, in the elaborate fashion of the age—not merely with
heightened initial letters and other purely decorative features, but

---

[7] It may be mentioned that this scene figures on a fresco in one of
the Jewish catacombs, and there may have thus been a continuity of
tradition from classical times.

often also with miniatures illustrating the details of the text. Elijah Levita, indeed, complained that his co-religionists in Italy attached more importance to the beauty of a manuscript than to its accuracy.

Unfortunately, this work remained generally anonymous in Italy. We know of some splendidly gifted Spanish illuminators of the time (such as Joseph ibn Hayyim, who was responsible for the famous Kennicott Bible in Oxford) and some extremely capable Germans (such as Joel ben Simeon, author of several beautiful codices of the Passover ritual, or *Haggadah*—some of them apparently executed in Italy, where he had settled); but there is very good reason to imagine that in many cases, if not in most, such work was entrusted to Gentile hands, after the Jewish scribe had completed the actual text. It is true that it has proved impossible to substantiate the claims that an exquisite little liturgical miscellany which purports to have been presented in the fourteenth century by a learned cardinal to Galeotto Malatesta, Lord of Rimini, is to be ascribed to "Ziotto da Fiorenza" —that is, Giotto—as is asserted in an early manuscript note. For, lovely though it is, the volume obviously belongs to the mid-fifteenth century. But the illuminations in certain other Italian Jewish manuscripts of the period are of such perfection that they must certainly have been the work of miniaturists of the first rank, who were in all probability non-Jews.

One may mention, for example, the superb codex of Avicenna's *Canon* which is the greatest treasure of the library of the University of Bologna, with numerous lavishly illuminated pages in the very finest tradition of the Tuscan school. The history of this extraordinary volume itself suggests its importance. It was formerly in the Dominican convent in that city, having been brought there perhaps at the time of the persecution of Hebrew literature in 1553. It was unsuccessfully competed for by the Grand Duke of Tuscany who wished to purchase it in 1587; it was carried off to Paris by Napoleon in 1796 and restored after Waterloo. Other exceptional Hebrew illuminated manuscripts of outstanding importance include the code of Jacob ben Asher in the Vatican (MS. Rossi 555), copied in Mantua in 1436 and probably illuminated there; the miscellaneous Rothschild Codex 24 in the Umbro-Florentine style now in the Bezalel Museum, Jerusalem; the code of

Maimonides illuminated in the style of Matteo de Ser Cambio of Perugia (and conceivably an early production of this master), formerly in Frankfort and now in a private collection in New York. These examples are chosen almost at random out of many. Often there is no Jewish flavor in the decorations. But there are the two Bible manuscripts in Florence, referred to above, which were written probably by a convert and for a non-Jew, the illuminations in which, in the finest Tuscan tradition of the fifteenth century, actually embody representations not only of the creation of the world by "God the Father," but also of the crucifixion, the saints, the Trinity and the Holy Ghost! In one case (Biblioteca Medicea Laurenziana, Cod. Plut. I.31), the illuminations are from the hand of Franceso d'Antonio del Cherico, one of the greatest Florentine masters of the time. The Jews introduced the tradition of manuscript illumination into two categories of personal document: the marriage contract (*Ketubah*) and the Book of Esther read on the feast of Purim (*Megillah*). These are common enough from the beginning of the seventeenth century and doubtless existed earlier, but so far as I am aware none in either category is extant which can be termed a specimen of Renaissance art in the strict sense.[8]

The art dealer fills a specific function in a sophisticated society; and the purveying of works of art, ancient and modern, was an essential factor of cultural activity in the Renaissance period. Into this, the Jews necessarily entered in more than one way. For, as jewelers, it was part of their normal activity to buy and sell goldsmiths' work of the type in which such artists as Benvenuto Cellini excelled; while, as dealers in second-hand articles, paintings, sculptures and antiques inevitably came into their possession from time to time. This aspect of the Renaissance has not yet received adequate treatment; but when it does, numerous Jewish names will certainly emerge. Cosimo de' Medici, Grand Duke of Tuscany, was in touch with Jewish merchants in Venice from whom he purchased antiques, which at that time were brought thither

---

[8] The earliest I can trace at present is one written at Castelnuovo, near Siena, in 1567 (now in Jerusalem). A fine specimen in the John Rylands Library at Manchester is dated 1521, but by a posterior hand, and actually belongs to the period about 1600.

in considerable quantity from the Levant. In 1561, he acquired from one of them an entire collection of ancient coins. Apparently, David Finzi, of Mantua, whose collections of Jewish and non-Jewish coins are mentioned by Azariah de' Rossi,[9] also engaged in this type of business. Abraham Colorni, whose name is mentioned elsewhere in these pages, dealt in antiques among his many other occupations, his studio at Ferrara being famous for its stocks; though to be sure, in view of his reputation, it is likely that their authenticity was not always above question. Among his clients, however, was the Duke of Savoy, who purchased from him some classical medals. The silver fruit-bowl (*pomeria*) presented by the Commune of Ascoli to Maria Orsini in 1493 was bought from the Jew Manuel. There was in 1529 a goldsmith named Master Raphael in Urbino, who sought out antique figures and similar objects for the ducal court; whether he was a Jew is not recorded, but it is likely enough. Such activity was especially marked at the court of Mantua. A jeweler named Orso ("Orso Hebreo joieler") of Venice, and his brother, were the official gem purveyors here in 1525 and furnished the reigning family with jewels. It should be noted that "jewels" at this time signified a good deal more than precious stones, and "jewelers" fashioned as well as sold the trinkets in which they dealt. In the middle of the seventeenth century there was a Mantuan Jew named Giuseppe Colorni who served the Gonzaga family in the same capacity. About this time, an Italian Jew named Jacob Carpi, something of an artist as well as an art expert, settled in Amsterdam and became known as a picture dealer—the first of a long line whose tradition has remained significant even today.

At the close of the sixteenth century, the Jew David de' Cervi of Rome (son or brother, probably, of the Joseph de' Cervi who was permitted by the Emperor Rudolph in 1577 to work at his craft in the castle of Prague without interference from the native craftsmen) seems to have been one of the best known and most active court jewelers in Italy. He enjoyed the most illustrious clientele, was often employed in procuring works of art for the Gonzaga dukes, and through their means, perhaps, was introduced to the court of Savoy. When in 1605 the marriage between Mar-

---

[9] See below, p. 329.

gherita of Savoy and the Prince of Mantua took place—one of the most magnificent spectacles of the age, to which we will have occasion to refer more than once later on—it was he who supplied the superb jewelry presented to the bride. Subsequently, we find him active in the imperial court in Prague.

In view of the fact that the Italian Jew did not in fact object to the representational arts so strenuously as is generally thought, as the preceding pages have made clear, it is a little surprising that so few of their portraits of the Renaissance period have survived. Nevertheless, from the seventeenth century they are not uncommon, and a certain pious Italian rabbi of the time, far from objecting to portraits, recommended that pious Jews should keep miniatures of their parents constantly with them, so as to be fortified by their recollection and example. It is, however, remarkable that the only portraits traceable anterior to the seventeenth century which were commissioned by Jews are, not paintings (which even from the point of view of the rigid interpretation of biblical law were perhaps admissible), but "graven images," in the form of three-dimensional medallions which were at all times considered more objectionable than two-dimensional art. The earliest such productions known (apart from a mysterious medallion of perhaps 1503, with a long and strange Hebrew inscription, which may possibly be intended to represent Benjamin, son of the physician Elijah Beer—unless it is the head of Jupiter!) is of Elias de Lattes (grandson of the papal physician Bonet de Lattes) and his mother Ricca, executed in 1552 by an unidentifiable artist, probably in Rome. Two more were made by the fashionable medalist Pastorino de' Pastorini: the one, of Abraham Emanuel Norsa (1557), and the other, a year or so earlier, of the ex-marrano recently returned to Judaism, Gracia Nasi—not the famous *grande dame* of that name, alias Beatrice Mendes, but her niece and namesake, then in her eighteenth year. The latter's pride in her new-found Jewishness is demonstrated by the fact that, whereas the age is given in Latin, the name is in Hebrew; a testimony, too, perhaps to Pastorino's own breadth of mind. (The work, signed with the initial "P," has however been ascribed also to another eminent artist-engraver, Giovanni Paolo Poggini.) It is a fine piece of portraiture, showing the young woman dressed in the height of mid-sixteenth century fashion—her décolleté bodice, with a heavily embroidered collar supporting the back of the neck, large pearls in her headdress, elaborate earrings and necklace and a cascade of veiling which falls over her shoulders.

Though no painted portraits commissioned by Italian Jews at this period are extant, as has been mentioned (I know of none anterior to 1600, though there are a fair number later), they were sometimes taken as subject-matter by artists. Bernard Berenson has conjectured that a famous painting by Giovanni Bellini shows turbaned Levantine Jews at Venice. Jewish types may be seen perhaps also in Carpaccio's "Healing of the Possessed" in the Accademia in that city, as well as in Gentile Bellini's "Procession in the Piazza of S. Marco." The eminent scholar Elijah del Medigo may be represented in Benozzo Gozzoli's "Adoration of the Magi" in Florence. More important as a document is a *predella* in the ducal palace at Urbino by Paolo Uccello, executed for the Confraternity of Corpus Christi in 1467-68, showing the acquisition of the Host from an impoverished woman by a Jew—incidentally, an admirable representation of the interior of a Jewish banking establishment at the time—and its subsequent desecration, followed by the barbarous execution of the entire family of the culprit. But the only assuredly identified portraits of the period, so far as I am aware, are in a painting at Mantua by one of the school of Mantegna, which commemorates a curious episode. A certain Daniel Norsa, head of one of the most affluent families of that city, bought a new house which had on the wall a painting of the Madonna. The bishop permitted him to have it removed; nevertheless, the mob resented the action as sacrilegious. It happened that just about this time, on July 6, 1495, Giovanni Francesco Gonzaga, Marquess of Mantua, had fought an indeterminate battle at Fornovo against the French, which he decided to consider as a victory, and determined to celebrate it in style. Accordingly, he confiscated the house where Daniel Norsa had committed his "sacrilege," tore it down, and erected on the site a church dedicated to the Virgin of Victory. It was for this that Mantegna executed his great painting, now in the Louvre, known as "La Madonna della Vittoria." One of his pupils, moreover, made another painting for the church, depicting the enthroned Virgin as she holds a model of the building. Daniel Norsa and his family are shown below, the men distinguished by the Jewish badge on their breasts, and all with understandable pathos on their faces. This is an invaluable representation of a typical Jewish family in upper Italy in the Renaissance period, and has thus a documentary value far above its considerable artistic merit.

For further representations of Jewish scenes in Italian art we have to wait for a much later period. In the Rococo period Alessandro Magnasco (1667-1749) delighted in fanciful synagogue interiors (based, it is said, on that of Leghorn), showing an impossible architecture peopled with preposterous figures, and bearing only a remote relationship to fact—a fashion set before his day in a less extreme manner by the Dutch painter Pieter Saenredam (1597-1665) in a painting now in Turin. It was, however, only in the second half of the eighteenth century that the great painter Pietro Longhi (1702-85) and the mediocre engraver Giovanni Maria delle Piane (1764-1818) set down pictorially the lineaments of Italian—or at least Venetian—Jewish life, in the manner in which Rembrandt van Rijn and Bernard Piccart had already done for Holland.

TEN

Physicians, Quacks *and* Charlatans

Jewish physicians in the age of the Renaissance were especially numerous in Italy: so numerous that in some settings the typical figure of a physician was that of a Jew. This was not because they breathed the spirit of the new age, but rather because in a way they were the custodians of the spirit of the old.

The unquestioned penchant of the modern Jew for medical science is not of particular antiquity, in terms of the tremendous sweep of Jewish history. It is true that, as early as the very beginning of the Christian era, the Latin encyclopaedist A. Cornelius Celsus mentions some prescriptions in the name of Jewish practitioners; that four centuries later the Patriarch Gamaliel, the head of Palestinian Jewry, is cited as a medical authority; and that probably as far back as the seventh century, the mysterious Asaf Judaeus, who apparently flourished in Syria or Mesopotamia, compiled an important Hebrew medical treatise, in which, in advance of his time, he hints at the hereditary character of certain maladies. Such names are exceptional in that remote period; Jews became prominent in medicine only when they entered into the flood-tide of the intellectual life of the Arab world of the Middle Ages. To this environment belong the most significant figures, such as Isaac Israeli of Kairouan (known to European scholars as Isaac Judaeus) in the tenth century, whose treatises on fevers and on pharmacology in their Latin translations were of extreme importance in European medical study in and even after the Middle Ages; or Moses Maimonides in the twelfth, whose medical writings (apart from the philosophical works by which he is best remembered today) were studied in European universities four or five hundred years after his death.

Throughout the Moslem world, in the pre-Renaissance period, Jewish physicians were highly esteemed for their ability. In the

Christian world an additional factor came into consideration. For here, owing to their mobility, their linguistic knowledge and their cosmopolitan outlook, the Jews personified the traditions and reputation of the Arabic medicine in which they had been brought up and to which they had access—whether in the originals or in Hebrew translations. Hence, when a ruler or prelate took a Jewish physician into his service, it was not simply out of belief in his competence, but because he was thought to have at his command vast stores of secret medical doctrine which was unknown to or even kept from Christians.

We have already seen in a previous chapter how important a part was taken by Jewish translators in Spain, in Italy and in Provence in the process of transmission whereby Arab science reached Christian Europe. By the fourteenth century, the medical schools of Montpellier and Padua had probably absorbed everything that was worth absorbing in the Islamic medical tradition and had little or nothing left to learn in this sphere; though indeed they continued long after to base themselves on it, and the works of the Arab writers (in particular Avicenna) were their fundamental textbooks. From now on, Jews began to enroll in the European medical schools in the face of much opposition; and (at least in the countries under Aragonese influence, in particular Sicily) we find that Jews, wherever they had studied, were not admitted to practice until they had been examined for proficiency by the local medical authorities—a procedure which in earlier days would have been preposterous. Nevertheless, owing both to their ability and to their background, Jewish physicians remained disproportionately prominent and active in southern Europe. It is true that the Church rigidly forbade true believers to have recourse to infidel medical practitioners, who might thus acquire an improper influence over them and even (it was actually believed) deliberately prevent them from receiving the last sacraments if their illness was likely to prove fatal. Considerations of health were paramount; and the mere fact that the Jews had access to foreign languages and strange lores still gave them at this period an almost unfair advantage.

Hence there was in Italy, in the age of the Renaissance, a galaxy of physicians of note who were in attendance on Popes, prelates, princes and nobles. From the thirteenth century at least, pontiff after pontiff had a Jew in his employ as his personal medical attendant, and almost every ruler in Italy followed this example. The rabbinical literature shows that Jews served as military physicians, accompanying the armies in the field. There were what we would today term specialists as well. The Sforza dukes of Milan had their teeth attended to by two Jewish dentists, "famous in their art." When, in 1442, the Ferrarese knight Filippo Trombetta was suffering from serious eye trouble, two of the three expert oculists in the country who were recommended to him were Jews: Master Helia of Milan and "the most learned eyemaster, the Jew Izach" of Cremona. (The third specialist was Venanzio da Camerino.) Many cities engaged a Jew as communal physician for a term of years. The roll of illustrious Italian Jewish practitioners in the Renaissance period is almost unending, and they include some of the most brilliant figures of the age.

One may take the example of Elijah ben Sabbetai Beer, the first of the Jewish physicians to be given the rank of knight because of their skill (as was not exceptional at the time—perhaps to overcome the opposition of the universities to granting them the degree of doctor, which was considered to imply the knightly dignity). In 1405, he was granted the rights of citizenship by the civic authorities in Rome; he was in the service of Pope Martin V and his successor, Eugenius IV; at another stage of his career, he was court physician to the Duke of Ferrara; he lectured in medicine at the University of Pavia—one of the few authenticated instances of a Jew who had such an official appointment; and we find traces of him in other places in Italy from time to time. Such was his reputation that in 1410 the ailing Henry IV of England, disregarding the fact that Jews had long been excluded from his kingdom, summoned him from Bologna to London as his personal medical attendant, in the hope that he might be able to effect a cure. Not only was he empowered to practice medicine in any part of the realm; but he brought with him a household of ten persons, who obviously were intended to constitute the statutory quorum (*minyan*) for Jewish public worship. It is interesting to note, incidentally, that in the previous year the famous or fabulous Mayor of London, Richard Whittington, had invited a Jewish physician from France, Samson of Mirabeau, to attend on his wife in her last illness.

Of Elias Sabot (as he is called in the English documents) a curious, and typically Renaissance, relic survives—if the ascription is correct, which is not quite certain: a large medallion, struck in honor of his son Benjamin, bearing a typical Greek head, a long and enigmatic Hebrew inscription, and on the reverse the Latin words (also hardly capable of interpretation): *Post tenebras spero lucem felicitatis iudex dies ultimus. D.III.M.*[1] This Elijah is not to be confused with another Jewish physician of the same name about whom a gruesome tale is reported. It was said that, in 1408, near the Porta Nuova, he murdered a certain Moses who was his professional rival and who had outvied him for the favor of Ladislaus King of Naples (then in control of Rome). How preposterously Renaissance in spirit!

To give a complete roll of the eminent Jewish physicians who worked in Italy during the Renaissance period and attended on Italian princes, ecclesiastical and secular, would take too long, for there was hardly a court in the country that did not know them. But every now and again there is recorded an especially dramatic episode which associates them vividly with some famous Italian name or scene.

When Pope Innocent VIII lay on his death-bed in 1492, so feeble that he could take no nourishment except woman's milk, it is said that a Jewish physician (his identity cannot be established) attempted a startling remedy: he wished to restore the Holy Father's health by a blood-transfusion. Three ten-year-old boys were, it is told, chosen for the purpose and were paid a ducat each for their services. But they died in the course of the experiment, and the Pope obtained no benefit. He had been unconscious at the time, and is said to have been indignant when later he was told of what had been intended. Doubt has been cast on the tale by recent inquirers, and it may be entirely untrue; certainly, the details were piled on in such a way as to make it appear that the Jew's conduct had been particularly heinous. But if authentic, the episode would be of great importance in medical history, since it is apparently the earliest scientific experiment of the sort (or one of the earliest) on record.

---

[1] See illustration following p. 276.

It is possible (though no more) that the audacious experimentalist referred to in this anecdote is to be identified with Samuel Sarfati (= The Frenchman), who deserves separate treatment on account of his family as well as on his own merit. He was body-physician to both Alexander VI (Innocent's successor) and Julius II, on whose accession he presented the petition of the Roman Jews asking for the confirmation of their privileges, and delivered an address which made a considerable impression. The Pope, on appointing him to his service, later empowered him to attend on Christian patients without formality and freed him from the obligation of wearing the Jewish badge. On account of his interests in France he was also granted a safe-conduct and protection by King Louis XII. His medical reputation stood very high. It was jealously noted by his competitors that Pope Julius trusted him more than any Christian physician in his service. If one story told about him is true, he had excellent reason. In the torrid summer of 1511 the Pope suddenly fell ill. Four days later he fell into a coma, from which his medical advisers (who previously had been prevented by Sarfati from overdosing him with rhubarb) did not think he would emerge. The rumor spread that he was dead, the palace servants began to plunder the papal chambers, and the cardinals prepared for a conclave. Only the Jewish physician refused to give up hope, and reaped the reward when his master recovered consciousness, demanded a drink of wine, and before long resumed his former almost demoniac activity.

On his actual death a year and a half later, Samuel (whose house was plundered in the disorders traditional on such occasions) was for a time in the service of Pope Leo X, who sent him to Florence to attend on his brother Giuliano when he was ill in 1515. He commanded such confidence that, on his recovery, the latter kept him in his service, though he sent all his other physicians away. He is mentioned by Antonfrancesco Grazzini ("Il Lasca") in his *novelle* as one of the outstanding Italian physicians of his day.

Samuel Sarfati's son, Joseph (known to his Christian colleagues as Giuseppe Gallo), was a less eminent physician but a more interesting character, whose vicissitudes greatly impressed contemporaries. He seems to have cut something of a figure in literary circles, for besides his medical training he had some philosophical and mathematical competence, knew some Oriental tongues (including Arabic), mastered the Greek language and literature and could write Latin verse as well as prose in a style sufficiently elegant to satisfy the exacting standards of the humanists. He was apparently in practice on his own account, when his father died in Florence, probably about 1520, leaving a considerable property. A servant stole the whole of Joseph's portion from the chest in which it was stored and fled with it to Constantinople. When Joseph followed him there (obviously a considerable treasure was involved) the thief ingeniously denounced him to the Turkish authorities as a papal spy. Police were sent to arrest him and he was wounded in the tussle, but managed to get away and return to Rome. Here Pope Clement VII renewed his father's privileges in his favor, and he was able to set up in practice again. He became very successful, built up a fashionable clientele, was accepted in the papal court and had entrée to the palaces of some of the most influential of the cardinals, for one of whom he composed a Hebrew epitaph. At the same time he was regarded as a leading member of the Jewish community, and was able not only to extend his hospitality to David Reubeni when he was in Rome but also to advance his cause materially. He was at the height of his reputation at the time of the disastrous sack of Rome in 1527, which in one sense ended the heyday of the Renaissance there. His house was pillaged from top to bottom, and he was held to ransom, but after four days managed to escape at night while his captors were sleeping off their potations. In his flight he contracted some infection, was suspected of having the plague, was driven away from the little town where he sought refuge, and died unattended in a miserable hovel, more from thirst and hunger than from disease. The whole story is recounted at considerable length by Giovanni Pierio Valeriani, who may have known him personally, in his pessimistic work on the Vicissitudes of Scholars (*De litteratorum infelicitate*, Venice, 1620), one of the classics of this age, in which moral judgment is so characteristically tempered by human sympathy. It has been necessary to revert to Giuseppe Gallo more than once elsewhere in these pages, for he was a memorable figure in Italian Jewish letters, a poet of ability though not always of restraint, and author of one of the earliest dramatic experiments in the Hebrew language.

The Medici seem to have had something of a preference for Jewish medical advisers, whether at the Vatican or at their palaces in Florence. Lorenzo de' Medici's brother, Giuliano, for example, had turned to a Jewish practitioner named Moses (probably to be identified with a Spaniard, Moses son of Joseph, who figures in the records about this time) to attend on his light-of-love Simonetta Vespucci ("La Bella Simonetta") in her last illness in 1476—a memorable death-bed, if it is true that it inspired Poliziano's poem, "La Giostra," and Botticelli's painting, "La Primavera," which is believed to depict the entry of the soul of the frail beauty into a new life.

Another famous death-bed scene of Renaissance Italy was that of Lorenzo the Magnificent himself, in the prime of his life in 1492, when Savonarola came from San Marco and exhorted the dying man to repent. His regular medical attendant was an old friend, Piero Leone, who was accused of gross incompetence and committed suicide when he realized the outcome of his bungling. Ludovico il Moro, Duke of Milan, was informed how serious Lorenzo's condition was, and sent one of the most eminent physicians in his duchy to assist in the case—the Jew Lazzaro da Pavia. While in practice at Faenza, Lazzaro had become so popular among the townsfolk that Bernardino da Feltre, the zealous Franciscan friar, was utterly scandalized and demanded that he be expelled. When he arrived at the Villa Medici at Careggi, in the first week of April 1492, he found the patient in a critical state. Not despairing, he prescribed a new potion, composed, it is said (but one wonders whether a skilled physician of this enlightened age would have been quite so credulous), of crushed pearls and precious gems. As the compound was being prepared, Lorenzo feebly inquired of his friend, the poet Poliziano, who was in the room, what the newcomer was doing, and greeted the draught in excited and eager tones. But it did him no good, and he passed away very shortly thereafter. It was universally believed at the time that, had Master Lazzaro come earlier, his cures would have proved effective. In the following year, Piero de' Medici, Lorenzo's son, was poignantly reminded of the circumstances of his bereavement when he received a letter of May 21, 1493, from one Puccio Pucci, describing a joust at Faenza in the presence of

Catarina Sforza. In the course of this, one of her pages broke his leg, besides receiving injuries in the head and arm. They had forthwith sent for "maestro Lazero hebreo," who was considered (wrote Pucci) wonderful in surgery.

Another instance: When Ercole d'Este, Duke of Ferrara, was wounded in the foot in 1467 at the Battle of Molinella, fighting against the Florentines, he was attended and cured with medicinal draughts by a Jewish physician named Jacob. The duke never wholly recovered, remaining lame until the end of his days. An interested observer of the treatment of the illustrious patient was the young Berengario da Carpi, subsequently to be one of Italy's most famous anatomists, whose father was a close friend of this Jacob. Many years later, when he was Professor of Medicine at Bologna, Berengario described the episode in his once-standard work on fractures of the skull, *Tractatus de fractura calvi sive cranei* (ed. Venice, 1535, f. 61). Here he told also how, on another occasion, under the mistaken impression that he was a relative of the patient, this same Jewish practitioner, who normally kept his cures a profound secret, took him into the country when he went to collect the medicinal herbs of which he made use. Berengario was thus able to remember and later to record the recipe used, as he did also (f. 79) in the case of another, unnamed, Jewish physician whom he refers to as his close friend. The latter's medicinal treatment for lesions was, we hear, considered a specialty of the Jewish physicians at this time.

It was not unusual among Jews for medicine to be practiced in the same family, generation after generation, almost as a hereditary craft. Such was the case at this time with one family in particular, whose members were in contact with some of the most resplendent courts and some of the most outstanding persons in Renaissance Italy, over a period of something like two hundred years. The dynasty in question is that of Portaleone, which derived its name either from the quarter adjacent to the main Jewish settlement in Rome or else from a suburb of Mantua: they Hebraized this as *miShaar Aryeh*, that is, "from the Lion's Gate." The first of them to be mentioned in our records is a certain Benjamin Portaleone, known in the outer world as Guglielmo, or William. (We have seen the reason for this name-correspondence above.) He lived in Naples, where he was in the service of the licentious Ferrante (Ferdinand) I, who raised him to the dignity of knighthood. Subsequently, the latter sent him to attend on his kinsman, Galeazzo Maria Sforza, Duke of Milan, on whose death in 1476 he made his way to Mantua, the original home of his family. Here he served three Gonzaga rulers in succession—Luigi III, Federico I, and Giovanni Francesco, in whose employ he still was at the time of his death, apparently in 1500.

Dr. Guglielmo Portaleone's elder son, Abraham, was body-physician to Guidabaldo di Montefeltro, Duke of Urbino. Later, on returning to Mantua, he was similarly in attendance on the Marquess Giovanni Francesco II and his son Federico II, the first duke. He had a very great reputation in his day: so much so that when, in the winter of 1525, Giovanni delle Bande Nere, the famous *condottiere*, progenitor of the later Grand Dukes of Tuscany, was wounded in a skirmish a few days before the Battle of Pavia, Abraham was sent by his noble master to attend on him in Parma, whither the wounded man had been conveyed. The patient's cousin, Pope Clement VII, wrote letters both to the duke and to the Jewish doctor expressing his personal gratitude for this care. The scribe carelessly began the latter with the conventional words "to my beloved son" (*dilecto filio*) which he subsequently deleted! The Holy Father expressed his regret that Master Abraham was not a Christian, but promised him a reward for his services, which were in fact successful. But on November 24th of the following year, Giovanni was again wounded in the same leg, more severely, in a skirmish against the imperial troops in the marshes near Mantua. He received no attention for twenty hours, after which he was taken into the city to the Gonzaga palace. Now the same expert was again sent for, but this time he arrived too late. Gangrene had apparently set in; and though Master Abraham amputated, the patient died a few days later, the Jewish physician, of course, being accused in those credulous days of having poisoned the wound.

One other memorable patient of his is recorded. His master, the Marquess Giovanni Francesco Gonzaga, was famous in his day for his love of animals. In 1513, one of his favorite dogs died—the grief-stricken owner suspected, by poison. Master Abraham, his physician, was thereupon instructed to perform a post-mortem on the unfortunate animal to ascertain the cause of death—with what result is not stated.

This Dr. Abraham Portaleone's brother, Eleazar or Lazzaro, followed the same profession and also had a distinguished clientele, which included the townships of Sermide and Rovigo, Count Giovanni Sassatello, the General of the Republic of Venice, and Luigi III, Marquess of Mantua and his family. Lazzaro's two sons, Abraham and David, both received the authorization of the Pope, in 1518, to attend on Federico II. In the next generation, one member of the family, Judah or Leone, was a surgeon with a distinguished court practice; another, Meir or Lucido, received license to practice from Pope Clement VIII, as well as from the duke.

Their cousin, a third Abraham Portaleone, David's son, who graduated at Pavia in 1563, and was accepted three years later as a member of the College of Physicians in Mantua, was the most illustrious of the clan in his generation. From 1573, he was in attendance on Duke Guglielmo and his successor, Vincenzo I, and was in addition a medical writer of great reputation. At the suggestion of Duke Guglielmo he composed two medical works in Latin—the one, on general medical practice (*Consilia medica*) and the other, in the form of dialogue, on the medicinal use of gold, *De auro dialogi tres* (Venice, 1584), which was dedicated to his patron. Another book of his in Hebrew on biblical archaeology, entitled *Shilte haGibborim* or "The Shields of the Mighty" (Mantua, 1612), is noteworthy for exemplifying the Renaissance spirit in Hebrew literature and will accordingly have to be dealt with more fully elsewhere in this volume. He also left an ethical will, embodying a confession whose devotional spirit is all the more remarkable because its author was one of the most eminent physicians of the country. Among other matters, he ordered that his body should not be buried until three days after his death— an early and valuable protest against a practice which then led to hasty and sometimes premature burial.

His son, a second David, was also in the service of successive dukes, and had a fashionable clientele among the Mantuan aristocracy. When he died, the spirit of the Counter Reformation had triumphed in Mantua, and the ban on the employment of Jewish physicians was on the whole rigorously applied. But the reigning

duke, Carlo I, apparently could not accustom himself to the idea
of not having his health supervised by a member of this family.
He accordingly applied to the Pope for a special license for his
former physician's son, another Guglielmo, who had graduated
at Siena in 1639, to attend henceforth on Christians as well as
on Jews (to whom his practice had previously been restricted).
So far had the atmosphere in Italy changed now that even an
application under these august auspices was refused. There is
extant an entire volume of medical correspondence in Italian between successive bearers of the name of Portaleone and some of
the outstanding Italian consultants of the time, extending from
1582 to 1645. But, after Guglielmo's day, its members no longer
attained much distinction. Here accordingly we take leave of this
great clan of Jewish physicians.[2]

Another characteristic figure of the sixteenth century and
victim of the period of reaction was David de' Pomi, born in
1525 in the once-flourishing community of Spoleto in Umbria.
His family—in Hebrew *Min haTapuhim*—was among the oldest
in Italy, having been one of those founded according to tradition
by the four princely houses of Jerusalem carried by Titus as captives to Rome. His father had been ruined in consequence of the
wars which ravaged Italy in the first half of the sixteenth century; and the son, who had hoped to live from his private means,
had to depend for his livelihood on the practice of medicine. Into
this, he had been initiated by his uncle, Vitale Alatino (whom
we have already encountered), subsequently graduating from
the University of Perugia (1551). He attended in succession on
Count Niccolò Orsini and the Sforza family. Subsequently, he
set up at Chiusi and, after the beginning of the restrictive legislation, was empowered to continue to practice there among the
Christian population, as the result of what he assures us to have
been a brilliant Latin oration delivered in 1565 before Pope Pius

---

[2] The dramatist and impresario Leone de' Sommi Portaleone, of
whom we have spoken elsewhere in this volume, seems to have belonged to a cadet branch of this same family. When the present writer
first went to Italy in 1920, he found that the cook in the pension where
he stayed in Florence was a Jewish woman of the old ghetto type,
named Portaleone.

IV and his attendant cardinals. The Pope died, however, five days later and his successor, the austere Pius V, annulled the grant. In consequence, David de' Pomi went to live and practice at Venice, whither the reaction had not as yet penetrated.

Here he attained a considerable reputation, both as a physician and as a writer. He published an Italian translation of Ecclesiastes, dedicated to Cardinal Grimani, with an appendix on human misery and its avoidance, dedicated to Margaret of Savoy (Venice, 1571). He wrote a treatise, which unfortunately has not been preserved, to prove the divine origin of the Venetian republic. When the practice of medicine was forbidden to Jews at Venice also, he took up his pen again, and in 1588 there appeared his "Apology for the Jewish Physician" (*De medico hebraeo enarratio apologetica*), preceded by a commendatory letter from the printer, Aldo Manuzio the younger, one of the leaders of Venetian intellectual life at the time. In this work, written in elegant Latin, the veteran scholar proved from the classical Jewish literature, supported by the example of history, the falsehood of the charges leveled against the Jewish people as a whole, and against Jewish physicians in particular; and he concluded by adducing a number of examples of Jewish practitioners, ancient and modern, who had earned a reputation by their skill and devotion.

In the more restricted field of medical science, he produced a work on maladies of the breast, neither better nor worse than others of the period, which he dedicated to the doge and senate (Venice, 1588). At the time of the plague of 1572, he wrote a memorandum on how to free a town from contagion, containing some sound sense as well as some typical sixteenth-century nonsense; this, too, was subsequently published (Venice, 1577). But his most memorable and most characteristic work was outside the sphere of medicine: his encyclopaedic dictionary in three languages, Hebrew-Latin-Italian, entitled *Zemah David* or "The Plant of David," which he dedicated to the benevolent Pope Sixtus V (Venice, 1587). In the sometimes lengthy expositions of biblical and talmudic terms which this work comprises, there is often a good deal of curious and interesting lore. He describes (f. 36a) a syphon, and mentions what interest the device had aroused when it was exhibited in Venice in the previous year, although it was known (as he correctly states) to the scholars of the Talmud. He puts forward the theory that the Lord's "sore and great and strong sword" mentioned in Isaiah 27.1 implies the Bombard, and mentions how after the Battle of Lepanto he presented the doge a memorandum showing how that great victory had been foretold in this verse. Under the heading "Tarshish," which he believed to signify the jacinth, he has a curious dissertation (f. 232 a-b) on the origin of precious stones from rainfall; elsewhere (f. 86-7) he tells how he was accustomed to carry a jacinth about with him as a specific against plague when he went to visit his patients. He thought fit to include a discourse running to four columns (150-152) about the mythical river Sambation, which according to legend ceased to flow on the Sabbath: in this he mentioned incidentally a detail recently heard in conversation with a certain "great theologian," whose name however he does not give. In speaking of the substance *neter* or "nitre" mentioned by Jeremiah 2.22, he has a brief scientific note on the subject (f. 105-6). But this is amply counterbalanced by an amazing description (f. 62b) of what he terms the buffalo's egg. The book is a curious mixture of learning and credulity; but the former predominates.

This list of names of illustrious Jewish medical practitioners in the age of the Renaissance is already overlong. Yet the subject cannot be left without paying some attention to a different and indeed more significant side of the question, namely, the actual contribution of Jewish physicians of this period to medical science. In connection with this, it is necessary to take a somewhat different factor into consideration. The most memorable of those who will have to be taken into account belong to the category of the marranos, who have already been mentioned more than once, that is, the crypto-Jews of Spain and Portugal who, driven into Christianity, sometimes by sheer force, in the fourteenth and fifteenth centuries, managed to preserve their secret allegiance to Judaism and to transmit it to their descendants generation after generation, and even century after century. In their ranks, the proportion of physicians was for one reason or another extremely high; and they comprised a few medical writers of the very highest distinction. To take one example only: Garcia d'Orta, who had emigrated to the Portuguese possession of Goa in India, then at the height of its prosperity, is spoken of as the most important figure in the study of materia medica and pharmacology from the time of Discorides down to the seventeenth century; and his great work on medical botany, *Colloquios dos simples e drogas medicinães* (1563), was probably the greatest scientific monument of the Portuguese Renaissance. This learned composition includes the earliest descriptions by a European of tropical diseases, including cholera, and gives accounts of various medicinal plants which are still unsurpassed.[3]

It has recently been discovered that this great figure in the history of medicine was a Jew in everything but name. His forebears had been victims of the forced conversion in Portugal in 1497; some of his closest relatives were persecuted by the Inquisition as secret Judaizers; and one of his sisters was burned alive at an auto-da-fè. Only his death in 1568 saved the great physician himself from arrest and trial on the same charge; but twelve years later he was condemned posthumously, and his bones were dug up and burned, together with his effigy. He, indeed, never declared his Judaism publicly. On the other hand, many other Portuguese physicians of eminence did so, and became faithful sons of the synagogue: for example, Abraham Zacuto, or Zacutus Lusitanus, who settled in Amsterdam and published between 1629 and 1642 various works on general practice which were at one time much esteemed and ran into many editions; or Roderigo de Castro, who became a pillar of the synagogue in Hamburg and laid the basis of the science of gynaecology in his *De universa mulierum medicina* of 1603, and of medical jurisprudence in his *Medicus politicus* published posthumously in 1662.

In specific association with the Italian Renaissance, the most eminent and the most interesting of the marrano physicians—or of those at least who publicly declared their adherence to Judaism,

---

[3] The competence Jews were believed to have in this is shown also in the *Liber de balsamo* by Prospero Alpini (1533-1617), the first Director of the Botanic Garden at Padua, the form of which is a discussion at Cairo between the author, an Egyptian physician named Abdella, and a Jew named Abdachim. In the fifteenth century a Jew named Hayyim of Cyprus is said to have composed a work on the medicinal plants of Sardinia.

for there were many here too who did not[4]—was the person who
called himself, and is known to posterity by, the name of Amatus
Lusitanus, or Amatus the Portuguese. (The first name is probably
a Latinization of the Hebrew *Habib*, or perhaps *Oheb*.) In his
early years, as a Christian, he had been known as João Rodrigues,
and it was under that appellation that he graduated in Salamanca
about 1532. He then migrated, via Antwerp, to Italy, living first
at Venice and then at Ferrara, where for a time he held some sort
of university appointment in the medical school. He had a highly
distinguished clientele, including among the Jews Doña Gracia
Mendes, the redoubtable aunt of the Duke of Naxos, and her
household; and among the general population Pope Julius III, the
ambassadors of Spain and Portugal, and members of the ducal
House of Colonna. He was living in Ancona as a Jew at the time
of the frightful persecution of the marranos there in 1555/6, and
escaped to Pesaro, leaving his personal property and his manuscripts behind. Later, he crossed the Adriatic to Ragusa and finally
settled in Salonica, where he died. Precisely at what stage of his
life he publicly declared his adherence to Judaism is not quite
clear, but his later publications leave no doubt as to his religious
allegiance.

The career of the sixteenth-century marrano physician, who
was forced to leave his native land, lived a wandering existence,
attained a great reputation and had a distinguished clientele, is
not uncommon. It is of interest also for the medical historian that
Amatus, rather than as was once claimed Giovanni Battista Canano
(who witnessed his dissections), was responsible for the discovery
of the valves of the veins and their importance in the circulation
of the blood, and that he anticipated Vesalius in the operative treatment of empyema. But what gives him his importance in the intellectual history of the Renaissance is his writings. Apart from one
or two minor publications, these are mainly comprised in his seven

---

[4] A case in point was the illustrious Roderigo da Fonseca, who was
Professor of Medicine successively at Pisa and then (1615-22) at
Padua, and wrote numerous books on the subject from 1586 onward.
It is virtually certain that he was a "New Christian," but he remained
ostensibly a devoted son of the Church.

volumes of *Centuriae* or "Centuries," each containing the medical histories in Latin of one hundred cases which had come to his attention or in which he had effected a cure; the first part appeared at Florence in 1551, the last at Venice in 1566, and collected editions at intervals throughout the following century. At one time, they were used as clinical handbooks. But today, they constitute an almost inexhaustible source of information on medical history and (as is now being realized more and more) on social life and even individual biography in the sixteenth century. The episodes are treated in a highly personal fashion and with a strong sense of dramatic value. We are introduced to many distinguished names and personalities. We are told how, in Ragusa, the author was consulted by the judges in the case of a woman who was accused of having made a young man deaf by witchcraft, and how he demonstrated that the mishap was in fact due to syphilis. In a minor work, conceived on similar lines (*In Dioscoridis . . . de materia medica*, Venice, 1553), we are given details of the death of Don Samuel Abrabanel of Ferrara, the leading Jew of the city,[5] by taking an overdose of a drug. He tells us (*Centuria* IV.42) how, going one day into a book-shop, he met Azariah de' Rossi, the most brilliant figure in the Hebrew literary renaissance, was consulted by him as to his health, and describes in detail his appearance, his symptoms and his cure.[6] We are introduced to Jews living in England, at a time when no Jews were supposed to be there, and to marranos fleeing from Portugal to Italy together with their Negro slaves. It is a vast source of information, as yet most imperfectly explored.

Amatus Lusitanus, notwithstanding his flashes of insight, belonged essentially to the medieval school of medicine, not fundamentally changed since the days of the Arab scientific hegemony and still regarding Avicenna as the ultimate authority. The climate of the Renaissance was introduced into medical study by Andreas Vesalius, the greatest anatomist of all time. His *Tabulae anatomicae* of 1538, based on experiment and not on tradition, applied the new spirit to medical observation and made possible the subsequent revolution in the art of healing; the publication is regarded

---

[5] See p. 54.

[6] For De' Rossi, see pp. 318-334.

as opening a fresh age in the history of science in its more general sense. In this work, the author is at pains to give where possible the Hebrew equivalents for the organs which he describes. In this connection, he introduces us to a friend who helped him in his work, Lazarus de Frigeis, whom he calls a distinguished physician and his intimate acquaintance. With him he systemically studied Avicenna—apparently (though this is not certain) in a Hebrew version. (It is possible too from the phraseology that he had still another Jewish assistant.) Who Lazarus de Frigeis was cannot now be ascertained. It is just possible that he was the Jewish physician, Maestro Lazzaro ebreo, who was active in Venice in 1516-19; or conceivably he is the same as the Rhineland scholar Lazarus (Eleazar) of Mainz, physician in the household of the Emperor Ferdinand, who had scientific interests and composed a work in German on the nature of precious stones. However that may be, his association in this most significant work of the Renaissance era is of exceptional interest, for it shows us a Jew ranged by Vesalius' side on the threshold of modern science.

It is fantastic to find how implicitly some of the enlightened, skeptical Renaissance humanists believed in astrology and allowed their actions or their campaigns or, in the case of physicians, even their cures to be determined by the study of the stars. On the other hand, the fact cannot be too strongly emphasized that the pseudo-science, which still has so many votaries today, must be based on careful and accurate astronomical observation and calculation; for obviously, if it is desirable to undertake some action when a specific planet is in the ascendant, the time and period of that condition of the skies, and when it is likely to recur, must be determined precisely. Hence the astrologer had to be at the same time an astronomer, and indeed in the Middle Ages it was impossible to draw a precise line between the one and the other. By the same token, it is obvious that the call for astrology inevitably brought about considerable technical advances, the improvements in the astronomical instruments and tables of the Middle Ages receiving their impetus from astrological requirements.

In this respect, the Jews were children of their age, with perhaps one reservation: that the somewhat complicated requirements of the Jewish religious calendar, which ingeniously adjusted a precise lunar month to a cycle based on the solar year, imposed on all rabbinic scholars a minimal, and sometimes more than a minimal, astronomical knowledge, whatever their attitude toward astrology. Some rabbis, to be sure, poured scorn upon this latter "science": for example, in the Middle Ages it received no more trenchant condemnation than in a famous letter written in 1199 by Moses Maimonides in response to an inquiry on the subject by the scholars of Marseilles.[7] On the other hand, Jews are to be numbered among the most devoted "astronomologers" (if one may be permitted to coin the omnibus word) of the Middle Ages, and as such were responsible for some noteworthy advances in astral observation. In their outlook, they were essentially medieval, and thus it would be out of place to deal with them in this work. The work of some of them, however, links up with the new age. Thus, the improved quadrant known as Jacob's Staff, which was in use until relatively recently, was based on an invention which the fourteenth-century Provençal Jewish scholar, Levi ben Gershom, described in his philosophical classic *The Wars of the Lord*, in an astronomical section which was translated into Latin for Pope Clement VI and thus came to the notice of the great German scholar Johann Müller of Königsberg (Regiomontanus) in the fifteenth century.

Similarly, an improved astrolabe was devised for nautical use, on the eve of the great maritime discoveries, by a group of Portuguese scholars two of whom were Jews—the royal physicians Master Rodrigo and Master Joseph Vecinho. The great astronomical tables used in conjunction with these instruments, which accompanied the early explorers and were used by Columbus, were those prepared by Jewish scholars at the court of Alfonso the Wise of Castile. The more practical sets drawn up by Abraham Zacuto of Salamanca (who later entered the service of the king of Portugal) were edited by the Joseph Vecinho who has just been mentioned, and published by the Jewish printer Samuel

---

[7] The only literary production of Joseph Nasi, Duke of Naxos, is a little work, *Ben Porath Joseph* (Constantinople, 1577), reporting discussions on the subject in his palace of Belvedere, in which he took up the same attitude.

d'Ortas.[8] The writings of Zacuto and the *Sphaera mundi* of the thirteenth-century Irishman John Holywood (known as Sacrobosco)—the standard medieval astrological textbook—were brought together for more serious purposes in the earliest of all navigation manuals, *Regimento do estrolabio y do quadrante*, the first known edition of which appeared anonymously at Lisbon in 1509. This is so fundamental that, as has been said, all later manuals of the sort, to the present day, are no more than revised and enlarged editions of it. The authorship is unknown, but it has been ascribed, very plausibly, to this same Vecinho—possibly after his enforced conversion to Christianity in 1497 under the name of Diego Mendes. Later still, the marrano element in the country produced the greatest of Portuguese sixteenth-century scientists—Pedro Nuñes, Royal Cosmographer and Professor of Mathematics at Coimbra, whose *Treatise on the Sphere* (1537), opened the way for Mercator's work, and thus for the whole system of modern cartography.

Contemporary Italian Jewry produced no scientist who even approached this level. Yet there were a few Italian Jewish scholars of the Renaissance period who at least deserve mention in this connection. The most interesting in some respects was Mordecai ben Abraham Finzi of Mantua, recently identified, as has been mentioned above, with the financier Angelo Finzi, characteristic combination of scholar and businessman, who opened a loan-bank there in partnership with his brother, in 1435. He composed in, or translated into, Hebrew a whole series of treatises on mathematics and astronomy—in the latter case, without any specific astrological intentions, though no doubt they were implicit in his work—as well as a composition on mnemotechnics by his fellow-countryman Pietro Francesco of Orvieto. His anonymous *Tables of the Duration of Days*, printed at Mantua some time before 1480, is not only the earliest scientific publication in Hebrew, but at the same time (with only one possible exception) the earliest publication of a living author in the Hebrew language. He seems to have been in close touch with Mantuan intellectual and humanistic life, at that time very intense. Among his works is a description of the new astronomical instrument known as the celidario (a sort of

[8] See p. 177.

astrolabe) recently devised by Bartolomeo Manfredi, the famous local scientist and clock-maker, whom he knew personally. Elsewhere he cites a piece of information, regarding the construction of another instrument of the sort, which he had received orally "from the mouth of Master Bartolomeo delli Orologii in this city of Mantua."

Far more prominent, though perhaps less gifted, than Finzi in the world of learning a generation later, was Bonet (Bonetto) or Jacob de Lattes, who was papal physician under Alexander VI and his successors. A Provençal by birth ("Lattes" is a little place not far from Montpellier), he was the progenitor of the illustrious family of that name which was subsequently to furnish many persons of distinction to Italian Jewry. In the full medieval tradition, he was an astrologer as well as a physician, publishing in broadside form an annual astronomical calendar (*prognosticon*) to foretell the events of the coming year, at least between 1493 and 1499: that of 1498 was dedicated to the Cardinal of Valencia (that is, Cesare Borgia) and his kinsman the Cardinal Borgia. What is perhaps most amazing is that in this publication the author confidently announced the coming of the Messiah in 1505. He may have been credulous, but he was not lacking in technical ability, and before he left France he had invented an astronomical ring-dial—a sort of miniature astrolabe worn on the finger—to measure solar and stellar altitudes; by this means it would be possible to determine the time by night as well as by day. This he described in a little composition in Latin, which was first published as an appendix to a doggerel work by a contemporary Italian writer (Giuliano de Dati, *Calculatio composta in rima*, Rome, 1493), again independently in 1498 and repeatedly thereafter down to the middle of the century—for example, at Paris in 1507, 1516 and 1527 as an appendix to Sacrobosco's treatise on the sphere,[9] and further in 1534, 1538 and 1557. In the dedication to Pope Alexander, the author apologized—with reason—for his poor Latin, and

---

[9] In the margin to this edition, at the side of a harmless flight of fancy where the author said that "The work of Thy fingers" in Psalm 8.4 refers to the eclipses, the printer Henri Estienne noted tartly: "How ridiculous" (*phantastica sunt haec*).

reverted again to the subject at the end of his treatise, which closes with an execrable dystich in that language:

> Reader, forgive my errors and grammatical infelicity;
> By faith I am a Jew, and am deficient in Latinity.[10]

When the French mathematician-philosopher Charles Bouelles (Bovillus) was in Rome in 1507 (he recounts in his theological work, *Dialogi de Trinitate*, Paris 1519), he met Dr. Bonet de Lattes in the Jewish quarter one Sunday afternoon, was introduced to him and went to his residence in order to inspect this invention of his. (The marble tablet which distinguished his house, inscribed in Hebrew with his name, was found in the bed of the Tiber not long ago.) He describes how the upper floor had been converted into a synagogue, where he saw the Ark containing the Holy Scrolls, hidden by a curtain, and the other normal Jewish ritual paraphernalia; and here one of Bonet's sons, who proved to be extremely well-versed in Aristotle, was sitting deeply immersed in philosophical study. A lengthy theological discussion ensued between the young man and the French visitor, but it remained on a friendly basis. Some time before this, under Pope Leo X, when Johann Reuchlin was assailed by the Dominicans of Cologne in connection with his defense of Hebrew literature and his book *Augenspiegel* which he had published, was condemned by them, he sent Lattes a lengthy letter in the language of the Bible begging him to use his influence with the Holy Father to secure the withdrawal of the case from Dominican jurisdiction. A Christian scholar writing—in Hebrew—to solicit the intervention of a Jew with the Pope in his dispute with the friars: this sums up in a sentence the spirit of Renaissance Italy!

The family of Bonet de Lattes maintained his distinction among Roman Jewry. This was especially true of his son Immanuel, also a physician, who was likewise highly esteemed at the court of Pope Leo X, translated a book for him from Hebrew into Latin which was considered to be for the general utility of Christendom, and was suitably rewarded for it. He maintained his connec-

---

[10] *Parce precor rudibus, que sunt errata latino;*
Lex hebrea michi est: lingua latinus minus.

tion with Provence, where the family had originated, and in 1529 was engaged by the City Council of Avignon to give a series of public lectures on the art of medicine. There is an interesting relic of the family in a medal struck in 1552, bearing on one side the portrait of Immanuel's daughter-in-law, Rica de Lattes, and on the other that of her son, Elijah.

Numerous other scholars of some note, whose names we have already encountered—especially physicians—were not only believers in but even vigorous exponents of astrology. Maestro Calo, or Calo Calonymus (Calonymus ben David), who was so active as a scientific translator in the early sixteenth century, is recorded to have foretold the war which was to be waged against Venice by the League of Cambrai; similarly, in March 1513, he respectfully urged the doge not to be alarmed by the eclipse of the sun, which he was confident augured no ill to the Republic. There is extant in Parma (Codex de' Rossi, 336) a volume containing astronomical treatises compiled and horoscopes cast by this typical child of his age before he left Naples, where his father, David Calo, also figures in the records as the royal astronomer. Even Leone Ebreo (Judah Abrabanel) is referred to as following the same calling.

More typical perhaps than these scholars of the Renaissance atmosphere, if not of the Renaissance outlook, were the charlatans whose astrological pretensions were not balanced by any real astronomical knowledge, but who were able nevertheless to batten on the credulity both of the masses and of the classes. Among these there were not a few Jewish cheapjacks, whose alien background and reputation for the possession of recondite knowledge no doubt added to their professional glamor. Indeed, a series of "Prognostications of the Most Excellent Astrograph Zacut, of Ferrara," who obviously was a Jew and perhaps of Abraham Zacuto's own family (or Abraham Zacuto himself?), were published annually in Italian in that city, after the style of *Old Moore's Almanac*, between about 1525 (if not earlier) and 1535. Apart from this, we have many other indications of the sort. We know, for example, of Messer Vitale Cannaruto (de Cannarutis), who was described in 1488 as Astrologer Royal to the Crown of Naples; and it is probable too that the "philosophers" Minach and Sabatello of San Severino, whom we encounter here in 1491, owed this title to similar pretensions. Filippo Maria Visconti, Duke of Milan, who was reputed to do nothing without seeking the guidance of the stars, had a Jew named Elias among the astrologers in his service. To the present day, one of the characteristic surnames among Roman Jewry is "Dello Strologo" (= "son of the Astrologer"), which presumably derives from some long-distant ancestor who was reputed to be proficient in the study of the stars. The most famous of all astrologers of this or of any other age, Nostradamus, was the grandson of the Jewish physician of King Réné of Provence, who had become converted to Christianity and was henceforth called after the Virgin Mary (Notre Dame).[11]

But by this time the specific Jewish competence in these matters was waning, and Jewish writers were avidly attempting to assimilate the latest advances of European science and in some cases to render them available to their co-religionists. In the seventeenth century, for example, Joseph Baruch d'Urbino of Mantua rendered into Hebrew the works of Piccolomini, one of the most popular astronomical writers of the sixteenth century. Beyond the borders of Italy, meanwhile, David Gans of Prague (1541-1613) participated in astronomical observations in the Prague observatory, carried on a scientific correspondence with Johann Müller (Regiomontanus), was in contact with Kepler and Tycho Brahe, and was commissioned by the last-named to translate from Hebrew into German the Alphonsine Tables, drawn up by medieval Jewish scholars in Spain. But, though acquainted with the work of Copernicus (which he attributed to the Pythagoreans!), Gans in his own writings followed the superseded Ptolemaic system. The *Porto Astronomico* by Rabbi Emanuel Porto, of Trieste, *ove si ha la dottrina di fabricare le tavole dei seni tangenti . . .* (Padua, 1636), is unimportant save as a curiosity.

In modern times, Jews have shown a considerable proclivity

---

[11] The German convert Paolus Riccius, who became Professor of Philosophy at Pavia (above, p. 145) also dabbled in astrology. Among the by-products of his interest was a controversy with the theologian Maier Eck, Luther's great antagonist, on the highly modern question of the possibility of the existence of life on the stellar bodies.

toward mathematics, and in the Middle Ages too their contribution to that subject was of great importance. The twelfth-century scholar Abraham bar Hiyya of Barcelona, by his translations and original work, laid the foundations of the study of higher mathematics—especially geometry—in Europe, and is (though not only for that reason) one of the most noteworthy figures in the history of medieval science. More dramatic was the history of the very popular astronomical and mathematical work of the fourteenth-century Provençal scholar Immanuel Bonfils of Tarrascon, entitled *Shesh Kenafayim* or "The Six Pinions." This, translated early into Latin, and later from Latin into Russian, was among the most important of the works by which mathematical studies were first introduced into that country.

It is not surprising, therefore, to find that some Jews contributed to this study in the Renaissance period as well. A number of Jewish writers of the age, moreover, composed Hebrew works in which they endeavored to give some idea of mathematics to their co-religionists. Among the writings of Mordecai Finzi of Mantua, for example, was a translation from the Latin of a work on algebra by the Arab, Abu Kamil Shuya, and a more or less original treatise on geometry which he entitled *Hokhmat haMedidah* or "The Science of Measuring." Later on, some popularizing works of this type—such as, *Ober laSokher* (Venice, 1627) by Emanuel (Menahem) Porto, Rabbi of Trieste, who has been mentioned above— were published and seem to have achieved some measure of success.

It was characteristic that the basic Jewish literature could sometimes plunge the student into these apparently remote studies. In his *Guide for the Perplexed* Moses Maimonides had devoted a chapter (I.lxxiii) to discussing twelve propositions which were accepted by the Arab philosophers, including the problem of the difference between commensurable and incommensurable lines. The elucidation of this subject engaged the attention of Moses Provenzal, the learned and enlightened Mantuan rabbi, who composed a brief geometrical treatise in Hebrew explaining it. This was published as an appendix to the Sabbionetta edition of the *Guide* in 1553 (though possibly printed earlier). It was considered to be of sufficiently general interest to appeal to a wider public. Accordingly, one of the author's friends, Joseph Shalit of Padua (known also as printer and typographer), translated it from Hebrew into Italian (perhaps after the author's manuscript), this appearing in Mantua in 1550 under the title *Opera nova di giometria in dimostrare come possano uscire due linee sopra una superficie, le quali procedendo non possano incontrarsi mai* (dedicated to the illustrious Spanish statesman and poet, Diego Hurtado de Mendoza, friend and patient of Jacob Mantino). The brilliant Venetian mathematician Francesco Barozzi, something of a Hebraist in his own right, who was to end his days miserably because of his dabbling in the magical arts, was so impressed by it that he translated it, with Maimonides' original, into Latin and included it with twelve other methods of solving the problem in a publication of his own (Venice, 1586).

Technology was making blundering advances throughout the Renaissance period, and every now and again we find traces of Jewish participation in it. One of the earliest patents on record was granted by the Venetian senate in 1508 to a Jew from Padua named Joseph (Giuseppe ebreo da Padova) for an invention no details of which however are available to me. Notwithstanding the prejudice against the Jews, at this time very strong in this city (where they were as yet not allowed to settle permanently), no difficulty was experienced in a matter of this sort. Some years before this, that same august body had authorized the association of a number of Jews with a Christian mechanic in developing a machine that he had devised, as no differences of creed should be taken into account in matters in which the public weal was concerned. The nature of this invention is not specified—it was presumably concerned with manufacture, perhaps of textiles. We know of a Jew named Solomon who had a reputation as an engineer second to none in Italy in his day. In 1444, Lionello d'Este, Lord of Ferrara, informed the civic authorities there that he had "engaged as Engineer Magister Solomon the Jew" and requested them to make arrangements for his payment. In this same year, a plan was put forward for the diversion, for sanitary reasons, of the waters of the river Brenta. Master Solomon happened to be in Venice at the time, and the senate ordered that he be consulted in this matter, "for it is understood that he has a pefect mastery and skill in the matter of leveling the waters." Another Italian Jewish "engineer" of the period was Isaac of Noyon, known as

"Magister Achino ingegnere," who offered his services to the Duke of Milan in 1437 to construct a bridge over the river Po.[12] In 1515, much interest was aroused by a report that some Roman Jews had invented an improved process for the manufacture of saltpeter (potassium nitrate), the principal ingredient in the manufacture of gunpowder, which would produce a far greater supply at lower cost. The Cardinal Giulio de' Medici (later to be Pope Clement VII), learning of this, wrote to his cousin Lorenzo in Florence urgently recommending him to invite these Jews to work for him, either there or at Pisa, as this would be of the utmost utility to the state.[13]

Outside the realms of medicine and "astronomology," little scientific literature was produced at this time by Italian Jews. In 1582, however, a certain Jewish physician of Ferrara named Raphael Mirami (of whom little or nothing else is known) published an ingenious work on the refraction of light (*Compendiosa introduttione alla prima parte della specularia*), which he dedicated to Antonio Montecatini, the duke's Secretary of State (the second part bore the name of one Camillo Giglioli). In this work there is an appendix showing how to construct a sun (or moon) dial-clock in a shady place, by an ingenious use of reflectors. For such a purpose the finest mirrors would obviously be required, and for this it would no doubt have been possible to avail oneself of the vegetable oil for which a patent was received in 1588 from Pope Sixtus V by a Jew of French descent, Meir son of Gabriel Magino of Venice; it was claimed that this oil produced remarkable results

---

[12] A Jewish construction engineer, Mendel Isaacovitch, whose specialty was bridge-building, is recorded in Poland also at the close of the sixteenth century: in 1592, he was entrusted by King Sigismund III with a personal mission to Vienna.

[13] Late in the seventeenth century, Samuel and Joseph Saltiel introduced to the Duchy of Savoy a process of smelting gold without fire (presumably, that is, through the use of acids). Outside Italy, the outspoken Joachim Gans (Gaunse) of Prague, a kinsman of the historian David Gans, worked in the capacity of mining engineer in England and made some important technical innovations. Dr. Abraham Portaleone refers in his *Shilte haGiborim* to a work written in 1561 by Meshullam da Volterra, of Pesaro, which dealt with the nature of precious stones and casting precious metals.

in polishing mirrors and cut glass. This same Magino also invented a new process for silk manufacture and received from the same Pope a monopoly for this on condition that the profits were shared with the pontiff's sister. By way of specification Magino published an entire book devoted to the subject, in the form of dialogue. As part of his reward, and to make his work easier for him, he was empowered to live outside the ghetto for the next fifteen years—by now, a rare and coveted privilege. The essential part of the new process seems to have been the reputed discovery of how to obtain cocoons from the silk-worm twice in a year. But it does not seem as though his enterprise was particularly successful, for later (1597) he turns up in Lorraine, as Maggino Gabrieli, still with ambitious new projects stirring in his brain.

The practice of alchemy had been very common in Italy in the fourteenth century, but the scientific spirit of the Renaissance undermined the fashion to some extent. Nevertheless, there were still many persons who searched desperately after the secret of manufacturing precious metal, and Jews were apparently to be found among them, at least in proportion to their numbers. An affluent Jewish loan-banker in Modena, in the middle of the sixteenth century, became so impassioned an experimentalist that he actually handed over to a swindler all the gold and silver in his possession in complete confidence that he would get it back artificially augmented; in fact, the result was that he was lured to his death. We owe these details to his nephew, Leone Modena, who was not warned by this example, but himself became a devotee of the pseudo-science. In 1603, he joined in the alchemical experiments of a Roman Jewish physician who should have known better. Subsequently, Leone's own son set up a laboratory for the purpose in the ghetto of Venice in conjunction with a Catholic priest. Modena now confidently anticipated an income of a thousand ducats a year with a minimum of labor. On one occasion he even sold some silver which he actually believed to have been made out of lead. Unfortunately, the young man was poisoned by the arsenic fumes used in his work, and with his death another hope of restoring the family fortune ended in disaster. To be sure, this alchemical interest was not confined to Italy. At the court of Prague, where the study was avidly pursued, a Polish Jew, named Mordecai of Nelle, was the official royal chronicler for all activities and experiments of the sort. Here, however, the theory had been seriously put forward that there was a short cut to the mastery of the secret in the fact that gold could literally be distilled out of a Jew's body!

Mention has been made more than once in various connections in the foregoing pages of that extraordinary person, part certainly impostor, and part possibly genius, Abraham Colorni. A summary account of his career may fittingly close this chapter. He was born in 1544 in Mantua, but we know nothing about his life until he emerged a quarter of a century later as an architect in the service of Alfonso II, Duke of Ferrara. He seems to have had a share in the construction of the sumptuous ducal villa known as the Palazzo della Mesola, and at the same time assisted in designing the fortifications of the city, at that time considered one of the constructional marvels of Europe. For (if it is permitted to select one out of the large number of occupations that engaged his attention) his specialty was military engineering. He invented all manner of ingenious devices, some of them strikingly modern, for facilitating the art of war—bridges that could be thrown over rivers or moats in a few minutes, thus rendering the strongest fortress vulnerable; boats which could be reduced into the smallest possible space and thus be of inestimable value for night attacks; folding ladders, equally useful for assaulting bastions or for extinguishing fires; and similar devices. He invented new methods for the manufacture of gunpowder, for the firing of artillery, for mines; he described with gusto a series of musical instruments which in an emergency could be converted into weapons; he boasted that he could save a beleaguered army by the use of sunken trenches. On one occasion he is reported to have offered for the consideration of the Venetian government an expensive plan to exterminate entire crowds in church or at a banquet without arousing suspicion, the solitary remedy being an antidote which he was prepared to sell along with his specific. His most remarkable invention, if the report is true, was an anticipation of the quick-firing guns of the nineteenth century. The Duke of Ferrara was, in fact, sufficiently impressed to order from him two thousand arquebuses, able to fire ten shots without reloading. There is no documentary evidence that they were delivered, but the fact that the inventor remained in favor seems to suggest that the project was not completely fraudulent: moreover, shortly thereafter he offered similar warlike instruments to the Pope. In the more peaceful arts, he had a special ability in stucco-work; he manufactured improved clocks and sundials; he anticipated and perhaps manufactured a taximeter. In 1589, lent by Alfonso d'Este to his brother-in-law, the warlike Giacomo II, Duke of Savoy, who suffered severely from gout, Colorni constructed a horse-drawn invalid chair for his use. He was a skilled swordsman and duelist. He was an expert juggler. He could perform feats of legerdemain. He has been spoken of as the man who invented card-tricks, at which he was adept. He boasted that he could escape from any prison by secret means. In 1580, he received a license to publish a work entitled *Euthimetria*. No copy of this (if it appeared) has survived. Raphael Mirami, however, informs us that it gave instructions for the use of mirrors in measuring heights, distances and depths. He also compiled a volume of mathematical tables and a treatise entitled *Chiriofisonomia*, directed against the "superstitions" of physiognomology and chiromancy, at the express request of Vincenzo Gonzaga, Duke of Mantua, to whom it was dedicated. This alone, his admirers said, was sufficient to preserve his fame for posterity. Another *magnum opus* of his was a translation from the Hebrew of the magical treatise, the *Key of Solomon*, which he made for the same ruler. This is extant in Italian, French and in Spanish, and was considered by Napoleon sufficiently interesting or useful for a finely-decorated copy of the last-named version, executed as recently as 1778, to be included in his personal library at St. Helena. The only one of his works to be published, however, was an ingenious but involved guide to secret writing, entitled *Scotografia, overo scienza di scrivere oscuro . . . per qual si voglia lingua . . . et per cifra et per contra cifra* (Prague, 1593).

This versatile son, or stepson, of the Renaissance was clearly a highly entertaining companion. It is not remarkable that he had a number of Gentile admirers, who praised his achievements in prose and verse. Above all, he was in close touch with the ingenious Canon Tommaso Garzoni, who admired his ability devoutly, hoped for his conversion, and described his inventions, at great length, in his curious and at one time extremely popular encyclopaedia of queer trades, *La Piazza universale di tutte le professioni del mondo* (first published in Venice, 1592), which included also a sonnet in his honor.

Colorni remained active at the courts of Ferrara and Mantua for some ten years. He was then summoned to Prague by the Emperor Rudolph II, who delighted in every sort of magical and supernatural experiment, so that his court resembled a vast al-chemical laboratory. Thence, after some years, he went on to Stuttgart, at the invitation of the Duke of Württemberg. But here he failed to give satisfaction—German princes apparently required more solid results than those of Italy—and his visit ended in a prison. For once at least his pretensions were justified by results, for he escaped and made his way back to the court of Mantua where, notwithstanding the protests of his last employer, he was again benignly received. He died not long thereafter, in 1599, at the age of fifty-five, and his secrets with him. Whether he was an inventor born before his time or a mere charlatan, or as is more probable a combination of both, it is impossible to say.

ELEVEN

The Jews *and* the
Renaissance Theater

The rabbis of antiquity, in second- and third-century Palestine, objected to the theater, considering it a center of utter immorality, the antithesis to the synagogue and house of study. It must be remembered, of course, that what they had in mind was not the sublimity of Attic drama but the pornographic comedies of provincial touring companies. Nevertheless, Jewish actors were known, even in that age. There was one, Alytiros, at the court of Nero; others—including an actress, whose sarcophagus is preserved —are buried in the Roman catacombs; and as early as the second century B.C.E. an Alexandrian Jew named Ezekiel (Ezekielos) composed a drama in the Greek style and language, of which some fragments have been preserved, on the subject of the Exodus.

In the Middle Ages, the Jews, sharing the outlook of their neighbors, developed in their own quarters a similar cultural life, which likewise groped toward a vague dramatic expression associated with various religious manifestations. Synagogue poets, like those of the Church, wrote moral dialogues between Man and his Soul, or between the spirits of Good and Evil, which were essentially dramatic in conception if not in presentation. It is true that the Jews could have nothing in the nature of the passion play which at Easter-tide recalled to the Christian faithful the climax of the earthly career of Jesus of Nazareth. On the other hand, owing to the accident of juxtaposition in the religious calendar (unless it was that both inherited independently the same pre-Christian tradition) their Purim celebrations inevitably took on something of the color of the Catholic carnival-tide at which crude dramatic representations provided in the comic spirit the counterpart to the "divine tragedy" which was in preparation.

From a very early date, we read of Purim pageants, in which the part of Haman would be represented sometimes by a malefactor, upon whom condign punishment might thus be inflicted. (A case in point is recorded from Manosque, in southern France, in 1306. It was perhaps a similar episode which led the Jews of the tiny community of Stamford, in England, to be accused in 1222 of "making a game" in mockery of the Christian faith.) From this it was clearly an easy step, under external influence, to more methodical dramatic performances. Thus, the Purim play had its beginning; taking as its subject first and foremost the story of Mordecai and Esther, with Haman as its butt, and then extending to a few other biblical subjects, within a very limited range, such as the Sale of Joseph or the story of David and Goliath. Full documentation and texts are available only from a relatively late date—not perhaps before the seventeenth century; but (as will be seen) there can be no doubt that the practice was adequately developed at the time of the Renaissance, and hence existed even before.

In Italy, at the time of the Renaissance, the institution was fully established and generally familiar. "This night," wrote Marin Sanuto, the Venetian diarist, on Saturday, March 4, 1531 (the day following Purim), "there was performed among the Jews in the 'Geto' a very fine comedy; but no Christian could be present by order of the Council of Ten. It ended at ten o'clock at night."

It seems pretty certain that this was an annual event well known in Venice, and that in other years Christians had flocked to attend—otherwise, the Council of Ten would have known nothing of it beforehand. We have to imagine, too, that it was something more than one of the traditional Purim buffooneries, for Italian Jews were by now beginning to be affected by the new currents in dramatic literature. Already the drama in a European sense had been introduced into Hebrew by Giuseppe Gallo (Joseph Sarfatti) in an adaptation of the famous Spanish comedy *Celestina* (the author of which, as is now known, was a marrano, Fernando de Rojas). This, however, remained unpublished, and knowledge of it has only recently come to light.[1]

---

[1] As early as 1488, the Turkish Karaite, Caleb Afendopolo, had written an elementary biblical drama on Abner ben Ner and the court of King Saul. This, however, links up rather with the medieval tradition.

There was another connection between the Jews and the incipient drama of the late Middle Ages. In the passion plays, the Jews figured as the villains of the piece; and the spectators clearly did not differentiate between the Jews of antiquity and those of their own day. It was natural that they should be introduced into the carnival-tide antithesis to the passion play. This tradition, too, goes back to an early date. We are told that at Huesca in Spain, in 1279, the rabble carried out a mock-baptism after the manner of the Torah, to the accompaniment of ribald hymns, and the proceedings ended with a parody of the Jewish custom of electing a "Purim king," who was then cacophonously escorted through the streets. In Rome in the Renaissance period, plays mocking Jewish life and customs which were known as *giudate* (= Jeweries) were an essential part of the traditional popular drama acted on ox-carts around the streets during the carnival season. These were forbidden in the sixteenth century owing to the unpleasant atmosphere which they caused. Nevertheless, long after this, the Fishermen's Guild was accustomed to present, as its dramatic *chef d'oeuvre* at this season, burlesques of Jewish ceremonial, such as the mock-funeral of a rabbi. (It was only in 1768 that this practice was stopped.) From this, it was a short step to the anti-Jewish drama in the regular theater, of which Elizabethan England provides classical instances. Burlesque Jewish characters thus figure in two of the comedies of Ariosto—*Il Marescalco* and *La Cortigiana*—setting an example which knew many imitations.[2]

For a long time, a play on the subject of Abraham and the Sacrifice of Isaac, by the Mantuan rabbi Moses Zacuto (1625-97) was thought to be the earliest dramatic experiment in Hebrew. The connection with Mantua is in any case significant. For Giuseppe Gallo see pp. 144 f. and 217 f.

[2] The contemporary Jew sometimes figures, too, in the "Sacre Rappresentazioni" or morality plays, such as the well-known *Agnolo Ebreo* (Agnolo = Angelo = Mordecai: see above p. 19). Agnolo's Christian wife persuades him to abandon the practice of usury and give his money away in alms. Heaven compensates him for this by enriching him miraculously: he picks up money in the street and finds a jewel in the belly of a fish. Realizing that only the God of the Christians can make him rich, he becomes baptized. This conveyed at least a better impression than the habitual passion plays or outright anti-Jewish burlesques. A Jewish sorcerer figures also in the "Sacra Rappresentazione," *Teofilo*: see above, p .67.

To burlesque Jews, when there were Jews available who could be forced to burlesque themselves, was superfluous; and from the thirteenth century at the latest the Jews were compelled—certainly in Rome and at Marsala in Sicily, presumably elsewhere as well—to join in the carnival-time buffooneries by acting as mounts for the soldiers or populace in their races. The *Corso degli ebrei,* or Race of the Jews, which later became a feature of the carnival in Rome, was clearly connected with this. From this it was not a difficult transition for them to be compelled to provide buffoons at all times for the diversion of the powerful, not only in the Christian, but also in the Moslem world—as for the sultan in Constantinople, at least from the sixteenth century on. Parallel, therefore, to the spontaneous development of an incipient drama among the Jews of the Renaissance period, we find that histrionics of a different sort, which, however, may have proved useful in a way, were thrust upon them.

The first record of serious participation that I have been able to trace thus far comes from Pesaro, the seaport on the Adriatic coast (later incorporated in the Duchy of Urbino) which was in the second half of the fifteenth century an appanage of the House of Sforza. In October 1489, Giovanni Sforza, Lord of Pesaro, was married in this city to Maddalena Gonzaga, sister of the Marquess of Mantua, the Duke and Duchess of Urbino being among the guests. The *pièce de resistance* of the resplendent wedding celebrations was a dramatic performance based on the story of Judith and Holophernes, which according to a report sent home by the bride's brother was staged by and at the expense of the local Jewish community. Unfortunately, no other details have been preserved. But though it is the first recorded, it was not necessarily the first instance of such dramatic representations by Jews of the Renaissance period in honor of reigning families: the inconsequential way in which it is mentioned makes it in fact probable that this was usual. The story of Judith and Holophernes was a favorite subject of the anonymous popular drama published in this age; and the interesting problem presents itself whether these and other publications of a similar nature were not perhaps written in some cases by Jews and for performance in the Jewish quarter. The story was certainly a popular one among them, as we see from numerous representations on Italian ritual objects and references in religious literature. And it is significant that the theatrical tradition is known to have persisted in the ghetto of Pesaro down to the end of the eighteenth century, when a local rabbi, Daniel Terni, wrote various quasi-dramatic compositions for public performance there.

At the period with which we are dealing, the stage was not wholly professionalized; it was only in the process of being organized in a modern sense. Dramatic representations were generally given by amateurs or quasi-amateurs, sometimes perhaps with professional participation; not yet in specially-built places of public resort, but sometimes in the marketplace or inn-yard, and at other times in the spacious salons of the nobility who sponsored the productions for the delectation of their friends. Especially prominent in this sort of activity in Renaissance Italy was the ducal House of Gonzaga, which made the city of Mantua famous in the sixteenth century for the scale, magnificence and perfection of its court pageantry and public spectacles, organized on the slightest pretext. The stage at this period was in this category; and Mantua thus became one of the centers of the new Italian drama, which was to have such important repercussions. The dukes provided the impetus, the patronage, the setting. But, there being no professional dramatic companies, the actual performance was left to or imposed upon their faithful subjects.

Among these, there was a sizable Jewish community. As we have seen, it was not very ancient, nor was it particularly well populated. In the sixteenth century, it comprised something less than two thousand people (the exact figure given for 1584 is 1,844)—some of them descended from very old Italian Jewish families, others from more recent Germanic immigrants from over the Alps, by now, however, thoroughly Italianized in speech and outlook. They were profoundly influenced by the brilliant atmosphere of the environment, the Renaissance culture—especially perhaps in its more superficial and languorous aspects—being more acclimatized among them probably than anywhere else in Italian Jewry. They had an absorbing interest, it seems, not only in music but also in the drama. Their performances speedily acquired a considerable reputation among their neighbors. So great was the enthusiasm which this species of diversion aroused that in 1564 the far from unenlightened Rabbi David Provenzal felt impelled to warn his community against allowing it to obtain too strong a hold. Thus it happened that, when successive dukes of Mantua desired to have a performance for the delectation of the court or the entertainment of some visiting ruler, it was very frequently to the Jews that they turned, enjoining them to stage the spectacle, whether comedy or tragedy, which was required.

How far back this tradition went cannot be precisely ascertained. The first mention is said to be of 1525, but it is possible to add a few years to the conventional record. In 1520, Cardinal Ercole Gonzaga gave a great banquet in order to celebrate in fitting fashion the accession of his brother, the Marquess (later, from 1530, Duke) Federico. In the fashion of the time, he desired to round off the festivities by having a "comedy" presented before his guests. His literary factotum, Mario Equicola, accordingly wrote in his name to the Duke of Ferrara, his former patron, asking him to send to Mantua for this purpose two Jewish actors, Solomon and Jacob (*Salamone e Jacopo ebrei*), who obviously enjoyed some reputation in this field. What the comedy was in which they acted we do not know. But this episode is of exceptional importance, not only because it throws back the association of the Jews with the Mantuan theater for an appreciable time, but also because it shows that those of Ferrara too (whose records have not been sufficiently investigated from this point of view) were of importance in the same sphere. The case of Pesaro has already been discussed. It becomes increasingly probable that this was a commonplace throughout Italy at the time.

In any case, by 1525, the participation of the Jews in the state performances at Mantua was regarded as a normal thing. In that year, the ducal secretary, writing to the Marchioness Dowager in Rome about the carnival celebrations, observed: "Tomorrow another comedy will be recited by the Jews, having been composed by them." (The last words are intriguing. Are we to understand that they were ordered to reënact their Purim play—this would have been the right season for it—or that they already had at this time some competent playwright among them, as they had, as we shall see, a little later on?) Again, in August 1549, on the occasion of the marriage of Duke Francesco (Federico's successor) and Catherina, daughter of the King of the Romans and niece of the Emperor Charles V, two "comedies" were presented—one by "our Mantuan actors" and the other by the Jews. Since the German visitors could not understand Italian, there was a musical diversion as well, to save them from being bored; almost certainly, this was also entrusted to the Jews, being another of their specialties.

As to the nature of this spectacle, we again have no inkling. But we are told what it was that the Jews performed at court in 1563, in honor of the visit of the Archdukes Rudolph and Ernest of Austria—Ludovico Ariosto's *Suppositi*, a rather dreary comedy in the classical Latin tradition, distinguished only for its purity of language. "It was acted admirably, and there was music by first-class performers, and above all the setting was very fine, with magnificent vistas and splendid lighting effects," wrote an eye-witness. Again, we learn that during the carnival of 1568 the Jews put on a new comedy, *Le Due Fulvie* by the Mantuan amateur Massimo Faroni, which had been duly approved by the Academy. A gentleman of the court had been appointed to supervise the production, as was usual on such occasions: it happened to be Bernardo Tasso, whose son, Torquato, was already at work on his *Gerusalemme liberata*.

Another comedy was produced by the Jews for the carnival of 1582. It was not very good in itself, the inquisitive Duke of Ferrara was informed, but the *mise en scène* was magnificent and there were exceptionally fine *intermedi*. (These *intermedi* or *intermezzi* [interludes], of which we shall hear a good deal henceforth, were the musical or spectacular diversions between the acts, which sometimes outdid the plays themselves for brilliance and had a greater appeal to some sections of the audience. In the long run, this extravagance almost stifled the Italian drama, the *intermezzo* becoming more important than the play and the spectacle more important than the action.) At the end, a *moresca* (ballet) was performed by the duke's pages, with torches on their heads: "a delightful spectacle, well worth seeing." Some of the specifications for the costumes and properties used, apparently on this occasion, under the direction of this same Massimo Faroni, have recently come to light in the archives of the Mantuan Jewish community. Another performance which attracted attention was given in 1584 to celebrate the marriage of the dissolute heir-apparent, Prince Vincenzo, *en secondes noces*, to a daughter of the Grand Duke of Tuscany. As the latter was told by his secretary, who had escorted the bride to her new home: "Yesterday, a comedy was presented by the Jewish actors (*istrioni hebrei*). It was not at all badly recited, with pleasing though commonplace and inexpensive *intermezzi*." The play chosen on this occasion was the popular *Ingiusti Sdegni* by the Abbé Bernardo Pino of Cagli (a work more remarkable indeed for its moral elevation than for its artistic merit); and the performance was presumably diversified by the dances commissioned for it in the previous year from the Jewish ballet-master Isacchino Massarano, of whom more will be said later.[3]

Not only the duke, but the heir apparent too, Don Vincenzo Gonzaga, availed himself of the services of the Jewish theatrical company. In 1582, we find him informing his father, now a valetudinarian, that to celebrate his birthday he had decided to have a comedy presented by the Jews at Mantua, and asking his permission; it would not be noisy, the young man dutifully promised. (Possibly he had in mind Leone de' Sommi's *Il Giannizero*—of which more below—which was first produced about this time.) In the following year he wished to have a similar performance to enhance the carnival diversions, but since he could not be in Mantua then, he asked for permission to substitute for it a tragedy by Manfredi, which he said would not be a terrifying one. The duke refused permission, however—he did not like tragedies—and suggested that the performance should take place somewhere else. In 1587, Vincenzo wanted two comedies performed for the carnival in the castle theater—one by the Jewish players and the other by Christians. The duke gave his consent, but on this occasion the Jews' performance did not in fact take place, as they were not allowed enough time for preparations and rehearsals.

On the death that summer of his father, whose last days had been solaced by the playing of his Jewish favorite Abramino dell' Arpa,[4] Vincenzo himself became duke. The full spirit of Renaissance splendor now became installed in Mantua as nowhere else in Italy, or indeed in Europe. Every form of art was lavishly encouraged,

───────────
[3] See below, p. 284 f.
[4] See below, p. 283 f.

without regard to expense. The court was everywhere famous for the richness of its collections, the magnificence of its costumes, and the frequency as well as the fantastic splendor of its pageants. Although he was by no means pro-Jewish (he expelled all "foreign" Jews from the city in 1590, and it was in his days that the reaction against Mantuan Jewry began), the most resplendent of the Jewish theatrical performances certainly took place during his reign, after which the House of Gonzaga began to decline.

Already in the autumn following the new duke's accession, the community was commissioned to produce a "comedy or pastoral," probably to celebrate His Serene Highness' birthday. But this time they were forewarned by experience. Would he decide on the piece as soon as possible, they requested, so that there would be enough time for them to learn and rehearse their parts? In the following years, other performances are mentioned, though we have no details, and it is probable in fact that these court functions had by now become annual events. In successive years, from 1596 on, we have positive evidence of this from incidental mentions in the archives of the Jewish community itself, though in 1597 the performance that had been prepared was canceled owing to the death of the Duke of Ferrara that October.

The performance of the otherwise-unknown comedy, *Accesi da amor* ("Inflamed by Love") during the carnival of 1605 must have been especially resplendent. Over eighty members of the Jewish community who participated (including one who was designated as rabbi) were exempted from the obligation of carrying a lantern at night, as had been enjoined on all good citizens by the duke's officials in order to prevent disorder. The *intermezzi* for this performance were arranged by Federigo Follino, the court Master of Ceremonies ("soprintendente alle feste del nostro palazzo"), a man accustomed, as has been said, "to translate life into choreography." The accounts of this performance too have recently come to light in the archives of the Jewish community. It should be noted that the information that has been given above is mostly derived from incidental mentions in a wide variety of scattered sources: there can be no doubt that many other performances took place which have escaped record.

We do not know very much about what might be termed the logistics of these presentations, as far as the Jewish community was concerned. They were obviously regarded as official affairs, communications on the subject being made by the ducal officials to the *Massaro*, or head of the community as representing his co-religionists; the latter in turn appointed a special commission to supervise the arrangements. Participation was not always spontaneous; on one occasion, in 1587, we find the Jews requesting that a court gentleman should be appointed as soon as possible to supervise the proposed production, so that he should be able to procure them the effects that they needed and put pressure on any person who refused to collaborate. For the wealthy merchant and banker class, this did not present any great material problem; but use had to be made also of the services of the poor, who earned their living by manual labor, and had to be compensated for the loss of their time. Special spectacular effects were presumably paid for by the duke, but the normal expenses had to be shouldered by the community, their lord thus economizing substantially by making use of their services; in March 1592, it was determined, however, that the commission in charge of the arrangements should not be authorized to spend for the purpose more than twenty-five *scudi* from the communal funds.

Sometimes religious scruples, too, had to be taken into consideration. In 1581, the duke was informed by the gentleman whom he had commissioned to supervise the production that "the Jews insist on beginning the comedy early, so as to finish it before their Sabbath commences. Otherwise, it will be garbled, as they may not do anything of this sort after nightfall." If a performance was planned for the Jewish Holy Day season, there might be more serious complications. This was the case, for example, in the autumn of 1588, when the date chosen for the "comedy or pastoral," which they were commissioned to perform happened to fall on the Jewish New Year feast—"one of their most solemn days"—which continued over forty-eight hours, and was immediately followed that year by the Sabbath. They therefore requested the duke to change it to the day before or the day after—otherwise, the spectacle would be shorn of many attractive features, such as fires and music and other delights, which the Jewish Law did not permit on a feast-day.

Unfortunately, we are not informed about the actual personnel:

how interesting it would be to learn of some famous scholar or talmudist who participated, and what role he played! The only name actually mentioned in connection with any of these performances (other than in the list referred to above) is that of the young Angelo (= Mordecai) Sacerdote (= Cohen) who was one of the dancers, under the direction of Isacchino Massarano, in a spectacle performed in 1591, when with the others he was escorted by the beadle before the duke and warned to be regular in his rehearsals.[5] There can be little doubt, however, that one of the occasional participants was that intriguing figure Simone Basilea of Verona, who was reputed to be able "to present without assistance, with his own voice, comedies of many personages" (perhaps what we would term today a *diseur* rather than or as well as a ventriloquist). He was for that reason given by successive dukes the guerdon, denied to persons of greater but less resplendent potentialities, of being allowed to dispense, when performing outside the city, with the distinctive badge, the wearing of which had recently been reimposed on the Mantuan Jews.[6]

How did this handful of Mantuan Jews, absorbed in their economic life and by no means unmindful of Hebraic culture, manage to launch scenic productions which were so ambitious and obviously so successful? The answer lies in the character and ability of a single person, one of the most remarkable characters that Italian Jewry of the Renaissance period produced.

Mention has already been made repeatedly in these pages of the famous Mantuan family of Portaleone which generation after generation provided the ducal court with its physicians. Several

---

[5] Through the courtesy of the finder, Mr. S. Simonsohn, lists of the performers in the "comedy" of 1605 now lie before me. They include various identifiable names—such as Lazzaro d'Italia, presumably to be identified with the Hebrew printer Eliezer d'Italia. It was on this occasion that "Madame Europa" sang so sweetly in one of the *intermezzi*.

[6] Basilea having been recommended for this favor by one of the Medici, it is probable that his performances were familiar also in Florence. The Ferrarese court jester, Scoccola, who figures prominently in the famous fresco by Francesco Cossa in the Palazzo Schifanova, is said to have been a Jew; but I can find no authority for this statement.

of its members were distinguished by the supplementary appella-
tive, of uncertain origin, "of Sommo," or De' Sommi. Out of
this line of scholars, philosophers and physicians emerged somewhat incongruously the person who is to engage our attention
now—the first theatrical impresario of modern times. Leone de'
Sommi Portaleone, son of Isaac Portaleone, was born in 1525 or
thereabouts, almost certainly in Mantua, where he was educated.
His early days were uneventful, so far as is known, but it is interesting to note that he was a pupil of that same Rabbi David
Provenzal whose disapproval of dramatic performances has been
mentioned above, for whom he transcribed a work of Ibn Ezra
in 1538. He seems to have been a private pedagogue in his youth,
his surviving works including a short treatise on Hebrew calligraphy which he composed for the benefit of his pupils. Since
he was an expert in this subject, the synagogue may have called
on his services, so that he wrote biblical scrolls for liturgical use;
indeed, his erudite relative, Dr. Abraham Portaleone, reports in
his encyclopaedia *Shilte haGibborim* his recipe for making the ink
for this pious purpose. Like every literate Italian Jew, he wrote
poetry; and when the Hebrew poetasters throughout Italy initiated one of their artificial Renaissance controversies on the merits
and defects of womankind, he contributed to it an amusing macaronic composition, half in Hebrew and half in Italian,[7] "The
Shield of Women"; this he dedicated to Hannah Rieti, wife of the

---

[7] This ingenious trifle has stanzas of eight lines, of which the first,
third, sixth and seventh are in Hebrew, the second, fourth, fifth and
last in Italian. The original editor, Adolph Neubauer, not realizing that
the two components made sense only when taken in conjunction,
published the Hebrew in one periodical and the Italian in another, to
the preposterous confusion of posterity! The flavor can be appreciated
from a couple of actual stanzas:—

שמעו נא את דברתי
Donne sagge honeste e belle
כי אתודה דברתי
Contra queste chiurme felle
Degli vecchi che a la stelle
העלו את חרפתכן
ואני מגן לכן
Per diffendervi a ogni via.

Mantuan communal magnate Reuben Sullam and perhaps the mother of the Moses Sullam to whom Salamone de' Rossi was to inscribe his synagogue music.

An intelligent, versatile, literate person of this type, living in Mantua in the sixteenth century, would inevitably be drawn into the theatrical activities of the Jewish community—and, if he showed particular merit, beyond them. This is clearly what happened to Leone de' Sommi. No doubt he began as a youth witnessing the theatrical productions of his fellow-Jews, then went on to act in them. Of this there is no positive evidence, though it is almost certain from what we know of his later career. He showed such competence that in due course he was entrusted with supervising the productions and writing the plays that were performed, until in the end he became known as the most capable worker in this field in Mantua, and perhaps in the whole of Italy. For many years, his services were constantly being called upon by the ducal court, whether as playwright or as impresario, whenever any great spectacle was intended. On one occasion, a specially composed piece, *Gli Sconosciuti* ("The Unknown") was presented there before a brilliant company, including the dukes of Mantua and Ferrara, four cardinals, and a great number of the nobility and gentry; the *intermezzi* (on the subject of Psyche) being also apparently his composition. Another of his plays, *Onesti amori* ("Chaste Love") was composed to celebrate the remarkable qualities of the Duchess Eleanora, "whose virtue the world admires and heavens honor": (*le honora*) he observed, in a gallant and perhaps excusable pun. In 1582, his *Il Gianizzero* ("The Janissary") was staged—very probably by the Jewish theatrical company, to celebrate the heir-apparent's birthday.[8] Certainly, he was in close touch with the court. We find him writing to a member of the ducal family in

---

ואת יפה רעיתי
Che mi chiami a questa impresa
לעורר מליצתי
Delle donne alla difesa
Dammi aiuto a la contesa
נגד דברי תועה
שעשו אם אל רעה
Et co'l mondo villania.

[8] See above, p. 250.

1579, in a free and easy fashion, asking that one of his poems (presumably dramatic) should be returned to him, as he had been thinking about it during a recent indisposition and wanted to write a new prologue before it was produced.

Under the circumstances, De' Sommi naturally became familiar with the predilections of his ducal masters, and was consulted regularly in connection with them. On one occasion, when the Jewish community was instructed to see to a production for some state occasion, they found difficulty in making a selection, since Leone de' Sommi, who knew His Serene Highness' tastes, was away in Piedmont. When, in 1580, arrangements were being made for the ill-starred betrothal of the heir-apparent with Margherita Farnese, daughter of the Duke of Parma (the couple lived together for only a few months), Duke Guglielmo summoned him to Revere to discuss what performances should be staged in honor of the event, at the same time telling him to see that his coreligionists made their preparations for the "machinery" (*apparecchio*) in good time, as their services were certain to be required.

From the middle of the sixteenth century, the drama in Italy had been regarded as a special care of the academies—formerly devoted to classical learning, but now to less serious subjects. Almost every town of any importance came to have its own, generally bearing some fantastic name. Their activities included, besides occasional banquets, the recitation of verses and the presentation of plays—sometimes acted by the members themselves, sometimes by young amateurs under their direction, less frequently by paid actors. One such academy was founded and endowed at Mantua in 1562 by a member of the reigning family, Don Cesare Gonzaga, Duke of Ariano, himself an amateur playwright of some slight merit, who called it the Academy of the Enamored (Accademia degli Invaghiti). In 1566, he procured from Pope Pius V, who was his uncle, letters patent giving the institution official status and empowering it by virtue of this to confer the degrees of doctor and notary public, to legitimize bastards and to crown poets: a combination of functions which was not then considered incongruous. This was immediately followed by a "brief" declaring all the members of the body to be knights (*cavalieri*) and permitting the papal arms to be incorporated in the badge which they were empowered to wear.

Don Cesare had dramatic activities especially at heart when he called this foundation into being. He was anxious therefore to include among the members Leone de' Sommi, the Jew, Mantua's outstanding expert in theatrical matters. However, his broadmindedness was not shared by his collaborators. Objections were raised, above all, by the Rector of the Academy, the well-known litterateur Benedetto Marliani (his "academic" name was Incitato) who maintained that it was impossible for a Jew to enjoy the rank of *cavaliere*, like other members of the foundation. This as a matter of fact was questionable; a few Jewish physicians had been raised to that dignity in the previous generation, including at least one member of the Portaleone family. However, the argument was given greater weight by the fact that it was considered improper for a Jew to wear the papal arms. It was in vain that Gonzaga pleaded, and that De' Sommi wrote a wistful poem of expostulation to his adversary:

> Why therefore am I daubed with brand of shame,
>   Only because my rites are held remote
> From those you keep, and my laws not the same?

But it was of no avail. Marliani maintained his objection, and the founder had to be content with appointing his protégé "Academic Writer" (*Scrittore accademico*). This implied, presumably, that he was, as it were, its official poet and playwright, and composed such dramas and comedies as were commissioned from him. At least one of these is recorded: *Drusilla*, a "pastoral tragedy" (*favola tragica pastorale*) dedicated to Don Cesare, which was included in the inventory of his son's library. When his patron died, in 1575, De' Sommi composed a pastoral fable, *I Doni* ("The Gifts") to console the academy in the affliction felt for the loss of its founder.

He continued to enjoy the friendship and patronage of Don Cesare's son, Fernando (Ferrante) Gonzaga—himself a playwright, though not of any note—who succeeded his father as "Protector" of the Accademia degli Invaghiti. In 1580, we find the latter in correspondence with the duke asking for Leone to be exempted from the obligation of wearing the Jewish badge (in the form of patches of orange color on jerkin and cloak) which had been imposed in "enlightened" Mantua in 1577 as a sop to the papal demand for anti-Jewish measures. He was a man of *virtù* (that is, versatile ability), wrote his patron, and had acquired much merit with the academy of Mantua for the long services that he had rendered to it with his writing; and he accordingly deserved—an invidious manner of expressing it!—to be separated from the vulgar mass of the Jews. Another restriction enforced after 1577 was the prohibition to own real estate, and in 1585 Sommi applied for exemption from this as well.

It has been pointed out that dramatic representations were at this time given mainly in the palaces of the nobility, or else in the open air; the theater, in the modern sense, was only now beginning to emerge. But Leone de' Sommi had already grasped the spirit of the new era. In 1567, he petitioned the duke for a license to be allowed to "set up a room in Mantua, for presenting comedies by those who go reciting them for payment," and to have sole rights for this for ten years; in return, he undertook to give annually two sacks of grain in charity for distribution to the poor. This would have been virtually a public theater in the present-day sense, though not specifically constructed for the purpose; and one of the very first on record in modern times. It is probable enough that, among those who "go reciting comedies for payment," Leone had in mind his own co-religionists, who as we have seen specialized in this sort of thing: in any case, this is valuable evidence of the existence at this time in Mantua of bands of professional actors. The application was supported by Francesco Gonzaga, Count of Novellara (another son of the founder of the Accademia degli Invaghiti, who also shared his father's tastes). Whether or not it was granted, and the theater came into being, is unknown. But there is perhaps an allusion to it in a racy story told by the ingenious Tommaso Garzoni in his absurd collection (without any bearing on the Jews) entitled *La Sinagoga degli Ignoranti* ("The Synagogue of the Ignorant"). He tells in this how, on the day of the *frascata*, Leon the Jew of Mantua gambled his hose-points away: "so that, being doorman that day, he held his hose up with one hand, while with the other he held up the curtain, everyone who entered laughing immoderately about this." I am inclined to identify this *Leone ebreo mantovano* with Leone de' Sommi, who is likely enough to have shared in the gaming propensities of his age and associates, and to think that here we have a glimpse of an episode in the history of the theater which he founded. It is possible, however, that *frascata* (that is, arbor) refers to the "tabernacle" associated with the Jewish feast of Succoth.

De' Sommi's activity was not confined to Mantua. We know, for example, that he was frequently in the Duchy of Savoy, at which court too he was a familiar figure. In 1584, he dedicated his *Nozze di Mercurio e Filologia* ("Wedding of Mercury and Filologia," based on a book by Marciano Capello: the reference in the last name is to the virgin, not the science, so entitled) to Duke Carlo Emanuele I, begging him to see to its production on the stage. This proved difficult, owing to its particularly spectacular qualities, which were presumably responsible for the fact that it had not already been seen in Mantua; though it inspired the *intermezzi* produced there on a particularly brilliant occasion several years later. On the other hand, De' Sommi's *La Fortunata*, first staged in Mantua, was seen twice before the court in Turin—the first time probably during the festivities to celebrate the duke's wedding, and again in 1585, when new *intermezzi* were composed for it. There was another occasion when the presentation of a play in Mantua, for which his presence was needed, was held up until his return from Piedmont. So greatly was he appreciated here that the complete manuscript collection of his works was ultimately acquired for the ducal (later royal) library in Turin, where they were preserved for over three hundred years. In all probability, he was in touch with the other courts of northern Italy as well.

He did not only write plays; he was considered expert in presenting them, as well as in everything calculated to enhance the magnificence of the occasion. In 1587, we find him writing to the Duke of Mantua that, as requested, he had devised some new tourneys and other spectacles. When, in 1584, the duke was preparing to have Guarini's *Pastor Fido* put on the stage in Mantua, and was in correspondence about it with the author, the latter wrote to him that there should be a choir of nymphs: "but this is still in the hands of Leone," he observed, obviously referring to De' Sommi.

Again, in the autumn of 1591, the poet Manfredi, then at Nancy, sent the Duke Vincenzo a new "sylvan" dramatic poem which he had composed, in the hope of having it performed at court. He was sure that, if this took place, the production would be entrusted to the aging "Messer Leone" and some six weeks later wrote to him anxiously about it, telling him so and giving detailed instructions about the costume. It was important to remember, he observed, that the action was staged in Assyria, where robes were worn long (as was still the case!). Hence, the shepherds' vestments should reach below the calf, and the nymphs' to the very heel. "I need not tell you anything more," he concluded, "knowing that you are a master of that art." An indication of the importance which the Jews had in the spectacles of the Mantuan court may be found in the fact that a communication to much the same effect was sent by the author to "Messer Isacchino hebreo (that is, Isacchino Massarano), the master of dancing" (*maestro di ballare*), since he was certain to be entrusted with the supervision of the ballet. A third letter was written to the individual who was expected to supervise the musical accompaniments. For the sake of symmetry, one might have hoped that this would be Salamone de' Rossi, the Jewish court musician; but in fact it was the Flemish composer, Jaques Wert.[9]

Whether Manfredi's instructions were carried out we do not know: by the time his letter reached Mantua—indeed, before it was written—Leone de' Sommi had died of fever on September 10, 1590, in the Contrada del Camello in that city, after an illness of seven days, at the age of sixty-five.[10]

---

[9] Recently-discovered documents show that De' Sommi was even more interesting and more versatile than was hitherto believed. He apparently wrote a polemical work against Christianity: about 1592, a Piedmontese Jew named Moses Melli was accused of having among his papers a writing of Leone Sommi containing "irreverence" against Jesus (R.M.I., xxi.329). In 1587, according to an as yet unpublished record in the Mantuan archives, he and two other Jews made an agreement to exert themselves to procure the election of their master, the Duke of Mantua, to the throne of Poland, dividing all prospective expenses as well as profits thereafter among themselves.

[10] So the official "necrology" of the city of Mantua. But there is some little doubt about this. The local antiquarian, Bertolotti, who first published this note (substituting, however, "May" for "September"), questioned whether the reference was to the impresario-playwright, since he believed that he found a reference to him as still alive in 1610,

But his reputation survived him. In the autumn of 1598, Guarini's pastoral tragicomedy, *Il Pastor Fido*, was revived in three performances at the Theater of the Castle (recently built by Duke Vincenzo, to replace the original Court Theater in the riding-school destroyed by fire in 1591, under suspicious circumstances, and holding, it was said, 6,000 persons), Margaret of Austria, the bride of Philip III of Spain, being present with a brilliant retinue. A contemporary pamphlet by a certain G. B. Grillo gives full details of the *intermezzi* accompanying the performance, which were, we are told, similar to those composed in 1584 by the Jew Leone de' Sommi, on the subject of the marriage of Mercury and Filologia.

He left a mass of original literary material—perhaps greater in bulk than the work of any other Jewish writer of his generation and immeasurably greater than that of any other Jewish writer in the vernacular. Apart from his scattered Hebrew compositions, no fewer than sixteen volumes of his manuscript works in Italian were formerly preserved in the great Royal (now National) Library at Turin. These comprised four volumes of original poetry, eleven of plays (including at least six comedies, three pastoral fables and several *intermezzi*), and two—the most memorable part of the collection—of prose. Among the poetical material were translations into *ottava rima* of forty-five biblical psalms, accompanied by the original Hebrew (the first work of this type to be undertaken, so far as our knowledge goes), and large numbers of poems dedicated in many cases to the Gonzaga, with a few to Lucrezia, to the members of the Accademia degli Invaghiti, or to the Pope as its protector. Unfortunately, almost all this material was lost, before it had been properly examined, in the great fire of 1904, when the Turin Library and most of its irreplaceable manuscripts were destroyed (one of the greatest literary disasters of those puny years of pre-atomic tranquility). Of De' Sommi's most important composition, however, there was another copy in the Library at Parma, in the collection assembled by the great

---

when the duke wrote that he was awaiting the arrival of "Lioni" with the costumes before beginning a theatrical performance. On the other hand, there is extant an epitaph by Daniel Fano which repeatedly gives the year 5362 (that is, 1591/2) as the year of death, though curiously omitting the exact date.

eighteenth-century Christian Hebraist G. B. de' Rossi, and it is this above all that has secured De' Sommi's reputation for posterity.

For this purpose, the "Dialogues on the Theater" (*Dialoghi in materia di rappresentazioni sceniche*) is perhaps the most memorable contribution by a professing Jew to general literature in the age of the Renaissance, after Judah Abrabanel's "Dialogues of Love." The work, which consists of a fictitious conversation between "Massimiano," "Santino" and "Veridico" (= the Truthteller, representing De' Sommi's own considered opinions), was ostensibly compiled in 1556; but since it refers to events of a later date than this, it was either revised subsequently or else this is a copyist's slip, perhaps for 1565. The dialogues are four in number, and deal, sometimes artlessly and sometimes with real insight, with every aspect of stagecraft; it is in fact our most valuable source of information on the methods of scenic production at that time, being a generation earlier in date as well as far more alert than the first published work of the sort, Ingegneri's *Della poesia rappresentativa e del modo di rappresentare le favole sceniche* (Ferrara, 1598).

The first dialogue discusses principally "the origin of comedies, and certain laws relating thereto, and whether it is meet that they should be in prose or in verse, together with various observations about tragedies and other scenic plays." The second "explains why the comedy is divided into five acts, and what division and proportion every scenic poem should rightly have." The third— the most valuable—"discusses the proper manner to recite and how to dress, and everything that generally pertains to the actors, with many necessary instructions and reminders." The fourth "treats of the condition of the apparatus and of scenes of every sort, and the order and diversity of the *intermezzi*."

Within this setting, there is a vast amount of information on theatrical conventions and methods of the sixteenth century, much naivete, a good deal of misplaced learning, and at the same time some sound theatrical common sense which is by no means out of place even today. A true son of his age, De' Sommi traces the origin of the theater to Moses—the reputed author according to rabbinic tradition of the Book of Job—for that "most elegant and philosophic tragedy, with only five human interlocutors, which, though not composed for representation on the stage (*albeit it has been repeatedly*) was nevertheless composed in the style of a colloquy." Conceivably, in the mention of the public representations of the drama of Job, we may have a reference to the Mantuan Jewish theater in its more solemn moments. To look back to the Bible for early examples of literary forms is not, as we now see, purely a modern fashion.

De' Sommi is excessively conventional in the second dialogue, where he points out with approval that the ancients did not permit personages to enter the stage more than five times, though regard for some such restriction might make many contemporary comedies less confusing. He is perhaps sounder when he goes on to insist that the stage should never be left empty. We get some impression of the splendor of the spectacles at Mantua when he speaks of the scenic apparatus. His Massimiano describes the extravagance of the setting at the court on the occasion of the marriage of Duke Guglielmo with Eleanora of Austria in 1561—used only for a tourney that one evening, and then destroyed, though it would have made a marvelous permanent stage. (What waste, the modern man would say; what magnificence, sighed the child of the Renaissance!) He then goes on to discuss lighting effects, and emphasizes the use of mirrors in this connection; possibly he was influenced here by the treatise on the refraction of light by his co-religionist, Raffaelo Mirami of Ferrara.[11]

He is at his best, however, when he discusses the actors. He points out that it is important, not only to fit the character to the part, but also to disguise his normal appearance; clearly, a sound precept in the circumstances with which he had to deal, as otherwise the audience would tend to think of the individual whom they knew in their daily life, and not the personage he was supposed to represent. He insists that the most important thing is good enunciation, and that nothing must be allowed to interfere with this. He therefore disapproved of the wearing of masks or false beards; it is easy enough to convey an impression of age by painting the chin or by wearing a white wig. In this connection, he speaks of his own experience on the stage, and mentions several contemporary actors—especially the Roman actress

---

[11] Above, p. 238.

Flaminia, whom he considers the greatest of his day, quoting a couple of sonnets (perhaps his own) in her honor. He pays due regard to gesture, in a manner which gives a pretty graphic picture of the crudities of the contemporary theater. Attention must be devoted to this, not only by the person who is speaking, but by everybody else who is on the stage, who must demonstrate their feelings by their demeanor. Thus he says a servant should tear his neckerchief to pieces between his teeth to give the appearance of anguish, or throw his hat into the air to indicate joy; or that the nit-wit must indicate his character by catching flies or searching for fleas . . .

He indicates that it was proper to introduce to the stage an element of license (*qualche parte licenziosetta*, he delightfully puts it), provided it bears some "proportionate relation with the subject." He, moreover, indicates the proper vehicle for material of the sort: "That which the audience finds most amusing is for the licentious, smutty, or spicy portions to be allotted to two comedians, not to say clowns, one young, one old, who have been expressly invited for this purpose, and who season their contributions with a quantity of pleasantries." In those of his plays that survived the Turin fire, we see how he acted upon his own precept. They lack indeed the consistent pornography of (for example) Macchiavelli's *Mandragola*; but they are hardly adapted for a Victorian drawing-room.

There are in the dialogues a number of oblique references to his own dramatic works. For example, he describes in laudatory terms the prologue to his prose-comedy *La Fortunata*, presented for the first time, as he informs us, in Mantua four years previously (probably in 1552), in which Fame and Fortune made their appearance. (It was to be revived twice in Turin, as has been mentioned above.) He refers almost certainly to his *L'Irifile* in speaking of the ingenious prologue to a tragicomedy presented at Mantua in the carnival of the previous year (that is, 1555 or 1556), in which the author included a dialogue between Tragedy and Comedy and had the happy idea of introducing Virgil himself to settle their dispute. He probably alludes to this production also when he describes "a pastoral fable in five acts recited not long since in Mantua," in the Great Hall of the ducal palace. The name Veridico, which he gave to the participant in the dialogues who

expresses his own considered opinions, is that of one of the characters in this play (the text of which is still extant): it has been
conjectured that he himself took this part in the production, and
that he regarded it as one of his more successful roles. One may
assume that the performances under his direction were introduced,
as he insisted that every dramatic performance should be, by a
fanfare of trumpets.

Although De' Sommi may have had a considerable personal
influence on the development of Italian stagecraft, his work did
not. His "Dialogues" were unpublished in his day, and the original
text has remained so even now; so that Ingegneri's far inferior
work enjoys the credit of being the first on the subject to appear.
His significance in theatrical history was first properly realized
by the great Italian Jewish literary historian Alessandro d'Ancona,
who, though he overlooked him in the first edition of his classical
study of the origins of the theater in Italy, made amends in the
second (Turin, 1891) in which he devoted a good deal of space
to him and his work. The original Italian text of the "Dialogues"
has even now not been printed in full. But in 1937 it was published
at last in an English translation, with a proper appraisal of its
importance, as an appendix to the new edition of Allardyce
Nicoll's fundamental work on the development of the theater.

About the literary quality of De' Sommi's plays there is little
to be said. They are no better, and no worse, than the normal
uninspired standard of the Italian drama of the sixteenth century.
The tragedies and pastorals are written in the polished, turgid
verse characteristic of the age. (There is, incidentally, much use
of the echo-device, which was to become popular also in Italian
Hebrew poetry.) The plots are highly involved, with the usual
preposterous sequence of coincidence and disguise. The entire lack
of Jewish coloring, or rather the omnipresence of pagan atmosphere and mythology, is noteworthy. Obviously, the author had a
pretty good knowledge of the classical background—typical in
this, too, of the educated Jew of the upper class in sixteenth-
century Italy. If *L'Irifile* is indeed of 1555 or 1556, it is one of the
earliest of the pastoral plays which were so fashionable in Italian
literature of the time; it was preceded and presumably influenced
by Agostino Beccari's *Sacrificio*, presented at the court of Ferrara
in 1554 and published there in the following year, but has the

advantage of many years over Tasso's *Aminta*, first presented at a court feast in 1573, which in turn influenced Guarini's memorable *Pastor Fido*, begun (though not produced) seven years later. Since De' Sommi was probably acquainted personally with both of these great figures in Italian literature, the coincidence is not perhaps entirely one of time.

The suggestion has been made that at one time William Shakespeare toured Italy with a company of English strolling players, acquiring his knowledge of things Italian and visiting those cities which he mentions in his plays, including (or, according to one view, especially) Mantua; though his ignorance of Italian geography would be inexcusable in the most hurried tourist of today. If he was ever in this city, it is probable that he would have made the acquaintance of Leone de' Sommi, the Jewish impresario, and learned some of his views on dramatic production. There is, to be sure, very little in common between the "Dialogues," centered upon the spectacular productions of the ducal court at Mantua, and the insistent simplicity of Shakespeare's dramatic conceptions. But the principles of acting are certainly those upon which the English playwright must have insisted in his own productions.

In view of his influence at court, De' Sommi's services were often called upon by his co-religionists; and he did not betray their confidence in him. On March 13, 1566, he took up the case of the Mantuan rabbi Moses Provenzal, who had been threatened with excommunication by some of his colleagues because he had criticized a divorce which they had legalized: Duke Guglielmo was requested to order the dispute to be remitted to an impartial rabbinical tribunal for adjudication. On another occasion, he even championed a Jewish butcher who had been fined by the community for putting up his prices during Lent, when he lost his non-Jewish clientele and his expenses were accordingly increased. In 1577, he was the mouthpiece of the community when they asked for the legal recognition of the decisions of the rabbinical courts, and in 1578 when they begged the duke to grant no individual exemptions from the duty of paying communal taxation (which would enhance the general burden) and to see that the Jews of the smaller places in the duchy shouldered their fair share. Again he intervened, in 1588, when the Jewish community had to complain about the conduct of the silk-guild, which was presumably attempting to drive the Jewish manufacturers out of business; and in the last year of his life, in 1590, he similarly took up the case of the Jewish petty brokers. Even applications for the extension of the Jewish cemeteries at Mantua and Viadana were presented through him.

In the annals of Hebrew literature, too, the name of De' Sommi is of genuine importance. For, in the characteristic spirit of the Italian Jew in the age of the Renaissance, he expressed his literary interests also in the sacred tongue, in which he composed a pastoral drama, only recently discovered and published: "The Comedy of Wedlock" (*Zakhuth Bediḥuta deKiddushin*). This, the first extant specimen of original dramatic literature in Hebrew, is in much the same style and shows much the same inspiration as the author's Italian compositions, though lacking their licentiousness and making a fitful attempt at introducing a Hebrew atmosphere and allusions. De' Sommi's name is not, as a matter of fact, specifically attached to the work; it was, however, composed toward the end of the sixteenth century by a Mantuan Jew named Judah or Leone, the ascription to him being thus virtually certain. Its significance for Jewish cultural history is considerable. It was written, as is made obvious from various allusions in the text, for public performance *in Hebrew* on the Feast of Purim. (The Mantuan Jewish public was, it seems, exceptionally well versed in that language.) Moreover, from the fact that at least two (acting?) copies were to be found in the library of a Mantuan Jewish scholar of a later generation, it is probable that it continued to be performed from time to time long after the author's death.

We are accustomed enough in these days to persons of the type of De' Sommi: it is not perhaps unfair to call him the Max Reinhardt of the sixteenth century. But his twentieth-century counterparts—and again, Max Reinhardt may be taken as the example— tend to be attached to Judaism and Jewish life only nominally if at all. De' Sommi was unlike them in that he was not merely an eager Jew, but one who was steeped in traditional life. It seems almost paradoxical in these degenerate days to find this man of the highest general culture, theatrical entrepreneur, and frequenter of courts and palaces, living the life of a profoundly observant Jew. Mention has been made already of his Hebrew writings and of his Jewish communal activity. But there is perhaps greater significance in an episode of his last days. Repentance in old age was characteristic of the Renaissance. There is no evidence that De' Sommi lived a licentious life. But he must have been to some extent removed from normal Jewish activities; and it was typical of the period that toward the end of his days he built a synagogue, which probably continued in use until the Mantuan Jews were shut up in their ghetto in 1612.

Somewhat surprisingly, the Jewish theatrical activities at the court of Mantua survived even this reactionary step. A newly-found document gives intimate details of the preparations for the comedy which was to have been presented by the community for the carnival in 1615. The rehearsals were completed, the day arrived, and the players were dressed up in their costumes and waiting to appear, when a message was received from His Serene Highness, Duke Ferdinand, that because of his *balletto* (possibly an informal open-air dance, not a ballet in the modern sense) the performance was to be postponed until after Easter; the *balletto* and *moresco* were, however, to take place as arranged. Later on, he intimated that he wanted to have the proposed performance revised, with more attention to the dances; and when in the autumn everything was ready, he again postponed it all until the following carnival-tide, in the spring of 1616. The result obviously pleased him, as a second performance was commissioned for the following Whitsuntide. The total expense involved to the community was something like 5,000 lire.

Under the new circumstances, however, this Jewish participation in the Mantuan theater must have had a diminished vitality, and there can be little doubt that a fatal blow was inflicted by the sack of the city at the hands of the German troops in 1629 and the temporary expulsion of the Jews. This does not imply, to be sure, that the Jews lost their interests entirely: as late as 1646, requirements for the "commedia" are mentioned in a receipt for articles purchased for the community; and there can be no doubt that more or less private theatricals continued in the Mantuan ghetto, as in others, even later than this.

That there was similar activity elsewhere, over so long a period, on the same scale and with the same exalted patronage, is hardly likely. But it is obvious that the Mantuan episodes reflected what

must have been a general tendency. The courts of Turin and of
Ferrara have already entered to some extent into our picture. A
more widespread devotion to the drama in the Jewish community
is found in particular at Venice. The Purim production in the
ghetto here in 1531 has already been mentioned. Clearly, it was
not an isolated occasion. It is known how on the same festivity,
in 1558, the ghetto players performed a polished play on the subject of Queen Esther specially written by the eminent marrano
poet Salamone Usque (the most gifted translator of Petrarch into
Spanish); he had the assistance of a certain Lazzaro Levi, who was
perhaps responsible for the Italian version. It was apparently a
great success. Though intended in the first place for the Jewish
community, it was publicly presented the following year, presumably by the ghetto players, before a select company of Venetian nobility and gentry; and it was revived a generation later, in
1592, in the presence of a similarly distinguished audience. Some
years later, a new presentation was suggested. Leone Modena, who
was Lazzaro Levi's nephew, now volunteered to adapt the play
for the purpose in accordance with the new dramatic conceptions
that had arisen in the course of the previous half-century—in
particular as exemplified in a recent turgid epic on Queen Esther
by Antonio Ceba of Genoa, which had been a great literary success. The details regarding the performance of this version are not
preserved, but it was published at Venice in 1619 with a dedication to the Jewish poetess, Sarah Coppio Sullam, whose family,
as has been seen, was distinguished for its wider cultural interests.
It may be that she had introduced Modena to Ceba's poem, for
which she had great admiration—the author's reaction to this being
his attempt to convert her to Christianity.[12]

This was not the only original dramatic composition written at
this time in the Venetian ghetto. The ubiquitous Leone Modena
himself composed an original pastoral comedy "Rachel and Jacob,"
of which we happen to be informed—although the text has not
survived—because on one occasion he was compelled to pledge
his only copy with a friend. Moreover, in 1611 he edited a pastoral play by his colleague Angelo (Elchanan Judah) Alat(r)ini—
also known as a composer and translator of religious poetry. His

[12] See p. 57.

pupil, Benedetto Luzzatto, published at Venice in 1631 a pastoral fable in five acts, entitled *L'Amor possente* ("The Power of Love"), which he dedicated to Don Foresto d'Este, a member of the ducal house of Modena.

As in Mantua, Venetian dramatic interest received regular expression. In the winter of 1605, a comedy was produced by the Jews in Venice with *intermezzi* in which Leone Modena's brother-in-law sang. Obviously, this was no isolated occasion. Some time in the first half of the seventeenth century (the exact date is not ascertainable, but it was certainly before 1647), a regular theater was set up here in the ghetto. Possibly this may have been a result of the influx of refugees from Mantua in 1629, who gave such a stimulus to local musical life as well.[13] It can hardly be doubted that Modena as usual was active in this. Some of his colleagues, on the other hand, objected on religious grounds—a punctiliousness unknown, it seems, in liberal-minded Mantuan Jewry. Azariah Picho, famous as a preacher, whose works are still popular as pietistic handbooks, wrote aghast to Samuel Aboab, then rabbi at Verona, asking whether in his opinion it was proper for "a permanent theater-house to be established in the camp of the Hebrews, for men, women and children to gather therein to listen to mockeries and ribaldry." Aboab (*Responsa* § IV) disapproved as violently as his extensive Hebrew vocabulary permitted, holding that it would bring the most chaste of women into contact with those of lowest character and inevitably corrupt the young. As a matter of fact, the ghetto public was too restricted to make such a venture successful, and nothing is heard of it thereafter. We know, on the other hand, that throughout the age of the ghetto, Italian Jewry continued to maintain something of its theatrical interests, and that dramatic representations were indulged in from time to time, even in little communities such as Pesaro or Gorizia or Siena, down to the late eighteenth century. All this, however, is far removed from what was known in Mantua, in the heyday of the Renaissance period, when that city was a center of Italian drama and the local Jewish community was one of its mainstays.

---

[13] Below, p. 300.

TWELVE

Music *and* the Dance

"What doth Music say to the Gentiles? 'Certes, I was stolen from the land of the Hebrews' (Genesis 40.15)" ingeniously observed the Italian Jewish poet, Immanuel of Rome, in one of his pastiches. Obviously, this was no more than a display of verbal virtuosity; yet there must have been a perceptible Jewish inclination to music at the time when he wrote, in the early fourteenth century, in order to give it an element of verisimilitude. There was perhaps some historical basis for such a point of view in remoter antiquity. For it is probable that the early Christian Church used in its worship the psalmody as well as the psalms of the synagogue and temple, the characteristics of which are preserved in the Gregorian chant and plain-song, the basic ecclesiastical element in European music being thus traceable in the last instance to a Jewish background.

This, however, is a conclusion of modern scholarship. In the Middle Ages, it was far from obvious. Though in some recitative parts of the synagogal liturgy (such as the reading of the biblical lessons) an individual tradition of great antiquity was perpetuated, the tunes used for the congregational or domestic singing of hymns were of the same type as those used in the outside world on similar (or, sometimes, less solemn) occasions: frequently, indeed, not merely of the same type, but actually the same. The nineteenth-century Protestant revivalists in England were not the first to decide that it was not right to leave all the best tunes to the Devil, and very often catchy melodies which were popular in street or market-place were adapted by the Jews for their hymns of praise; at a somewhat later period a note would sometimes be appended indicating the secular tune ("Three colors in one," or the like) to which they were to be sung. The rabbis protested vigorously. "What shall we say and how shall we justify ourselves," cried one popular preacher, Judah Moscato, "as regards some of the synagogue cantors of our day, who chant the holy prayers to the tunes of popular songs of the multitude, and thus, while they are discoursing on holy themes, think of the original ignoble and licentious associations!" Objections were naturally yet stronger in certain cases, when the words of the hymn were similar in sound to those of the ditty. But even so the practice continued; and to this day in some Italian synagogues on the Rejoicing in the Law a lovely hymn is sung, with the refrain *Amen, Shem Nora* (= "Amen, the awesome Name") which originates in a Spanish love-lyric, "Ah! mia Señora."

An indication of the European orientation of Jewish music in the medieval Christian environment is provided by the fact that we now already begin to have specimens of musical notation of Hebrew texts in a western medium. The oldest extant is an elegy on the death of Moses, for the Rejoicing in the Law or perhaps Pentecost, which was found in the Cairo Genizah in a thirteenth-century manuscript, accompanied by interlinear musical notation in what are known as "neumes"—the system used at this period by the Church. This has recently been published as a phonograph record, and the resemblance to the Gregorian chant is obvious to the least expert ear. It must remain an open question whether this was wholly a result of environmental influence, or whether the original Jewish tradition on which the Gregorian chant was based still retained its vitality in the synagogue at this time. However that may be, in this manuscript (which, notwithstanding the fact that it was discovered in Egypt, is almost certainly of Italian —perhaps Lombard—provenance) the melody is recorded in a typically western medium, which must have been familiar therefore among Jewish cantors and singers even at so early a date.

For our next specimens we have to wait a good while. An illuminated Hebrew Bible written in Spain about 1400 embodies in its decorations to the "Song of Songs" a strip of the musical notation from which the singer is seen to be chanting the text. This fragment is in the usual style of the Roman plain-song notation of the fourteenth century, and uses only three lines, in the manner of the church song-books. Probably, this is "the most ancient noted Jewish biblical melody." Dating to the second part of the fifteenth century is a motet of three parts—cantus, tenor and contratenor—of about 1450-60, written in northern Spain, contained in a manuscript of the Bibliothèque Nationale in Paris. In this case, the words (written in Latin characters) are a curious but unmistakable Hebrew jumble, embodying the essential phrases of the *Kedushah* or *Trishagion: Kados, Kados, Kados* . . . ("Holy, Holy, Holy, is the Lord of Hosts"). That this was set down for the use of marranos, as has been suggested, is more than unlikely, and the purpose as well as the interpretation remain somewhat mysterious, though the Jewish associations are certain.

To be sure, certain rabbis of the Middle Ages (and they included even Maimonides) objected to music *per se*, except at the celebration of weddings, for which it was regarded as essential. Some considered such manifestations of joy to be improper while the Temple lay in ruins; others, with sensual secular melodies in mind, were thinking of it rather from the point of view of puritan morality. On the other hand, some Jewish scholars of repute, such as Saadiah, the great tenth-century Gaon of Sura, showed a lively understanding of the theory and philosophy of music, apparently based on close study. Important, too, in this connection is a treatise on harmonious numbers, now extant only in Latin, composed in the fourteenth century, by the Provençal Jewish mathematician-philosopher, Levi ben Gershom, or "Ralbag," at the personal request of Philippe de Vitry, Bishop of Meaux, originator of the "new art" in music.

One of the few early attempts to treat the subject systematically in Hebrew is an unpublished work in which a certain Judah ben Isaac—otherwise unknown, but presumably an Italian—presented to Jewish readers the substance of a famous musical treatise by the early fourteenth-century theorist, Marchetto of Padua. A number of other writers, moreover, touched on the matter incidentally, in various connections. The eloquent Judah Moscato, for example, assigned pride of place in his popular collection of sermons, *Nefuzoth Judah*, first published in 1589, to a homily (a passage from which has just been quoted) on music. In this he displayed much curious learning, and ingeniously attempted to distinguish between the genius of Jewish and of occidental music, which made it inadvisable in his opinion to adapt Hebrew psalmody to alien strains. Similarly, Samuel Archevolti, the poet-grammarian, devoted to the subject chapters xxxi-xxxiii of his well known work on prosody, *Arugath haBosem* (Venice, 1602). In this he bravely attempted to reconcile familiar classical assertions with Jewish prejudices. Music, he conceded, is of the spheres. Given to mankind by Tubal Cain, as the Bible vaguely suggests, it was lost in consequence of the Flood, and was then renewed first by Pythagoras, and then (!) by King David, the royal psalmist. The eminent physician, Abraham Portaleone, in his encyclopaedic *Shilte haGibborim* on biblical and Hebrew antiquities, which was completed in 1607 (its genesis and nature are described elsewhere in this volume),[1] made a lengthy digression while discussing the Temple worship to consider music in general and instrumental (or as he terms it "artificial") music in particular. In dealing with these topics, in a succession of twenty diffuse and learned chapters, he makes it clear how the Mantuan Jews of his day discussed among themselves the position of music among the ancient Hebrews and its nature. Leone Modena, himself no mean performer, wrote a panegyric of music which breathes his personal enthusiasm.

The interest was, to be sure, not merely theoretical. In the musical pageantry of the Renaissance period, Jewish groups were sometimes prominent in Italy, as they were indeed throughout the Mediterranean area, especially in Spain. In 1469, for example, when the city of Palermo celebrated the fate-fraught marriage of the Infant Ferdinand (later King Ferdinand the Catholic) of Aragon to Isabella of Castile, four hundred young Jews clad in silk danced to music in the procession—no doubt, in the semi-Saracenic fashion still traditional on the island.

The houses of the cultured loan-bankers in the north of the country naturally knew much the same sort of diversions as their Christian neighbors. The Messianic adventurer, David Reubeni, tells us how, when he was staying with the erudite and polished Jehiel Nissim of Pisa in 1524, the latter's wife, Diamante, with her daughter and a number of her damsels, tried to solace his melancholy with music and dancing, though he pretended that his mind was above such things; how the town instrumentalists performed at his host's house in expectations of largesse; and how

---

[1] See pp. 222 and 254.

Madonna Diamante played, in their villa outside the city, for company which included several distinguished patrician visitors.

Obviously, if the Jews indulged in such diversions, they had to learn them. In the Renaissance period in Italy, it was in fact regarded as part of the duty of a Hebrew teacher in cultured households to give instruction to his pupils, not only in Bible and Talmud, but also in the allied subjects of singing, music and dancing. One pedagogue of the period, in a letter to a favorite pupil, admonished him not to neglect to practice his playing on the lute and fife—but only at night, after his father had gone to bed. The learned Leone Modena, who himself had studied these diversions in his youth, could find no higher praise of his own brother-in-law than to say that he was expert in these subjects, while his son-in-law was a dancing master by profession. When, in 1697, an attempt was made to reduce what was regarded as the excessive luxury prevalent in the Venetian ghetto, it was prohibited for a dancing-master to be employed in a bridal house, whether after a marriage or before; though it is unknown how effective this provision was.

It was not only in the households of their fellow-Jews that these experts found an outlet for their virtuosity. Such was their proficiency that one of the characteristic occupations of Italian Jews in Christian society in the Renaissance period was teaching the arts of music and the dance—then, as we shall see, a wholly integral part of polite education. Sometimes they had a highly distinguished clientele. In the early part of the fifteenth century, for example, a Jew named Musetto (= Little Moses) was dancing-master to the children of Malatesta V, Lord of Pesaro. Obviously, he was highly regarded, for when he came to San Marino in 1429 to claim his dowry, which had been deposited with a local Jew, he bore with him a very warm letter of recommendation to the Captains Regent of the Republic from his employer's wife, Camilla Sforza.

We know, however, of the prevalence of this calling most of all because of the opposition that it aroused. For it ran clear against the policy of Holy Church, which objected strenuously to any close association between Jews and Christians and even to normal social intercourse between members of the two faiths; and relations between the dancing-teacher and his pupils were in every sense extremely close. It is under the circumstances not wholly to be wondered at that in 1443 the authorities at Venice ordered the immediate closing of the schools of music, dancing and similar accomplishments kept by Jews, and prohibited them to teach these subjects henceforth under pain of six months' imprisonment and a fine of 500 ducats. But, as has often been said, medieval legislation prescribed an ideal rather than laying down a rule of actual conduct, and so little was this provision obeyed that in future years it was periodically reënacted. The situation at Venice was paralleled elsewhere. In 1466, for example, the fantastically anti-Jewish Fra Bernardino da Feltre compelled the authorities at Parma to expel certain Jewish women who had been engaged in teaching music and dancing to the ladies of that city. We will see later some other examples from various parts of the country relating to the subsequent period.

This anonymous activity provides something of the background for the work of a handful of Jews of the Renaissance period whose activity in the realm of music and the then-allied arts was of considerable significance, and cannot be overlooked in any study of the subject. The dancing-instructors who have been spoken of above should not be evaluated in modern terms. The exercise, as has been pointed out, played an important part in the lives of educated men and women in Italy at this time. As practiced in the upper level of society, it was a refined and complicated art, wholly different from the spontaneous prancing of the peasant and artisan. It was highly conventionalized, and some of those teaching it—who obviously needed qualifications of a higher type than mere agility and sense of rhythm—enjoyed great prestige. There are extant a handful of scientific treatises written by some of them on the subject. One of the most important of these is the *Trattato del' arte del ballo*, or "Treatise on the Art of Dancing," by Guglielmo ebreo (= William the Jew) of Pesaro. (The name need not surprise us: as we have seen, it was frequently used among the Jews of this period as a sort of homonym for Benjamin.) About his life, we know relatively little. He was a pupil, as he himself tells us, of Domenico (Domenichino) da Piacenza, the founder of the new school of dancing which emerged at the resplendent court of Lionello d'Este at Ferrara, and the inventor of the contrasting sets of measures which he called the *balletto* and was the ancestor of the modern ballet. The Jewish virtuoso styles himself the other's most devout disciple and fervent imitator and incorporated many of his dances in his own compilation. He must have been close to the brilliant and versatile circle which was gathered about the court of the Medici in Florence in the middle of the fifteenth century. For in his composition (written not later than 1463, and it may be added in the purest Tuscan), there are included two dances composed—obviously as a very young man, for he was born only in 1449—by Lorenzo the Magnificent himself. Another indication of the high regard in which Guglielmo was held in Florence is the fact that one codex of his work contains a lengthy poem in *terza rima* in his praise by the eminent humanist Giovanni Mario Filelfo (son of the even more famous though morally contemptible Francesco Filelfo), whose daughter Theodora was one of his pupils ("Canzon morale di Mario Philelfo ad honore et laude di maestro Guglielmo Hebreo"):

> How great have been the honors on him poured
> And guerdons for his dancing and his skill,
> By many a king and marquess, duke and lord . . .

words which suggest that he was a familiar figure in other courts of Italy besides that of the Medici. Seeing him dance, Filelfo adroitly observed, even Cato would have given up his legendary severity; while Diana herself would have been seduced by his skill and grace.

We have indeed a dazzling glimpse of his activity when he organized the *divertimento* at the marriage of Costanzo Sforza with Camilla d'Aragona at Pesaro in 1475. It was a memorable occasion, and he was able to enlist practical assistance from his coreligionists. Half of the banquet was organized under the Sign of the Sun, the other half under that of the Moon. At one point, the Jews of Pesaro went in procession past the bridal couple, with great pomp. In their midst was a wooden elephant, on which rode the Queen of Sheba, sitting on a gold throne under a canopy of silver; then came two more elephants bearing towers on which were a number of beautiful young women bearing lilies and oriflames. When she arrived abreast of the happy pair, her wooden steed was stopped and the Queen of Sheba descending from her baldanquin delivered an address in Hebrew, as a prelude to presenting the wedding gift from the Jewish community. She then danced away with her lovely escort. A character representing Rehoboam ("Roboano": though it is not easy to imagine why) then gave a complimentary address soliciting the favor of the ruling house for their Jewish subjects. Thereafter the interlude closed with a performance by twelve youths representing the labors of agriculture, and other similar dances by 120 youths and maidens, who made their way into the dining room to the sound of musical instruments. All these dances were composed by Guglielmo ebreo himself, who, we are told, was responsible for introducing the fashion of the *moresche*, embodying not only dances but also mimicry before the grand spectacles.

There is reason to believe that in middle life Guglielmo da Pesaro became converted to Christianity. Of the extant fifteenth-century manuscripts of the *Trattato* two are anonymous, three bear Guglielmo ebreo's name in this form, and the remaining one, in the Bibliothèque Nationale in Paris (Fonds It. 476)—which must be relatively late, as four chapters not in other copies are added to the theoretical section—is ascribed to Giovanni Ambrogio da Pesaro. This is no copyist's error, for throughout the manuscript this name is substituted for Guglielmo ebreo's wherever it occurs, and even Guglielmo's original dances are entered under the other name. There does not seem to be much doubt that the two persons were identical—all the more so since the same place of origin is given in both cases—and that in due course Guglielmo the Jew became, as a Christian, Giovanni Ambrogio.

This identity being established, we are now able to add a further and hitherto unrecorded chapter to the Jewish dancing-teacher's career. It seems that in 1463 he was in the service of Galeazzo Maria Sforza, Duke of Milan, for whom a handsomely written and illuminated codex of his Treatise (also in the Bibliothèque Nationale, Fonds It. 973) was copied in that year by an expert scribe; it is the only one of the series to be dated. A delightful miniature in this volume shows three dancers with their little fingers interlocked performing a *bassa danza*, the "Queen of Measures," to the music of a harp. It may be that here we have in the central figure a portrait of Guglielmo himself. At this time he was still a Jew, his name being given as Guglielmo ebreo. His baptism as Giovanni Ambrogio—a probable name for a convert in Milan, the city of St. Ambrose—must have taken place soon thereafter. In due course, he was sent by the Duchess Bianca Sforza to Naples to her young daughter Ippolita, the bride of the Duke of Calabria, heir to the Neapolitan throne (later Alfonso II) as dancing-master to the royal children; in particular, he was to teach them the new fashionable Milanese dance, the *ballo lombardo*, out of which the famous *gagliarda* was to develop in due course. There is extant a letter which Giovanni Ambrogio wrote in 1470 to the Duchess of Milan extolling the future queen's charms and reporting on the progress which his pupils had made. Later on, we find him in the service of the court of Ferrara where, in 1481, he was dancing-master to the seven-year-old daughter of the ducal house who was to become famous as Isabella d'Este, Duchess of Mantua—assuredly, no mean exponent of the art. This is the last mention of him that has thus far been traced.

The work by which his name is remembered was, however, written by Guglielmo ebreo, obviously before his conversion. In this, he approaches his subject seriously, for he had a lofty conception of his function. He writes:

> The art of dancing is, for the generous hearts that love it, and for the gentle spirits that have a heaven-sent inclination—rather than an accidental disposition—thereto, a most affectionate matter, entirely different from and basically opposed to the vicious and mechanic common people, who so frequently, by their corrupt spirit and depraved minds, turn it from a liberal art and virtuous science into a vile adulterous affair, and who more often in their dishonest concupiscence disguised as modesty make the dance a procuress, through whom they are able to arrive stealthily at the satisfaction of their desires.

He goes on to enumerate the six primary requirements in a dancer—"measure," or ability to keep time; "memory" for the correct sequence of movements; attention to the space available; dexterity; manner; and corporal movement—all of which are lengthily if not too clearly expounded in the treatise. A lady moreover had to pay attention to other matters besides these:

Her glance should not be proud or froward, darting hither and thither, as many are accustomed. Let her keep her eyes for the most part decently directed downward; not, however, as some do with her head sunk on her bosom, but straight and in a line with the body, as Nature teaches almost of itself . . . At the end of the dance, when her partner leaves her, she should face him squarely and, with a sweet regard, make a decent and respectful curtsey in answer to his.

It would take too long to analyze in detail the theoretical part of the treatise. Guglielmo does not, however, confine himself to this, but goes on to give a description of numerous dances, which he divides into two main groups—the dignified *basse danze* (ancestors of the minuet) and the livelier *balli*. He thus provides the richest storehouse of Italian Renaissance dances known to us. In some cases, the names of the authors are indicated. Many are ascribed to his master, Domenico da Piacenza; a couple, as has been mentioned, are by Lorenzo the Magnificent; and one, entitled *Partita crudele* ("Cruel Parting"), is by a co-religionist of Guglielmo, Giuseppe ebreo (unknown from any other source). Curiously enough, the last is omitted in the codex of the *Trattato* written after the author's conversion and ascribed to Giovanni Ambrogio.[2] Eleven of the dances are specifically ascribed to Guglielmo himself: one of them, called "Caterva," was written, we are informed, in Bologna, while another was composed for Madonna Suena Colonna, a member of one of the most distinguished Roman patrician families. It may be added that in the *Libro dell' arte del danzare* by our author's contemporary, Antonio Cornazano, which in the theoretical part is superior to the *Trattato*, no original dances are mentioned. Apart from this, Guglielmo's work is unquestionably more valuable from the practical standpoint.

Guglielmo wrote too early for publication in the modern sense—the first printed book devoted to dancing is *L'art et instruction de bien dancer*, produced in Paris about 1490, of which only a single copy has survived. But his work seems to have been studied a good deal, at least six manuscripts of it being extant. It is only in

---

[2] The same is the case, however, with the two by Lorenzo the Magnificent, so that racial or religious susceptibility was not necessarily responsible for the omission.

the course of the last century that the work has been published, in three separate editions—in one case specifically for its linguistic importance. Thus at last Guglielmo ebreo da Pesaro entered into his own.

The arts of music and dancing were closely interconnected at the time of the Renaissance, as has been indicated, and Guglielmo da Pesaro's composition of dances implied in most cases also the composition of the accompaniment. In the next generation, there were a number of instrumentalists of Jewish birth (and in those days the instrumentalist was composer as well) who were of more than ordinary ability and fame. Outstanding among these was a certain Jewish lute-player from Germany—obviously of low character—who settled in Florence. Here he was taken up by the Medici and was induced to be baptized, assuming the name Giovanni Maria, in honor of Cardinal Giovanni de' Medici (later Pope Leo X). He seems to have imbibed the spirit of Renaissance Italy to the full, for in 1492 he was condemned to death and confiscation of his goods for a murder in which he was implicated. By now, however, he had left the city. Whether he is identical with the singer and composer Giovan Maria da Crema, who supervised the musical education of the Gonzaga princes at Mantua a few years after this, is not quite certain. Before long we find him (after an interlude at Urbino) in Rome, where his patron, the cardinal, had gathered round him a number of able musicians, in whom he took special delight. When the cardinal became Pope, his favorites had an opportunity for further advancement. Giovanni Maria (whose son Camillo, a musician like himself, likewise enjoyed the papal favor and patronage) now received a regular allowance of twenty-five gold ducats. It seems that this income was secured upon the revenues of the little fortress-town of Verocchio, of which he was now made castellan, with all its revenues and the title of count (June 22, 1513). It was a unique guerdon, perhaps, even for this period; and when the inhabitants raised objections, the Pope took firm steps to see that his instructions were obeyed. Nevertheless, after a time, we find Giovanni Maria in Venice, where he had a brother living. Here, too, he entered the ruler's employment, but changed his instrument, becoming the doge's fife-player (*pifaro del doge*). Leo missed him sorely, and in May 1520, the Venetian representative in Rome wrote to the signoria requesting them to do the Holy Father the favor of sending Giovanni Maria back there for a time to perform certain pieces of music. He was accordingly permitted to return for one year, though when it came to the point, the Pope apparently would not let him go. On his patron's death, he went to Mantua to seek employment, with letters of recommendation from his friend Baldassare Castiglione, author of *Il Cortegiano*, and the Cardinal de' Medici, later Pope Clement VII, who wrote of him: "I believe your Excellency knows how attached the late Pope of blessed memory was to the virtue and grace of Jo: Maria the musician . . . who, accompanied by his art, served him until the last days of his life."

It was not long before he again returned to the papal city, and the Venetian envoys who were sent to congratulate Pope Hadrian VI on his accession reported how on May 20, 1523, "Zuan Maria" and three other lutenists with whom he played a quartet provided the musical entertainment on the occasion of a great banquet at the papal court, he himself plucking the strings with marvelous effect.

His original compositions were popular in his day far beyond the boundaries of Italy. The Venetian resident at the court of Henry VIII of England sent home for a number of his works in 1515. As late as 1552, the German musician Hans Gerle of Nuremberg included eight of his preambles and six dances in a collection of compositions by the most renowned lutenists. He also seems to have earned a reputation for his performances on wind-instruments, for he was, as we have seen, referred to as a fife-player, and Andrea Calmo included in his *Lettere Piacevoli* an epistle addressed to him under the name: "M. Zuan Maria del Cornetto, kinsman of the Muses." There can thus be little doubt that he is to be identified with ". . . quel si nomato Cornetto padoano, Zan Maria," who is praised so highly by Teofilo Folengo in his *Orlandino* (IV.27). It is remarkable that, though baptized, he continued to be known by his sobriquet "Jew" ("Gianmaria Giudeo"), and many authors (including even Burckhardt, the great historian of the Renaissance, and Rieger, the chronicler of the Jews in Rome) did not suspect that he had left his faith.[3]

Jewish musicians and instrumentalists were in the public eye above all at Mantua, under the marquesses and dukes of the House of Gonzaga. Of the courts of Renaissance Italy, this was in many ways the most magnificent; and the Jewish community too, as we have seen, seems to have been affected by the Renaissance spirit to an unusual degree. It was here, for example, that Jewish participation in the drama came to be of such great importance; and the long and important musical tradition among the Jews of the city was in close connection with this. From the first half of the sixteenth century, we find a whole series of Jewish vocalists and instrumentalists in the ducal service here, contributing greatly to the brilliance of the scene.

In 1542, mention is made for the first time, in a letter in the Gonzaga archives, of a Jew known as Abramo dell' Arpa ("Abraham of the Harp") who took part that year in a dramatic spectacle at the ducal court, being cast in the role of the god Pan. He made himself such a name that shortly thereafter he was summoned to Vienna as music-teacher to the children of Ferdinand I of Austria, but was soon back in Mantua, where he remained in the ducal service for many years. He is mentioned in 1553 as one of the musicians drawing a regular salary from Duke Guglielmo. Although two years later we find him in Rome, under the appellation "Abraham the Musician of Mantua," he later returned to that city where he got into trouble, being imprisoned by the ducal order in December 1566. But his disgrace was not lasting, and before long he was active again. By now he was aging, and his nephew, Abramino (= Little Abraham) dell' Arpa came into prominence by his side. On one occasion, in 1587, the two collaborated in the musical

---

[3] According to all the authorities the famous viola-player of this period, Giacomo di Sansecondo, Giovanni Maria's contemporary, who was painted by Raphael, was also a Jew. This is based on a misreading of a passage in Burckhardt's *Renaissance*, in which he is mentioned immediately after Giovanni Maria. The inference is false. The name should accordingly be deleted from the standard Jewish books of reference. Burckhardt and those who follow him are in error in stating that it is in the *Orlandino* that the reference to "Giovan Maria da Corneto" (*sic*) is to be found.

entertainment which accompanied the great banquet given on the lake on St. John's Eve when Cardinal Gaetano, the Legate of Bologna, came to Mantua to baptize a new-born member of the ducal family. That year Duke Guglielmo retired, a dying man, to the lovely seclusion of the palace he had rebuilt—without wanton paintings—among the gardens at Goito, high above the Mincio; and Abramino had to accompany him, to cheer his last days with music.

More prominent and more versatile than either of these two was Jacchino or Isacchino (that is, Little Isaac) Massarano. He was proficient in many branches of musical activity. He taught; he sang soprano; he played the lute; he composed; and above all he was regarded as an expert on choreography and all that pertained to it. In 1583, he was commissioned to provide the dances for the forthcoming performances of *Gli Ingiusti Sdegni* by Bernardo Pino[4]; and in the following year, when the Mantuan heir apparent visited Ferrara, he was sent to supervise a similar performance there. In 1591, Guarini's *Pastor fido*—the most famous play of its day—was presented on the stage of the ducal palace, and he was commissioned to compose and supervise for the performance the Blindfolded Dance (*Balletto della cieca*) by Amarilli; his absence from the city for a few days threw the whole production back. ("He had an expert devise the choreography of the ballet, incorporating therein an imitation of those actions peculiar to the familiar game of blind man's buff," the author wrote of himself in his note to the 1602 edition of his work, in an obvious reference to this occasion.) In this same year, he was commissioned by the poet Manfredi to supervise the dances for his new "sylvan" poem, the production of which he hoped would be entrusted to Leone de' Sommi.[5] He certainly needed no detailed instructions, Manfredi wrote, but he was to pay particular attention to the choir's four *canzonette*, which were to be danced as well as sung, the varying speeds at which they were to be performed being minutely prescribed. Whatever may have been the case with some others,

---

[4] See above, p. 260.
[5] See above, pp. 254 ff.

Isacchino was obviously not dependent on musical activity for his sustenance, for he lived in such style that one evening in 1594 he was host to the duke and other members of the ruling family, with the gentlemen of their train, at an entertainment in his house.

Another performer of note at the Mantuan court, though in a different sphere, was a certain "Madama Europa," as she was called: a sister of the composer Salamone de' Rossi, of whom more later, and perhaps daughter of Azariah de' Rossi, the most important Jewish literary figure of the Renaissance period in Italy, after whom one of her sons was named. Why she adopted the curious sobriquet by which she figures on the court accounts and registers is unknown. It is likely that the key is provided by her prominence on a certain occasion, memorable in the history of Italian drama and music, when the Jewish contribution was very much in evidence. It happened in March 1608, at the time of the marriage of Francesco Gonzaga, the duke's son, Prince of Mantua (later himself to reign as duke, though only for six months) with the Infanta Margherita of Savoy. The wedding festivities were of incredible luxury, the jewelry with which the bride was decked having been provided by the Roman Jew, David de' Cervi. As part of the celebration, Monteverdi was commissioned to write a play set to music, like *L'Orfeo*, which had pleased the duke so much the previous year. The outcome was the Master's earliest opera, *L'Arianna*, to the libretto by the Florentine Ottavio Rinuccini, now presented on the stage for the first time: an epochal event in musical history, for it was in this work that the composer first revealed the emotional and dramatic value of discords, thereby decisively influencing future developments. No pains were spared to make the spectacle as perfect as money and industry could achieve: the actors, we are told, studied their parts for no less than six months, so as to be letter-perfect. Among them was the Jewish singer, Madama Europa, whose name is recorded among the participants, though her role is not stated. For full measure, Guarini's play, *L'Idropica*, was staged on this same occasion by the Compagnia de' Fedeli—similarly for the first time, since it had been mislaid somehow since 1584, when it had been written.

In the fashion of the day, the play was supported and nearly overwhelmed by a series of *intermezzi*, or musical interludes be-

tween the acts,[6] the prologue to these was likewise composed by
Monteverdi, on themes by Chiabrera. In the second of the series—
apparently old stock, which had already been presented some time
before—the lady who now concerns us was in all probability the
unnamed singer who took the part of Europe: it is likely that she
had figured in the same role at the previous performance also, and
owed to this fact the name by which she had become known.
In any case, her performance on that memorable occasion in 1608
made a great impression. "Understanding music to perfection, she
sang to the great pleasure and greater surprise of the audience,
her voice being so delicate and sweet, and her simplicity bringing
tears to their eyes." Nevertheless, according to report, she owed
her favor at court to the charms of her body as well as of her
voice; and the records reveal something of her strained relations
with Madama Sabrina, her rival for the ducal affections, with intimate details of their merits, quarrels, and reconciliations.[7]

Singers and instrumentalists were known elsewhere in Italy. But
only in Mantua, as far as is known, was there a sequence of Jewish
composers who published their works. Madame Europa's own son,
Anselmo (= Asher) de' Rossi (his mother presumably married
a cousin) was a case in point; for he was among the collaborators
in Federico Malgarini's collection of "Motets . . . written by
various musicians, servants of the Lord Duke of Mantua" (Venice,
1618), his contribution being a composition for three voices entitled *Aperi oculos meos* ("I opened my eyes"). Similarly, Davit
(David) da Civita published at Venice in 1616 a collection of
seventeen madrigals for alto, basso and basso continuo, entitled
Premitie Armoniche ("Harmonious first-fruits") which, as his
"most faithful and devoted servant," he dedicated to the Duke of
Mantua himself. A good deal more prolific was Allegro Porto,
another contemporary. Musical publications of this age are pro-
digiously rare, many surviving in only a single copy—others perhaps were even less fortunate, so that to state dogmatically that

---

[6] There is a fuller description of this feature elsewhere in this volume, pp. 249 ff.

[7] King Henri IV of France, no mean judge, considered that the
Signora de' Rossi, who once accompanied the Duchess of Mantua on
a visit to his court, had the most beautiful hands in the world. But his
reference was probably to a lady in waiting, not to the Jewish singer.

certain compositions were unpublished is hazardous. It is conse-
quently difficult to obtain a complete and detailed picture of the
production of some minor composers. But, in the great musical
collection brought together in the eighteenth century by King
João of Portugal, and destroyed in the Lisbon earthquake of 1755,
it is known that there were four works by Allegro Porto. He
published in 1625 two collections of madrigals for five voices—
one of them dedicated to the Holy Roman Emperor Ferdinand II
(whose empress was a daughter of the Duke of Mantua), as well
as a collection of musical pieces in the new style (*Nuove Musiche*,
Venice, 1619) dedicated to Count Alfonso da Porzia, chamberlain
of the Duke of Bavaria. A further collection of his, of madrigals
for three voices "with some arias and a romanesque dialogue"
(the first part alone is recorded, but perhaps there were others),
published first in 1619, was reissued in the nineteenth century.

It is partly because of the large amount of research that has
been done on this subject in the Mantuan archives that we receive
the impression that the Jewish participation in the musical renaissance was concentrated at the court of the Gonzaga. But there
is reason to believe that they were little less prominent at the close
of the sixteenth century in other Italian courts. We know, for
example, how the dukes of Savoy took into their service at Turin
various members of the De' Rossi family of Mantua—in particular
Angelo de' Rossi (who may well be identical with the Anselmo
de' Rossi whom we have mentioned above) together with his sons
Giuseppe and Bonaiuto. He first came to Savoy in the service of
Amedeo di Savoia, the brilliant bastard son of Duke Emanuele
Filiberto. In his service he achieved such success that he was later
taken over by his half-brother Duke Carlo Emanuele I, "the
Great," under whose auspices the court of Turin began to acquire
a brilliance almost rivaling that of Mantua. Angelo de' Rossi figured during his reign as composer of ballets, player of the lute,
and music teacher to the young princes, as well as to the pages
about the court. His sons, on the other hand, who retained their
position after their father's death, were accomplished players of
the guitar. As part of his remuneration, Anselmo was authorized
to maintain a loan-bank at Rocconigi, near the country seat where
the dukes spent much of their leisure: he was thus available whenever his services might be needed. On one occasion, we learn,

when foreign princes were expected at court, the duke provided him with a new suit of clothing, so that he would make a good impression on the distinguished visitors. Giuseppe de' Rossi continued in the service as court musician at Turin into the second half of the seventeenth century, being exempted from the application of the sumptuary laws (regulating and restricting extravagance in costume) enacted by the Jewish community in 1651: it was obvious that one who had to appear as resplendently as possible at court could not be subjected to petty restrictions of this sort!

Another Jewish musician who added to the brilliance of the court of Savoy at this period was one Benedetto Sessigli, also a lute-player. On one occasion, when a water-entertainment was being held by the duke in the park of his villa at Mirafiori, near Turin, he was one of those who performed in the duke's own barge, but lost his footing and fell into the water. He was fished out not much the worse, but the duke had to replace his instrument.

Standing head and shoulders above all other Jewish musicians of the Renaissance period, and a very considerable musical figure in his own right, was Salamone de' Rossi. It was once believed that he was a son, and he was certainly a close relative, of Azariah de' Rossi ("Min haAdumim"), the typical savant of Italian Jewry of the Renaissance period; it is significant, and highly characteristic of the age, that in the same family Hebraic and secular interests, synagogal inspiration and court activities, were so intimately connected.

Like Monteverdi himself, the renewer of Italian music (who received his first appointment at the Mantuan court in this capacity about the same time), Salamone originally made himself known as a viol-player, apparently entering the ducal service together with his sister on the accession of Duke Vincenzo in 1587; like most players on this instrument he also sang. From this he went on to original composition, being taught, as he states, all he knew by the duke's salaried musicians—doubtless including the Church composer, Ingegneri, Monteverdi's master. From 1602 to 1613, when he removed to Venice, the last-named was "maestro di capella" at the ducal court, and De' Rossi worked under him. Successive rulers conferred on him as on other Jewish virtuosi in their employment the somewhat invidious sign of favor, that he might go about, whether within or without the city of Mantua, without wearing the stipulated Jewish badge, this being intended (as Duke Vincenzo phrased it) as a demonstration of "how dear to us is the service that Salamone Rossi the Jew has performed for us for many years past by his virtue in music and playing." At one time it seems that De' Rossi had his own company of musicians (the members of which, one may imagine, were also Jews) with which he traveled about to give performances. (This may have been the reason for the concession just mentioned.) When, in 1612, Alessandro I, Prince of Mirandola and Concordia, was expecting a visit from his father-in-law, the Duke of Modena, he sent to Mantua asking the State Counsellor to send him "the Jew Salamone" and his company to give a concert in honor of the guests. In 1622, De' Rossi was still in the employment of the Duke of Mantua as viol-player, at a yearly salary of 383 lire, and he doubtless continued to fill this function until his death, probably about six years later. It is surely significant that Jewish instrumentalists were so prominent in the environment for which Monteverdi composed some of his most memorable music.

De' Rossi's chief importance lay, however, in his original musical compositions, of which large numbers are recorded, ranging in date from 1589 to 1628. At the resplendent festivities in 1608 to celebrate the marriage of the Prince of Mantua, when Monteverdi's *L'Arianna* was first performed, he composed the music for the first intermezzo, and he also collaborated in those intermezzi with which Guarini's *L'Idropica* was diversified. (The prologue to these was written by Monteverdi himself.) This was the occasion, it will be recalled, when his sister so distinguished herself with her singing. Long before this, his first published work had appeared—a collection of nineteen canzonette for three voices which was published in Venice in 1589; the first, "Voi due terrestri numi," celebrated the marriage in the previous year of Duke Vincenzo to the daughter of the Grand Duke of Tuscany and was presumably sung at the wedding celebrations—which were enlivened also (as we shall see) by a comedy produced by the Jewish theatrical company. A further volume of this work appeared three years later.

Salamone de' Rossi was especially noteworthy for his madrigals, in which he anticipated Monteverdi by some years. Of these, he produced no fewer than five collections. The first comprising twenty-one songs (*Il primo libro de Madrigali a cinque voci*) also dedicated to Duke Vincenzo, had what is to be considered a remarkable success, seven editions (some of them, however, known at present by only one copy, or even a single part) appearing in his lifetime. Four further volumes of madrigals, making five in all, appeared in Venice in the course of the next few years (ii, 1599, 1602, 1605, 1610; iii, 1603, 1609, 1620; iv, 1603; v, 1614). In addition, he produced a volume of "Madrigaletti" for two voices (Venice, 1628) and so on.

Still more important probably than this was his instrumental music, in which he showed himself something of a pioneer, but which he did not start publishing until he had earned a reputation with his songs. It was only in 1607 that he produced his first collection of these (intended for three instruments and produced in as many parts—"canto primo," "secondo" and "basso") under the title *Sinfonie et gagliarde a tre, quatro & a cinque voci, per sonar due viole ouero doi cornetti & un chittarrone o altro istromento da corpo* (the *gagliarda* was a French dance, very popular at that time which, as we have seen above, had developed out of the *ballo lombardo*). This (which proved very successful and was republished in 1608, 1622 and 1623) was succeeded by other similar collections (*Il secondo libro delle sinfonie è gagliarde*, 1608; *Sonate, gagliarde, brandi e correnti a due viole col basso per il Cembalo*, 1623; *Il terzo libro de varie sonate, sinfonie, gagliarde, brandi e correnti, per sonar due viole da braccio, & un chittarrone o altro simile stromento*, 1623, 1638; *Il quarto libro de varie sonate, sinfonie, gagliarde, brandi, e correnti per sonar due violini et un chittarrone o altro stromento simile*, 1622, 1642). Two of the compositions in the third collection are to airs by Giovanfrancesco and Giovambattista Rubini (not of course to be confused with the famous nineteenth-century singer of the same name!); one of the compositions in the last was not unjustifiably entitled "the Modern" (*Sonata prima, detta la Moderna*). From the titles that have been quoted, it can to some extent be realized how his musical range and conceptions developed: for that reason it has been thought desirable to give them at length. The publication of 1628 was described as De' Rossi's thirteenth *opus*, and the tale was not yet complete—no slight record for a composer of that time. Besides all this, several contributions by him are to be found in composite volumes of the period—for example, in *Il Parnasso* (Antwerp, 1613), and *Il Helicone* (*ibid.*, 1616). One work with which he was associated—his only approach toward opera—has special interest. In 1617, the Florentine Giovanni Battista Andreini produced a "sacred representation," *La Maddalena* (Venice, 1617) in which certain "most excellent musicians" of the day collaborated. De' Rossi's contribution was the concluding *balletto* for three voices, to the accompaniment of three *viole da braccio* (violins) entitled "Spezziam pront' ò vecchiarelle." The other collaborators in this work included A. Guivazzani, Muzzio Effrem, and above all the great Monteverdi.

Some indication of the consideration in which Salamone was held and the extent of his connections in courtly circles is conveyed by the names of the persons to whom he dedicated his works. Such courtesies were at that time in the nature of an expression of gratitude for favors received or expected; yet they nevertheless imply fairly intimate relations. De' Rossi's first publication was, as we have seen, inscribed as from one in duty bound to the Duke of Mantua; other works bore the names of Felicità Guerrera Gonzaga, Marchioness of Pallazuolo; Francesco Ludovico Gonzaga, another member of the ducal family; Alessandro Pico, Duke of Mirandola—the same who later invited the musician to his court; the Duke of Modena and Reggio; the Count of San Secondo; Guglielmo Andreasi, Count of Rhodes; the Prince of Guastalla, and so on.

De' Rossi's place in musical history is assured. Alfred Einstein, the historian of the Italian madrigal, pronounced his works as having been written with an easy grace, and his *Madrigaletti a due voci* as the most enchanting duets and most perfect in form until the little masterpieces of Carissimi and L. Rossi, long after his day. His songs displayed charm, though no great originality. His instrumental music, on the other hand, reveals a remarkable virtuosity, the more noteworthy since in his day its use as an independent medium was not yet fully recognized. A pioneer in the development of instrumental variations, he was, as we see in his 1602 collection, one of the first, if not the first, to transfer the new monodic style to instrumental music. In his *Sinfonie e gagliarde* of 1607 he first established the trio sonata, the classic medium of baroque secular music, subsequently developed so superbly by Biagio, Marini and others. Hugo Riemann spoke of him as "undoubtedly the most important representative of the new style in the instrumental field . . . and the manner of his conception long remained a model for its simple form." He anticipated Monteverdi in his wholehearted support of the "modern" tendencies now beginning to show themselves in music, which were before long to bear such notable fruits. Egon Wellesz, indeed, goes so far as to consider him the inventor of the symphony in its modern sense.

Unlike some of the others who have been mentioned in these pages, and perhaps unlike most other eminent Jewish musicians until Ernest Bloch and Darius Milhaud in our own day, Salamone de' Rossi was an important figure in Jewish cultural life as well. For he made a memorable attempt—unparalleled, it may be said, until the nineteenth century—to introduce the spirit of the musical Renaissance into the service of the synagogue.

From the purely aesthetic standpoint, synagogal music has always suffered in the past from certain drawbacks. One was an excessive conservatism: the Jewish musical tradition was a composite one, but to adhere unintelligently to its every detail was regarded by some as a requirement of "orthodoxy." Another was what may be termed extraneity: Jews moved from one land to another, and in their new home sometimes considered the musical tradition they had brought with them as essentially Jewish, whereas it was merely foreign. A third was the very piety of the worshiper. He prayed, and was not content to be prayed for; and he did not mind very much at what speed or in what key he performed his religious duties. And, finally, it was considered improper to have instrumental music in the synagogue, which, apart from aping Gentile practice, would usurp the prerogative of the destroyed Temple of Jerusalem. Indeed, it was in any case forbidden for a Jew to play any musical instrument on the Sabbath or major festivals.

There were exceptions, to be sure; and they illustrate to some extent the degree of the influence of the Renaissance spirit on Italian Jewish life. In Padua, there was an organized synagogue choir at the end of the sixteenth century, Benzion Zarfati (later rabbi in Venice) being among those who sang in it. About the same time a *Hazzan* or synagogue reader in Casale Monferrato, Abraham Segre, who had a proper musical training, compiled a collection of liturgical melodies for his disciple and successor, Jacob Finzi; only a fragment has been preserved. A younger contemporary of De' Rossi, Abraham Joseph Solomon Graziani, the bibliophile-rabbi of Modena, formally permitted the use of the organ in synagogue, influenced perhaps by the fact that one had been introduced in Prague for the service which inaugurated the Sabbath; and when once a new Scroll of the Law was dedicated in one of the neighboring communities, the versatile Leone Modena composed a special hymn "to be sung to music" for that event. On one festive occasion early in the seventeenth century, when he was living in Ferrara, the congregation in the principal synagogue there had the agreeable surprise of hearing a choir of half a dozen youths render certain hymns with all the conventional artificial graces. The extreme pietists rose in protest against so un-Jewish an innovation. Modena, with some of his colleagues, retorted in a formal responsum in which he convincingly (from his point of view) demonstrated that there could be no objection to this in rabbinic law, and that it was the duty as well as the privilege of any person who possessed a beautiful voice to exercise it as best he could to the glory of God. On this same occasion, or another like it, he produced a further responsum discussing whether it was permissible to repeat the Divine Name in the musical setting to a hymn.

His arguments were doubtless cogent; but there is no evidence that the experiment was widely imitated. Indeed, the exceptions that have been mentioned above barely prove the rule. Both the dedication of a *Sepher Torah* and the reception of the Sabbath partook in the Jewish mind of the character of bridal celebrations, when music was considered not merely permissible but necessary; and it is certain that normally, notwithstanding the persistence of some extraordinarily beautiful synagogal melodies and cantillation, and the efforts made to find cantors endowed with fine voices, the

Synagogue's appeal did not depend on aesthetic values. An eyewitness tells us how in Venice, during the service on the Rejoicing in the Law (and the same applied doubtless to other cities), in an endeavor to supplement the singing of the joyous hymns "since they do not use instruments, some clap with their hands above the head, some smite their thighs, some imitate castanets with their fingers, some pretend to play the guitar by scraping their doublets." Clearly, there was little aesthetic appeal, whether to the eye or to the ear.

Indeed, notwithstanding the admitted competence of Jewish musicians, synagogal music was, it seems, a byword for inelegance. It is easy to understand the reason. A Catholic, accustomed to the pomp and ceremony of a great church, where the organ played and a trained band of celibates performed a stately and tuneful ceremonial, would pass outside or peer within the synagogue in which a couple of dozen pious householders competed in vocal, and perhaps untuneful, piety. He did not realize the fact that a population of a couple of hundred souls could not maintain the same pomp of worship as one of several thousand or even tens of thousands; still less did he realize the different approach to public worship of the two sections, one of them centering upon the priest and his functions, the other practicing a complete religious egalitarianism. He accordingly received the impression that the synagogue service was necessarily untuneful, and Jewish music a succession of cacophony. Hence, at the very period when Jews were collaborating so intimately in Italian musical life, as shown above, there developed what might perhaps be termed a musical anti-Semitism. Pseudo-Jewish motifs thus appear in a number of musical productions of the time, linking up with the Jewish scenes in plays which are discussed elsewhere in this volume.

An outstanding instance is the scene in Orazio Vecchi's famous madrigal-opera *L'Amfiparnaso* of 1597, in which the clown Francatrippa goes to pawn his clothes with the Jews. They refuse however to do business since it is their Sabbath, and they are at prayer in the synagogue:

> He shakes the door and hears a noise,
> Of monstrous shouting by the boys.

This—one of the most characteristic passages in Vecchi's work—is conveyed monotonously, however, rather than untunefully, in mock-Hebrew:

> Ahi Baruchai
>   Badamai Merdochai
> An Biladan
> Ghet milotran
>   La Baruchabà.[8] . . .

> Oth Zorochoth
>   Ashach muflach
>   Lochut zorochot
>   Calendala Balachat. . . .

There are several parallel passages in musical works of the time, most of them light-hearted enough. Thus in the *Villotte del Fiore* by Filippo d'Azajolo, published in 1569, a burlesque piece entitled "Ebraica" figures by the side of a "Todesca" and a "Bergamesca," parodying German and Bergamese styles. Adriano Banchieri introduces in his *La Barca di Venezia a Padua* (1605) two Jewish comic figures, Betell and Samuel, as "Interlocutori di Barca"; among his compositions for three voices there is a "Mascherata degli ebrei"; and in his *Pazzia Senile* ("Aged Folly") of 1598 (republished 1621: "the first comic opera," as it has been termed) there figures a song entitled "The Jewish Synagogue," in which the monotonous noise "tic tac tic" is intended to represent its musical atmosphere. Many similar vocal caricatures may be found in the literature of the Renaissance in Italy, all, however, fairly good-humored and never rivaling the coarse anti-Semitic satires of contemporary Germany, such as the preposterous *Judentäntze* and caricatures for the lute which had been included by Hans Neusiedler in 1544 in his *Lautenbuch*.

The foregoing illustrates to some extent the atmosphere in which Salamone de' Rossi made his most memorable musical

---

[8] = *Baruch haBa* ("Blessed be he who comes"): a traditional salutation among Jews, which seems to have caught the fancy of the Italians, and gave the title to a famous anti-Jewish comedy of the eighteenth century.

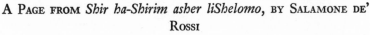

A PAGE FROM *Shir ha-Shirim asher liShelomo*, BY SALAMONE DE'
ROSSI

Courtesy of the Library of the Hebrew Union College, Cincinnati

contribution, which gives his name a special importance in Jewish cultural history. In the year 5383 according to the Jewish reckoning (1622/3) he produced in Venice a volume of synagogal music, on which he had been working for some time, entitled: *HaShirim asher liShelomo*—"Songs that are Solomon's," an ingenious modification of the first phrase of the Song of Songs. This collection (the original of which is preserved in the Ambrosian Library at Milan) comprised "Hymns, songs, and praises, brought together according to the science of playing and music, for 3, 4, 5, 6, 7 and 8 voices . . . to praise the Lord and to hymn His most high Name in all manner of holiness." It was dedicated to Moses Sullam, head of one of the most prominent and wealthy Mantuan families, who had been among the composer's supporters from his earliest days, had helped in his musical training, and had been one of those who persuaded him to publish the work. Since Mantua did not have the conveniences for a production of this sort, it was printed (like all De' Rossi's other works) in Venice, being seen through the press by his friend, Leone Modena, who was himself something of a musician and also had been anxious to see it in print. The latter, moreover, provided the work, in the fashion of the day, with an approbation in Hebrew in which he insisted, perhaps a trifle optimistically, that the words would not suffer because of the musical rendering; and he appended to it the responsum demonstrating the permissibility of trained singing in the synagogue which he had prepared at the time of the dispute at Ferrara seventeen years before. He had something of a personal interest, in fact: for among the half-dozen hymns included in the collection was one, for the marriage service, the words of which he had composed.

"The Songs that are Solomon's," as published, consisted of thirty-three compositions assembled over a long period of years; all had been performed before they were printed—presumably in one or the other of the Mantuan synagogues following the Italian rite, which is that adopted in the text. As was usual at the time, the various vocal parts were printed separately, not the complete score (it was not until the nineteenth century that an enthusiast produced a new edition in this form); the Hebrew text being printed, in order to correspond with the music, from left to right. The pieces selected are all taken from the synagogue service, and include psalms, hymns and prayers for the Sabbath and festivals (such as the *Kaddish*): some are for choir and soli, others have from three to eight parts. Some idea of the general atmosphere may be obtained from the fine rendering of Psalm 126 ("When the Lord returned the captivity of Zion") published recently as a phonograph record. It is pure Italian Renaissance music, wholly lacking in traditional elements, and without any trace of the Arabic or eastern European influences which have now come to be considered typically "Jewish"; Samuel Naumbourg, however, the nineteenth-century enthusiast who reëdited the collection, was of the opinion that De' Rossi introduced into his work a cadence in the minor (to be found in fact in some twenty out of the thirty-three compositions) which he considered to distinguish it from the contemporary Church music. It is noteworthy that the composer's sacred music is technically far more simple than his secular compositions, perhaps reflecting the general tendency of Church music at the time, but perhaps to make easier its performance in the synagogue by relatively untrained persons.

How far and for how long De' Rossi's attempt to reform synagogal music succeeded in establishing itself is unascertainable. From his own statement, that all of these compositions had been performed before their publication, it is obvious that during his lifetime he was able to introduce them into at least one of the Mantuan synagogues, and no doubt Leone Modena and other enthusiasts did what they could elsewhere. But the times were not propitious. The ghetto was beginning to establish its stranglehold on Italian Jewish life; the community of Mantua was about to enter a period of tribulation; the forces of conservatism were too strong; besides, the composer overlooked, as others have done, the fact that the familiar and the traditional has a devotional apart from its aesthetic value. From the prodigious rarity of Salamone de' Rossi's synagogal music (the only complete set recorded in any library in the world is one in Paris) it would seem that the original issue was almost thumbed out of existence. But it was never republished. In the following century, the Venetian patrician Benedetto Marcello used among the themes for some fifty psalms, which he published in 1724-27, about a dozen tunes which he had heard in the synagogues of Venice. But they were almost all, whatever their origin, of a "traditional" nature, this compilation being a precious store-house of ancient synagogal melodies which shows little if any contemporaneous influence from the outside world. Incidentally, the editor observed that notwithstanding his endeavors he was not able to find any notated music in the synagogues of Venice or any other place. Obviously, De' Rossi's gallant experiment of a hundred years before had failed.

In the Bodleian library of Oxford there is, however, a copy of part of De' Rossi's work which penetrated to northern Europe and was obviously much studied there. It contains the autographs of a couple of cantors who made use of it, as well as scraps of musical notation (including some in the tonic solfa, written in Hebrew characters—perhaps a unicum). A former owner, Moses ben Abraham of Nikolsburg, appended to this a note to the effect that "the Lord favored me, so that I studied in this book of music . . . to chant songs and praises in the synagogue and to exalt Him in exultant voice." It may be, therefore, that vague echoes of Salamone de' Rossi's compositions merged in the end into the vast tradition of central European synagogal melody, to which it helped to introduce some echoes of the new Italian style.

This Jewish interest in music, which received its most remarkable exemplification in Mantua, largely through the genius of a single person, was certainly not confined to that city. Indeed, we owe our knowledge of this activity partly to the sheer accident that so much research happens to have been conducted on the musical and artistic life at the court of the Gonzaga, and it is likely enough that if similarly detailed inquiries were carried out in other Italian centers, further discoveries of the sort might be made in this field. Isolated scraps of information from various places seem to add up to a consistent picture. It is known, for example, that in the Duchy of Monferrat, Jews were accustomed to frequent Christian houses, "to sing, play music, and dance," this being forbidden (except where special license was forthcoming) at the beginning of the reaction in 1577. A certain dancing-teacher named Leone ebreo is recorded as having so greatly pleased the ladies of Reggio that in 1603 they petitioned the duke for permission for him to transfer himself and his household to that city to continue his activity among them. In 1621, David Finzi, of Modena, "who possesses the virtue of playing instruments," petitioned the duke for leave to settle in Carpi in order to teach that art, "having been so requested by the gentlemen of Carpi." In Pesaro, now part of the Papal States, we find in 1626 a Jew named Samuel the Musician (Samuelle Sonatore). A Jewish copyist at Ferrara in 1472, Mordecai ben Abraham Farisol (probably son of the better-known Abraham Farisol), signed himself "Mordecai haMenagen" ("The Musician") and the family used as a sort of rebus of their surname the musical notes *fa, re, sol,* as mentioned above. An Abraham ben Eleazar haMenagen was a member of the Roman community in 1545 and the ancestor of a distinguished family of the ghetto period—including at least one eminent rabbi—who took that, or the Italian equivalent "Sonatore," as their surname. It is conceivable that this Abraham was one of the two Jewish musicians in the service of a certain great lady in the papal capital whose services were utilized in order to secure the release of a Jew who got himself into trouble there. Jewish players were in any case familiar enough here at this time.[9]

In Venice especially, with its exceptionally high degree of interest in such activities, there seems to have been a long and persistent musical tradition, second only to that in Mantua. As we have seen, it went back to the first part of the fifteenth century, at which time the teaching of dancing and music was already a characteristic, although proscribed, Jewish activity. This interest long continued uninterruptedly. It may well be that the composers David Civita and Allegro Porto, who have been mentioned above, were natives of Venice, where their works were published, although associated with Mantua. We are informed of several notable Venetian Jewish singers and musicians of this period. Andrea Calmo, in his burlesque *Lettere Piacevoli* (ii.33), writing in the middle of the sixteenth century, lavished compliments on a Venetian Jewess named Madonna Bellina, "a pillar of music," who he said played and composed to admiration, sang like a thousand nightingales, and had no fault other than her religion. About the same time the blind poet Luigi Groto ("Il cieco d'Hadria") composed a sonnet at the request of a certain Rosa Levi (later to be

---

[9] Elias Vannini, the composer of Church music, who made his contribution from the shelter of a Carmelite monastery, is also said by some writers to have been a Jew, though apparently only on the insufficient score of his biblical name.

converted to Christianity, on which occasion he delivered a pompous oration) in memory of her brother, "a most excellent Jewish musician," who "held the palm in singing and playing" and "showed his singular art at royal entertainments and in elevated scenes." A certain Rachel, who was said to be gifted with a voice of unusual beauty, was a familiar figure in the salons of the nobility in the first decade of the seventeenth century. Salamone de' Rossi was a frequent visitor to the city, where he had many acquaintances; and the rabbinate were happy to grant him a fifteen-year copyright for his publication. Doubtless they did this at the request of their versatile colleague, Rabbi Leone Modena, who had a good tenor voice, numbered music among the accomplishments which he had mastered in his younger days, and remained passionately devoted to it; it was he in fact who, as we have seen, saw De' Rossi's synagogal compositions through the press—a difficult task, as he points out in his preface, since the Hebrew had to be printed backwards! But he was not alone in his passion. In 1605, his young son Mordecai, writing to his uncle Moses, after a dramatic performance in which he had figured, slyly misquoted the Book of Exodus: " 'Then Moses sang'—in the *intermezzo*."

The musical life of the Venetian ghetto was sporadic and unorganized. But, in 1628, it was unexpectedly reinforced. The Germans were besieging Mantua, which they captured in July, and their implacable anti-Jewish tendencies were strengthened by the fidelity of the Jews to the House of Gonzaga. Accordingly, they were expelled. (The history of this tragic episode was recounted by Abraham Massarano, probably the son of the *maître de ballet* Isacchino who has been mentioned above, in his moving little volume, *haGaluth vehaPeduth*.) The exclusion did not last for long, but many of the exiles sought refuge in Venice, including several who were devotees of music—some, perhaps, having figured in the concerts at the ducal court. (It may be that Salamone de' Rossi, who is known to have survived until about this time, was one of them.) Thus stimulated, the Venetian ghetto established a musical academy, perhaps in imitation of an institution which may have existed formerly in Mantua. Though known to the outside world as "The Company of the Musicians of the Ghetto of Venice," it took as its name, in the mock-modest fashion of the time, L'Accademia degli Imperiti, or Academy of the Unskilled; with the pathetic Hebrew parallel, *Bezokrenu et Zion*, "When we remembered Zion" (though indeed they had taken down their harps again!).

For a brief time it flourished. It numbered vocalists as well as instrumentalists, and it seems even some original composers. It was supported by certain of the wealthier members of the community; it exchanged courtesies and compositions with similar bodies in the outer city; and Leone Modena himself acted as *maestro di cappella* as well as secretary. Performances took place on two evenings in every week.

That autumn, one of the more affluent supporters was, as it happens, chosen as Bridegroom of the Law in the Spanish synagogue on the feast of the Rejoicing in the Law at the conclusion of Tabernacles. In his honor his colleagues participated in the services that day, organized in two antiphonal choirs (*cori spezzati*) in the style recently popularized in Venice by Giovanni Gabrieli, the musical director of the Church of San Marco. The proceedings, which attracted many members of the nobility, lasted until long after nightfall. The rabbis would not permit the use of the organ that had been introduced into the synagogue for the occasion, but it seems that other instruments were played. The actual music used on this occasion (or one very similar in every respect about the same time) has by a lucky chance been preserved.[10] One would like to think that some of De' Rossi's compositions were included.

This miniature musical renaissance did not last for long. In the following year, there was an outbreak of plague in Italy, which raged in Venice for sixteen months, not sparing the ghetto. Large numbers of persons died; many others fled; and several of the members and supporters of the Accademia degli Imperiti were among them, including some of the finest performers. Though the society continued to exist for some years, it was henceforth only a ghost of its former self; its meetings became infrequent, and the performances fell far below the previous standard. When, in 1639, a newly-formed body in the outer city suggested an interchange of

---

[10] In an important contemporary manuscript in the Naumbourg Collection in the Hebrew Union College in Cincinnati.

courtesies, as in the old days, Leone Modena had to write, regret-
fully, stating that it was beyond his power to promise any collaboration which could repay the effort. It is probable that the body
came to an end not long after.

Indeed, the anti-Jewish reaction which had by now set in, and
the ghetto system, which had been established with the professed
object of cutting off all social contact between the Jews and the
outside world, was fatal to the former amosphere. It took some
little time for the new spirit to prevail, but as the seventeenth century advanced, its hold became more and more effective. In Rome
among other restrictions issued in 1598, it was sternly forbidden
for Jews to frequent Christian houses in order to teach music,
singing and dancing; and when the ghetto system was introduced
into Mantua in 1612, the same prohibition was extended even
there, with the reservation that in certain cases the duke might
grant exemption. The succession of Jewish musicians of original
ability rapidly dwindled. There is a remarkable illustration of this
in the fact that when, in the second half of the seventeenth century, the religious confraternity *Shomerim laBoker* desired to have
a jovial hymn beginning *Ahai veReai* chanted in dialogue-form by
four voices at its annual feast on Hosha'anna Rabba, there was
apparently no composer in the ghetto who could be entrusted with
the task, and they approached the well known Church musician,
Carlo Grossi of Vicenza, who was to be appointed *maestro di
cappella universale* at Mantua in 1687. The music, accompanied by
the words of the hymn transliterated into Latin characters, is thus
embodied, rather incongruously in the latter's publication, *Il
Divertimento de' Grandi . . . Con un dialogo amoroso & uno in
idioma Ebraico* (Venice, 1681). In De' Rossi's day, it will be
recalled, the process had been in the reverse direction.

Nevertheless, the musical tradition in Italian Jewry did not die.
There are still extant manuscript specimens of synagogal music of
the late seventeenth and eighteenth centuries which show that
some cantors at least were fully alive to the musical currents of
the outside world. Handel's oratorio, *Esther*, was translated into
Hebrew by a contemporary Venetian rabbi, Jacob Raphael
Saraval, obviously for presentation in a Jewish musical circle. As
late as 1785, the cardinal legate of Ancona found it necessary to

prohibit once again the teaching of dancing by Jews, though only ten years earlier according to one report a couple of them had been specifically granted the privilege of giving instruction in music and the dance. Jewish instrumentalists remained numerous in Italy. Of this, there is a remarkable demonstration in the fact that at the very close of the eighteenth century, in an enumeration of the occupations of Mantuan Jews by the learned physician-polemist Benedetto Frizzi, he mentions among a total population of only some 2,000 no fewer than fifteen professional musicians who, to earn a living, must necessarily have performed mainly for a Gentile clientele. At Verona, too, the Jewish musicians were well known in the eighteenth century, one of them being that Giacobbe (James) Basevi Cervetto who settled in London and was responsible for the introduction of the violoncello into England. Nor should it be forgotten that Mozart's librettist, Lorenzo da Ponte (to whom is due no small part of the enjoyment of *Don Giovanni*) was by birth a Jew of Ceneda. It thus becomes clear that the remarkable participation of Jews in the musical life of modern Europe and America is basically not a recent development, but has a memorable ancestry extending back to, and antedating, the Renaissance.

THIRTEEN

The Renaissance *in*
Jewish Literature

A celebrated Italian rabbi of the Renaissance period, David del Bene, is said to have been so deeply immersed in the spirit of the environment that once, while preaching in the synagogue in Mantua, he enthusiastically referred to the Holy Diana (*Quella Santa Diana*). True or not, this story illustrates the profound impact of general culture on Jewish intellectual life at this time—the subject with which we must now deal.

The tradition went back to the very dawn of the Renaissance period. We have already seen that at the beginning of the fourteenth century Immanuel of Rome reflected the prevailing spirit in his highly licentious poetry, where adolescent jokes alternate with improbable stories of amatory conquest. Moreover, he not only copied phrases, but even adapted entire poems by Italian authors of the period (apart from his remarkable imitation of Dante's *Divina commedia*, with which we have dealt at length). No major poet among the Italian Jews in later generations approached him in eroticism, or indeed in genius. One legacy which he bequeathed to Hebrew literature had a long influence. As has been mentioned, he was the first to adapt into Hebrew (as well as the first Jew to use in the vernacular) the fourteen-line sonnet which had recently been perfected by the Italian writers, and which through the clearness and beauty of its structure had come to be the classical medium for poetical writing in that country— not only, alas, among those who were able to manipulate it to the best advantage. The sonnet, according to the great historian of the Italian Renaissance, became for Italian literature a condenser of thoughts and emotions such as was possessed by the poetry of no other people.

It was similarly to remain for centuries, and indeed throughout the ghetto period, one of the favorite vehicles of expression among the Italian Jewish poets, under the name "Golden Song" (the Hebrew word for "gold" having the numerical value fourteen). There was hardly a writer of the Renaissance period who did not try his hand at it—though as among their neighbors, the bad, insignificant or even ludicrous sonnets enormously outnumbered the good.

Indeed, the fashions of the environment are reflected in nothing more vividly than in the place that the writing of poetry occupied in the scheme of Italian Jewish education as early as the beginning of the fourteenth century and down to the close of the eighteenth. Instruction in this subject was part of the normal duties of the Hebrew pedagogue, together with the teaching of Bible and Talmud. Every possible event in the life of the individual or of the community was saluted in a flood of verses, sometimes published, or presented within illuminated borders, or at a later date perhaps printed on silk. The inclusion of versification in a "dead" language in the scheme of education will seem less bizarre if it is recalled that Latin and Greek verse composition remains part of the classical curriculum in the English "public schools" to this day. We have seen elsewhere in this volume that, in the early sixteenth century, dramatic literature too began to appear in the literary activity of Italian Jews, at first through the medium of translations, then in original compositions. The echo-poem, in which the repetition of the last one or two syllables gives answer or emphasis to the poet's lines, was absurdly popular in all European literature at this time, and especially in Italy after Guarini had renewed the fashion. It was widely used also by the Hebrew poets of that country, some virtuosi, however, managing to manipulate their phrases so ingeniously that the Hebrew words evoked Italian echoes. So too the macaronic admixtures of vernacular with Latin, which became popular in the early sixteenth century, found its imitators under circumstances which gave the authors' ingenuity even greater play. Some writers produced poems in which Hebrew and Italian lines figured alternately; a few managed to compose poems the phonetic sounds of which made equally good (or bad) sense whether read as Hebrew or as Italian.

The best known instance of this curious genre was an elegy written in 1584 by the irrepressible Leone Modena, at the age of thirteen, in memory of his teacher; he prided himself long afterward that it was still admired by the virtuosi, Christian as well as Jews:

קינה שמור אוי מה כפס אוצר בו
Chi nasce, muor. Oimè, che pass' acerbo!
כל טוב אילים כוסי אור דין אל צלו
Colto vien l'uom, così ordina 'l Cielo
משה מורי משה יקר דבר בו
Mosè morì, Mosè: già car'di verbo
שם תושיה און יום כפור הוא זה לו
Santo sia ogn'uom, con puro zelo
כלה מיטב ימי שן צרי אשר בו
Ch'alla metà, già mai senza riserbo
ציון זה מות רע אין כאן ירפה לו
Si guinge, ma vedràn in cangiar pelo
ספינה בים קל צל עובר ימינו
Se fin' abbiam, ch'al cielo vero ameno
הלים יובא שבי ושי שמנו
Ah! l'uomo va, se viv' assai, se meno.[1]

Not only the spirit and the outward form, but the actual matter of the literature of their neighbors continued throughout the Renaissance period to find an echo, or even imitation, in the Jewish community. The first literary exercise of that ubiquitous figure Leone Modena, in the second half of the sixteenth century, was as has been mentioned an experiment in translating some of the less reputable portions of Ariosto into Spanish; indeed, there is in the Bodleian Library (MS. 2001) a sixteenth-century text of the great Italian epic, in a Spanish translation transcribed into Hebrew characters, perhaps for the use of a member of the Sephardi community in Venice. Daniel da Rossena (one of the participants in

---

[1] Two slightly different versions of this poem are given by the author in his writings. The correspondence between the Hebrew and Italian texts will become clearer if the reader remembers the variants in the Italian (especially Venetian) pronunciation of Hebrew at this time, when apparently the *sh* sound was pronounced *s,* and *g* pronounced *i* or *y.* Modena's *tour de force* was imitated on a tombstone in the seventeenth century, and plagiarized by the London Jewish physician Ephraim Luzzatto in the eighteenth.

the poetical battle in praise or blame of women which has been mentioned elsewhere) made at the beginning of the sixteenth century a free version in Hebrew rhymed prose of the romance of Bernabo and Luciana. This was not an isolated instance, for in Provence, not long before, Bonastruc Avigdor had similarly rendered *Peter of Provence and the Fair Magalona,* while, largely for the use of the German Jews in Italy, Elias Levita had composed on a secular model a Yiddish "romance," *Paris and Vienna* (reprinted Verona, 1594: no copy of the first edition is known—it was no doubt thumbed out of existence[2]). More important than this was his adaptation of "Bevis of Hampton" (Isny, 1541), which introduced the phrase *Bove-Maʻaseh* into colloquial Jewish speech as a synonym for an old wives' tale. Even in Turkey, a certain Jacob Algaba achieved a Hebrew version of Amadis de Gaule (Constantinople, 1540?). At this time, certainly, the Jews did not live in an intellectual ghetto.

The Italian scholars of the period prided themselves on a return to the purest literary standards of classical antiquity, as a reaction against the barbarism of medieval ecclesiastical Latin. This was paralleled by a striking revival of literary Hebrew among the Italian Jews. Everyone could read it, most persons could write it, an epigram or poem in it received general appreciation, and as in our own day, the neo-Hebrew literature covered every aspect of intellectual activity. Communal secretaries were chosen not infrequently only on the strength of their Hebrew style. Indeed, the vitality of Hebrew was such as to retard the development of Jewish literature in Italian, which was to a great extent made unnecessary, and attained real significance only in relatively modern times. The purity of the Italian diction and prosody was admired and envied in all parts of the Jewish world; while, on the other hand, the Italian rabbis sometimes sneered at the barbarous and inelegant—not to say ungrammatical—phraseology of even the most learned visitors from beyond the Alps. There was, however, a difference—and for the better—between the flowing, easy style of the Italian Jewish humanists and the sometimes stilted Latin of their Christian neighbors. Some of them, indeed, such as the

---

[2] This work is said to have appeared also in Italian shortly afterward.

chronicler Joseph haCohen, author of the historical martyrology
"The Vale of Tears" (*Emek haBakha*) tried to imitate slavishly
the biblical style, in the same way as the Christian scholars attempted to be Ciceronian; and there were others who obscured
their meaning in an almost impenetrable tangle of clichés, to such
an extent that it was impossible for the reader to comprehend what
they meant unless he knew it already. But the ordinary writer of
the period used a simple, flowing narrative style, as clearly differ-
entiated from the medieval as it was from the biblical standards,
and demonstrating its vitality both by linguistic innovations and
by unabashed borrowings from the Italian vocabulary.

The artificial revival of Latin among the humanists extended to
conversational as well as literary use. This too had its echo in a
revival of spoken Hebrew among the Jews, anticipating in certain
respects the renewal in contemporary Palestine—with the reservation that the sacred language had always known a relatively considerable vitality, if only as a means of communicating with co-
religionists in or from distant parts. Thus at the beginning of the
sixteenth century, when the Jewish community of Padua was a
melting-pot for groups from all parts of the Jewish world, a
talmudist from France used to carry on his discussions with other
scholars in that tongue, this being the only common medium of
communication among them.

Later on, however, the speaking of Hebrew on occasion became
a virtue rather than a necessity among the more cultured elements,
many persons making a point of using the language regularly
among themselves. In his work on prosody,[3] Samuel Archevolti
devotes a whole chapter (xxviii)—obviously not intended as a mere
academic exercise—to the purity of Hebrew speech and diction.
Azariah de' Rossi tells that in his day, although the Jews lived in
an Italian-speaking environment and were linguistically assimilated
to it, "the intelligentsia, who are many, express themselves, speak,
and write in the Holy Tongue," though not presumably in their
normal activities. Even Christians who were interested in Hebrew
studies followed this example; we have pointed out that Giannozzo
Manetti, the Florentine humanist, is said to have insisted on speak-

[3] See below, pp. 273 f.

ing Hebrew with the convert whom he had as his instructor in that language.

As was the case with the Christians, so the Jewish writers now began to discover themselves physically as human beings; and a new literature, of personal values, began to emerge in the Hebrew language. The first biography in all Jewish literature after biblical times was that of Isaac Abrabanel, published in 1551 by a Mantuan rabbi, Baruch Uziel Forte ("Hazachetto," in the hybrid Hebrew-Italian diminutive form usually employed).[4] Leone Modena was only one of those who wrote autobiographies, in which he was anticipated in Italian by a semi-illiterate huckster from Siena. In another connection, the story was told about the travelers who went to Palestine and wrote accounts of the land and of the way thither in a highly personal form, describing at length their individual impressions, experiences, adventures and vicissitudes, with results very different from the statistical, detached accounts of an earlier period. David Reubeni's story of his wanderings in Italy and elsewhere is so detailed as to partake almost of the nature of a diary. Detailed pen-portraits of individuals now begin for the first time to appear in Hebrew literature, paralleling the gradual appearance of painted portraits in Jewish homes. Abraham Farisol, for example, in his geographical work *Orhot Olam*, depicts the appearance of David Reubeni himself—"short of stature, thin of flesh, courageous, a great prayer, swarthy-skinned." Or Leone Modena describes his father, Isaac, who died in 1591: "Of middle height, lean and wiry of body, generally healthy, dark complexioned, with a short beard . . . neither extravagant nor niggardly, and loving laughter": nothing extraordinary to be sure from today's point of view, but in those times wholly novel. Many writers (and again Modena is an example, though one only out of many) carefully preserved copies of the letters they had written—not only because of their style or their learning, but for their inherent interest.

On the other hand, it is remarkable that, although there was an unquestionable revival of interest in history among the Italian Jews in the Renaissance period, this expressed itself through the medium of episodic chronicles, in the medieval style, rather than

---

[4] Forte = Hebrew *hazak* = strong: *-etto* is the diminutive ending.

of comprehensive histories in the modern sense, such as Macchiavelli and Guicciardini had by now introduced to European literature. It is enough to mention in this connection Joseph haCohen's
naive *History of the French and Turkish Monarchies,* or in the
Jewish sphere his martyrology, *The Vale of Tears,* to which
reference has been made just above; or *The Chain of Tradition*
by the banker Gedaliah ibn Jacchia of Imola, so replete with
legendary matter that his critics called it *The Chain of Lies.* The
most important historical work produced by a Jew in Renaissance
Italy is the tragic "Consolation in the Tribulations of Israel" (*Consolaçam às Tribulaçoens de Israel*) by the former marrano Samuel
Usque, published at Ferrara in 1553.[5] This stupendous work, however—more significant for its imaginativeness and its composition
than as a narrative of events—was written in Portuguese, and
belongs to the history of the Renaissance in Portugal.

This somewhat embryonic revival of interest in history was
accompanied by a manifestation among Jews, almost for the first
time, of an interest in geography as an academic field of knowledge, without any necessary practical application such as had
inspired the famous Jewish mapmakers of Majorca in the Middle
Ages. Now it was, for example, that the versatile Ferrara scribe
Abraham Farisol compiled his *Orhot Olam* or "Paths of the
World" (referred to above), embodying all the geographical
knowledge that he could collect from whatever source, oral as
well as written—the first published Jewish book to mention Christopher Columbus and the discovery of America.[6] Joseph haCohen,
too, supplemented his historical writings by a geographical treatise;
while geography was one of the subjects to be taught at the university preparatory courses which the brothers Provenzal wished
to set up in Mantua. Accounts of travel to the Holy Land were
eagerly collected, and primitive maps began to make their appearance. In many writings of the period we find an awareness of
geographical matters and problems—for example, when Hebrew
writers tried to identify, with whatever knowledge they had at
their command, the lands and places mentioned in the Bible.

---

[5] See pp. 55, 184.
[6] See above, p. 122.

With the close of the fifteenth century, Mantua—the home *par excellence* of the Jewish Renaissance in Italy—became the center of the movement for the introduction of the new humanistic spirit into Jewish scholarship. Hebrew education—and not purely in a talmudic sense—was particularly well advanced here. This is evident from the fact that down to the end of the eighteenth century those communal regulations which had to be generally understood —the laws governing taxation, and the "sumptuary laws" to control extravagance in personal life—were always published and circulated in Hebrew, and in Hebrew only. Obviously, this implies a very widespread understanding of the language, among all sections of the population and presumably among both sexes. However that may be, it was in Mantua that the synthesis between Hebrew and Renaissance culture reached its culmination. The process was assisted by the very early establishment of a Hebrew press in the city, no later than 1476—a year after the first known specimens of Hebrew printing.

One of the outstanding Jewish scholars of Mantua in the second half of the fifteenth century was a certain Judah, or Judah Leon, who had qualified as a physician, had received papal and imperial license to practice (probably accompanied by the dignity of knighthood), and accordingly was generally known as Judah Messer Leon; in the local records he is spoken of deferentially as "Leon the Jew, Doctor of Arts and Medicine, and Knight, as well as Doctor of the Hebrew Law." Perhaps he was a native of Naples, though this is not certain: for a time he was resident in Ancona, where he engaged in a number of polemics which attracted a great deal of attention among his contemporaries; he studied philosophy and composed commentaries on various works of Aristotle—including one on the *Later Analytics*, which one of his opponents condemned as an arrant plagiarism, having been translated (he said) from the Latin![7] He perhaps was author also of a commentary on the Book of Proverbs, in which there was discussed in the most serious fashion, but a shade incongruously, whether or not Petrarch's Laura was a real person. For a period of some ten years after about 1471 he lived in Mantua, where he fell afoul of the distinguished and intolerant talmudist, Rabbi

---

[7] Cf. above, p. 81.

Joseph Colon, and quarreled with him so violently and with such disturbing consequences that the duke restored quiet by banishing them both from his dominions. It has been conjectured that the dispute was about the vexing problem mentioned above, of whether the academic gown required the "fringes" prescribed by Mosaic Law! He then settled in Naples, as chief rabbi of the Jewish communities of the realm.

The most memorable literary production of this versatile and quarrelsome character was a Hebrew work entitled *Nofet Zufim*, or the "Flow of the Honeycombs" (Mantua, before 1480), which has the distinction of being the earliest Hebrew book by a living writer ever to be published. Formally, it is a textbook of logic, but in fact it is a great deal more. In it, the author sought to demonstrate that the Jews were not devoid of literary appreciation and taste. With this object, he approached the Bible from the purely literary point of view, showing for example the superiority of the oratory of the Hebrew prophets over that of the Greeks and Romans. One chapter of the work, on the nature of the state, may be considered the earliest Jewish experiment in the field of political science. Incidentally, the author endeavored to demonstrate that there was no necessary disparity between Judaism and secular studies, which contribute to a better appreciation of the products of the Jewish genius. To prove his thesis, he used such classical writings as were available to him; not indeed in Greek, of which he was ignorant, but a good deal in Latin—above all Cicero, and even Quintillian's newly-discovered *Institutio oratoria*, published in Rome in 1470, his conceptions being largely based on these two writers. This is perhaps the earliest of the long series of works in various languages treating the Bible as literature. It was an audacious attitude to take up in those days, when Jews as well as Christians considered that the Book of Books was too sacred to be judged by the same criteria as other writings; though Judah Romano, Immanuel of Rome's cousin, had anticipated this writer by nearly two centuries in comparing the tongue of Isaiah with that of Tully.

Judah Messer Leon inaugurated a fresh approach to the biblical literature. A century later, his fellow-townsman, Jedidiah Solomon Norsa ("Norzi" in the traditional Hebrew transcription), member of an ancient and distinguished Mantuan family hailing from Norcia in Umbria, initiated or rather renewed a fresh approach to the biblical text. It may be said that a thousand years before, in their attempts to establish a definitive and authoritative standard for the Holy Scriptures, the Masorites had anticipated in certain respects the methods of Renaissance scholarship—as indeed did the medieval commentators on the Talmud, always ready to consult variant readings or to suspect textual lacunae. But the Masoretic text itself had begun by now to exhibit variants. Norsa made it his life's work to reëstablish the authentic version and to produce a text of the Bible which should be as perfect as learning and industry could make it. For this purpose he assembled and compared ancient codices (including the famous Toledo Bible of 1277 now in the De' Rossi collection at Parma), searched out the copies made by the most esteemed scribes of more recent times, checked them against the newly printed editions, examined the citations which are scattered through the talmudic and midrashic literatures, and consulted Jewish writers on the Bible both ancient and modern, published and unpublished, noting the variants also in every other available source. He found that a Palestinian bibliomaniac of the time, Menahem Lonzano, had been working less systematically along somewhat the same lines, his researches being summed up in an essay in his *Shete Iadoth* (Venice, 1618); when Menahem came to Italy, in his old age, Norsa gave him the hospitality of his house, so as to profit by his erudition. He heard of another work on the subject by a medieval Spanish scholar, Meir Abulafia, as yet unpublished; to consult this, and to search out other biblical codices, it appears that he crossed the seas to the Levant and traveled from place to place, spending much time away from his home. All told, he used some sixty principal authorities for his purpose—a colossal number for those days. It was only after a lifetime of labor that his great work, *Goder Perez* ("The Repairer of the Breach") was completed. Not impressive in point of size, it was of vast significance, since, for the first time since the invention of printing, it established the traditional text of the Bible on a scientific basis, thus anticipating and facilitating the work of Kennicott in the eighteenth century, of Ginsburg in the nineteenth, of Kittle and Kahle in the twentieth. The sequel was, however, somewhat depressing. It was not until more than a century after Norsa's death that his work was published at Mantua, in 1712-14, under the title *Minḥat Shai* ("The Oblation": the second word comprises the initials of Solomon Jedidiah). Though it immediately became classical, the introduction did not appear with it, and was given by the rabbis of Mantua to a local nobleman, thus being published only in the nineteenth century. So far had the Renaissance spirit waned!

One of the typical aspects of Renaissance intellectual activity was archaeological research on the basis of literary texts. This received its most remarkable exemplification in all Jewish literature in the *magnum opus* of Dr. Abraham Portaleone. The author we have already encountered, as a member of the most eminent of the Italian Jewish medical dynasties of this period, body-physician to the Duke of Mantua, and author of two scientific works in Latin; he also composed in his later days a program of pious readings and studies for his children, characteristic of the versatility of the Italian Jewish mentality at this time. He was already, it seems, advanced in years, and paralyzed down one side of his body as the result of a stroke, when he began the composition of the work by which he is best remembered in Jewish literary annals, the *Shilte haGibborim* or "Shields of the Mighty" (finished 1607, published 1612)—the first printed Hebrew book, incidentally, in which modern punctuation, including the question-mark, is employed.

The motivation of the work was wholly medieval; the treatment, in some ways, surprisingly modern. Portaleone had what might be termed a pious obsession with the former service of the Temple in Jerusalem, and impressed on his three highly-educated sons the duty of rehearsing regularly the details of the sacrificial worship which should rightly have been performed there day by day. At the same time, he insisted that the recital should be clarified by the fullest possible comprehension of everything relating to the procedure and the setting, down to the last detail. His work thus became a systematic treatment of the archaeology and appurtenances of the Temple and everything connected with it, on the basis of the entire corpus of the classical Jewish literature—the Bible, the Talmud, the Midrash and so on—reinforced by all the extraneous literature, in whatever tongue, to which he had access. He thus deals in a succession of what might be termed antiquarian essays, distributed into four books and ninety chapters, with the Temple and its construction, the Sanctuary, the Altar, the Menorah (Temple Candelabrum), the Table of Showbread and other implements; the robes of the Priests and Levites and their functions; the High Priest's vestments, including the breastplate and the ephod with its jewels; the chants of the Levites and the instruments with which they were accompanied; the sacrifices, the public feasts and other special occasions; the prayers and the periodical reading of the Torah; and so on.

Each of these main headings gives occasion for limitless learned digressions. Few works perhaps even of that age of erudition are more erudite, and certainly none is more diffuse. In connection with the construction of the Temple, for example, the author embarks on a long discussion regarding ancient Jewish architectural terms and measurements. When he describes the psalmody of the Levites he embodies the veritable treatise on music, general and instrumental, that has been described above. The historical distinction between Priests, Levites and Israelites serves as the peg or the pretext for a discussion of political science, which in turn leads up to a consideration of national defense, military organization, tactics and instruments of war—all within the framework of an imaginary harangue delivered by the High Priest when he addressed the people before battle, in accordance with the prescription in the Book of Deuteronomy (20.1-9). In the course of this discussion, the suggestion is put forward that the biblical term *solelah* (that is, siege-works: cf. Isaiah 37.33) denoted artillery, in the modern sense! The main tactical principle the author laid down was, to be sure, sound, almost Churchillian—that the enemy should never be allowed to relax.[8] In this section, he managed, too, to include a few details about secret writing—for the High Priest had something to do with drawing up contracts.

His discussion of the stones of the High Priest's breastplate is sufficient to start him on a veritable and, in fact, valuable treatise on precious stones—especially, their medical use as indicated in

---

[8] In this connection it may be mentioned that the chronicler Gedaliah ibn Jacchia (see pp. 329 f.), was also interested in military matters and from the use of the Hebrew work *va-yeḥalek*, in Genesis 14.15, hazarded the opinion that Abraham introduced the practice of wearing a white shirt (*ḥalak*) over armor during a surprise night-assault.

ancient literature and current practice; in connection with all this, he naturally cites his own Latin work published not long before on the therapeutic application of gold. This in turn leads him on to a consideration of anatomy and (returning now to his point of departure) of trade in precious stones, the price of diamonds in the early Spring of 1606, the way to distinguish the true from the false, and then of tariffs and currency.

He now deals with the Temple sacrifices, which enable him to provide what is in effect a complete treatise on zoology and animal anatomy, with an entire section on the strange beasts with one horn recently discovered, such as the rhinoceros—a beast certainly familiar to his contemporary Vitale di Sacerdote of Nice, who wished to provide one for the zoological collection in the ducal park at Turin. There were, of course, other types of offering in the Temple, these giving him the opportunity to make a learned scientific comparison between liquid and dry measures and to describe his own experiments in this matter. He now proceeds to deal with the use of salt in the sacrifices, and then speaks of salts generally, including those of gold and of silver, and their medicinal value; as also of saltpeter and hence of gunpowder. This section of the work comprises an almost complete up-to-date treatise on chemistry and pharmacology, a subject on which he was certainly an authority. Soap and soap-making also find a place at this point. The Temple incense provides a starting-point for a description of spices generally.

A separate section at the end of the work is devoted to the alphabet and the art of writing, in the course of which the author endeavored to demonstrate that printing was not discovered in the fifteenth century, as was commonly held, but was familiar in the days of the Bible, as may plainly be seen from Job 19.23-4 ("Oh that my words were now written; Oh that they were inscribed in a book! That with an iron pen and lead they were graven in the rock for ever").

The author shows in every section of this curious compilation a vast if heterogeneous range of knowledge. He boasts that he made use not only of the writings in Hebrew of ninety-eight Jewish scholars, whom he enumerates in detail, but also of ten other languages—Aramaic, Persian, Arabic, Greek, Latin, Italian, Spanish, French, and Bohemian (that is, Czech). To this could also

possibly be added Portuguese, for he also quotes (perhaps, however, from a translation) the marrano physician Garcia d'Orta, of
whose Judaizing tendencies he was quite ignorant. To be sure, in
many cases it was a question only of citing one or two random
words in the languages mentioned; but he certainly had more than
a passing knowledge of the classics. He was naturally acquainted
with the standard Latin writers, from Virgil down to the comic
playwrights Terence and Plautus. But he showed also a greater
familiarity with Greek than perhaps any other Jewish writer of
the Renaissance period. He knew, for example, that there were
five different dialects in the Greek language, and classified the
poets accordingly. Moreover, he was anxious to spread a knowledge of classical studies among his co-religionists. Not only did
he include in his work what has been termed a systematic course
in Latin, but he even printed in it the Greek alphabet, with the
express purpose of assisting his fellow-Jews to master the rudiments of that language. Obviously, this would not get them very
far; so he advised them to buy Christian prayer-books which
comprised the evening and morning prayers in Greek, in order to
carry their studies a stage further. Graetz, the greatest of Jewish
historians, speaks of him as "half-mad." That is preposterously
unfair; but he was, to say the least, discursive to the verge of
eccentricity.

The most remarkable Jewish work of the Renaissance period
is, however, the *Meor Eynayim* or "Enlightenment of the Eyes"
of Abraham Portaleone's compatriot, Azariah min haAdumim or
(as he signed his Italian letters) Bonaiuto de' Rossi (generally
known by the hybrid Hebrew-Italian form, Azariah de' Rossi),
born in Mantua about 1514. We happen to know more about his
physique and appearance than we do of any other Jew of this
period. One day (it was in 1548 or 1549, and probably at Ferrara)
he dropped into a bookshop to inspect the latest publications.
There he found an acquaintance, the marrano physician Amatus
Lusitanus (of whom we have already spoken), who was discussing with a friend Galatino's learned polemical work against
Judaism, *De arcanis catholicae veritatis*, the first edition of which
had appeared thirty years before from the press of Geronimo Soncino at Ortona in the Abruzzi. Azariah ("the Mantuan Jew, a

TITLE PAGE OF THE *Sepher Meor Eynayim*, BY AZARIAH DE' ROSSI,
MANTUA, 1573
Courtesy of the Library of the Jewish Theological Seminary of America

great scholar both in Hebrew and in Latin letters," as Amatus describes him) joined in the conversation and gave his views—especially regarding the two scholars who appear in the work in defense of the Christian Hebraist Johannes von Reuchlin. When the discussion was ended, Azariah consulted Amatus in a professional capacity, for he was suffering from indigestion and insomnia, apparently accentuated by the long hours he spent at study and, in Amatus' opinion, by the rich food of the traditional Jewish cuisine; a course of treatment at the local medicinal baths had not improved his condition, and for the past year he had also had intermittent fevers. Amatus goes in some detail (*Centuriae* IV, § 42) into the symptoms of the disease and the cure that he prescribed, in which he regulated in the most minute manner everything concerning his patient, from his diet (with due regard to the Jewish ritual laws) to his hours of study and his marital relations; and he boasted that at the end of four months Azariah was completely cured, and became as strong as a boxer. Among other things, Amatus advised him to avoid a damp and misty climate, such as one finds at Mantua and Ferrara. It may be in consequence of this that Azariah removed to Bologna. At the time of the persecution of the Jews here in 1568, he was apparently one of those who escaped from the city by bribing the gate-keepers. He now made his way to Ferrara again, and he was living here when an external event prompted him to take up the work that has made his name famous.

In the early morning of Friday, November 18, 1571, between three and four o'clock, the city of Ferrara was shaken by an earthquake which caused great damage and some loss of life. Though (it seemed miraculous to them) none of the ten synagogues in the town was damaged, the Jews joined in the general exodus to the countryside, disregarding even the sanctity of the Sabbath in their terror. Something of the style of living among the wealthy at this time is conveyed by the information that half a dozen of the communal magnates were able to accommodate over one hundred persons in their gardens and courtyards. Azariah de' Rossi—whose house had been partly destroyed—was among the refugees. In these circumstances he made the acquaintance of a certain Christian scholar, a fugitive like himself, who in a highly characteristic fashion passed his time by studying the apocryphal

Letter of Aristeas—a famous piece of Judeo-Hellenistic literature, probably of the first century B.C.E., which describes in hyperbolic terms the magnificence of the Temple of Jerusalem and the legendary origin of the Septuagint Version of the Bible. A difficulty arising at one point, he asked his temporary Jewish neighbor what was the reading of the Hebrew in that passage. To his embarrassment, Azariah had to reply that no Hebrew text existed, and that the work, though Jewish in origin, was virtually unknown among his co-religionists.

It was this episode which determined him to devote his attention seriously to a project which had been in his mind already for some time past—the compilation of a work which should bring to the attention of the Jews those materials regarding Jewish antiquity extant in the classical languages (particularly Greek), and which should apply incidentally to Hebrew records the critical principles of the Renaissance. Within eighteen months he had completed it and it was published in the autumn of 1573 in his birthplace, Mantua, where he had taken up residence again to supervise the printing. He entitled it *Meor Eynayim*, or the "Enlightenment of the Eyes." It is in three parts, with some organic but no logical connection. The first gives an account of the Ferrara earthquake and the personal experiences which resulted from it; the second provides a Hebrew translation of the *Letter of Aristeas* which he had carried out within twenty days of the conversation referred to above; and the third—comprising the main body of the work, some 335 out of a total of 387 pages in the original edition—is taken up by a number of independent essays, divided into four sections, on various aspects of Jewish antiquity, considered in the light of classical literature and Renaissance principles of research.

After a defense of his conduct in bringing evidence from extraneous sources on Jewish studies—a procedure hardly known as yet, at least in a Christian environment; there had been greater freedom in the Moslem world of the Middle Ages—he goes on to consider in detail the importance in this connection of the writings of Philo of Alexandria (he translates the name *Jedidiah*) whom he for the first time reintroduces to the Jewish orbit; he severely criticizes him, on the other hand, for having treated the biblical narratives as mere allegories and questions his orthodoxy. This in turn leads him to give an account of the Jewish sects of the period of the Second Temple and to attempt to establish their relation to those mentioned in the rabbinical literature—a problem which still engages the attention of scholars.

Next he takes into consideration the origins of the Septuagint, so entertainingly described in the *Letter of Aristeas*, and points out certain discrepancies between this and the accepted "Masoretic" version of the Hebrew Bible. He advances the ingenious hypothesis (which some modern scholars have revived) that the reason for such differences is that the "seventy elders" did not translate directly from the Hebrew, but from an intermediate Aramaic text current in Palestine at the time of the Second Temple. He then speaks of the origin of the Jewish settlements in Alexandria and Cyrene, of Bar Kokhba's revolt against the Romans in 132-35, and other related matters, in the light of the classical sources.

Having now established his point, that extraneous records may throw considerable light on Jewish studies, he considers the position when the secular and the Jewish sources are in conflict. The haggadic (that is, non-legalistic) portions of the vast rabbinical literature contain a great number of stories which, he maintains, cannot be taken literally: for example, the legend, unknown to Roman writers, ascribing the death of Titus to a gnat which entered his brain on his return journey from Jerusalem to Rome. The third part of the work is devoted, in the same spirit, to an inquiry into Jewish chronology. This is followed by a consideration of certain significant passages of Philo, Josephus, and others, bearing on Jewish history, with translations of some texts. The fourth part deals with aspects of Jewish archaeology, including the High Priestly vestments, the structure and service of the Temple, and the history of the royal proselytes to Judaism in the last days of the Second Temple, Queen Helena and her sons, the rabbinic story about them being compared with the account in Josephus.

This is the content of the volume, in barest outline; it is too discursive to analyze in detail, without tedium to reader and writer alike. For what is remarkable about the work, more than the subjects that are treated, is the spirit of free inquiry in which they are treated. For the first time, the standards that had become established during the previous century for the study of classical texts and classical antiquities were applied to Jewish studies. Jewish students were not only informed of the mass of material comprised in the classical (particularly the Greek) literature which could throw light on their interests; they were also shown (and this was the daring part of the innovation) how the rabbinic texts should be handled in the light of such sources. Moreover, considering that a degree of authority and even of sanctity was at this period attached to the Talmud hardly less than that attached to the Bible itself, it was an object-lesson in criticism in a wider sense, the full implications of which were not confined to the Jewish community.

The wealth of literature cited in the work is dazzling. Apart from the Jewish writers, Azariah quotes—and with some degree of understanding—approximately one hundred authors, half of them Latin or Greek; though indeed he wistfully confesses that his knowledge of the latter language was by no means so good as he desired. Of the ancient poets, he knew Homer and Aesop, Terence, Virgil, Horace and Tibullus. The philosophers included, not only the inevitable Pythagoras, Aristotle and Plato, but also Seneca, Cicero, and Themistius; natural science is represented by Euclid and Pliny; geography by Strabo, Ptolemy and Solinus; medicine by Hippocrates, Dioscorides, and Galen. Among the historians, besides Herodotus, Xenophon, Livy, Suetonius, Tacitus, Plutarch and Caesar, there are also lesser-known authorities such as Dionysius of Halicarnassus, Diodorus Siculus, Dio Cassius, Eutropius, and so on. He even had some knowledge of the third-century Dalmatian jurist Herennius Modestinus. Not only this: he was familiar with the writings of the Church Fathers—Eusebius, Jerome, Augustine, Justin Martyr, Clement of Alexandria, and a host of others; not to mention medieval writers such as Isidor of Seville, Suidas, Thomas Aquinas and the pioneer of Hebrew studies in the medieval Church (though he did not know of this!) Hugo of St. Victor. It goes without saying that, like so many of his Jewish contemporaries he was well acquainted with the basic Italian writers, such as Dante, "the learned Christian poet," and Petrarch. In addition, no fewer than thirty-five contemporary writers on history and theology are cited; not only Italians, but also Spaniards, Germans and so on. Add to this the comprehensive knowledge that he shows of Jewish literature—ancient, medieval

and modern—and it will be realized that we are in the presence of
a scholar of utterly exceptional range and attainment. It is true
that, while he refers to the writings of his contemporary, Luigi
Guicciardini, he shows no knowledge of his more eminent kinsman, the historian Francesco, nor for that matter even of Macchiavelli. The reason was primarily that he was affected by the
absorption in antiquity which was the distinguishing feature of
the earlier Renaissance. Indeed, the conception of later, and still
less of contemporary, history had as we have seen hardly penetrated as yet into Jewish intellectual life.

As has been indicated, it was not only his learning, but also his
use of it, that is memorable. In every chapter there are ingenious
theories, some of which anticipate those put forward as novelties
in our own day, or brief considerations of problems regarding
which entire volumes were subsequently written. He adduced
evidence from the New Testament (f. 52b) to show that at the
beginning of the Christian era Hebrew had given way in Palestine
to Aramaic. He decides that Philo had no knowledge of the sacred
language, though his rabbinical friends in Mantua, the brothers
Provenzal, were somewhat shocked by this conclusion (52a).
After comparing upwards of fifty passages cited by the Alexandrian scholar from the Bible, he concludes that his Greek text was
not the Septuagint version (48a): a subject to which a learned
monograph has recently been devoted. The same is the case also
with another problem on which Azariah touched: Philo's relation
to talmudic law. He not only knew of the work on biblical antiquities ascribed to this same scholar and of the doubts regarding
its authorship, which he was inclined to think unfounded, but he
also cited for it more rabbinic parallels than any other later scholar
has done, down to the present day. He demonstrates that the
current Jewish year-reckoning, *anno mundi*, goes back only to
the close of the talmudic age (95a). He endeavors to show that
the author of the *Zohar* knew that the earth was round (57b).
He advances, after prolonged discussions with his friends, a theory
of biblical prosody (which achieved its effect by a regular number
of stresses in each verse or half-verse), near enough to the conclusions formulated in the eighteenth century by Bishop Lowth (who
indeed quotes him approvingly) and now generally accepted by
scholars. At every turn we are confronted with evidence of an

original and daring mind. His answers were not infrequently wrong; but his questions were always right.[9]

His intellectual curiosity rivaled his erudition. He ransacked libraries, he consulted manuscripts, he compared editions, he used the evidence of coins, he discussed problems with rabbis on the one hand and monks on the other. He asked Christian students of the classics whether there was any basis for the description of the coronation of Vespasian which figures in the writings of the Hebrew pseudo-Josephus (Josippon), and records their negative answer. (Scholars now believe that it reflects the procedure at the time of an early Holy Roman Emperor.) He inquired of a Benedictine monastery near Mantua whether they knew of any manuscripts of the Hellenistic Jewish writer Aristobulus, quoted by Eusebius, and was informed by them (52a) that they owned a copy, and that it was superior to Philo (alas, that it cannot now be traced!). He speaks longingly (*ibid.*) of the Medicean library in Florence, where he heard that another manuscript of this work was to be found. There is extant a letter in Italian which he wrote to the Abbot of Monte Cassino (the great center of learning in southern Italy), requesting his acceptance of a copy of his work—which the other was, it seems, able to read! The book ends in somewhat macabre fashion with the verses that the author had prepared to be inscribed on his tombstone; from his own copy in the Bodleian Library in Oxford, heavily annotated in preparation for a second edition, we learn that they are a translation of the Latin hexameters prepared by the peace-making Cardinal Gasparo Contarini (who died in 1542) for his own sepulcher.

The "enlightenment of the eyes" achieved by the *Meor Eynayim* was, as it turned out, too dazzling. The criticisms that the author had to face in Italy were more or less on an academic plane. His friend Moses Provenzal, who had considered him to be too hard on Philo, also thought that his correction of the traditional system of chronology was unjustified, and Azariah had to publish an appendix to his work of a few pages in which he dealt with the objection. The same point of view was adopted, more

---

[9] On the other hand, some of De' Rossi's learned statements seem to be based on faulty recollection: for example, his quotation (4.4) from Origen via Pico della Mirandola that Moses exhibited the Book of Job to the Israelites on the Sabbath.

326   THE JEWS IN THE RENAISSANCE

acrimoniously, by Isaac Finzi, Rabbi of Pesaro, who wrote a lengthy monograph on the subject, to which De' Rossi replied at similar length and with a display of erudition of the same type as in his main work; this entitled *Mazref laKesef* ("Purifier of Silver") was not published until long after his death.

Some obscurantist scholars took the matter up more fiercely, objecting not so much to details, as to the basic fact that the author attached an equal value to secular and to Jewish sources, and that he considered (as indeed many had done before him) that the talmudic legends need not be taken literally. The trouble was perhaps, in fact, not so much that Azariah displayed such independence of thought—that had been a commonplace in Jewish writing throughout the Middle Ages—as that the expression of this free attitude was concentrated in the covers of a single volume, devoted to little else; and that, thanks to the invention of printing, this volume could come into every hand. If he illustrated the spirit of the Renaissance, they on their side were affected by the spirit of the Counter-Reformation, which during the past few years had established a rigid censorship of literary productions. (The *Index librorum prohibitorum* had been published for the first time in 1564.) It was not that Azariah's work was considered abominable, but that it was considered dangerous; and a number of rabbis from various Italian communities (to be sure, not including some of the most important—Mantua, Modena, Florence) forbade its reading or even its retention without special license.

This did not go far enough for some of the extremists. There was in Judaism no supreme authority comparable to the papacy. They accordingly appealed to the greatest rabbinical authority of the age, Joseph Caro, author of the *Shulḥan Arukh* (who had indeed been referred to laudatorily in the *Meor Eynayim*, De' Rossi informing us that he had assisted in the collection of money in Italy for the publication of his works). This tremendous but essentially medieval Levantine scholar, who had passed his adult life beyond the reach of the new currents of European intellectual life, was horrified, and drew up a decree ordering the work to be burned. But he died before it could be promulgated, and the rabbis of Mantua determined on a compromise, forbidding the book to be read by any person under the age of twenty-five. Some copies of it still bear on the fly-leaves a formal rabbinic authorization to this effect, though none later than 1630.

The book then was not suppressed, as heretical works in the sphere of Christianity were suppressed in Italy at this time. But it was disapproved; and in view of the conditions that prevailed in Italian Jewry after the full effects of the ghetto system had made themselves felt, the results were not dissimilar. The impetus to a new approach to Jewish studies proved sterile. The *Meor Eynayim* had the unusual experience of being quoted and used by various Christian scholars; but it was never republished by the Jews until more than 200 years had elapsed. When in the nineteenth century the movement of the Science of Judaism had its beginning in Germany, De' Rossi's work became one of its classics, and only now were the ideas and hypotheses in which it abounds taken up and followed to their conclusion. It is symptomatic that what is still the standard edition is that edited by the great Zunz, the founder of the new school. A dozen generations after his death, De' Rossi became one of the fathers of the new Wissenschaft des Judentums.

It is inevitable that in the foregoing pages attention has been paid preëminently to a few outstanding individuals in whose writings the Renaissance spirit manifested itself. What is, however, more significant is the wide diffusion of this attitude of mind and this range of interest even among the ordinary householders. Everywhere, there were enthusiastic book-collectors, whose libraries were open for consultation by savants such as De' Rossi—for example, in the fifteenth century, Menahem of Volterra (whose collection is now in the Vatican), or in the sixteenth Baruch da Peschiera (whose books found their way to Turin and Parma). Solomon Finzi, son of the Mantuan scientist Angelo (Mordecai) Finzi, had in his library in the little township of Viadana a collection of two hundred volumes, at that time considered to be a number worthy of a great humanist: he may have been related immediately to the banking family of the same name in Bologna, later on, who were reputed to own a similar number of manuscripts, besides a rich collection of printed books. The largest Jewish library in Italy in the Renaissance period, however, was said to be that built up by successive wealthy and erudite generations of the Da Pisa family.

Mention has already been made of Benjamin d'Arignano of

Rome, also owner of a noted library, greatly used by the printers and editors of the period, who found his splendid collection of manuscripts invaluable in preparing their texts. These earlier collectors were all to be outdone in the seventeenth century by Abraham Solomon Graziani, whose abbreviated signature *Ish Ger*, accompanied sometimes by valuable annotations, is to be found in countless books in Jewish libraries throughout the world. In the true Renaissance spirit, these great libraries were utilized for the purpose of establishing accurate texts. For the *Tikkune haZohar* (Mantua, 1560) ten manuscripts were utilized; the Soncino edition of Kimhi's great dictionary was based on codices from France, Germany, Spain and Italy.

Like their Christian neighbors, the Jewish scholars turned as much as they could to archaeology to illustrate their literary researches. Obadiah (Servadio) Sforno, the Bible commentator and physician, compared the Mosaic "Urim and Tumim" with the pagan oracles. Visitors from Palestine brought home with them specimens of the ancient Jewish coins, which were eagerly studied. Vitale (Jehiel Nissim) da Pisa, economist as well as talmudist, who had recently received a shekel from Jerusalem, weighed it in Florence in 1527 so as to establish its relative value in Tuscan currency. A contemporary, Rabbi Moses Basola of Ancona, collected specimens while he was traveling through Palestine in 1522 (as Nahmanides had done, two and a half centuries before) and used them for the purpose of ascertaining the primitive Hebrew alphabet—information of which De' Rossi made eager use (f. 171-2); he was thus enabled to reproduce in his great work an engraving of a shekel of the "Fourth Year," unfortunately only approximately correct. This was the first such reproduction in Hebrew literature. However a generation before this the unbalanced French Hebraist Guillaume Postel (who piously endeavored to demonstrate that all languages derived from the Hebrew!) had already printed an engraving of a shekel, more accurately, in his *Linguarum duodecim characteribus differentium alphabetum* (Paris, 1538); while a year before the publication of the *Meor Eynayim*, the Spaniard Arias Montano had done the same in the appendix to the Antwerp Polyglot Bible of 1572, this being the first exact reproduction to be published. On the other hand, it was only in 1583—nine years after De' Rossi's publication—that the greatest Christian scholar of the day, J. J. Scaliger (following the example set a generation before by the reformer Melanchthon), brought the importance of the ancient Jewish coinage for scientific investigation to the notice of European scholarship generally.

Other aspects of numismatics also engaged the attention of Italian Jewish scholars of the age. Another of Azariah de Rossi's Mantuan friends, David Finzi, possessed a collection of ancient non-Jewish coins of the classical period, as well as some of Jewish interest. The specimen which De' Rossi cites (f. 174) purporting to have been struck by King Solomon, is of course an obvious fake, as are some others of biblical interest (all with "modern" characters) which came into circulation at this time. But this too accorded with the prevailing tendency, reflected in the medals bearing the likenesses of Dido, Priam, or even Adam and Eve, which were boldly struck and circulated in the Renaissance period. It was probably not obscurantism, but healthy skepticism, which must have prompted Abraham Portaleone to warn his fellow-Jews against wasting large sums in the indiscriminate purchase of old medals.

Such collecting could of course have a wider interest for scholarly purposes, as De' Rossi was not the only person to realize. While he was in the papal service in Rome, Obadiah Sforno, assisted by some like-minded friends, attempted to establish the nature of the coinage mentioned in the Talmud and its value in contemporary Italian currency. His pupil, Gedaliah ibn Jacchia (to whom we owe this information) incorporated in his rambling literary chronicle what is in effect an entire miniature treatise on the ancient Jewish weights and measures, which he endeavored to establish in terms of those current in Bologna, the metropolis of the area in which he lived.

Everywhere the Jewish humanists found others of like interests and breadth of knowledge with whom to discuss opinions or interchange views. De' Rossi for example was happy to know that his theory of Hebrew prosody was endorsed by his fellow-townsmen, the brothers Provenzal, whose opinion he so greatly valued. He was not the only member of his circle to be familiar with the writings of Philo, which he informs us (p. 45a) were venerated and eagerly studied by some of the finest intellects among his

330 THE JEWS IN THE RENAISSANCE

friends—all of whom presumably had also at least a smattering of Greek. Nor were the classic Greek philosophers alien to the Jewish scholars of this age, as we have seen; though there were some among them, like Johanan Alemanno,[10] who stoutly maintained that Plato derived his ideas from the Hebrew prophets.

The knowledge of the classical languages was not by any means confined to professional savants. Gedaliah ibn Jacchia shows a range of reading hardly less than that of De' Rossi himself, though far less well organized, and cites a comparable number of classical and patristic writers (including, for example, St. Augustine). Moreover, he goes out of his way to include in his work, quite gratuitously, a section on classical paganism. The traveler Meshullam of Volterra casually quoted Pliny in his Hebrew account of his experiences on the way to Palestine. The pious Obadiah di Bertinoro seems to be reflecting his own conclusions when he says in his Mishnah commentary (Shekalim III.2) that no European language is as beautiful as Greek.

David Messer Leon wrote poems in Latin, and Abraham Jaghel, the imitator of Dante, had enough Greek to translate part of the apocryphal *Fourth Book of Ezra* into Hebrew. Abraham Farisol used Ptolemy's geography in compiling his own (written, as he ingenuously tells us, in the hope of providing a counter-attraction to the lascivious works of fiction which were in increasing vogue even among the Jewish community). Simone Luzzatto, Modena's colleague in the Venetian rabbinate, clearly shows in his Italian philosophical dialogue *Socrate* a good training in Greek as well as Latin.[11] An unsubstantiated report speaks of one Enoch of Ascoli,

[10] See above, p. 120.

[11] Having devoted in these pages so much space to Leone Modena, it might be expected that I would speak also at length of his slightly junior contemporary and colleague in the rabbinate of Venice, Simha (Simone) Luzzatto (c. 1582-1663), author of *Socrate* (Venice, 1651) a philosophical dialogue in Italian championing the freedom of the human intellect; and a politico-economic treatise, *Discorso circa il stato degl'Ebrei* (1639), which obviously reflects the influence of the sixteenth-century theorist Giovanni Botero. But, whereas Modena was essentially a belated product of the Renaissance, the writings of Luzzatto—of remarkable interest in themselves—were rather an anticipation of the "modern" age. Moreover, he did not leave behind him, as the other did, such a vast mass of personal material illustrating the social and intellectual background of the period.

who at the end of the fifteenth century traveled through France, Germany, Greece and the Balkans to find and purchase manuscripts (obviously, if the tale is true, in the classical tongues) for Pope Nicholas V. There has already been occasion to mention above the classical interests of Judah Messer Leon, Girolamo Soncino, Giuseppe Gallo, and others.

Jacob Mantino, whose long series of translations testify to his knowledge of Latin, and who was not unfamiliar with Greek, knew of the existence of Etruscan—fresh at that time on the horizons of scholarship—and hazarded the opinion that it derived from Assyrian.

Proud of their competence in the classical languages, some Jewish scholars attempted to apply it to their Hebrew studies, in the hope of being able to prove the superiority and priority of the latter. Rabbi David Provenzal, we are informed by De' Rossi, compiled a vocabulary of over 2,000 words, which he opined from their sound to have percolated from Hebrew into Latin and Greek: a timid approach, we may perhaps consider it, to comparative philology. Unfortunately, this work has not been preserved, but we have a few specimens of the excursions of others into this same hazardous realm. For example, a certain Elijah Melli, of Mantua, communicated to Abraham Jaghel a whole list of Italian words which in his opinion derived from the Hebrew: a tribute, however, more to his ingenuity than to his philological acumen.[12] The silver-tongued preacher Judah Moscato, who was intimate both with De' Rossi and the Provenzal family, showed himself in his justly-celebrated collection of sermons to be not only thoroughly versed in the classical languages and literatures but also to some extent imbued with their spirit. He believed indeed that ancient civilization derived from Judaism, and all languages of culture from Hebrew. This was in his opinion an additional reason for Jews to familiarize themselves with these branches of knowledge as a matter of duty. He even attempted to derive the name of the Muse of Tragic Poetry, Calliope, from the Hebrew *kol yaphe* ("beautiful voice," which is indeed its meaning

---

[12] *E.g., Ospedale* = אסף דלים; *miracoli* = מי ראה כאלה; *ambasceria* = בשורה. The details are included by Jaghel in that extraordinary though little-known work *Ge Hizzayon*, for which see above, p. 105.

in Greek, except that the order of the two component parts is reversed). When in the middle of the sixteenth century the proposal was made to call a literary society which the Jews had established at Ferrara by the name "Accademia," some zealots objected to the application of this pagan name to a Jewish body, until De' Rossi (p. 173b) naively demonstrated that this Greek term was in fact derived from the Hebrew words *Eked* (= Assembly) and *Adam* (= man); an interesting point, in view of the similar objection raised in 1953 when it was desired to establish an "Academy" of the Hebrew language in Jerusalem. It may be an echo of this somewhat bizarre identification that the Jewish law-court at Mantua (*Beth Din*) was officially called "L'Accademia degli ebrei" down to the end of the eighteenth century.

There were even cases in which Jewish scholars addressed themselves to the Christian world on humanistic subjects in Latin; for example, the talmudist and physician, Lazzaro (Eliezer Mazliah) da Viterbo, who wrote for the Cardinal Guglielmo Sirleto about 1580 a learned dissertation in that language, still unpublished, in which he vindicated the integrity of the Hebrew text of the Bible. The reason for this was the curious allegation that the Jews had deliberately introduced changes into the biblical prophecies relating to the Messiah, this explaining certain discrepancies between the Hebrew and the Vulgate version. Apart from the theological implications the question was one of considerable significance in an age when scholars such as Sirleto's correspondent, Francesco Vettori, were so busily engaged in searching out the oldest manuscripts of classical works and establishing the best, uncorrupted readings.

The new spirit inevitably pervaded the study of Hebrew grammar. It was not only a question of new theories and arguments, as when Elijah Levita demonstrated the "modernity" of the Hebrew vowel-points, but of the entire outlook. Moses ibn Habib, an immigrant from Spain who lived in southern Italy toward the end of the fifteenth century, had attempted to summarize the principles of the Hebrew language in catechic form in his little work *Marpe Lashon*, while in his *Darkhe Noam* (written in Apulia in 1486) he gave a survey of Hebrew prosody and versification based solidly on Aristotle's *Poetics*.

Abraham de' Balmes, in his *Mikneh Abraham*, postulated a philosophical basis to grammar, besides stressing the importance of syntax, which in his work first receives separate treatment. Samuel Archevolti, in his work on prosody, tried to establish a psychology of language, and was moreover the first person to give a general description of Mishnaic Hebrew.

To assume, as is so often done, that after De' Rossi's day Italian Jewry relapsed into an age of obscurantism is very far from the truth. It may be true that heresy-hunting was more common, that segregation in ghettos fostered the intellectual as well as the physical regimentation of its denizens, that the example as well as the fear of the outside world resulted in an imitation on a smaller scale in the Jewish communities of the attitudes of the Counter-Reformation. At the same time the spread in the Mediterranean world of the neo-mystical movement that had originated with Isaac Luria and his school in Safed not only diverted attention from the humanities, but also made rationalism into a superfluity; moreover, by attaching extreme importance to the numerical details of words and letters, it undermined the possibility of textual criticism. In some persons this spirit induced a tendency to withdraw from extraneous occupations: thus, as has been mentioned, Moses Zacuto, Rabbi of Mantua and at one time a fellow-student of Spinoza, professed repentance in his old age for his waste of time in studying Latin in his youth. Nevertheless, the Italian Jewish scholars retained on the whole a great deal of their breadth of interest. Notwithstanding the example that has just been mentioned, and notwithstanding the fact that in 1618 the Inquisition prohibited Jews from learning grammar or Latin with Christians, that language was still generally studied in the cultivated classes. Still, even now, every rabbi could (and did) compose Hebrew verses, and some of them Hebrew plays. Still, they wrote in an elegant style and accurate language; still, many of them had a university education and were the recipients of laudatory verses, in Hebrew and Italian, "on the day that the crown of medicine and philosophy was placed upon their heads." There doubtless was a recession in the intellectual life of Italian Jewry in these generations, but it can hardly be termed a reaction: and the flame which it preserved was to kindle in the eighteenth century in

northern Europe the revival out of which modern Hebrew literature was in the end to emerge.

With this record of incomplete fulfilment our survey may
fittingly conclude. For in so many ways, the achievement of the
Jews in the Renaissance fell short of what might have been anticipated, and of the expectations that had perhaps been aroused. It
was inevitable. The friendly relations between Jewish and non-
Jewish circles at the time have been emphasized in the foregoing
pages. But we have to remember that they were, if not the exception, certainly not the rule—and without this atmosphere the common cultural tradition could not produce perfect fruits. There
were everywhere interludes of reaction, toleration was at the best
tempered with contempt, and even under the most favorable circumstances there was a level of eminence, not very advanced,
above which no Jew, however talented, could rise. Moreover, a
permanently close relationship in the modern sense between fol-
lowers of opposing faiths was then out of the question, or nearly
so.

In consequence, there could be (and there were) promising
initiatives in those fields of activity that have been dealt with in
these pages, but in most cases they were imperfectly developed
and ultimately proved sterile. Finally, from the middle of the sixteenth century on, the ghetto reaction suppressed even within the
Jewish community such progress as had begun. Healthy collaboration now became impossible. What we have seen in fifteenth
and sixteenth century Italy is thus no more than a timid anticipation of the process which was to leave so profound a mark on
European cultural life four and five hundred years later, was to
achieve so much, and was to experience so tragic a fate.

Nevertheless, the record is by no means negligible. There were
some aspects of the cultural ferment of the time in which the
Jews took a significant share. There was none the fringes of
which they did not at least touch. Above all, their personalities
and characters reflected the spirit of the age, Italian Jewry during
these years thus displaying much of the warmth, the color, and
the human interest which give Renaissance Italy its perennial fas-
cination and delight.

ABBREVIATIONS

ASI	Archivio storico italiano
GSLI	Giornale storico della letteratura italiana
HUCA	Hebrew Union College Annual
JJS	Journal of Jewish Studies
KS	Kirjath Sepher
JQR	Jewish Quarterly Review
JQR NS	Jewish Quarterly Review, new series
MGWJ	Monatschrift für die Geschichte und Wissenschaft des Judenthums
RI	Rivista israelitica
REJ	Revue des études juives
RMI	Rassegna mensile di Israel
PAAJR	Proceedings of American Academy for Jewish Research
VI	Vessillo israelitico
ZfHB	Zeitschrift für hebräische Bibliographie

Jubilee and memorial volumes of essays by various hands (*Festschriften*) are all referred to, for convenience, as ". . . Studies."

My references to periodicals are sometimes by year and sometimes by volume, as I have sometimes used offprints from publications the full run of which was not accessible to me.

Date and place of publication of volumes are added only where it is likely to be useful to the student.

Bibliographical Note

It would be easy to multiply references in this work almost indefinitely, but that would increase its bulk, diminish its readability, and be of little solid use to the serious student. General guidance on the literature will be given in the following pages: detailed references follow, in the notes to individual chapters, only for data which cannot be readily ascertained.

For further information regarding the persons mentioned in the text, recourse should be made to the usual works of reference: in the Jewish sphere, to the *Jewish Encyclopaedia*, *Universal Jewish Encyclopaedia*, *Encyclopaedia Hebraica*, and (for the letters A-L) the German *Encyclopaedia Judaica*, which in this subject had the inestimable benefit of the collaboration of Umberto Cassuto. As regards Italian non-Jews mentioned in these pages, the *Encyclopedia Italiana* is the fullest source of information and guidance.

The old bibliography of Italian Jewish history by G. Gabrieli, *Italia Judaica* (Rome, 1924), is now superseded by the far fuller work of Attilio Milano, *Bibliotheca historica Italo-Judaica* (Florence, 1954), with elaborate indices.

The Jewish background, so far as Italy is concerned, may be studied in C. Roth, *History of the Jews in Italy* (Philadelphia, 1946; revised text soon in Hebrew and in Italian). In addition, there are a number of important works devoted to certain Italian communities from which a great deal of the material in this volume has been derived. Where Rome is concerned, the data are mainly from Vogelstein-Rieger, *Geschichte der Juden in Rom* (Berlin, 1895-96); for Florence, U. Cassuto, *Gli ebrei a Firenze nell'età del Rinascimento* (Florence, 1918); for Venice, C. Roth, *History of the Jews in Venice* (Philadelphia, 1930). The interested student is advised to make judicious use of the indices to these volumes if he requires further guidance on matters or personalities connected with one or the other of these cities. In addition, there is much important source material regarding Modena and Ferrara *etc.*, in A. Balletti, *Gli ebrei e gli Estensi* (2nd ed., Reggio Emilia, 1930), and regarding Naples in N. Ferorelli, *Gli ebrei nell' Italia meridionale* (Turin, 1915). Almost every detail regarding the Renaissance scene at the court of Savoy and in Turin is derived from the articles by Salvatore Foa in *RMI* 1955 (subsequently published in volume form).

On the relations of the Popes (and the Church in general) and the Jews at this period there is ample guidance in the work of Vogelstein-Rieger mentioned above and the others on the Jews in Rome by Berliner, Blu[t]stein, Natali *et al.* A good deal of additional material is to be found in the documents (in chronological order) published by M. Stern, *Urkundliche Beiträge über die Stellung der Päpste zu den Juden* (Kiel, 1893).

A large number of subsidiary studies by M. A. Shulvass on aspects of Jewish life in the Renaissance period have appeared in various Hebrew and English periodicals, in America and Israel, during the past few years: *e.g.*, "The Knowledge of Antiquity among the Italian Jews of the Renaissance," PAAJR, XVIII: "The Religious Life of the Italian Jews in the Age of the Renaissance," *ibid.*, XVII (Hebrew): "Talmudic Study among the Italian Jews in the Age of the Renaissance" (*Horeb* X, [N.Y. 1948: Hebrew]). More specifically, A. Lewkowitz, *Das Judentum und die geistigen Strömungen d. Neuzeit. I: Die Renaissance* (Breslau, 1929), is of importance for the study of the subject, though S. Mézan, *De Gabirol à Abravanel: Juifs espagnols promoteurs de la Renaissance* (Paris, 1936) touches on it only incidentally.

Much use will be made throughout these pages of the writings of Leone Modena. (I propose to use this form, which he himself prescribed in his *Autobiography*, throughout this work, and regret that I did not do so previously. He insists that by his day "Modena" no longer indicated a place of origin but was a surname, the prefix "Da" being therefore superfluous.) A great deal has been written about him: the most recent work by Ellis Rivkin (Cincinnati, 1952: based on his articles in *JQR* 1947-51) contains exhaustive bibliographies, which it is needless to repeat here. In these pages, particular use is made of his *Autobiography* (ed. Abraham Kahana, Kiev, 1912; some excerpts in English translation in L. W. Schwarz, *Memoirs of my People*, Philadelphia, 1943) and of his Letters, *Leo Modena's Briefe und Schriftstücke* (ed. L. Blau, Budapest, 1905-1906, with an important introduction). I have referred also to his manuscript writings in the British Museum [now published in great part in Israel by S. Simonsohn].

Another volume of memoirs much used here is the "Travel-Diary" of David Reubeni, the fullest edition of which with very ample annotations is by A. Z. Aescoly (Jerusalem, 1940); excerpts also in Schwarz, *op. cit.*, and in E. N. Adler, *Jewish Travellers* (London, 1930). This work also contains passages from the accounts of various Italian Jewish travelers to Palestine, the originals of which are most readily accessible in a series of volumes edited by A. Yaari, who has also edited separately (Jerusalem, 1949) the work of Meshullam da Volterra, to which I not infrequently refer (see below).

For the Renaissance background in general, the best guide even now is Jacob Burckhardt's *The Civilisation of the Renaissance in Italy*, first produced in 1860; the student is advised to make use of the fifteenth (or a subsequent) German edition, which has slight additions to the text and large additions to the notes by L. Geiger and W. Götz, or one of the English editions based on it; the use of one of the illustrated editions (*e.g.*, those produced by the Phaidon Press) will add greatly to the reader's enjoyment and comprehension. The leisurely, discursive work of John Addington Symonds, *The Renaissance in Italy* (7 vols., 1875-81) still retains much of its charm.

On a far smaller scale, and for the most part more recent, are:— W. H. Pater, *Studies in the History of the Renaissance* (1873); A. H. Hudson, *The Story of the Renaissance* (1912); R. A. Taylor, *Aspects of the Italian Renaissance* (1923); H. O. Taylor, *Thought and Expression in the Sixteenth Century* (1920); R. Roeder, *The Man of the Renaissance* (1933); C. K. Ferguson, *The Renaissance in Historical Thought* (1948); M. F. Jerrold, *Italy in the Renaissance* (1927); B. L. Ullman, *Studies in the Italian Renaissance*; Will Durant, *The Renaissance* (1953); F. Clement (ed.), *The Civilisation of the Renaissance* (1929); J. R. Hale, *England and the Italian Renaissance* (1953); H. S. Lucas, *The Renaissance and the Reformation* (1934); P. O. Kristeller, *Studies in Renaissance Thought and Letters* (1956).

Especially important works in languages other than English include: L. Geiger, *Renaissance and Humanismus in Italien und Deutschland* (1882); E. R. Labande, *L'Italie de la Renaissance* (1953); H. Baeyens, *Begrip en probleem van de Renaissance* (1952); P. Monnier, *Le Quattrocento* (2nd ed., 1920); K. Burdach,

Reformation, Renaissance, Humanismus (1918; Italian trans., 1935); F. Fiorentino, *Studi e retratti della Rinascenza* (1911); V. Zabughin, *Storia del rinascimento cristiano in Italia* (1924); N. Festa, *L'Umanesimo del Rinascimento* (1935); C. Angeleri, *Il problema religioso del Rinascimento* (1952); *Il Rinascimento: significato e limiti* (Atti del V convegno internazionale sul Rinascimento, Florence, 1958); G. Gentile, *Studi sul Rinascimento* (2nd ed., 1936); E. Walser, *Gesammelte Studien zur Geistesgeschichte der Renaissance* (1932); E. Garin, *Medievo e Rinascimento* (1956); G. Saitta, *L'Umanesimo, Il Rinascimento* (1949-1951); *Actes du colloque sur la Renaissance* (Sorbonne, 1958).

Guidance on contemporary publications is given in the *Renaissance News*, published quarterly for the American Council of Learned Societies.

The admirable work in Hebrew by M. A. Shulvass, on Jewish life in Renaissance Italy, appeared only after this book (the publication of which has been delayed by reasons beyond the author's control) was completed. The Hebrew work by E. Shemueli, "Men of the Renaissance" (1956) does not deal specifically with Jewish aspects.

Notes

ONE

THE BACKGROUND OF RENAISSANCE JEWISH LIFE

p. 3.   The fullest account of the subject dealt with in this chapter is a work by the present writer, C. Roth, *History of the Jews in Italy* (Philadelphia, 1946). Since this was published, some important additional material has been published, especially by A. Milano in successive issues of *RMI*. Guidance as regards individual places can be found in G. Gabrieli, *Italia Judaica*, and the later *Bibliography* by A. Milano, both referred to above.

p. 12.   The description *Kiryah haAlizah* was applied to Mantua by Azariah de' Rossi in his *Meor Eynayim*; but I fancy that I have encountered it in other writers of the period.

p. 17.   The personality of Anselmo del Banco (together with his brother, Hayim Meshullam) was brought into Jewish historiography for the first time in my *History of the Jews in Venice*: the details are mainly from the Italian sources scattered about the fifty-eight (!) volumes of M. Sanuto's *Diarii* (Venice, 1879-1903), supplemented by Elijah Capsali's Hebrew *Chronicle of Venice*, partially published by N. Porgès in *REJ*, vols. LXXVII, LXXVIII, LXXIX. For the Da Pisa family, see Cassuto in *RI*, vols. v and vi, and D. Kaufmann in *REJ*, XXXI and XXXII; also in his *Gesammelte Schriften* (Frankfort, 1908). For the Norsa family, see P. Norsa, *Una Famiglia di Banchieri; la famiglia Norsa* (Naples, 1953-58), and A. Marx in his *Studies in Jewish History and Booklore* (New York, 1944).

p. 19 f.   The involved question of the correspondence of Hebrew and Italian nomenclature was fully dealt with for the first time by Cassuto in a special chapter of his work on the Jews of Florence.

TWO

THE JEWS IN RENAISSANCE SOCIETY

p. 21 ff. For the relations of the Medici and the Jews, see Cassuto's *Ebrei a Firenze* and his article, *La famille des Médicis et les Juifs* in *REJ*, LXVI (1923), 132-45.

p. 22. Most of the persons mentioned here are spoken of in greater detail elsewhere in this volume, with the exception of Ishmael da Rieti, for whom see, in addition to Cassuto's *Firenze*, also A. Marx in L. Ginzberg Studies (N.Y., 1946, Hebrew section); and in M. Schorr Studies (N.Y., 1945); for Dattero ebreo, see below, Chapter IX. For Noah Norsa, see A. Marx, in Chajes Studies (Vienna, 1932), reprinted in his *Studies in Jewish History and Booklore* (N.Y., 1944); also Paolo Norsa, *Una Famiglia di Banchieri: La famiglia Norsa* (Naples, 1953). For Joseph da Fano, *JJS*, I, 144-46. The sources relating to the Abrabanel family may be traced in B. Netanyahu's biography *Don Isaac Abravanel, Statesman and Philosopher* (Philadelphia, 1953).

p. 23 f. For the sources on David Reubeni see above p. 339.

p. 24. Sumptuary Laws: see L. Finkelstein's *Jewish Self-Government in the Middle Ages* (N.Y., 1924), for texts and translation.

p. 25. Purim King: see *Meor Eynayim*, 1st ed. (1573) pp. 40-41 and *REJ*, X (1885), 186.

p. 28. Provenzal's responsum and the other relevant documents on tennis playing were published by I. Rivkind in the Hebrew periodical *Tarbitz*, LV, 366-76, and their significance in the history of the game discussed by R. W. Henderson, in *JQR* NS, XXVI, 1-6. Scaine's treatise on tennis referred to in the text was recently published in English translation by W. W. Kershaw, with notes by P. A. Negretti, under the auspices of the Royal Tennis Club.

p. 30 f. As mentioned above, descriptions of travels to Palestine by various Italian Jews of the Renaissance period are to be found in a series of volumes edited by A. Yaari, and there are some

English versions by E. N. Adler's *Jewish Travellers* (London, 1930).

p. 33 ff.   The question of higher education among the Italian Jews in the Renaissance period is discussed in an essay in my *Personalities and Events in Jewish History* (Philadelphia, 1954), and the training of Jewish physicians at this period in my article in *Speculum*, XXVIII (1953): some data also in H. Friedenwald's writings on the *Jews and Medicine* to be referred to below in the bibliography to Chapter XII.

p. 34.   Judah del Bene's complaint is in his *Kissaoth leBeth David* (Verona, 1646), f. 24; for Ishmael da Rieti's *Yeshiva* at Siena, see A. Marx's article on him referred to above.

p. 36.   Bruno's interest in a Jewish preacher is mentioned in the Diary of G. Cotin for 20.iii.1586 (cf. *Nuova antologia*, September, 1902) and unconvincingly discussed in Z*f*HB, VII, 28-29.

p. 38.   For Jewish preachers and preaching in the age of the Renaissance, see studies by I. Bettan in *HUCA*, VI, VII, etc. (also published separately).

p. 39.   For university teaching by members of the Del Medigo family, see Joseph del Medigo's *Sepher Elim*, p. 299; of Judah Minz, Neppi-Ghirondi, *Toledoth Gedole Israel*, p. 122; of Don Judah Abrabanel (Leone Ebreo), *RMI*, 1930, 355, and Netanyahu, *op. cit.* L. Münster, in *RMI*, 1954, 310-21, proves pretty conclusively that Jacob Mantino (for whom see below, Chapters IV and XII) did not teach at the University of Bologna, though Pope Clement VII managed to get him temporarily on the payroll. Cf. T. Momigliano, in *VI*, LXV, 384-7 (*Un ebreo professore di medicina a Perugia*), for another doubtful case.

p. 42.   In S. Asaf's admirable source-book for the history of Jewish education, II, 115-20, is the Hebrew text of the appeal of Provenzal for the establishment of an advanced Jewish college for secular studies, an English version of which is in J. R. Marcus, *The Jew in the Medieval World* (Cincinnati, 1938), pp. 381-93.

THREE

MANNERS AND MORALS

p. 44 f.   Material relating to the moral standards of Italian Jewry
in the Renaissance period is collected in M. Güdemann, *Geschichte
des Erziehungswesens und der Cultur der abendländischen Juden*
(Vienna, 1884-88, also available in Hebrew), in the concluding
portion of the work. I fancy that he is here perhaps too favorable
toward the native Italian Jews.

p. 45.   For the conditions in Florence referred to in the text,
see not only Cassuto's work, but also M. Ciardini, *I banchieri
ebrei in Firenze* (Florence, 1907). He tells here (p. 10) how
Bonaventura da Volterra was sentenced on a charge of "carnal
violence"; his subsequent pilgrimage to Palestine in fulfilment of
a vow is presumably to be related to this.

p. 45.   The curious story of the marriage at Urbino by consummation is in a responsum published by A. H. Freimann in his
Seder Kidushin . . . (Jerusalem, 1945), pp. 135-36. That Jewish
women called on the Madonna is told by the apostate Giulio
Morosini in his *Via della Fede*.

p. 48.   An episode of an over-scented Jew is told maliciously
by T. Garzoni, *La Piazza universale di tutte le professioni del
mondo* (Venice, 1616, etc.), discorso lxxix.

p. 49.   The recipe book of Caterina Sforza is cited in the biography by P. O. Pasolini (Rome, 1893), III, 527, 608-609; English
translation of the letter in J. R. Marcus, *Jews in the Medieval
World*, pp. 399-400: for Esperanza Malchi, see my *Anglo-Jewish
Letters*, pp. 38-39.

p. 49.   For the women peddlers of Casalmaggiore, see Responsa
of Meir of Padua, n. 26; for the innkeeper in Padua, those of
Joseph Colon, n. 160; for the women-doctors, my article in *Speculum*, XXVIII, 841-42; for education by women, Asaf's source-
book, IV, 112, 121.

p. 52.   For women acting as *shoḥet*, see Duschinsky in *Gaster
Studies*; also Immanuel Lattes' Responsa, pp. 137-40 and M. Mortara, *Indice . . dei rabbini . . in Italia*, p. 54. The Hebrew literature

about women is described by Steinschneider in *Letterbode*, XII, 49-95.

p. 52.   There is an article on Jewish women copyists by A. M. Haberman in *KS*, XIII, 114-20, and also a separate monograph by him on women printers, etc. (Berlin, 1933). For the Del Banco prayer-book, see *ZfHB*, IX, 160.

p. 55 f.   The fullest account of Doña Gracia Mendes is my biography (Philadelphia, 1947; also in Hebrew and in Spanish); there is in this work some account of certain of her contemporaries. For Bienvenida Abrabanel, see also Netanyahu's work on Isaac Abrabanel.

p. 57.   Deborah Ascarelli's poems were republished by her descendant, Pellegrino Ascarelli (Rome, 1925). On Sarah Coppio Sullam, see the monographs by L. Modona (Bologna, 1887), and E. David (Paris, 1877); some of her correspondence is in an English translation in F. Kobler, *A Treasury of Jewish Letters* (Philadelphia, 1953), II, 436-48.

p. 58.   The violent episode in the Verona synagogue is recounted by Joseph Colon in his *Responsa*; the racy Siena ghetto diary was published by me in *HUCA*, V. For the attempt against the Grand Signor, see now F. Babinger in *Rivista degli studi orientali*, XXVI, 87-113.

p. 59 ff.   For Jewish dabbling in magic, etc., see (besides the paragraphs devoted to the subject by Burckhardt), J. Trachtenburg, *The Devil and the Jews* (New Haven, 1943), and references in Lynn Thorndike, *History of Magic and Science in the Sixteenth Century*, vols. v and vi. For the witchcraft accusations at Mantua, *REJ*, XXV, 108; at Reggio and Modena, Balletti, *op. cit.*, pp. 168-69; and for the episode of Dianora, Modena, *Letters* (ed. Blau), pp. 132-33.

FOUR

THE LATIN RENAISSANCE AND THE JEWISH TRANSLATORS

The fundamental work on the activity of the Jews in the work of translation and as cultural intermediaries in the Middle Ages is M. Steinschneider, *Hebräische Übersetzungen des Mittelalter* (Berlin, 1893); on this are based most of the later literary treatments, such as the chapters in *The Legacy of Israel*, ed. Abrahams, Singer and Bevan (Oxford, 1927) and in my own *Jewish Contribution to Civilisation*.

p. 66.   The work of the Jewish intermediaries in France is discussed in the sections by Renan (and Neubauer) in the *Histoire littéraire de la France*, vols. XXVII ("Les rabbins français du commencement du xive siècle") and XXXI ("Les écrivains juifs français du xive siècle").

p. 67.   The work of the Spanish writers is admirably described by J. Millás y Vallicrosa, *Estudios sobre historia de la ciencia española* (Barcelona, 1949); the ground is covered also to some extent in F. Vera's *Los judios españoles y su contribución a las ciencias exactas* (Buenos Aires, 1948).

p. 74.   The work of Elijah del Medigo is minutely described, with full references, in Cassuto's book on Florence, so often referred to in these pages. There is an excellent monograph on Jacob Mantino and his circle by D. Kaufmann in *REJ*, XXVII, "*Jacob Mantino: une page de l'histoire de la Renaissance.*" See also V. Ravà in *VI*, LI, 310-13, and *RMI*, 1944, 310-21. Various physicians and scientists mentioned in this chapter are dealt with by H. Friedenwald in his writings on Jewish medicine, to be referred to in the bibliography to Chapter X. R. Caggese's *Roberto d'Angiò* describes the activities of some of the Neapolitan translators, for which see also Cassuto in *VI*, LIX (1911), 282-85, 338-41, 422-24.

p. 74.   For the Jewish collaboration in the 1550-52 Aristotle, etc., see L. Minio Paluello, "Note sull' Aristotele Latino" in *Rivista di filosofia neo-scholastica*, XLII.

Cf. also E. Franceschini, "Le versioni latine medievali di Aristotele e dei sui commentatori nelle biblioteche delle Tre Venezia," in *Miscellanea Ferrari* (Florence, 1952), 313-26.

p. 82. Moses Alatino describes at length the circumstances under which he made his translation in the preface to be published version; see for him also *RMI*, 1950, 210; De' Rossi, preface to *Meor Eynayim*; and Balletti, *op. cit.*, p. 79.

FIVE

IN THE STEPS OF DANTE

p. 86 f. The Islamic (and, indirectly, Jewish) background of Dante's writings, were the subject of Miguel Asín y Palacios, *La escatología musulmana en la Divina commedia* (Madrid, 1919; inadequate English version, tr. H. Sunderland, London, 1926); attention was called to Ibn Gabirol in this connection by R. Ottolenghi, *Un lontano precursore di Dante* (Lugano, 1910). See now, however, for the authentic Arabic model of his picture of the After-World, J. Muñoz Sendino (ed.), *La escala de Mahoma* (Madrid, 1949).

p. 87. The Almanac of Jacob ben Machir has been published under the title *Almanach Dantis Alighierii, sive Profhacii Judaei montispessulani almanach perpetuum ad annum 1300 inchoatum*, ed. J. Boffito and C. Melzi d'Eril (Florence, 1908); for its use in the *Divina commedia*, see M. A. Orr, *Dante and the Early Astronomers* (London, 1913; new ed., 1956).

It may be mentioned that the *Divina commedia* has been partially translated into Hebrew in the same meter as the original by S. Formiggini and S. Sabbadini (Trieste, 1867-9); some cantos more competently by Z. Jabotinsky in *haTekufah*, vol. XIX, and now in full by L. Olswanger (Tel Aviv, 1944-55).

p. 88 ff. On Immanuel of Rome, see the somewhat antiquated work by L. Modona, *Vita e opere di Immanuele Romano* (Florence, 1904); it contains the text of all of his Italian poems, as does also the edition of the *Mahberoth Immanuel* published by M. A. Haberman (Tel Aviv, 1946); the vision of the After-World has been published in a poor English translation in rhymed prose, H. Gollancz, *Tophet and Eden* (London, 1921).

p. 88 ff.   On the relations between his writings and those of Dante, concerning which a great deal of unsound and conjectural material has been published in the past, see the two admirable monographs of U. Cassuto, "L'elemento italiano nelle Maḥberoth Immanuel," in *RI*, II and III, and his *Dante e Manoello* (Florence, 1921; also partially in German, *Jahrbuch für jüdische Geschichte und Literatur*, 1920-21). [There has now appeared a further edition of Immanuel of Rome's poetical works, Hebrew and Italian, ed. D. Yarden, 1957.]

p. 88 ff.   My account of the genesis of Immanuel's imitation is based, however, on my own researches, as published in the Jubilee Volume for S. Asaf (Jerusalem, 1953); *RMI*, XVII: and *Modern Language Review*, 1953. In the last two, the interchange of sonnets with and between Cino da Pistoia and Busone da Gubbio can be conveniently consulted; for my translations of these, I have made partial use of those in the essay by J. Chotzner in his *Hebrew Humour and other Essays* (London, 1905).

p. 103.   Coming now to Dante's minor imitators, Ahitub of Palermo's "Composition of the Basket" is published by J. Schirman in *Mitteilungen des Forschungsinstituts für hebräische Dichtung*, I. Moses da Rieti's *Mikdash Meät* was edited by J. Goldenthal under the curious title, *Il Dante ebreo, ossia, il piccolo santuario* (Vienna, 1851); for the author, see, besides the usual works of reference, *RMI*, VI, 259. Its historical content has never yet been properly assessed, but the action of the poem is well analyzed by M. Waxman, *History of Jewish Literature*, II, 75-77; see *ibid.*, 88-91, for Moses Zacuto and his work.

p. 106.   The descriptions of the After-World by Zacuto and Olmo were published in Italian translation by C. Foà (Finale 1901, 1904).

p. 107.   The interchange of sonnets between Peregrini and Salamone ebreo is published by Norsa in the "prestampa" of his *Una famiglia di banchieri* referred to above.

p. 107.   M. Steinschneider's monographs on the Italian literature of the Jews appeared in *Il Buonaroti*, 1871-76 (supplemented by M. Soave in *VI*, 1877-80): *VI*, 1877-80; and *MGWJ*, 1898-1900.

p. 110.   There are two monographs on Didaco Pyrrho—by T. Cheira (Florence, 1826) and M. Grunwald with A. Casnacich (Frankfort-o-M., 1883).

SIX

WITH THE HUMANISTS OF FLORENCE

p. 111 ff.   The material on the Jews in the humanistic circle in Florence has been exhaustively collected by Umberto Cassuto in his *Ebrei a Firenze*, especially part III, chapter iii.

p. 117.   For Flavius Mithridates and his work, see the references in Chapter VII, p. 145. The Hebraic influences on Ficino and Pico are considered in the monograph by A. Lewkowitz (referred to above, p. 338), pp. 21-32.

p. 119.   Selections from Johanan Alemanno's *Heshek Shelomo* were published under the title *Shaar haHeshek* (Leghorn, 1790), and others of historical significance by J. Perles in *REJ*, XII, 245 ff.

p. 121.   No full study has been devoted to Abraham Farisol; for his work as copyist see Alexander Marx Studies, I, 244-46; selections of his *Magen Abraham* have now been published by Löwinger in *haZofeh*, XII, 277-97. The Oxford (1691) edition of the *Orḥot Olam* is accompanied by a Latin translation.

p. 128.   For Pico's cabbalistical interests see the imperfectly-informed work of G. Oreglia di Santo Stefano, *Giovanni Pico della Mirandola e la Cabala* (Mirandola, 1917?); for his relations with Reuchlin, the essay by Israel Abrahams in *Hebrew Union College Jubilee Volume* (1925), pp. 317-31: and for Reuchlin's own Hebrew studies, S. A. Hirsch, *A Book of Essays* (London, 1905). [Latest on the subject: F. Secret, *Le Zohar chez les Kabbalistes Chrétiens de la Renaissance*, Paris, 1958.]

p. 128.   There are very many monographs on the life and writings of Leone ebreo: *e.g.*, in German by B. Zimmels (Breslau, 1886 and Vienna, 1892) and H. Pflaum (Tübingen, 1926), in Portuguese by Joaquim de Caravalho (Coimbra, 1929), in Italian by Fontanesi (1923), E. Solmi (1903) and I. Sonne (1934), and in Hebrew by J. Klausner in the periodical *Tarbitz*, III, 67-98 (with exhaustive bibliography).

p. 129.   For his life in S. Italy see B. Netanyahu's life of Isaac Abrabanel, and N. Niccolini in *La Critica*, XXVIII, IV (cf. *RMI*, 1951, 76).

p. 130.   The standard edition of the "Dialoghi" is now the well-edited work by S. Caramella, in the classical series *Scrittori d'Italia* (Bari, 1929); the first edition has been reissued in facsimile, with very ample introduction, etc. by C. Gebhardt (Heidelberg, 1929).

p. 133.   The problems of the original language and the Hebrew version are discussed by I. Sonne in Simḥoni Studies (Hebrew, Berlin, 1929) and in *Tarbitz*, III, 287-313.

p. 135.   Its influence on Spinoza is discussed by E. Solmi, *Benedetto Spinoza e Leone ebreo*, 1903.

p. 136.   For Garcilaso's version, see J. Luis Lanuza, "La Traducción del Indio a León Hebreo," in *Davar* (Buenos Aires, 1954).

SEVEN

THE CHRISTIAN HEBRAISTS

p. 137 ff.   For Hebrew studies in the Middle Ages, the fullest guidance is now B. Smalley, *The Study of the Bible in the Middle Ages*, second ed.; the Poblet episode may be found in Martene-Durand, *Thesaurus novus anecdotorum*, IV, 292.

p. 139.   For the beginnings of the study of Hebrew in Florence, see Cassuto and the authorities there cited, especially the "Lives" (*Vite*) of Vespasiano di Bisticci, see below.

p. 139.   Nicholas de Cusa's Hebrew interests are described in *MGWJ*, XLIII, 250-66, and Lewkowitz, *op. cit.*, pp. 44-49, and Marco Lippomani's in M. Steinschneider, *Letteratura italiana dei Giudei*, pp. 50-51.

p. 139.   The Hebrew studies of G. Manetti are described in Vespasiano da Bisticci, *Vite di uomini illustri;* for those of Bartolo, see Savigny, *Droit . . . au moyen age*, IV, 224. For Manetti's translation of the Psalter, which he carried out at the court of Alfonso I of Naples (to whom it was dedicated), see S. Garofolo, "Il Salterio di Asaf in una traduzione umanistica inedita dall' ebraico, in *Miscellanea Biblica . . . B. Ubach*, ed. R. M. Diaz, Barcelona, 1953. Further light on the subject in hand is to be found in the same scholar's "Gli Umanisti italiani del secolo xv. e la Bibbia" in the composite volume *La Bibbia e il Concilio di Trento*.

p. 141.   For the later period generally, see J. Perles, *Das studium der hebräischen Sprache in Deutschland von Ende des xv. bis zur*

Mitte des xvi. Jahrhunderts (Breslau, 1870) and his studies, *Beiträge zur Geschichte der hebräischen und aramäischen Studien* (Munich, 1884).

p. 142 f.   Tiraboschi in his *Storia della letteratura italiana*, book III, cap: 2, devotes some space to the fifteenth-century Hebraists elsewhere (Andrea Biglia, Pietro Rossi of Siena, Paolo da Canale, Palmieri, Virgilio Zavarisi, Giulio Campagnola); Paolo Canale is recorded also by Pierio Valeriano in *De litteratorum infelicitate*, Venice, 1620. Cf. also G. C. Giulari, "Dei Veronesi cultori delle lingue orientali," in *Riv. Or.*, 1867-68, 388-410, 511-38. See also generally L. Kukenheim, *Contributions à l'histoire de la grammaire … hébraïque à l'époque de la Renaissance* (Leyden, 1951), and his articles in *Acta orientalia*, XI (1951); some details and references in P. Browe, *Die Judenmission im Mittelalter und die Päpste* (Rome, 1942).

p. 142.   For Elijah Halfon see Kaufmann's monograph on Mantino in *REJ*, XXVI.

p. 143.   The document on the Ferrara academy is in Balletti, pp. 96-97: cf. my *Italy*, p. 214.

p. 145.   For Guidacerio, see H. Galliner in *Historia Judaica*, II, and Marx, *Studies in Jewish History and Booklore*, pp. 312-14.

p. 145 f.   The enigmatic figure of Guglielmo da Moncada, alias Flavius Mithridates, has been treated of most recently by M. D. Cassuto, "Wer war der Orientalist Mitridates?" in *Zeitschrift für die Geschichte der Juden in Deutschland*, 1934-35, pp. 230-36, and F. Secret, "Qui était l'orientaliste Mithridate?" in *REJ*, XVI (CXVI), 96-102, together with the earlier study by G. Baruch in *Archiv für Kulturgeschichte*, 1905, 15 ff.

p. 146.   For Savonarola's interests, see Ridolfi's biography (Florence, 1952) I, 193; II, 15, 148, 230; and Cassuto, *Firenze*, p. 324.

p. 147 f.   For Isabella d'Este's interest, see *GSLI*, XXXIII, 26, and for Caterina Cibo, J. G. Meuschen, *Courieuse Schau-Bühne Durlauchtisgst-Gelehrten Dames* (Frankfort-am-Main, 1706), p. 44.

p. 147.   For De' Rossi and Luigi Gonzaga, see *REJ*, XII, 263.

p. 148.   For Widmanstadt, see *REJ*, I, III, and XVII; the works of Vogelstein-Rieger on Rome and of Cassuto on Florence; Steinschneider's Catalogue of the Hebrew MSS. in Munich; and most recently H. Striedl, "Die Bücherei des Orientalisten J. A. Widmanstetter," in F. Babinger Studies (1952).

p. 151.   Much on the Vatican Library is in Cassuto, *I manoscritti Palatini ebraici della Biblioteca … Vaticana* (Rome, 1935): its admission book has been published, ed. Bertolo (Rome, 1942).

p. 156.   The biography of Egidio da Viterbo by G. Signorelli (Florence, 1929) pays inadequate attention to his remarkable Hebrew interests.

p. 156f.   There has been as yet no adequate treatment of Elias Levita, but there is some useful information in L. Geiger, *Das Studium der hebräischen Sprache in Deutschland* (Breslau, 1870), where there are also some other sidelights on Hebrew studies in Italy.

p. 158 ff.   The material dealing with the debates of Hebrew scholars regarding the divorce of Henry VIII is assembled by Kaufmann in *REJ*, XXVII and XXX; see also my *Anglo-Jewish Letters*, pp. 21-22, and *History of the Jews in England*, p. 146.

p. 163.   The historians of Hebrew printing in Italy (for more details on which see Chapter VIII) do not seem to have paid attention to the attempt to secure papal intervention at Venice in 1518, for which see M. Stern, *Urkundliche Beiträge*, pp. 73-74.

p. 163.   For the press in Rome in 1536, see *REJ*, XXVII, 210-11 and 233-34.

p. 164.   The Hebrew evidences on the burning of the Talmud have been collected by A. Yaari in a little centennial brochure (Tel Aviv, 1954); cf. *idem, Meḥkrei Sefer* (Jerusalem, 1958), pp. 198 ff.

EIGHT

THE PRINTED BOOK

p. 165.   The most pleasant guide to the early history of Hebrew printing—not, however, very reliable, and now not up to date—is Amram, *The Makers of Hebrew Books in Italy* (Philadelphia, 1909). In Hebrew, there is a concise survey of the history of the Hebrew book in general by A. M. Haberman (Jerusalem, 1945). Scattered monographs by Steinschneider, Freimann, Marx, etc. in German, by Marx, Bloch, Sonne, etc. in English, by Yaari, Sonne, Haberman, etc. in Hebrew, help to fill out the details of the picture.

p. 165 f.   For the remarkable Avignon episode of 1444, see Abbé Requin, *L'Imprimerie à Avignon en 1444* (Paris, 1890).

p. 173.   For the 1476 (?) Spanish incunable, see Sonne in *Bibliofilia*, XXXIX and *KS*, XIV.

p. 174.   The present chapter deals mainly, not with Hebrew printing, but with the participation of Jews in general printing, a subject discussed by the present writer in an article with full references in *JJS*, 1953, 116-30. Previous to this, attention had been paid in this connection only to the printers of the Soncino family, who have formed the subject of monographs by Soave, Manzoni, Sacchi and Castellani in Italian, Haberman in Hebrew, and M. Marx in English (in *HUCA*, XI).

p. 175.   The interesting question of the interchange of the decorative borders between Hebrew and non-Hebrew printers, dealt with already by A. Marx in his *Studies in Jewish History and Booklore*, pp. 289-91, is the subject of an article by the present writer in *Bodleian Quarterly Record*, 1953, 295-303.

p. 180.   On Hebrew printing in Venice, see the chapter in my *History of the Jews in Venice*, substantially reproduced by a different author in *Bulletin of the New York Public Library*, 1932.

p. 180.   For the Jewish interest in the paper-trade of the dukes of Urbino (which included the products of the famous mills of Fabriano) see G. Luzzatto, *I banchieri ebrei in Urbino*, pp. 26-27: cf. also A. F. Gasparinetti, *The Papers, Paper-Makers and Paper Merchants in Fabriano*, 1938, and A. Zonghi, *Watermarks*, 1954.

NINE

ART AND ARTISTS

p. 189.   The best general introduction to the subject of Jewish art and Jewish artists throughout the ages (overlooking a composite volume edited by myself which is now in preparation) is F. Landsberger, *A History of Jewish Art*, Cincinnati, 1946, based in part on studies by the same author and by the present writer in *HUCA*, XVI, XVII, XVIII, etc., where more exact references may generally be found. Landsberger has also devoted articles in subsequent volumes of *HUCA* to kindred subjects.

p. 191.   For the medieval Jewish artists in Perpignan and Spain, see A. Rubío y Lluch, *Documents per l'historia de la cultura cataluny mig-eval* (Barcelona, 1921) and for the Levi family *Sefarad*, IX, 359.

p. 192.   The artist Moses da Castellazzo is the subject of articles in *REJ*, XXII, XXIII, XLV, and in *Bibliofilia*, IX, 22 ff.; the new information regarding him derives from *Maria Savorgnan–Pietro Bembo: Carteggio d'Amore, 1500-1*, ed. C. Dionisotti (Florence, 1950), letters 65, 66, 67, 75.

For the Jewish bookbinder Meir Jaffe, see Landsberger in *HUCA*, XV, 534-42; for bookbinders and other craftsmen at the papal court in Avignon, K. H. Schäfer, *Die Ausgaben der apostolischen Kammer;* adequate guidance in the indices.

p. 197.   The Jew Samson who made the dog-collars for the Duke of Savoy is recorded in Balletti, p. 165, note.

p. 199.   For the Jewish majolica-workers, Campori, *Majoliche di Mantova*, and an approaching monograph of my own on the Italian majolica Passover plates.

p. 204.   For the synagogal frescoes in Carpi, etc., cf. Balletti, p. 100.

p. 206.   I have described the Cardinal's Hanukkah Lamps in an article in the London *Jewish Monthly*, December, 1949.

p. 206.   For the Jewish metal-workers in Spain and Provence, see *Sefarad*, IX, 359; A. Rubió y Lluch, *Documents per l'historia de la cultura cataluny mig-eval* (Barcelona, 1921), II, 84, 190, etc.

p. 206 f.   There is as yet no adequate treatment of medieval Hebrew illuminated manuscripts, though there is a well-illustrated work by E. Munkásci on some of those in Italian libraries (Budapest, c. 1938), and a few have been described by F. Landsberger in *HUCA*. XV, XXI and XXIII, and by the present writer in *Sefarad*, XII ("The Kennicott Bible").

p. 207 f.   Cf. also H. Rosenau in *Bulletin of John Rylands Library*, 1954. The MS. ascribed to Giotto is discussed by E. Panofsky, "Giotto and Maimonides in Avignon," in *Journal of the Walters Art Gallery*, IV (1941); it is in fact of the second half of the fifteenth century and of the Umbro-Florentine school (with Ferrarese reminiscences) akin to the manuscript 25 now in the Bezalel Museum, Jerusalem.

p. 208.   The "Christian" Hebrew Bibles referred to in the text are described by P. D'Ancona, in *La Miniatura Fiorentina* (Florence, 1914), nos. 207 and 785.

p. 208.   For the Jewish art-purveyors, see Cassuto, *Firenze* p. 180; Balletti, pp. 164-65; Luzio-Renier, *Mantova e Urbino* (1893), pp. 284-86, and Bertolotti, "Artisti in relazione coi Gonzaga" in *Atti di storia . . . provincie modenesi e parmensi* (1885). Joseph de' Cervi was working in 1577 under royal auspices at the Hradcány castle in Prague; cf. *Jewish Social Studies*, XVI (1954), 341.

TEN

PHYSICIANS, QUACKS AND CHARLATANS

p. 213 ff.   The fundamental work on Jewish physicians of the Middle Ages and after is *The Jews and Medicine: Essays*, by Harry Friedenwald (2 vols., Baltimore, 1944), together with his slender volume, *Jewish Luminaries in Medical History* (*ibid.*, 1946): these two works give comprehensive guidance to all the earlier literature.

Very much in this field is still to be discovered. Prof. U. Middeldorf, of the University of Chicago, writes to me: "In my researches in Florentine archives I once came across an account book of a Jewish physician of the 15th century, who apparently took care of the inmates of a convent for years. Unfortunately, I did not make a note."

p. 215 f.   For Elias Sabot (Elijah ben Sabbetai) see the detailed article by L. Munthner in Astorre Mayer Studies, Jerusalem, 1956. He was also in Basle (*Encylopaedia Judaica*, III, 1136) and went on a diplomatic mission for the Count of Savoy (*REJ*, IL, p. 259). For the reputed murder, see the chronicle in *Muratori*, XXIV, 993; and for the medallion (said also to celebrate the death of the Borgia Pope Alexander VI!), S. Ferrarès in *Revue numismatique*, 1910, 160-230, and M. Parriset, in *Mémoires de l'Académie des Sciences de Lyon*, 1907, 87 ff. The Jewish dentists, etc., are mentioned in E. Motta's *Oculisti dentisti e medici ebrei nella seconda metà del secolo xv*, in Corradi's *Annali universitari di medicina*, 1887.

p. 217.   On Samuel Sarfatti and Giuseppe Gallo, see Cassuto, *Firenze,* and the authorities there cited.

p. 219.   Simonetta Vespucci is linked with Botticelli's "Primavera" in *Arte,* 1897, 321-40.

p. 219.   For Master Lazzaro and Lorenzo de' Medici, cf. Cassuto, *Firenze,* pp. 182, 184, 272-73; and for his attendance on the page, Pasolini, *Caterina Sforza,* III, 182.

p. 220 ff.   For the physicians of the Portaleone family, see Colorni, in *Annuario di studi ebraici,* i, 176-82; Mortara, *REJ,* XII, 114-16; D'Arco and Braghirolli, *Documenti inediti intorno a Maestro Abramo Medico mantovano* (Mantua, 1867), and Kaufmann in *JQR,* IV, 333 ff. and in *Gesammelte Schriften,* 303-18; S. Schiller-Szinessy in his preface to his edition of Kimhi's commentary on Psalms, pp. xiv-xvi; and Stern, *Urkundliche Beiträge,* I, 179-80. For Abraham Portaleone's attendance on Giovanni delle Bande Nere and the Pope's letters of thanks, see *ASI,* 1888, p. 193, and 1858, II, 14; and for his autopsy on the marquis' favorite dog, *GSLI,* XXXIII, 48 and *Il Medico,* VII, 17.

p. 222.   Following a medical catalogue I formerly ascribed to Dr. Abraham Portaleone II, the first modern work on otology (the science of the diseases of the ear); I now discover that this was based on a misreading of the title of his work on the medical use of gold (*De auro*).

p. 222.   The case-book of Guglielmo Portaleone, 1582-95, is MS. Kaufmann 458 (Budapest); his escape from murder in 1576 is chronicled in *Otzar Nehmad,* III, 140.

p. 225 f.   On Garcia d'Orta, there is an important monograph by A. da Silva Carvalho (Coimbra, 1934), and there is one on Amatus Lusitanus (Porto, 1907) by M. Lemos, who has written also on other marrano physicians; there is a good deal about Amatus also in my *House of Nasi* (2 vols., Philadelphia, 1947-48). He is, of course, amply dealt with by Friedenwald in *Jews and Medicine* (see above) and in a recent Portuguese commemorative volume. A statue to his memory now stands in his native city.

p. 229.   Lazarus de Frigeis, Vesalius' Jewish collaborator, is discussed in an article by S. Franco in *RMI,* XV, 494-515, and incidentally but penetratingly by C. Singer and C. Rabin in their *Prelude to Modern Science* (Cambridge, 1946). For Lazarus of Mainz, see A. Kohut Studies, p. 63.

p. 230.   For the work of A. Zacuto and J. Vecinho, see among many other works B. Penrose, *Travel and Discovery in the Renaissance* (Cambridge, Mass., 1952) p. 65: and my own articles in

Sefarad, 1949 and 1954, and in *JQR*, 1937. The standard monograph on the former is by F. Cantera Burgos (Madrid, 1931).

p. 232.   I have unfortunately not been able to consult the biography of B. Manfredi by F. Gabotto (Turin, 1891).

p. 233.   For the episode of Bonet de Lattes and Bovilles, see J. Guttman, *Aus der Zeit der Renaissance*, in MGWJ, XLIII, 250 ff.

p. 234.   For the Jewish court astrologers, etc. in southern Italy, see Ferorelli, *Italia Meridionale*, p. 116 ff.

p. 237.   For the Jewish engineer Master Solomon see *VI*, 1906, 530-32: Zendrini, *Memorie storiche delle lagune di Venezia*, 1811, I, 102: Balletti, p. 54: for Isaac of Noyon, Landsberger, *Jewish Art*, p. 284: for the saltpeter manufacture, Cassuto, *Firenze*, p. 194: for Meir Magino, Vogelstein-Rieger, II, 180, *REJ* XXXI, 75 and 88 ff. and *MGWJ*, 1861, 277.

p. 239.   The Modena alchemist was an uncle of Leon Modena; see his *Autobiography*.

p. 240 ff.   On Colorni, there are two monographs by A. Jaré (Ferrara, 1874, 1891) and one by the present writer (*RMI*, IX 147-58; in English in *Personalities and Events*, pp. 296-304. Cf. also *RI*, II, 26.) His vital dates result from the Mantuan Necrology, consulted for me by Prof. V. Colorni. Napoleon's copy of the *Key of Solomon* translated into Spanish by Dr. Espinoza (later in the library of Sir Hudson Lowe) was included not long since in a London bookseller's catalogue.

ELEVEN

THE JEWS AND THE RENAISSANCE THEATER

p. 244.   The part of the Jews in the development of the theater in Mantua was first revealed by A. d'Ancona in the *second* edition of his *Origini del teatro italiano* (Turin, 1891); précis by C. Dejob in *REJ*, XXIII, 75-84; there is an adequate bibliography of the subject in Y. Schirman's edition (Jerusalem, 1946) of De' Sommi's Hebrew play, *The Comedy of Wedlock*, to be referred to below.

So far as Mantua is concerned, I have been favored by Dr. S. Simonsohn with further information bearing on the subject which he discovered in the archives of the Jewish community.

p. 245 f.   For the *giudate*, and the Jewish type in the Italian theater of the Renaissance period, see E. Re in *GSLI*, LX, 383-99.

p. 246.   For the dramatic performance by the Jews at Pesaro in 1489, see Luzio-Renier, *Mantova e Urbino* (1893), p. 49; it is curious that this city saw also the publication of the burlesque *Ragionamento fra due ebrei* in 1586 (perhaps earlier also).

p. 248.   For the early performance at Mantua by Jews from Ferrara, see *GSLI*, XXXIV, 9.

p. 256 ff.   The Accademia degli Invaghiti in Mantua is described by I. Affo in *Vita del cav. Marliani* (Parma, 1780).

p. 257.   Much has now been written on De' Sommi: see especially, in addition to Schirman's writings (referred to elsewhere), Peyron in *Atti del reale Acc. di Scienze di Torino*, XIX, 743-58, and in *VI*, 1883, 373 ff.; *RMI*, VIII; *GSLI*, IV, 296-97; D. Kaufmann, *Gesammelte Schriften*, III, 303-18.

p. 257 ff.   The record of De' Sommi's dramas and their vicissitudes is complicated. Apart from his various Hebrew writings, sixteen volumes of his manuscript works in Italian were formerly preserved in the Royal Library of Turin. These comprised, besides the famous *Dialoghi* on the theatrical art, four volumes of poems and no fewer than eleven of original plays. Unfortunately, this vast mass of material was lost (with the exception of one volume) before it had been properly examined, in the great fire of 1904 when the library, with most of its irreplaceable manuscripts, was destroyed. There was, however, another copy of the "Dialoghi" in the library at Parma, and it is from this that the recently-published translation was made. His *Irifile*, or *Hirifile Pastorale*, contained in the only volume of the plays which survived the fire, was described at some length by Abd-el-Kader Salza in *GSLI*, LIV (1899). The same writer had in preparation an edition of his *Tamburo*, described as the most polished of his comedies, but it apparently did not appear. In addition, his *Le tre sorelle* ("Three Sisters"), composed in 1588 and dedicated to Duke Vicenzo Gonzaga, is preserved in the Municipal Library of Mantua. His intermezzo *Amore e Psyche*, was however published in full by Ugo de Maria in a volume devoted to the treatment of that topic in Italian literature. The argument of his *Nozze di Mercurio e Filologia* was edited by A. Neri in *GSLI*, XI, 414. Lost

plays, other than those mentioned elsewhere in these pages, in-cluded as we know *L'Adelfa*, *La Diletta*, and *La Fortunata*.
p. 270.   Terni's play is in MS. Montefiore 387.

TWELVE

MUSIC AND THE DANCE

p. 271 ff.   The fullest possible guidance on everything connected with the Jews and music is to be found in *Bibliography of Jewish Music*, by Alfred Sendrey (New York, 1951). There are also numerous monographs on the subject, such as A. Z. Idelsohn, *Jewish Music* (New York, 1929); P. Gradenwitz, *The Music of the Jews* (New York, 1949); A. M. Rothmueller, *The Music of the Jews: an Historical Appreciation* (London, 1953). (Others by G. Saleski, New York, 1929; A. I. Cohon, New York, 1923; H. Berl, Stuttgart, 1926; A. L. Landau, Cincinnati, 1946.) For the theoretical background, reference may be made to a series of articles by E. Werner in *HUCA*, XVI-XVII and *PAAJR*, XVI, etc. The recordings to be referred to in the text are in an album published by the Union of American Hebrew Congregations: others both of Jewish and of secular music by De' Rossi have been published since this book was written.
p. 272.   The specimens of early Jewish musical notation are dis-cussed by Werner in *PAAJR*, XVI, and B. Szabolsci in Löw Studies (Budapest, 1947).
p. 275.   For the dancing-master Musetto see *REJ*, XLVIII, 242.
p. 276 ff.   The fullest account of Guglielmo da Pesaro and his work is by O. Kinkeldey in A. S. Freidus Studies (New York, 1929), to which I am indebted for some phrases and renderings. But he did not take into account the identification of Guglielmo with Giovanni Ambrogio, the material concerning which is col-lected by A. Michel, *The Earliest Dance Manuals*, in *Medievalia et humanistica*, III (1945), 117-31; cf. also G. Mazzi in *La bib-liofilia*, XVI, I (14-5), 185-209, and now also N. Sorell, "Gugli-elmo ebreo, Co-founder of the Ballet," in *Menorah Journal*, 1954,

79-95, and M. Dolmetsch, *Dances of Spain and Italy, 1400-1600* (London, 1954). Kurt Sachs, *World History of the Dance* (New York, 1937) is from my point of view unreliable.

p. 277 f.   The wedding pageant at Pesaro in 1475 is graphically described in a contemporary publication, recently republished *per nozze* from the original manuscript with many illustrations (see list of illustrations). The detail that the Jewish participation was directed by Guglielmo da Pesaro is added by F. Reyna in his *History of the Dance* (Paris, 1956). See final note on p. 363.

p. 281 f.   The material regarding Giovanni Maria is collected by P. Canal, *Della musica in Mantova*, pp. 25-26; Vogelstein-Rieger in their history of the Jews in Rome; and Cassuto, *Firenze;* but there are many references to him in other contemporary sources. Burckhardt's data are slightly erroneous.

p. 283.   For Abramo dell'Arpa's work at Vienna, see Grünwald, *Jews in Vienna*, p. 78, and in Rome, Vogelstein-Rieger, II, 122.

p. 283 f.   For the Jewish musicians in Mantua, see in particular E. Birnbaum, *Jüdische Musiker am Hofe von Mantua von 1542 bis 1628* (reprinted from *Kalender für Israeliten für das Jahr 5654;* Vienna, 1893); some documents also in d'Ancona, *Origini del teatro italiano* and in the works of Canal and Bertolotti on music in Mantua: see also the chapter devoted to the subject in Ademollo, *La Bella Adriana*, and Maria Bellonci, *Segreti dei Gonzaga* (Milan, 1947: also in English). Some occasions for the performances of the Jewish musicians are described in A. Nemmi, "Gli 'Intermezzi' del Pastor Fido," in *GSLI*, XI, 403-405; and A. Hartmann, "Battista Guarini and Il Pastor Fido," in *Musical Quarterly*, XXXIX (1953), 415-25.

p. 285 ff.   A great deal is now available specifically on Salamone de' Rossi, especially A. Einstein, "Salamone Rossi as a Composer of Madrigals," in *HUCA*, XXIII (II), 383-96; see also H. Riemann in *Alte Kammermusik: Handbuch d. Musikgeschichte: Musikgeschichte in Beispielen*, n. 81. The records produced by the Union of American Hebrew Congregations include his rendering of Psalm 126. That he (and his sister) were the children of an Azariah de' Rossi emerges from the Mantuan Jewish archives, but the author of the *Meor Eynayim* complains that he had no surviving son.

p. 299 f.   For the musicians at Reggio and Modena, see Balletti, p. 165 ff.; at Turin, S. Cordero di Pamparato, *I musici alla corte di Carlo Emanuele I*, 1900; for Mordecai Farrisol, Codex Turin n. 5; for Abraham Menaghen at Rome, Vogelstein-Rieger, II, 271;

and the two musicians employed there, Marx in Schorr Studies, p. 213.

p. 301 f.   For the musical academy of the Venetian ghetto, see a chapter "When we remembered Zion" in my *Personalities and Events in Jewish History;* the original documents are published in the original Italian article in *RMI*, III. In some points I have modified my conclusions since then. The music used in the Venice synagogue on the occasion described was conjecturally identified by Werner in *HUCA*, XVIII. The reference to the dancing teachers in Ancona in 1775 derives from Kurt Sachs, *World History of the Dance* (New York, 1937), which contains however, as has been indicated, many misstatements and should not be relied on.

THIRTEEN

THE RENAISSANCE IN JEWISH LITERATURE

p. 305.   Further details regarding the persons mentioned in this chapter and their background may be found in M. Waxman's *History of Jewish Literature* (4 vols., New York, 1930-41) and other similar works.

p. 305.   For the rabbinical objections to the sermons of (Eliezer) David del Bene (in Hebrew, *mehaTob*), see Kaufmann in *JQR*, VIII, 513 ff.

p. 307.   I have dealt with the echo-poem in Hebrew literature in an article in *Mellilah*, III-IV. Leon Modena's bilingual poem is printed in his volume of sermons, *Midbar Jehudah*, and often subsequently. For Leone de' Sommi's experiment with alternating lines, see above, p. 254.

p. 308 ff.   For Hebrew speaking in the age of the Renaissance, see my *Personalities and Events*, pp. 136-142 ("Was Hebrew Ever a Dead Language?"); *REJ*, LXXIX, 35; De' Rossi, *Mazref laKeseph*, p. 102. Christian scholars, too, spoke Hebrew, and the case of G. Manetti mentioned above (Chapter VII) was not unique. The Hebrew chronicler Benjamin Nehemiah ben Elhanan, imprisoned in Rome by the Inquisition in 1559, met in prison two scholars who spoke Hebrew in the purest fashion.

p. 310 f.   Jewish historiography in the age of the Renaissance is described by A. A. Neuman in a series of essays in his *Landmarks and Goals*, Philadelphia, 1953: attention may be called also to the vivid Chronicle of persecutions under Pope Paul IV published by Sonne in *Tarbitz*, II and separately, Jerusalem, 1954.

p. 312 ff.   For Judah Messer Leon, see especially H. Rosenberg's monograph on the scholars of Ancona prefaced to his edition of the Hebrew writings of Rabbis Vivante and Tedesco (Ancona, 1932); Colorni in *Annuario di Studi Ebraici*, I; and Shulvass in *Zion*, XII, 17-23.

p. 313 f.   Thus far there is no adequate monograph on J. S. Norsa, considered by the older generation of Italian Jews as one of the half-dozen foremost scholars who ever emerged in that environment. I venture to question whether the statement in the preface to his work (published by A. Jellinek, Vienna, 1876) really implies that he traveled overseas.

p. 315 ff.   For the Portaleone family see the references above in Chapter X; unfortunately no monograph has been written on the literary work of Abraham Portaleone.

p. 319 ff.   On Azariah de' Rossi, see especially a series of articles by S. Baron in Israel Abrahams Studies and in *REJ*, 1929 (of which I have made much use), by R. Marcus, *HUCA*, XXI; and by G. Kisch, *ibid.*, XXIII, 2; on the polemic about the work, see D. Kaufmann, *REJ*, XXXIII, XXXVIII. There is a contemporary monograph on the Ferrara earthquake: I. Ant. Buoni, medico ferrarese: *Dialogo del terremoto* (Modena, c. 1571)). The encounter and consultation with Amatus Lusitanus is described by H. Friedenwald in *The Jews and Medicine*, II, 391-403. For Italian interest in the *Letter of Aristeas* in the Renaissance Period, see A. Vaccari, 'La Lettera d'Aristea in Italia' in his *Scritti di erudizione e di filologia*, Florence, 1952. But none of the scholars whom he mentions is identifiable with De' Rossi's interlocutor.

p. 325.   For Rossi's correspondence, cf. *REJ*, XXX, 313-16.

p. 325 f.   For the intellectual outlook of some of Rossi's contemporaries, see M. Shulvass in *PAAJR*, XVII; in *Talpioth*, 1950 (on libraries), and in *Horeb*, 1938, etc.

p. 327 f.   For some Jewish book-collectors in Renaissance Italy, C. Bernheimer, *Palaeografia ebraica* (Florence, 1924), N. Allony in *Aresheth* I (1959), 44-60, 489-490; *KS* XXXII, 307; *REJ* (1958), 124 ff., and A. Marx, *Studies*, pp. 198-237.

p. 328.   For Vitale da Pisa's experiment with a *Shekel*, see *REJ*, XXVI, 95.

p. 330.   Simone (in Hebrew, Simha) Luzzatto's *Discorso* has been edited in Hebrew translation with biographical introduction, etc. by M. Shulvass and R. Bachi (Jerusalem, 1951), the latter's contribution being published also in Italian in his *Israele disperso e ricostruito* (Rome, 1952).

p. 332.   Lazzaro da Viterbo's dissertation on the integrity of the Bible was described by Kaufmann in *JQR*, VII, 283 ff.

p. 277.   I now find that the authority for the statement that the memorable pageantry at Pesaro at the time of the ducal wedding in 1475 was directed by Guglielmo ebreo (in conjunction with Domenico da Piacenza) is the Paris codex of his *Trattato dell' arte del ballo* (Fonds It. 476). Here he boasts how during his thirty years of activity he had presided in the same way over pageants of dance at Florence, Urbino, and Naples; at Milan, when the Sforza received the Duke of Cleves; at Mantua during a visit of the Pope; and at Venice, where the Emperor Maximilian created him a knight (Reyna, *Des origines du ballet*, Paris, 1955).

Index